CW01336505

THE
ESSENTIAL BRITISH
PRICE GUIDE
TO COLLECTING
45/78 rpm SINGLES
1950 – 1960

Compiled by

PAUL PELLETIER

Assisted by JOHN DONOGHUE

RECORD INFORMATION SERVICES

(PAUL PELLETIER)   ESTABLISHED 1974

208 STANSTEAD ROAD, FOREST HILL
LONDON SE23 1DB

First published in 1991 by RECORD INFORMATION SERVICES

ISBN 0 907872 27 1

COPYRIGHT 1991
PAUL PELLETIER/RECORD INFORMATION SERVICES

Typescript prepared by Paul Pelletier

Printed in the E.E.C. by P.R.I. APISM

'THE JIVE DIVE'

BUYS AND SELLS ALL COLLECTABLE RECORDS FROM THE 1950s ONWARDS

P.O. BOX 29, FELTHAM, MIDDLESEX TW14 0XP, ENGLAND

Telephone 081-890 8835

THE "ESSENTIAL" 1950s BRITISH SINGLES PRICE GUIDE

This Price Guide provides a complete listing of collectable and interesting Rock & Roll, Rhythm & Blues, Instrumental, Skiffle, Personality, Popular, Blues, Jazz, Comedy, Novelty, etc. records issued in Britain between January 1950 and December 1960. It also includes every entry in the British charts since their inception in 1952. The arrangement and content of the Price Guide has been carefully conceived as a significant improvement on similar publications. Most noticeable is the extensive cross-referencing, the inclusion of year of issue for every record, and the chronological listing of releases under each artist. The main weakness of previous guides which cover the 1950s is their failure to include 78 rpm records, despite the fact that 78s were still outselling 45s during 1958 and it was only in that year that two major companies (PHILIPS and PYE) began issuing all their single releases at 45 rpm. [The EMI Group (HMV, COLUMBIA, PARLOPHONE, etc.) began issuing popular 45s from January, 1953, followed by the DECCA Group (DECCA, BRUNSWICK, LONDON, pre-1956 CAPITOL, etc.) in October, 1954.] This Price Guide remains 45 rpm-centred but many interesting and collectable 78s are included which give depth to the whole 1950s decade. Indeed, because the Guide features every British chart entry of the period, then the inclusion of 78s was essential as so many were only available in that format.

It cannot be emphasised too strongly that this Price Guide is exactly that — a guide to the value of records. It does not seek to establish a fixed value for anything and to do so would be a folly. It does attempt to show a price range within which a collector can reasonably expect to buy a record or a dealer can reasonably value it. Ultimately, the worth of any second-hand item is determined by the price someone is either prepared to pay for it or sell it. It was intended to exclude singles with a value of under £2, but the inclusion of all chart records has meant a £1 - £2 category. Where shown, this low value is not a comment on the musical content of the record but probably reflects its abundance e.g. Guy Mitchell's hugely-popular "Singing The Blues". Even singles in the basic £2 - £4 category are worth less than their original 1950s purchase price, after taking inflation and increased standards of living into account.

Record values can be subject to fads, when an artist or single becomes particularly sought after for a while (premature death helps, such as the surge of interest following the demise of Elvis Presley in 1977). There are also U.K. regional variations, with higher prices probably easier to obtain in the South or Midlands. The greater the value of a single, the more likely it is to be sold by auction or negotiation rather than at a pre-set price. It is impossible to accurately value very rare and sought after singles such as Bobby Charles' "See You Later, Alligator". It must be remembered that only the most dedicated and relatively rich collectors can afford to spend hundreds of pounds on one record. Whether singles have an "investment" potential is a matter of opinion but generally, records of the 1950s have not maintained their value well over the last decade in relation to, say, 1960s records, nor even to the exotic prices some rare CDs obtain.

Although this Price Guide lists only commercially available records of the 1950s, an exception has been made for the PHILIPS JK 100 "Juke Box" series. In 1956, PHILIPS was producing only 78 rpm singles in Britain (although it was pressing 45 rpm E.P.s) but 45s were required for juke-boxes to promote new releases. PHILIPS thus introduced the special JK 100 45 rpm singles series which they supplied direct to juke-box distributors. Many of these singles are now sought after as they offer 45 rpm alternatives to otherwise 78 rpm only chart hits (like Guy Mitchell's "Singing The Blues") but heavy use on juke-boxes has made good condition copies very hard to find.

In general, demonstration records (review copies usually called "demos") of the 1950s are not so collectable as they have become for the 1960s onwards. This is due to their often crude and unattractive appearance which detracts from their finished-pressing value. An exception is the picture-covered series of demos issued by CAPITOL from 1956, usually with a photograph of the artist on the front together with biographical or recording details; such demos by an artist like Gene Vincent are much sought after and worth significantly more than an ordinary single. It should be noted that single-sided 45 rpm demos from the 1950s are fairly common, as are oddities (really test-pressings) from the DECCA Group which coupled recordings from different labels together; e.g. LONDON on one side and DURIUM on the other. Acetates (recordings individually cut by machine on special plastic 45 or 78 rpm discs) are too unique and varied to be included in any commercial Price Guide, although they can contain very interesting and valuable material.

One subject which causes endless confusion amongst collectors is export records. Through the 1950s, Britain exported millions of records each year to the Commonwealth and remnants of the Empire, and to many other countries including the U.S.A. (All releases in the U.S.A. on DECCA's LONDON label were manufactured in the U.K.; also British BRUNSWICK issues were pressed for export sporting the DECCA logo, an arrangement made necessary because of varying ownership of label trademarks in different countries). Because these export records bear the legend "Made In England", they are frequently mistaken for British releases on hitherto "undiscovered" series'. Certainly, some export series' were available in the U.K. to special order but in general, they were neither aimed at nor readily available for British consumption. Therefore, export releases are NOT included in this Price Guide, with the following exceptions: two COLUMBIA export singles made available in the U.K. became chart hits (Edith Piaf and Cliff Richard); two other export singles are included because they were the only 45 rpm pressings available of otherwise 78 rpm only chart hits (Perry Como and Humphrey Lyttelton). Future editions of this Price Guide will probably extend its coverage of export records.

Collectors generally have their own sources for finding or exchanging records, either through specialist shops, record fairs, mail-order, junk and charity shops, boot fairs, etc. There are now several magazines catering for collectors and dealers alike. The market leader is *RECORD COLLECTOR*; more recent is *RECORD HUNTER*, currently a pull-out section in *VOX*, and there is also *MUSIC COLLECTOR*. These three are monthly magazines and should be available through your local newsagent. *NOW DIG THIS* is for Rock & Roll enthusiasts (see opposite) and *IN TUNE* covers "Personality" singers between 1935 and 1960 (see next page). Anyone interested in advertising in future editions of this Guide should contact me.

It has taken over three years to bring this project to fruition, not helped by two house moves and many diversions (such as sleep). I must thank all those people whom I have consulted at one time or another, many preferring to remain anonymous. Apart from John Donoghue, my gratitude extends to John Repsch, Neil Rosser, Derek Mathews, Ray Wilks, David Anthonisz, Paul Fox, and Paul Bird for another apposite cartoon (page 212); never least is my printer John Relleen who has shown faith in me through thick and thin.

PAUL PELLETIER

EXPLANATORY NOTES: The Price Guide is arranged in alphabetical artist order and the singles listed in order of release. This chronological sequence produces occasional anomalies where 45 rpm pressings have been issued a year or more after the original 78. The first column shows the year of issue, followed by titles, label, catalogue number and value. Limitations of space have restricted the ability to show some titles in full; also the label is only shown for the first catalogue number where subsequent releases are from the same source. Apart from self-explanatory symbols used to give accompanying artist information, the following are important to note:

THE SYMBOL ø AFTER THE YEAR OF ISSUE INDICATES A BRITISH CHART ENTRY
THE SYMBOL º AFTER THE CATALOGUE NUMBER INDICATES A 78 rpm RECORD
CONTEMP. = CONTEMPORARY   G.T.J. = GOOD TIME JAZZ
V-CORAL = VOGUE-CORAL·   WARNER-B = WARNER BROTHERS

The price range given is for records in excellent condition, meaning that they both look and play well; they should also have clean labels and preferably be in the original paper sleeves. (Some original paper sleeves are themselves hard to find and may be sold separately from the actual records for prices up to £1 each.) Very few picture sleeves were made for 1950s British singles, but the few that do exist enhance the value of the record. Unless indicated otherwise, the price range is for 45 rpm singles only; 78 equivalents, where they exist, are worth perhaps a quarter to one-third of the shown value. The exception is for some very late 78 pressings made in 1960, which can be worth as much as or more than the 45; some of these late 78s are shown as separate entries in the listing because of their increased value. Values of DECCA Group singles, notably LONDON, can be crucially effected by such factors as triangle centres and gold lettering; later pressings of the same record may have a label change which adversely effects the value. Price ranges shown, in particular for LONDON singles, refer to first pressings.

As an example of cross-referencing, (qv MICKI MARLO) appears after PAUL ANKA's name on page 12 and when you refer to the MICKI MARLO entry you will find that Anka accompanied Marlo on one recording. You should also check under accompanying artist names: *e.g.* the JERRY LEWIS entry shows DEAN MARTIN accompanying Lewis on one side of a single and, conversely, the DEAN MARTIN entry shows JERRY LEWIS accompanying Martin on one side of another single.

Artists beginning with numbers (THREE, FOUR, etc.) or words like FABULOUS or ORIGINAL may be found under the second word: e.g. FIVE SMITH BROTHERS appear under SMITH BROTHERS. Artists not found in the main Guide may be included below under the second artist shown.

DAVE APPELL .... THE APPLEJACKS
MICKEY BAKER ... MICKEY & KITTY or SYLVIA
LEON BIBB .... PETE SEEGER
BARNEY BIGARD ORCH. ...... DUKE ELLINGTON
BING & SATCHMO .... LOUIS ARMSTRONG
ANN BLYTH .... VIC DAMONE
RAY BOLGER .... ETHEL MERMAN
CLAUDE BOLLING .... ROY ELDRIDGE
RICHARD BOONE .... JOHNNY WESTERN
THE BOWTIES .... IVY SCHULMAN
BOB BROOKMEYER .... BUD SHANK
PETER BROUGH & A.ANDREWS ... MAX BYGRAVES
PINEY BROWN .... EDDIE CHAMBLEE
TOMMY BROWN ..... GRIFFIN BROTHERS' ORCH.
DAWS BUTLER .... STAN FREBERG
JEAN CAMPBELL .... CYRIL STAPLETON
PEARL CARR .... TEDDY JOHNSON
CASCADING STRINGS .... JOHNNY GREGORY
CYD CHARISSE .... FRED ASTAIRE
CHICAGO BILL .... BIG BILL BROONZY
SEAN CONNERY .... JANET MUNRO
STEVE CONWAY .... VARIOUS ARTISTS
DAN DAILEY .... ETHEL MERMAN
BERYL DAVIS .... DAVID ROSE
LARRY DAY .... ALMA COGAN
TOMMY DEAN .... EDDIE CHAMBLEE
JIMMY DELL .... BARRY DE VORZON
PAUL DESMOND .... GERRY MULLIGAN
LOU DINNING .... DON ROBERTSON
SHIRLEY DOUGLAS .... CHAS McDEVITT
HARRY DOUGLASS .... DEEP RIVER BOYS
ECCLES .... THE GOONS
SONNY FARRAR .... THE STARGAZERS
JOSE FERRER .... ROSEMARY CLOONEY
BILLY FORD THUNDERBIRDS .. BILLY & LILLIE
LESLIE FYSON .... MICHAEL MEDWIN
BETSY GAY .... AL TRACE
JIMMY GIUFFRE .... HERB ELLIS
CHARLIE GORE .... RUBY WRIGHT
JOYCE GRENFELL .... NORMAN WISDOM
BUDDY HACKETT .... ALAN DALE
GILBERT HARDING .... HERMIONE GINGOLD
AUDREY HEPBURN .... FRED ASTAIRE
EDDIE JACKSON .... JIMMY DURANTE
KAY JUSTICE .... THE ESCORTS
ALAN KALANI .... THE SURFERS
HOWARD KEEL .. VIC DAMONE/KATHRYN GRAYSON
GRACE KELLY .... BING CROSBY
BARNEY KESSEL .... RICKY NELSON
EVELYN KINGSLEY .... THE TOWERS
EDDIE KIRK .... "TENNESSEE" ERNIE FORD
BERNIE KNEE .... BERNIE NEE
KNOTT SISTERS .... THE SHADES
LEE KONITZ .... GERRY MULLIGAN
PETER LAWFORD .... JIMMY DURANTE
BERNIE LAWRENCE .... STEVE LAWRENCE
EVELYN LAYE .... ANTON WALBROOK
LEADBELLY .... HUDDIE LEDBETTER
MARCI LEE .... JOHNNY OTIS

LITTLE EVA .... LUTHER & LITTLE EVA
LITTLE WILBUR .... WILBUR WHITFIELD
MARY MAYO .... BRUCE HAYES/JERRY VALE
BARBARA McNAIR .... BILLY WILLIAMS
THE MELLOMEN .. KIRK DOUGLAS/POUND HOUNDS
MEZZ MEZZROW .... SIDNEY BECHET
VELMA MIDDLETON .... LOUIS ARMSTRONG
SALLY MILES .... WALLY WHYTON
ANN MILLER .... KATHRYN GRAYSON
BOB MONKHOUSE .... DEREK ROY
Count JIM MORIARTY .... THE GOONS
DENNIS MORLEY .... WOOLF PHILLIPS
RICHARD MURDOCH .... DEREK ROY
PETE MURRAY .... BRIAN MATTHEW
DONALD O'CONNOR .... BING CROSBY
BRENDAN O'DOWDA .... RUBY MURRAY
KING OLIVER .... BLIND WILLIE DUNN
JANET OSBORNE .... DONALD PEERS
PARIS SISTERS .... GARY CROSBY
LEO PARKER .... BILL JENNINGS
PARLOPHONE POPS ORCH. .... RON GOODWIN
GARY PAXTON . HOLLYWOOD ARGYLES/SKIP & FLIP
LEONARD PENNARIO .... LES BAXTER
BILL PERKINS .... BUD SHANK
FRANK PERRY .... THE TOWERS
JON PERTWEE .... DEREK ROY
STEVE RACE .... VARIOUS ARTISTS
DON RALKE .... PETE CANDOLI
TED RAY .... DEREK ROY
TOMMY REILLY . L.DONEGAN/S.TERRY/J.WARNER
THE RINKY-DINKS .... BOBBY DARIN
RICHIE ROBIN .... GERRY GRANAHAN
NORMAN ROSSINGTON .... MICHAEL MEDWIN
ROSALIND RUSSELL .... EDITH ADAMS
ST. LOUIS JIMMY .... MEMPHIS SLIM
JIMMY SAVILLE .... THE VERNONS GIRLS
BOB SCOBEY'S FRISCO BAND .. SIDNEY BECHET
JANETTE SCOTT .... "GOOD COMPANIONS"
SHEPPARD SISTERS .... SHEPHERD SISTERS
THE SQUADRONAIRES .... RONNIE ALDRICH
DICK STABILE ORCH. .... RAY ANTHONY
RALPH STERLING .... BILL SNYDER
TRUDY STEVENS .... BING CROSBY
BILLY STRANGE .... CLIFFIE STONE
MONTY SUNSHINE .... CHRIS BARBER
DONALD SWANN .... MICHAEL FLANDERS
SALLY SWEETLAND . E.FISHER/SAUTER-FINEGAN
ERIC SYKES .... THE GOONS
THE TEENAGERS .... FRANKIE LYMON
TENNESSEE ERNIE .. "TENNESSEE" ERNIE FORD
AL VERLANE .... "PING PING"
RONNIE VERRELL . HAWKSWORTH-VERRELL GROUP
ANNE WARREN ...... TONY BRENT/RUBY MURRAY
SPEEDY WEST .... CLIFFIE STONE
MEL WILLIAMS .... JOHNNY OTIS
TONY WILLIAMS .. LINDA HAYES/THE PLATTERS
LIZ WINTERS .... BOB CORT
PATRICE WYMORE .... ERROL FLYNN
LEE YOUNG .... WOOLF PHILLIPS

74 Brockley Rise
Forest Hill
London SE23 1L

Tel: 01-690 1961

RECORD CARE

PROTECTIVE COVERS
AUDIO & CD ACCESSORIES

RECORD CARE ARE RETAIL and TRADE SUPPLIERS OF ALL YOUR
7", 10" & 12" PAPER, CARD and PLASTIC RECORD COVERS; Also
MAIL—ORDER PACKAGING NEEDS, plus CASSETTE and COMPACT
DISC LIBRARY CASES. SEND S.A.E. FOR RETAIL or TRADE LIST.

<u>7" WHITE PAPER COVERS (with or without centres)</u>
25 ..... £1.25; 50 ..... £2.25; 100 ..... £4.00

<u>7" WHITE or BROWN POLYLINED CARD COVERS</u>
25 ..... £3.90; 50 ..... £6.00; 100 ..... £11.00

<u>7" THIN POLYTHENE COVERS (200g)</u>
25 ..... £1.75; 50 ..... £3.00; 100 ..... £5.00

<u>7" THICK PLASTIC COVERS (800g)</u>
25 ..... £4.25; 50 ..... £8.00; 100 ..... £15.00

<u>7" CRUCIFORM POSTING UNITS (holds 2 to 10)</u>
25 ..... £5.25; 50 ..... £10.00; 100 ..... £19.00

<u>7" RECORD POSTING ENVELOPES</u>
25 ..... £4.50; 50 ..... £8.50; 100 ..... £16.00

<u>10" WHITE CARDBOARD COVERS</u>
25 ..... £3.90; 50 ..... £7.25; 100 ..... £13.50

RETAIL EXAMPLES ABOVE; SORRY — NO CHEQUES UNDER £5.00

PLEASE NOTE POST & PACKING EXTRA — RING/WRITE FOR QUOTE

SHIRLEY ABICAIR (*& HUMPHREY LYTTELTON)
56 Willie can/Happy trails .... PARLOPHONE MSP 6224 £ 4 – 6
57 Bimini/Where the sun always shines .... *R 4347 £ 2 – 4

THE ACCENTS
59 Wiggle, wiggle/Dreamin' and schemin' .... CORAL Q 72351 £ 9 – 12

SEPH ACRE & THE PETS
58 Rock and roll cha cha/You are my love .... PYE INT. 7N 25001 £ 4 – 6

ROY ACUFF & THE SMOKY MOUNTAIN BOYS
57 I like mountain music/It's hard to love (and not to be.) BRUNSWICK 05635 £ 4 – 6

BILLY ADAMS
59 Count every star/Peggy's party .... CAPITOL CL 15107 £ 4 – 6

CLIFF ADAMS ORCHESTRA
60ø The Lonely Man theme/Trigger happy .... PYE INT. 7N 25056 £ 2 – 4

EDITH ADAMS (*& ROSALIND RUSSELL)
55 Ohio*/A little bit in love .... BRUNSWICK 05406 £ 2 – 4

FAYE ADAMS
56 I'll be true/Happiness to my soul .... LONDON HLU 8339 £60 – 90

JOHNNY ADAMS & THE GONDOLIERS
59 Come on/Nowhere to go .... TOP RANK JAR 192 £ 4 – 6

MARIE ADAMS (qv JOHNNY OTIS)
59 What do you want to make those eyes at.../A fool in love CAPITOL CL 14963 £ 6 – 9

RITCHIE ADAMS
60 Back to school/Don't go my love, don't go .... LONDON HLU 9200 £ 6 – 9

RUSH ADAMS (& *LOULIE JEAN NORMAN/qv DAVID ROSE)
54 I'm sorry dear/No one to cry to .... PARLOPHONE MSP 6101 £ 2 – 4
56 Love plays the strings of my banjo/Kiss! Kiss! Kiss! . M–G–M SP 1162 £ 2 – 4
56 The birds and the bees*/My buddy's girl .... SP 1176 £ 2 – 4

THE ADDRISSI BROTHERS
59 Cherrystone/Lillies grow high .... LONDON HL 8922 £ 4 – 6
59 Un jarro/Saving my kisses .... HL 8973 £ 4 – 6
59 It's love/Back to the old salt mine .... COLUMBIA DB 4370 £ 6 – 9

BETH ADLAM w. BUZZ & THE BOYS
60 Seventeen/I'll walk into the sea .... STARLITE ST.45 024 £ 4 – 6

LARRY ADLER
56 Rififi/Malaguena .... COLUMBIA SCM 5217 £ 2 – 4

THE ADVENTURERS
59 Rip Van Winkle/Trail blazer .... CAPITOL CL 15108 £ 2 – 4

THE AFRO RHYTHM KINGS
54 Skokiaan/Bantu boogie .... LYRAGON J 732 º £ 4 – 6

ALYN AINSWORTH & HIS ORCH./*THE ROCK–A–FELLAS
59 Bedtime for drums/The cobbler's song .... PARLOPHONE R 4533 £ 2 – 4
59 18th–Century rock/Hell's bells .... *R 4594 £ 2 – 4

LAUREL AITKEN (& *THE CARIBS/+THE BLUEBEATS)
60 Sweet chariot/Nebuchnezer .... KALYPSO XX 15 £ 4 – 6
60 Cherrie/Aitken's boogie .... XX 16 £ 6 – 9
60 Boogie in my bones/Little Sheila .... STARLITE ST.45 011 £ 9 – 12
60 Honey girl/Drinkin' whisky .... *ST.45 014 £ 6 – 9

60	Baba kill me goat/Tribute to Collie Smith	KALYPSO	XX 19	£ 4 - 6
60	Boogie rock/Heavenly angel	BLUE BEAT	BB 1	£ 9 - 12
60	Mary Lee/Lonesome lover	MELODISC	+1570	£ 9 - 12

BILLY ALBERT "The Kid"

57	Black jack/The golden touch	V-CORAL	Q 72214	£ 2 - 4

EDDIE ALBERT (*& SONDRA LEE)

55	I'm in favour of friendship/Come pretty little girl ...	LONDON	HL 8136	£12 - 18
56	Little child (Daddy dear)*/Jenny kissed me		HLU 8241	£12 - 18

MEL ALBERT

59	Sugar plum/Never let me go	TOP RANK	JAR 178	£ 2 - 4

AL ALBERTS (of THE FOUR ACES)

58	Things I didn't say/God's greatest gift	CORAL	Q 72344	£ 2 - 4
59	Willingly/My love		Q 72352	£ 2 - 4
59	How soon? (will I be seeing you)/Taking a chance on love		Q 72363	£ 2 - 4

CRAIG ALDEN

60	Crazy little horn/Goggle-eye'd	LONDON	HLW 9224	£ 2 - 4

RONNIE ALDRICH & THE SQUADRONAIRES/*SQUADS (qv JOAN REGAN)

54	Coach call boogie/Donegal cradle song	DECCA	F 10248	£ 6 - 9
54	Wolf on the prowl/Mudhopper		F 10274	£ 6 - 9
55	Ko Ko Mo (I love you so)/Rock love		*F 10494	£ 9 - 12
55	Rock candy/Boom boom boomerang		*F 10544	£ 9 - 12
55	Rhythm 'n blues/Where ya gone, baby?		*F 10564	£ 9 - 12
57	Right now, right now/Rock and roll boogie	COLUMBIA	DB 3882	£12 - 18
57	Big band beat/Crazy bear		DB 3945	£ 6 - 9

ALFI & HARRY (actually DAVID SEVILLE)

56ø	Trouble with Harry/A little beauty	LONDON	HLU 8242	£12 - 18
57	Closing time/Safari		HLU 8494	£ 4 - 6

SANDRA ALFRED

58	Rocket and roll/Six day rock	ORIOLE	CB 1408	£ 6 - 9

RICHARD ALLAN *or ALLEN

60ø	As time goes by/Only one	PARLOPHONE	R 4634	£ 4 - 6
60	Everyday/Doctor in love		*R 4673	£ 2 - 4
60	Poetry in motion/Don't ever say you're gonna leave me .		R 4711	£ 2 - 4

ANNISTEEN ALLEN

55	Fujiyama Mama/Wheels of love	CAPITOL	CL 14264	£ 9 - 12
57	The money tree/Don't nobody move	BRUNSWICK	05639	£ 9 - 12

BARBARA ALLEN

59	Tommy's song/Never let me go	FELSTED	AF 115	£ 2 - 4

DEAN ALLEN

58	Rock me to sleep/Ooh-ooh baby baby	LONDON	HLM 8698	£12 - 18

JERRY ALLEN & HIS TRIO

54	S'posin'/When I needed you most	DECCA	F 10428	£ 2 - 4
55	Kind/Delaunay's dilemma		F 10443	£ 2 - 4

LEE ALLEN (& HIS BAND)

58	Walkin' with Mr. Lee/Promenade	H.M.V.	POP 452	£ 9 - 12
59	Cat walk/Creole Alley	TOP RANK	JAR 265	£ 6 - 9

MAURICE ALLEN

58	Rockhearted/Ooh baby	PYE	7N 15128	£ 4 - 6

REMEMBER! - THE SYMBOL º AFTER THE CATALOGUE NUMBER INDICATES A 78 rpm RECORD

REX ALLEN (qv TEX WILLIAMS)

57	Wrangle wrangle/Westward ho the wagons	BRUNSWICK	05677	£ 2 – 4
57	The little white horses/Drango		05675	£ 2 – 4
57	Money, marbles and chalk/Flower of San Antone		05699	£ 2 – 4
59	One more sunrise/The little old church in the valley ..	TOP RANK	JAR 188	£ 2 – 4

STEVE ALLEN (& HIS ORCH.) (*& JAYNE MEADOWS/qv GEORGE CATES)

56	The ballad of Davy Crockett/Very square dance	V–CORAL	Q 72118	£ 4 – 6
56	Memories of you/What is a wife?		Q 72126	£ 4 – 6
56	Goodbye/Let's dance		Q 72136	£ 2 – 4
56	What is a husband?*/What is a freem?		Q 72155	£ 4 – 6
56	Lola's theme/Conversation (on the telephone)		Q 72184	£ 2 – 4
58	Pretend you don't see her/But I haven't got him	CORAL	Q 72310	£ 2 – 4
58	Almost in your arms/Hula hoop	LONDON	HLD 8742	£ 2 – 4

THE ALLEY CATS

59	Last night/Snap–crackle and pop	VOGUE	V 9155	£ 9 – 12

GENE ALLISON

58	Hey, hey I love you/You can make it if you try	LONDON	HLU 8605	£18 – 25

LYNNE ALLISON

57	Mama from the train (A kiss, a kiss)/Song of the sparrow	COLUMBIA	DB 3867	£ 2 – 4
57	If only/The sky		DB 3906	£ 2 – 4

LAURINDO ALMEIDA QUARTET

56	Atabaque/Inquietacao	VOGUE	V 2382	£ 2 – 4

AMBROSE & HIS ORCH.

56	Lilacs in the rain/Deep purple	M–G–M	SP 1151	£ 2 – 4

LOLA AMECHE

53	Rock the joint/Don't let the stars get in your eyes ...	ORIOLE	CB 1143 ø	£ 6 – 9

THE AMES BROTHERS

53	You, you, you/My love, my life, my happiness	H.M.V.	7M 153	£ 6 – 9
54	Boogie woogie Maxixe/I can't believe that you're in.....		7M 179	£ 4 – 6
54	The man with the banjo/Man, man, is for the woman made		7M 209	£ 4 – 6
54	Hopelessly/One more time		7M 253	£ 4 – 6
54ø	The naughty lady of shady lane/Addio		B 10800 ø	£ 2 – 4
55ø	*as above*		7M 281	£ 9 – 12
55	Sweet brown–eyed baby/Sympathetic eyes		7M 310	£ 4 – 6
55	Merci beaucoup/Wrong again		7M 322	£ 4 – 6
55	My bonnie lassie/So will I		7M 331	£ 4 – 6
56	If you wanna see Mamie tonight/My love, your love		7M 410	£ 4 – 6
56	I'm gonna love you/It only hurts for a little while ...		POP 242	£ 6 – 9
56	49 shades of green/Summer sweetheart		POP 264	£ 2 – 4
57	Rockin' shoes/Tammy	R.C.A.	RCA 1015	£ 6 – 9
57	Melodie d'amour/So little time		RCA 1021	£ 2 – 4
58	A very precious love/In love		RCA 1049	£ 2 – 4
58	No one but you (in my heart)/Pussy cat		RCA 1091	£ 2 – 4
59	Red River Rose/When the Summer comes again		RCA 1104	£ 2 – 4
59	(Yes, I need) Only your love/Dancin' in the streets ...		RCA 1118	£ 2 – 4
59	Someone to come home to/Mason–Dixon line		RCA 1135	£ 2 – 4

EDDIE AMES

57	The bean song (Which way to.....)/I'd give you the world	H.M.V.	POP 311	£ 2 – 4

GENE AMMONS BAND

60	Ammons boogie/Echo chamber blues	STARLITE	ST 45.017	£ 9 – 12

MOREY AMSTERDAM

54	Somebody bad stole de wedding.../I wish I was a peanut..	M–G–M	SP 1086	£ 2 – 4

REMEMBER! – THE SYMBOL ø AFTER THE YEAR OF ISSUE INDICATES A BRITISH CHART ENTRY

ERNESTINE ANDERSON
59	Be mine/I don't see me in your eyes any more	MERCURY	AMT 1035	£ 2 – 4
59	My love will last/Call me darling		AMT 1073	£ 2 – 4
60	You, you, you/There are such things		AMT 1082	£ 2 – 4
60	A kiss to build a dream on/Come on, baby, let's go		AMT 1103	£ 2 – 4

LEROY ANDERSON & HIS "POPS" CONCERT ORCH.
55ø	Forgotten dreams/The last rose of Summer		05485	£ 4 – 6

SONNY ANDERSON
60	Yes, I'm gonna love you/Lonely lonely train	LONDON	HLP 9036	£18 – 25

THE ANDREWS SISTERS
57	Rum and coca-cola/No, baby	CAPITOL	CL 14705	£ 4 – 6
57	I'm goin' home/By His word		CL 14807	£ 2 – 4
58	One mistake/Melancholy moon		CL 14826	£ 2 – 4
58	Torero/Sunshine		CL 14878	£ 2 – 4
59	I'll be with you in apple blossom time/Oh! Johnny,......	BRUNSWICK	05782	£ 2 – 4
59	I've got an invitation to a dance/My love is a kitten .	CAPITOL	CL 14998	£ 2 – 4
60	Rum and coca cola/I'll be with you in apple blossom time		CL 15170	£ 2 – 4

EAMONN ANDREWS
55ø	The shifting, whispering sands (Parts 1 & 2)	PARLOPHONE	R 4106 º	£ 2 – 4
56	High wind/The legend of Wyatt Earp		R 4234	£ 2 – 4
57	The ship that never sailed/The magic tree		R 4318	£ 2 – 4

ERNIE ANDREWS
60	'Round midnight/Lover come back to me	VOGUE	V 9166	£ 4 – 6

JULIE ANDREWS (*& PHILIPPA BEVANS)
58	I could have danced all night*/Without you	PHILIPS	PB 846	£ 2 – 4
60	Tom Pillibi/Lazy afternoon	DECCA	F 11230	£ 2 – 4

LEE ANDREWS (*& THE HEARTS)
58	Teardrops/Girl around the corner	LONDON	HLM 8546	£25 – 40
58	Try the impossible/Nobody's home		*HLU 8661	£25 – 40

Mrs. NOEL ANDREWS & GUY TYNEGATE-SMITH
58	"How To Dance The Kwela Jive"	ORIOLE	CB 1448	£ 2 – 4

PATTY ANDREWS (qv BING CROSBY/JIMMY DURANTE)
55	Where to my love?/Without love	CAPITOL	CL 14324	£ 4 – 6
55	Suddenly there's a valley/Booga-da-woog		CL 14374	£ 6 – 9

JERRY ANGELO
59	Mary Lou/Crush me	PARLOPHONE	R 4548	£ 2 – 4

PAUL ANKA (qv MICKI MARLO)
57ø	Diana/Don't gamble with love	COLUMBIA	DB 3980	£ 4 – 6
57ø	I love you, baby/Tell me that you love me		DB 4022	£ 4 – 6
58ø	You are my destiny/When I stop loving you		DB 4063	£ 2 – 4
58ø	Crazy love/Let the bells keep ringing		DB 4110	£ 4 – 6
58ø	Midnight/Verboten! (Forbidden)		DB 4172	£ 2 – 4
58	Just young/So it's goodbye		DB 4199	£ 2 – 4
59ø	(All of a sudden) My hearts sings/That's love		DB 4241	£ 2 – 4
59	I miss you so/Late last night		DB 4286	£ 4 – 6
59ø	Lonely boy/Your love		DB 4324	£ 4 – 6
59ø	Put your head on my shoulder/Don't ever leave me		DB 4355	£ 2 – 4
60ø	It's time to cry/Something has changed me		DB 4390	£ 2 – 4
60ø	Puppy love/Adam and Eve		DB 4434	£ 2 – 4
60	My home town/Waiting for you		DB 4472	£ 2 – 4
60ø	Hello young lovers/I love you in the same old way		DB 4504	£ 2 – 4
60	Summer's gone/I'd have to share		DB 4524	£ 2 – 4

REMEMBER! – THE SYMBOL º AFTER THE CATALOGUE NUMBER INDICATES A 78 rpm RECORD

ANNETTE (Funicello) (*& THE AFTERBEATS)
59	Lonely guitar/Wild Willie	TOP RANK	JAR 137	£ 4 -	6
59	First name initial/My heart became of age		*JAR 233	£ 4 -	6
60	O Dio mio/It took dreams		JAR 343	£ 4 -	6
60	Pineapple Princess/Luau cha cha cha	*PYE INT.	7N 25061	£ 2 -	4

BILLIE ANTHONY (& *BIG BEN BANJO BAND/+ex-R.S.M. BRITTAIN)
54ø	This ole house/Oh, what a dream	COLUMBIA	DB 3519 º	£ 2 -	4
54ø	as above		SCM 5143	£ 9 -	12
54	Don't let the kiddygeddin/Teach me tonight		SCM 5155	£ 9 -	12
55	No more/Butterscotch mop		SCM 5164	£ 6 -	9
55	Tweedlee dee/Shake the hand of a stranger		SCM 5174	£ 9 -	12
55	Something's gotta give/Boom boom boomerang		SCM 5184	£ 6 -	9
55	The banjo's back in town*/Ten little kisses		SCM 5191	£ 4 -	6
55	Bring me a bluebird/The old pi-anna rag		SCM 5210	£ 4 -	6
56	A sweet old-fashioned girl/The treasure of love		SCM 5286	£ 6 -	9
56	Lay down your arms/One finger piano		DB 3818	£ 4 -	6
57	I dreamed/The charge of the Light Brigade+		DB 3874	£ 4 -	6
57	Rock-a-billy/A needle and thread		DB 3935	£ 9 -	12
57	One/It's fun finding out about London		*DB 3970	£ 2 -	4
57	Love and kisses/Everybody's buddy		DB 4021	£ 2 -	4
58	Careful, careful (Handle me with care)/You		DB 4141	£ 2 -	4
59	Yes, we have no bananas/Too late now		DB 4279	£ 2 -	4
60	A handful of gold/Sure fire love		DB 4394	£ 2 -	4

RAY ANTHONY & HIS ORCH. (*& DICK STABILE ORCH./qv GORDON MacRAE)
53ø	Dragnet/Bye bye baby	CAPITOL	CL 13983 º	£ 2 -	4
54	Woman's world/I don't hurt anymore		CL 14205	£ 4 -	6
55	Heat wave/Juke box special		CL 14243	£ 6 -	9
55	Baby you/Happy hornblowers		*CL 14275	£ 4 -	6
55	Sluefoot/Something's gotta give		CL 14306	£ 4 -	6
55	Learnin' the blues/Mmmm Mamie		CL 14321	£ 4 -	6
55	Pete Kelly's blues/DC-7		CL 14345	£ 4 -	6
55	Hernando's Hideaway/The bunny hop		CL 14354	£ 6 -	9
56	Flip-flop/Hurricane Anthony		CL 14525	£ 6 -	9
56	Cry me a river/Bullfighter's lament		CL 14553	£ 2 -	4
56	Rockin' through Dixie/Madeira		CL 14567	£ 4 -	6
56	The sleepwalker/Braziliera (Mexican storm song)		CL 14588	£ 2 -	4
56	I love you, Samantha/I am in love		CL 14648	£ 2 -	4
56	Love is just around the corner/Dancing lovers		CL 14670	£ 2 -	4
57	The girl can't help it/Rock around the rock pile		CL 14689	£ 9 -	12
57	Plymouth Rock/Calypso dance		CL 14703	£ 4 -	6
57	This could be the night/The incredible shrinking man ..		CL 14740	£ 2 -	4
57	The lonely trumpet/Cello-phane		CL 14752	£ 2 -	4
57	The bunny hop/The hokey pokey		CL 14769	£ 4 -	6
57	Drive-in/Show me the way to go home		CL 14775	£ 2 -	4
58	Peter Gunn/Tango for two (Mmm shall we dance?)		CL 14929	£ 2 -	4

RAYBURN ANTHONY
60	Who's gonna shoe your pretty..../There's no tomorrow ..	LONDON	HLS 9167	£ 6 -	9

VAL ANTHONY
53	Walk with the wind/No tears, no regrets	COLUMBIA	SCM 5079	£ 2 -	4
54	The heart of a fool/The Portuguese fishermen		SCM 5103	£ 2 -	4

THE APOLLOS
60	Rockin' horses/Just dreaming	MERCURY	AMT 1096	£ 6 -	9

THE APPLEJACKS (*w. DAVE APPELL)
55	Smarter/My heart will wait for you	BRUNSWICK	*05396	£12 -	18
57	Country dance/Applejack	COLUMBIA	*DB 3894	£18 -	25
58	Mexican hat rock/Stop, stop red light	LONDON	HLU 8753	£ 9 -	12
59	Rocka-conga/Am I blue		HLU 8806	£ 9 -	12
60	Circle dance/Love scene	TOP RANK	JAR 273	£ 4 -	6

CHARLIE APPLEWHITE

54	No one but you/Parade	BRUNSWICK	05358	£ 2 − 4
55	Prize of gold/Mister Publisher (have I got a song for..)		05411	£ 2 − 4
55ø	Blue star/A prayer was born		05416	£ 6 − 9

THE AQUATONES

58	You/She's the one for me	LONDON	HLO 8631	£18 − 25

TONI ARDEN

55	Beware/I'll step aside	H.M.V.	7M 314	£ 2 − 4
57	Little by little/Without love (there is nothing)	BRUNSWICK	05645	£ 4 − 6
57	My empty heart/Like a baby		05679	£ 2 − 4
58	Padre/All at once		05745	£ 2 − 4

THE ARIZONA BOYS' CHOIR

56	Ballad of Davy Crockett/Blue shadows on the trail	COLUMBIA	SCM 5215	£ 2 − 4

DEE ARLEN

59	Stay/Why should we wait any longer	PHILIPS	PB 950	£ 2 − 4

STEVE ARLEN

58	That's love/Easy 'n' free	MELODISC	1458	£ 9 − 12

KAY ARMEN

55	He/Suddenly there's a valley	M–G–M	SP 1146	£ 2 − 4
58	Ha! Ha! Ha! (Chella lla!)/Till	BRUNSWICK	05729	£ 2 − 4

ARMENIAN JAZZ QUARTET

57	Harem dance/Pretty girl	LONDON	HLR 8454	£ 4 − 6

RUSSELL ARMS

57	Cinco robles (Five oaks)/The world is made of Lisa	LONDON	HLB 8406	£ 4 − 6

LOUIS ARMSTRONG (& HIS ORCH./ALL STARS/etc.) (& *LOUIS JORDAN/+VELMA MIDDLETON/=THE COMMANDERS/#GARY CROSBY/%B.CROSBY [@BING & SATCHMO]/$NINA & FREDERICK)

50	Life is so peculiar/You rascal you	BRUNSWICK	*04627 º	£ 4 − 6
52ø	Takes two to tango/That's my desire+		04995 º	£ 2 − 4
53	King of the Zulus/Lonesome blues	COLUMBIA	SCM 5061	£ 4 − 6
54	Chicago breakdown/Twelfth Street rag		SCM 5118	£ 4 − 6
54	I'm not rough/Put 'em down blues		SCM 5142	£ 4 − 6
54	Basin Street blues − Parts 1 & 2	BRUNSWICK	05303	£ 4 − 6
54	Skokiaan − Parts 1 & 2		05332	£ 4 − 6
54	Muskrat ramble/Someday you'll be sorry=		05347	£ 4 − 6
55	Trees/Spooks		05364	£ 4 − 6
55	Ko Ko Mo (I love you so)/Struttin' with some barbecue .		#05400	£ 4 − 6
55	Pledging my love/Sincerely		05415	£ 4 − 6
55	Pretty little Missy/Bye and bye		05460	£ 4 − 6
55	Christmas night in Harlem/Christmas in New Orleans		05505	£ 4 − 6
56	Only you (and you alone)/Moments to remember		05512	£ 4 − 6
56ø	"Threepenny Opera" theme (Mack the..)/Back o' town blues	PHILIPS	PB 574 º	£ 2 − 4
56	Easy street/Lazybones	BRUNSWICK	#05574	£ 2 − 4
56ø	The faithful Hussar/The Memphis blues	PHILIPS	PB 604 º	£ 2 − 4
56	Now you has jazz%/High Society calypso	CAPITOL	CL 14643	£ 4 − 6
57	This younger generation/In pursuit of happiness	BRUNSWICK	05649	£ 2 − 4
59	The Mardi Gras march/I love jazz		05772	£ 2 − 4
59	The beat generation/Someday you'll be sorry	M–G–M	MGM 1035	£ 2 − 4
59ø	Mack the knife/The faithful Hussar	PHILIPS	PB 967	£ 2 − 4
59	The formula for love$/Struttin' with some barbecue+	PYE INT.	7N 25043	£ 2 − 4
60	Mahogany Hall blues stomp/On the sunny side of the	PHILIPS	JAZ 108	£ 2 − 4
60	Way down yonder in New.../Do you know what it means to..		JAZ 112	£ 2 − 4
60	Muskrat ramble/Dardanella	M–G–M	@MGM 1107	£ 2 − 4

GINNY ARNELL

60	Carnival/We	BRUNSWICK	05836	£ 2 − 4

CHICO ARNEZ & HIS LATIN AMERICAN ORCH. (qv JACKIE DAVIES)
59 Yashmak/Ain't she sweet .... PYE   7N 15196   £12 – 18

EDDY ARNOLD
55 The richest man (in the world)/I walked alone last night H.M.V.   7M 339   £ 4 – 6
57 Gonna find me a bluebird/Little bit .... R.C.A.   RCA 1008   £ 4 – 6
57 Scarlet ribbons/Bayou baby (A Cajun lullaby) ....:   RCA 1017   £ 2 – 4
58 My darling, my darling/Little Miss Sunbeam ....   RCA 1057   £ 2 – 4
59 Tennessee stud/What's the good (of all this love) .....   RCA 1138   £ 4 – 6
60 Just out of reach/Before this day ends ....   RCA 1212   £ 2 – 4

VIC ASH QUARTET
56 Blue Lou/Doxy .... TEMPO   A 135   £ 2 – 4
56 Early morning/Just one of those things ....   A 137   £ 2 – 4

IRVING ASHBY & HIS COMBO
58 Big guitar/Motatin' .... LONDON   HLP 8578   £ 9 – 12

JOHNNY ASHCROFT
59 A pub with no beer/Bouquet for the bride .... FELSTED AF 118   £ 2 – 4
60 Little boy lost/My love is a river .... H.M.V.   POP 759   £ 2 – 4

BUD ASHTON (& HIS GROUP)
Many releases by different guitarists under this pseudonym on EMBASSY – all £ 1 – 2

LYS ASSIA (*& THE JOHNSTON BROTHERS)
54 O mein Papa/Ponylied .... DECCA   F 10097   £ 2 – 4
54 The glow of a candle/My love, my life, my own ....   F 10278   £ 2 – 4
55 Apples, peaches and cherries*/Words of love ....,...   F 10516   £ 2 – 4
55 Arrivederci darling (Arrivederci Roma)/I'll be waiting   *F 10635   £ 2 – 4
56 My love/Someone ....   F 10675   £ 2 – 4
57 Through the eyes of love/Scusami ....   F 10930   £ 2 – 4

FRED ASTAIRE (*& CYD CHARISSE & CAROL RICHARDS/qv JUDY GARLAND)
57 Funny face/AUDREY HEPBURN: How long has this been going. H.M.V. POP 337   £ 2 – 4
57 Paris loves lovers*/All of you .... M-G-M   MGM 963   £ 2 – 4
57 The Ritz roll and rock/JANIS PAIGE: Satin and silk ....   MGM 964   £ 9 – 12

BENNY ATKINS
60 Lipstick on your lips/I'm following you .... MERCURY AMT 1113   £ 4 – 6

CHET ATKINS
59 Boo boo stick beat/Django's castle .... R.C.A.   RCA 1153   £ 4 – 6
60ø Teensville/One mint julep ....   RCA 1174   £ 4 – 6
60 "The Dark At The Top Of The Stairs" theme/Hocus pocus .   RCA 1209   £ 2 – 4

THE ATMOSPHERES
59 The fickle chicken/Kabalo .... LONDON   HLW 8977   £ 9 – 12
60 Telegraph/Caravan ....   HLW 9091   £ 9 – 12

WINIFRED ATWELL (*& TED HEATH MUSIC/qv VARIOUS ARTISTS)
51 The black and white rag/Cross hands boogie .... DECCA   F 9790 ♀ £ 2 – 4
51 Dinah boogie/Body and soul ....   *F 9822 ♀ £ 2 – 4
52ø Britannia rag/Dixie boogie ....   F 10015 ♀ £ 2 – 4
53ø Coronation rag/Bounce the boogie ....   F 10110 ♀ £ 2 – 4
53ø Flirtation waltz/Golden tango ....   F 10161 ♀ £ 2 – 4
53 Five finger boogie/Rhapsody rag .... PHILIPS PB 182 ♀ £ 2 – 4
53ø "Let's Have A Party" medley ....   PB 213 ♀ £ 2 – 4
54ø The story of three loves (18th variation..)/Moonlight...   PB 234 ♀ £ 2 – 4
54ø "Let's Have Another Party" medley ....   PB 268 ♀ £ 2 – 4
55 Song of the sea/The black mask waltz .... DECCA   F 10448   £ 2 – 4
55 Highland boogie/Concerto for romance .... PHILIPS PB 410 ♀ £ 2 – 4
55 Big Ben boogie/Winnie's waltzing rag .... DECCA   F 10476   £ 4 – 6
55 17th Century boogie/Stranger in Paradise ....   F 10496   £ 4 – 6
55ø "Let's Have A Ding Dong" medley ....   F 10634   £ 4 – 6

56ø	Poor people of Paris (Poor John)/Piano tuner's boogie .		F 10681	£ 6 – 9
56ø	Port–au–Prince/Startime		F 10727	£ 4 – 6
56ø	Left bank (C'est a Hambourg)/Rampart Street rock		F 10762	£ 4 – 6
56	Bumble boogie/St. Louis blues		F 10785	£ 4 – 6
56ø	"Make It A Party" medley		F 10796	£ 4 – 6
56	The Garden of Eden/Moonlight gambler		F 10825	£ 2 – 4
57ø	"Let's Rock 'N' Roll" medley		F 10852	£ 4 – 6
57	Spaceship boogie/Jane Street		F 10886	£ 4 – 6
57ø	"Let's Have A Ball" medley		F 10956	£ 2 – 4
58	Raunchy/Dugga dugga boom boom		F 10987	£ 2 – 4
58	Lazy train/At the Woodchopper's Ball		F 11036	£ 2 – 4
58	"Let's Go!" medley		F 11073	£ 2 – 4
59ø	The Summer of the seventeenth doll/Hawaiian cha cha ...		F 11143	£ 2 – 4
59ø	"Piano Party" medley		F 11183	£ 2 – 4
60	Rumpus/Silver shoes		F 11195	£ 2 – 4
60	"Tops In Pops!" medley		F 11208	£ 2 – 4
60	My old man's a dustman/Fings ain't wot they used t'be .		F 11226	£ 2 – 4

GEORGIE AULD (qv THE LANCERS/THE MODERNAIRES)

54	Manhattan/Solitaire	V–CORAL	Q 2002	£ 4 – 6
60	Hawaiian war chant/Sleepy lagoon	TOP RANK	JAR 281	£ 2 – 4

GENE AUSTIN (*& THE LES PAUL TRIO)

51	Ace in the hole*/I'm crying just for you	LONDON	L 567 º	£ 4 – 6

SIL AUSTIN

57	Slow walk/Wildwood	MERCURY	MT 132 º	£ 4 – 6
58	Fall out/Green blazer		MT 189 º	£ 4 – 6
58	Rainstorm/Don't you just know it		7MT 220	£ 9 – 12
58	Hey, Eula/The last time		7MT 225	£ 9 – 12

GENE AUTRY

59	Nine little reindeer/Buon Natale	LONDON	HLU 9001	£ 2 – 4

FRANKIE AVALON

58	Dede Dinah/Ooh–la–la	H.M.V.	POP 453	£ 9 – 12
58	You excite me/Darlin'	LONDON	HL 8636	£ 9 – 12
58ø	Ginger bread/Blue Betty	H.M.V.	POP 517	£ 6 – 9
59	I'll wait for you/What little girl?		POP 569	£ 4 – 6
59ø	Venus/I'm broke		POP 603	£ 4 – 6
59	Bobby sox to stockings/A boy without a girl		POP 636	£ 4 – 6
59	Just ask your heart/Two fools		POP 658	£ 2 – 4
60ø	Why?/Swingin' on a rainbow		POP 688	£ 4 – 6
60ø	Don't throw away all those teardrops/Talk, talk, talk .		POP 727	£ 4 – 6
60	The faithful kind/Gee whizz – Whilikins – Golly gee ...		POP 742	£ 2 – 4
60	Where are you/Tuxedo Junction		POP 766	£ 2 – 4
60	Togetherness/Don't let love pass me by		POP 794	£ 2 – 4
60	Green leaves of Summer/Here's to the ladies		POP 816	£ 2 – 4

THE AVON CITIES' JAZZ BAND (qv RAY BUSH)

56	Shim–me–sha–wabble/Hawaiian war chant	TEMPO	A 151	£ 2 – 4
60	Upper set/American patrol		A 169	£ 2 – 4

THE AVONS (*as THE AVON SISTERS)

59	Jerri–Lee (I love him so)/Baby–O	COLUMBIA	*DB 4236	£ 4 – 6
59ø	Seven little girls sitting in the back.../Alone at eight		DB 4363	£ 4 – 6
60	Pickin' petals/We fell in love		DB 4413	£ 4 – 6
60ø	We're only young once/I keep dreaming		DB 4461	£ 2 – 4
60ø	Four little heels/This was meant to be		DB 4522	£ 2 – 4

BOB AZZAM & HIS ORCH.

60ø	Mustapha/Tintarella di luna	DECCA	F 21235	£ 4 – 6

MONTY BABSON

59	All night long/The things money cannot buy	LONDON	HLJ 8877	£ 2 – 4

THE BABY DOLLS
60 Quiet!/Hey, baby! .... WARNER-B WB 16 £ 2 – 4

JOHNNY BACHELOR
60 Mumbles/Arabella Jean .... LONDON HLN 9074 £18 – 25

THE BACHELORS
58 Platter party/Love is a two-way street .... PARLOPHONE R 4454 £12 – 18
59 Ding ding/Please don't touch .... R 4547 £12 – 18
60 Lovin' babe/Why can't it be me .... DECCA F 11300 £ 4 – 6

JIM BACKUS (qv PEGGY LEE)
58 Delicious (The laughing song)/I need a vacation .... LONDON HLJ 8674 £ 4 – 6

GAR BACON
58 Mary Jane/Chains of love .... FELSTED AF 107 £ 6 – 9
59 Marshal, Marshal/Too young to love .... FONTANA H 196 £ 9 – 12

DOC BAGBY
58 Dumplin's/Sylvia's calling .... FONTANA H 106 º £ 4 – 6

PEARL BAILEY
54 She's something Spanish/What happened to the hair (on..) V-CORAL Q 2026 £ 4 – 6
56 Tired/Go back where you stayed last night .... H.M.V. POP 244 £ 4 – 6
56 That certain feeling/Hit the road to Dreamland .... LONDON HLN 8354 £12 – 18

BOB BAIN & HIS MUSIC
58 Wagon wheels/Strollin' home .... CAPITOL CL 14912 £ 2 – 4

ARTHUR BAIRD SKIFFLE GROUP
56 Union train/Union maid .... BELTONA BL 2669 £ 4 – 6

CHET BAKER (QUARTET)
56 My funny Valentine/But not for me .... VOGUE V 2377 £ 2 – 4
56 Just friends/Daybreak .... V 2381 £ 2 – 4
56 Winter wonderland/This time the dream's on me .... V 2232 £ 2 – 4
56 Long ago and far away/Bea's flat .... V 2309 £ 2 – 4

HYLDA BAKER
59 She knows y' know/Makin' love .... DECCA F 11186 £ 2 – 4

JEANETTE BAKER (Jeanette & Decky)
59 Everything reminds me of you/Crazy with you .... VOGUE V 9143 £40 – 60

KENNY BAKER (& HIS BAND/QUARTET/etc.)
53 Round about midnight/Afternoon in Paris .... PARLOPHONE MSP 6019 £ 2 – 4
53 Hayfoot, strawfoot/The continental .... MSP 6057 £ 2 – 4
54 Trumpet fantasy/Melancholy baby .... MSP 6062 £ 2 – 4
54 That's my desire/Stompin' at the Savoy .... MSP 6082 £ 2 – 4
54 I speak to the stars/Wanted .... MSP 6114 £ 2 – 4
54 Peg o' my heart/The other side .... MSP 6121 £ 2 – 4
56 Minute to midnight/Studio B boogie .... PYE JAZZ NJ 2000 º £ 2 – 4
56 Blues in thirds/Ding dong Daddy .... NJ 2010 º £ 2 – 4
56 Blues I love to sing/Baker's boogie .... PYE N 15059 º £ 2 – 4
58 Trumpet blues and cantabile/Bakerloo non-stop .... 7N 15146 £ 2 – 4
59 Cuban fiesta/Skylarks .... DECCA F 11130 £ 2 – 4

LaVERN BAKER (& THE GLIDERS)
55 Tweedlee dee/Tomorrow night .... COLUMBIA SCM 5172 £40 – 60
55 That lucky old sun/Play it fair .... LONDON HLA 8199 £25 – 40
56 Get up! Get up! (You sleepy head)/My happiness forever HLE 8260 £25 – 40
57 Tra la la/Jim Dandy .... COLUMBIA DB 3879 £40 – 60
57 I can't love you enough/Still .... LONDON HLE 8396 £25 – 40
57 Jim Dandy got married/Game of love .... HLE 8442 £40 – 60
57 Humpty Dumpty heart/Love me right .... HLE 8524 £18 – 25

- 17 -

58	Learning to love/Substitute		HLE 8638	£12 – 18
58	Whipper snapper/Harbour lights		HLE 8672	£18 – 25
59	I cried a tear/St. Louis blues		HLE 8790	£18 – 25
59	I waited too long/You're teasing me		HLE 8871	£12 – 18
59	So high so low/If you love me (I won't care)		HLE 8945	£ 9 – 12
60	Tiny Tim/For love of you		HLE 9023	£ 9 – 12
60	Bumble bee/My time will come		HLK 9252	£ 9 – 12

TWO-TON BAKER
55	Clink, clank (in my piggy bank)/Mr. Froggie	LONDON	HL 8121	£25 – 40

KENNY BALL & HIS (JAZZ) BAND
59	Waterloo/Wabash Cannonball	COLLECTOR	JDN 101	£ 4 – 6
60	Teddy Bears' picnic/Waltzing Matilda	PYE	7N 15272	£ 2 – 4

THE BALLADEERS
59	Tom gets the last laugh/Morning star	COLUMBIA	DB 4364	£ 2 – 4

THE BALLARAT Y.W.C.A. CHOIR
60	The happy wanderer/You'll never walk alone	STARLITE	ST.45 010	£ 2 – 4

HANK BALLARD & THE MIDNIGHTERS
59	Kansas City/The twist	PARLOPHONE	R 4558	£12 – 18
60	Finger poppin' time/I love you, I love you so-o-o		R 4682	£ 9 – 12
60	The twist/Teardrops on your letter		R 4688	£ 9 – 12
60	Let's go, let's go, let's go/If you'd forgive me		R 4707	£ 9 – 12

KAYE BALLARD
55	Triumph of love/Where were you last night?	BRUNSWICK	05376	£ 2 – 4
55	Don't you tell Pa/In love and out again		05436	£ 2 – 4

THE BANJO BOYS
55	Hey, Mr. Banjo/Kvi-vi-vi-vi-vitt	CAPITOL	CL 14298	£ 4 – 6

CHRIS BARBER'S JAZZ BAND (w. *OTTILIE PATTERSON/+LONNIE DONEGAN/=MONTY SUNSHINE)
51	Oh, didn't he ramble/(by CRANE RIVER JAZZ BAND)	ESQUIRE	12-013 º	£ 6 – 9
54	Chimes blues/Merrydown rag	DECCA	F 10417	£ 4 – 6
55	Bobby Shafto/The Martinique		F 10492	£ 4 – 6
55	It's tight like that/All the girls go crazy about the...		F 10666	£ 4 – 6
56	Tiger rag/Precious Lord, lead me on+	TEMPO	A 116	£ 4 – 6
56	Saratoga swing/Ice cream		A 132	£ 4 – 6
56	The world is waiting for the sunrise/St. Louis blues ..	DECCA	FJ 10724	£ 4 – 6
56	I never knew just what a girl could do/Storyville blues		FJ 10790	£ 4 – 6
57	Ice cream/Down by the riverside	TEMPO	A 160	£ 4 – 6
57	Bye and bye/MONTY SUNSHINE QUARTET: Old rugged cross ..	PYE JAZZ	NJ 2020 º	£ 2 – 4
58	Whistlin' Rufus/Hushabye		7NJ 2011	£ 4 – 6
58	Tuxedo rag/Brown skin Mama		7NJ 2004	£ 4 – 6
58	When the Saints go marching in (both sides)		*7NJ 2023	£ 2 – 4
58	High society/Papa De-Da-Da		7NJ 2007	£ 4 – 6
59ø	Petite fleur/Bugle boy march		7NJ 2026	£ 4 – 6
59ø	Lonesome=/There'll be a hot time in the old town tonight*	COLUMBIA	DB 4333	£ 4 – 6
60	Bill Bailey won't you please come home/Wild cat blues .	PYE JAZZ	7NJ 2030	£ 2 – 4
60	Bohemia rag/Swanee River	COLUMBIA	DB 4501	£ 2 – 4
60	The Mountains of Mourne/Real old mountain dew		*DB 4531	£ 2 – 4

CHRIS BARBER'S SKIFFLE GROUP/*WASHBOARD WONDERS (w. +JOHNNY DUNCAN/=DICKIE BISHOP)
51	Everybody loves my baby/Whoop it up	ESQUIRE	*10-180 º	£ 6 – 9
58	Doin' my time/Where could I go?	+PYE JAZZ	7NJ 2014	£ 4 – 6
58	Can't you line 'em/Gipsy Davy		=7NJ 2017	£ 4 – 6

DAVE BARBOUR & HIS ORCH.
59	Tough/Bu bam	ORIOLE	CB 1507	£ 4 – 6

RUE BARCLAY & PEGGY DUNCAN
54	River of tears/Tongue tied boy	LONDON	HL 8033	£12 – 18

KENNY BARDELL (qv KEN MACKINTOSH)
58	Salty salty is the sea/My darling, my darling	ORIOLE	CB 1420	£ 2 – 4

BOBBY BARE (qv BILL PARSONS)
60	I'm hanging up my rifle/That's where I want to be	TOP RANK	JAR 310	£ 6 – 9

BENNY BARNES
60	Token of love/That-a-boy Willie	MERCURY	AMT 1094	£ 2 – 4

BARRY BARNETT
58	Book of love/All I have to do is dream	H.M.V.	POP 487	£ 4 – 6
58	When/Secretly		POP 511	£ 4 – 6
58	My lucky love/Too young to love		POP 521	£ 4 – 6
58	Susie darlin'/Just a dream		POP 532	£ 4 – 6
59	The diary/Only one memory		POP 579	£ 2 – 4
59	Cuckoo girl/I'll string along with you		POP 627	£ 2 – 4

THE (ORIGINAL) BARNSTORMERS SPASM BAND
58	Whistling Rufus/Won't you come home, Bill Bailey?	PARLOPHONE	R 4416	£ 2 – 4
59	Stormin' the barn/That's all there is (there ain't no..)	TEMPO	A 168	£ 2 – 4

RIKKY BARON
60	Angry young man/My lonely heart	PARLOPHONE	R 4706	£ 2 – 4

THE BARONS
57	Don't walk out/Once in a lifetime	LONDON	HLP 8391	£60 – 90

DICKIE BARRETT
58	Smoke gets in your eyes/Remember me	M-G-M	MGM 976	£ 2 – 4

JOE BARRETT
55	I'm sincere/Why did you break my heart?	BRUNSWICK	05432	£ 2 – 4

RICHARD BARRETT & THE CHANTELS
59	Come softly to me/Walking through Dreamland	H.M.V.	POP 609	£ 6 – 9

THE (THREE) BARRY SISTERS (U.K.)
59	Little Boy Blue/My sweetie's coming to call	DECCA	F 11099	£ 2 – 4
59	Tall Paul/Till then		F 11118	£ 4 – 6
59	Jo Jo – the dog faced boy/I-ay ove-lay oo-yay		F 11141	£ 4 – 6
60	Spoilsport/Bonnie Prince Charlie		F 11201	£ 2 – 4

THE BARRY SISTERS (U.S.)
56	Cha Cha Joe/Baby come a little closer	LONDON	HLA 8248	£ 9 – 12
56	Till you come back to me/Intrigue		HLA 8304	£ 9 – 12
56	Sing me a sentimental love song/The Italian theme	COLUMBIA	DB 3843	£ 2 – 4
58	I hear bells/I get up ev'ry morning		DB 4215	£ 2 – 4
60	Misty/Why don't you do right?		DB 4562	£ 2 – 4

DAVE BARRY & SARA BERNER
56	Out of this world with flying saucers, Parts 1 & 2	LONDON	HLU 8324	£25 – 40

JOHN BARRY (SEVEN [plus FOUR]/*& HIS ORCH.) (qv DESMOND LANE)
57	Zip zip/Three little fishes	PARLOPHONE	R 4363	£ 9 – 12
58	Every which way/You've gotta way		R 4394	£ 9 – 12
58	Big guitar/Rodeo		R 4418	£ 4 – 6
58	Pancho/Hideaway		R 4453	£ 4 – 6
58	Farrago/Bee's knees		R 4488	£ 4 – 6
59	Long John/Snap 'n' whistle		R 4530	£ 4 – 6
59	Little John/For Pete's sake		R 4560	£ 4 – 6
59	Twelfth Street rag/Christella		R 4582	£ 4 – 6
60ø	Hit and miss/Rockin' already	COLUMBIA	DB 4414	£ 4 – 6
60ø	Beat for beatniks/Big fella		*DB 4446	£ 4 – 6
60ø	Blueberry Hill/Never let go		*DB 4480	£ 4 – 6
60ø	Walk don't run/I'm movin' on		DB 4505	£ 4 – 6
60ø	Black stockings/Get lost Jack Frost		DB 4554	£ 4 – 6

EILEEN BARTON
55	The year we fell in love/I don't want to mambo polka ..	V-CORAL	Q 72060	£ 4 – 6
55	Fujiyama Mama/I'd've baked a cake		Q 72075	£ 9 – 12
56	Cry me a river/Come home		Q 72122	£ 4 – 6
56	Teenage heart/My social hot dog		Q 72148	£ 4 – 6
56	I have to tell you/Spring it was		Q 72205	£ 2 – 4
57	Too close for comfort/Here I am in love again		Q 72250	£ 2 – 4
57	Without love/The scene of the crime		Q 72270	£ 2 – 4

BAS-SHEVA
55	Flame of love/I just wanna be your loving baby	CAPITOL	CL 14218	£ 4 – 6

COUNT BASIE & HIS ORCH./BIG BAND (& *ELLA FITZGERALD/+JOE WILLIAMS/qv BILLY
ECKSTINE/SARAH VAUGHAN)
59	The late late show/The M Squad theme	COLUMBIA	DB 4262	£ 2 – 4
59	April in Paris/Party blues+		*SCD 2116	£ 2 – 4
60	April in Paris/The midgets	H.M.V.	POP 733	£ 2 – 4
60	The golden bullet/Bluebeard blues	PHILIPS	JAZ 109	£ 2 – 4

ALFIE BASS (qv MICHAEL MEDWIN)
60	Villikens and his Dinah/Rat catcher's daughter	PYE	7N 15286	£ 2 – 4

SHIRLEY BASSEY
57ø	The banana boat song/Tra la la	PHILIPS	PB 668 º	£ 2 – 4
57ø	as above		JK 1006	£ 9 – 12
57	If I had a needle and thread/Tonight my heart she is....		JK 1018	£ 6 – 9
57ø	You, you Romeo/Fire down below		PB 723 º	£ 2 – 4
57	Puh-leeze! Mister Brown/Take my love, take my love		JK 1034	£ 6 – 9
58ø	As I love you/Hands across the sea		PB 845	£ 2 – 4
58ø	Kiss me, Honey Honey, kiss me/There's never been a night		PB 860	£ 4 – 6
59	Love for sale/Crazy rhythm		PB 917	£ 2 – 4
59	My funny Valentine/How about you?		PB 919	£ 2 – 4
59	If you love me/Count on me	COLUMBIA	DB 4344	£ 2 – 4
59	Night and day/The gypsy in my soul	PHILIPS	PB 975	£ 2 – 4
60ø	With these hands/The party's over	COLUMBIA	DB 4421	£ 2 – 4
60ø	As long as he needs me/So in love		DB 4490	£ 2 – 4
60	Birth of the blues/Careless love blues	PHILIPS	PB 1091	£ 2 – 4

ART BAXTER & HIS ROCK'N ROLL SINNERS
56	Jingle rock/Rock and roll rag	PHILIPS	PB 652 º	£ 9 – 12
57	Don't knock the rock/Rock rock rock		PB 666 º	£ 9 – 12

LES BAXTER & HIS ORCH./=DRUMS/+THE BOMBERS (*& LEONARD PENNARIO)
54	I love Paris/Manhattan	CAPITOL	CL 14166	£ 4 – 6
54	Midnight on the cliffs/Dream rhapsody		*CL 14173	£ 4 – 6
54	When you're in love/Romantic Rio		CL 14217	£ 4 – 6
55	Earth angel/Happy birthday		+CL 14239	£ 6 – 9
55	I ain't mad at you+/Blue mirage		CL 14249	£ 4 – 6
55ø	Unchained melody/Blue star (The Medic theme)		CL 14257	£ 6 – 9
55	Cherry pink and apple blossom white/Play me hearts and..		CL 14237	£ 4 – 6
55	Wake the town and tell the.../I'll never stop loving you		CL 14344	£ 4 – 6
55	The shrike/The toy tiger		CL 14351	£ 4 – 6
55	Take my love/If you've forgotten me		CL 14358	£ 4 – 6
56	Poor John/"Helen Of Troy" theme		CL 14533	£ 2 – 4
56	The trouble with Harry/Havana		CL 14546	£ 2 – 4
56	Tango of the drums/If you can dream		CL 14589	£ 2 – 4
57	Giant/There's never been anyone else but you		CL 14677	£ 2 – 4
59	Sabre dance/Milord		CL 15055	£ 2 – 4
60	Ooch-i-baba/Boomada		=CL 15140	£ 2 – 4

RONNIE BAXTER
60	I finally found you/Is it because?	TOP RANK	JAR 293	£ 4 – 6

BEA & DEE
59	Wishing time/Jerry	CAPITOL	CL 15066	£ 2 – 4

THE BEALE STREET BUSKERS

60	'Fraidy cat/Dusty	EMBER	EMB S107	£ 2 – 4

DEAN BEARD & THE CREW CATS

57	Rakin' and scrapin'/On my mind again	LONDON	HLE 8463	£60 – 90

PAUL BEATTIE

57	I'm comin' home/Nothing so strange	PARLOPHONE	R 4385	£ 4 – 6
58	Me, please me/Wanderlust		R 4429	£ 2 – 4
58	Banana/A house, a car, and a wedding ring		R 4468	£ 2 – 4
60	The big bounce/Slick chick		R 4664	£ 2 – 4

E.C. BEATTY

59	Ski king/I'm a lucky man	FELSTED	AF 127	£ 4 – 6

THE BEAU-MARKS

60	Clap your hands/Daddy said	TOP RANK	JAR 377	£ 6 – 9

THE BEAVERS

58	Road to happiness/Low as I can be	CAPITOL	CL 14909	£ 2 – 4

GILBERT BECAUD

59	The day the rains came/Les Marches de Provence	H.M.V.	POP 574	£ 2 – 4

SIDNEY BECHET (as +MEZZROW-BECHET SEPTET/=BECHET-SPANIER BIG FOUR/*& BOB SCOBEY'S
FRISCO BAND)

56	The onions/Ce' Moissieu qui parle	VOGUE	V 2328	£ 2 – 4
56	Viper mad/High society		V 2366	£ 2 – 4
56	Charleston/Swanee River		V 2367	£ 2 – 4
56	Casey Jones/Twelfth Street rag		V 2374	£ 2 – 4
56	If ever you go to Paree (Bonjour Paris)/El Doudou	DECCA	FJ 10734	£ 2 – 4
56	Everybody loves Saturday night/Laura	VOGUE	V 2378	£ 2 – 4
56	Theme & Army song from "The Threepenny Opera"		V 2394	£ 2 – 4
56	Society blues/Le marchand de poissons (Fish seller) ...		V 2354	£ 2 – 4
56	On the sunny side of the street/Summertime		*V 2379	£ 2 – 4
56	House party/Blood on the Moon		+V 2350	£ 2 – 4
56	Royal Garden blues/Mon homme		V 2391	£ 2 – 4
59	Petite fleur/Dans les rues d'Antibes		V 9141	£ 2 – 4
59	Si tu vois ma Mere (Lonesome)/Le marchand de poissons .		V 9157	£ 2 – 4
60	Sweet Lorraine/China boy	TOP RANK	=TR 5017	£ 2 – 4
60	Sweet Sue, just you/Lazy river		=TR 5018	£ 2 – 4
60	My woman's blues/What a dream	PHILIPS	JAZ 110	£ 2 – 4

BOB BECKHAM

59	Just as much as ever/Your sweet love	BRUNSWICK	05808	£ 2 – 4
60	Crazy arms/Beloved		05822	£ 2 – 4
60	Mais oui/Only the broken hearted		05835	£ 2 – 4
60	Nothing is forever/Two wrongs don't make a right		05837	£ 2 – 4

Her Grace The DUCHESS OF BEDFORD

57	Luck's in love with me/Mrs. GERALD LEGGE: I'm in love .	H.M.V.	POP 361	£ 2 – 4

MOLLY BEE

57	Since I met you, baby/I'll be waiting for you	LONDON	HLD 8400	£ 6 – 9
58	Going steady (with a dream)/Magic mirror	CAPITOL	CL 14849	£ 4 – 6
58	Please don't talk about me when I'm gone/Don't look back		CL 14880	£ 4 – 6
58	Five points of a star/After you've gone		CL 14949	£ 4 – 6

DOMINIC BEHAN

59	The bells of Hell/The Captains and the Kings	DECCA	F 11147	£ 2 – 4

BIX BEIDERBECKE & HIS GANG

· 60	Since my best gal turned me down/At the Jazz Band Ball	PHILIPS	JAZ 116	£ 2 – 4

REMEMBER! – THE SYMBOL ø AFTER THE YEAR OF ISSUE INDICATES A BRITISH CHART ENTRY

HARRY BELAFONTE

54	Hold 'em Joe/Suzanne (Every night when the sun goes....)	H.M.V.	7M	202	£ 4 – 6
54	I'm just a country boy/Pretty as a rainbow (after the..)		7M	224	£ 4 – 6
55	Close your eyes/I still get a thrill (thinking of you)	CAPITOL	CL 14312	£ 4 – 6
57ø	Banana boat song (Day–o)/Jamaica farewell	H.M.V.	POP	308	£ 6 – 9
57	Mama looka boo boo/Don't ever love me		POP	339	£ 2 – 4
57ø	Scarlet ribbons (for her hair)/Hold 'em Joe		POP	360	£ 4 – 6
57ø	Island in the Sun/Cocoanut woman	R.C.A.	RCA 1007	£ 4 – 6
57ø	Mary's boy child/Eden was just like this		RCA 1022	£ 4 – 6
58	Judy drownded/Lucy's door		RCA 1033	£ 2 – 4
58	Lead man holler/Haiti cherie		RCA 1035	£ 2 – 4
58ø	Little Bernadette/Danny boy		RCA 1072	£ 2 – 4
58ø	The son of Mary/I heard the bells on Christmas day		RCA 1084	£ 2 – 4
58	Silent night/The twelve days of Christmas		RCA 1085	£ 2 – 4
58	The banana boat song (Day–o)/Jamaica farewell		RCA 1089	£ 2 – 4
59	Times are gettin' hard/The waiting game		RCA 1103	£ 2 – 4
59	Turn around/Darlin' Cora		RCA 1116	£ 2 – 4
59	Round the Bay of Mexico/Fifteen		RCA 1125	£ 2 – 4

THE BELL NOTES

59	I've had it/Be mine	TOP RANK	JAR	102	£ 4 – 6
59	Old Spanish town/She went that–a–way		JAR	147	£ 4 – 6
59	That's right/Betty dear		JAR	201	£ 4 – 6

THE BELL SOUNDS

59	Marching guitars/Chloe	H.M.V.	POP	685	£ 4 – 6

BENNY BELL & THE BLOCKBUSTERS

57	The sack dress/Dr. Jazz	PARLOPHONE	R 4372	£ 2 – 4

FREDDIE BELL & THE BELL BOYS

56ø	Giddy–up–a ding dong/I said it and I'm glad	MERCURY	MT	122 º	£ 9 – 12
57	Hucklebuck/Rompin' and stompin'		MT	141 º	£ 9 – 12
57	Teach you to rock/Take the first train out of town		MT	146 º	£ 9 – 12
57	Big bad wolf/Rockin' the polonaise		MT	149 º	£ 9 – 12
57	Rockin' is my business/You're gonna be sorry		MT	159 º	£ 9 – 12

TONY BELLUS

59	Robbin' the cradle/Valentine girl	LONDON	HL	8933	£ 9 – 12

JESSE BELVIN

59	Guess who/Funny	R.C.A.	RCA 1119	£ 6 – 9

TEX BENEKE & HIS ORCH.

56	'S wonderful/Singin' in the rain	M–G–M	SP	1158	£ 2 – 4

BOYD BENNETT & HIS ROCKETS/+ORCH. (*w. BIG MOE/qv MOON MULLICAN)

55	Everlovin'/Boogie at midnight .... *PARLOPHONE	MSP 6161	£40 – 60
55ø	Seventeen*/Little ole you–all	R 4063 º	£ 9 – 12
55ø	*as above*	MSP 6180	£40 – 60
56	My boy – Flat Top/Banjo rock and roll	*MSP 6203	£40 – 60
56	Blue suede shoes/Oo–oo–oo*	MSP 6233	£40 – 60
58	Click clack/Move	R 4423	£25 – 40
59	Tear it up/Tight tights .... MERCURY	+AMT 1031	£12 – 18

CAROLE BENNETT

56	The little magician/I was your only love	CAPITOL	CL 14652	£ 2 – 4
57	Play the music/Miser's gold		CL 14692	£ 2 – 4
57	Haunted lover/Let the chips fall (where they may)		CL 14725	£ 2 – 4

DICKIE BENNETT

55	Stars shine in your eyes/There, but for the grace of....	DECCA	F 10595	£ 2 – 4
56	Dunaree doll/Can't we be partners (after the dance) ...		F 10697	£ 4 – 6
56	You don't know me/Cry upon my shoulder		F 10782	£ 2 – 4

JOE BENNETT & THE SPARKLETONES

57	Black slacks/Boppin' rock boogie	H.M.V.	POP	399	£25 – 40
58	Penny loafers and bobby socks/Rocket		POP	445	£40 – 60

KIM BENNETT (qv ROLAND SHAW)

55	Melody of love/Ding dong	DECCA	F	10460	£ 2 – 4
55	The Kentuckian song/Overnight		F	10599	£ 2 – 4
56	No, not much/You can't keep running		F	10706	£ 2 – 4

NICKY BENNETT

60	You understand me/Mr. Lonely	COLUMBIA	DB	4516	£ 2 – 4

TONY BENNETT

53	Congratulations to someone/Take me	COLUMBIA	SCM	5048	£ 4 – 6
55ø	Stranger in Paradise/Take me back again	PHILIPS	PB	420 ọ	£ 1 – 2
55ø	Close your eyes/It's too soon to know		PB	445 ọ	£ 2 – 4
56ø	Come next Spring/Afraid of the dark		PB	537 ọ	£ 2 – 4
57	Whatever Lola wants/Heart		JK	1008	£ 6 – 9
58	Young and warm and wonderful/Now I lay me down to sleep		PB	831	£ 2 – 4
58	Firefly/The night that Heaven fell		PB	855	£ 2 – 4
59	Being true to one another/It's so peaceful in the country		PB	907	£ 2 – 4
59	Smile (Theme from "Modern Times")/You can't love 'em all		PB	961	£ 2 – 4
60	Love look away/The cool school		PB	996	£ 2 – 4
60	Ask me (I know)/I'll bring you a rainbow		PB	1008	£ 2 – 4
60ø	Till/Ask anyone in love		PB	1079	£ 2 – 4
60	Marriage-go-round/Somebody		PB	1089	£ 2 – 4

JOHN BENNINGS & HIS RHYTHM & BLUES BAND

54	Timber/Third degree blues	ESQUIRE		10–376 ọ	£ 6 – 9

BOBBIE BENSON & HIS COMBO

58	Taxi driver, I don't care/Gentleman Bobby	PHILIPS	PB	854	£ 2 – 4

MARIE BENSON (qv VARIOUS ARTISTS)

55	Mambo Italiano/Mobile	DECCA	F	10452	£ 4 – 6

THE BENTLEY BROTHERS

59	Ma (she's makin' eyes at me)/Yes, we have no bananas ..	TOP RANK	JAR	208	£ 2 – 4

BRIAN BENTLEY & THE BACHELORS

60	Wishing well/Please make up your mind	PHILIPS	PB	1085	£ 2 – 4
60	First flight east/Sunday break		PB	1086	£ 4 – 6

BROOK BENTON (*& DINAH WASHINGTON)

56	Give me a sign/Love made me your fool	PHILIPS	PB	639 ọ	£ 4 – 6
58	A million miles from nowhere/Devoted	R.C.A.	RCA	1044	£ 4 – 6
58	It's just a matter of time/Hurtin' inside	MERCURY	AMT	1014	£ 4 – 6
59ø	Endlessly/So close		AMT	1043	£ 4 – 6
59	Thank you pretty baby/With all of my heart		AMT	1061	£ 2 – 4
59	So many ways/I want you forever		AMT	1068	£ 2 – 4
60	Baby (you've got what it takes)/I do		*AMT	1083	£ 6 – 9
60	The ties that bind/Hither and thither and yon		AMT	1097	£ 2 – 4
60	A rockin' good way/I believe		*AMT	1099	£ 9 – 12
60ø	Kiddio/The same one		AMT	1109	£ 4 – 6
60ø	Fools rush in/Someday you'll want me to want you		AMT	1121	£ 2 – 4

MILTON BERLE

56	In the middle of the house/Buffalo	V-CORAL	Q	72197	£ 6 – 9

SHELLEY BERMAN

60	"On The Phone": Hold on/Nephew trouble	H.M.V.	POP	732	£ 2 – 4

ROD BERNARD

59	Pardon, Mr. Gordon/This should go on forever	LONDON	HLM	8849	£12 – 18
59	One more chance/Shedding teardrops over you	MERCURY	AMT	1070	£ 4 – 6

ELMER BERNSTEIN (& HIS ORCH.)

56	Clark Street - Parts 1 & 2	BRUNSWICK	05544	£ 2 - 4
59ø	Staccato's theme/The jazz at Waldo's	CAPITOL	CL 15101	£ 4 - 6

CHUCK BERRY

56	Down bound train/No money down	LONDON	HLU 8275	£90 -120
57	You can't catch me/Havana moon		HLN 8375	£60 - 90
57	Roll over Beethoven/Drifting heart		HLU 8428	£18 - 25
57ø	School day (Ring! Ring! Goes the bell)/Deep feeling ...	COLUMBIA	DB 3951	£18 - 25
57	Rock and roll music/Blue feeling	LONDON	HLM 8531	£18 - 25
58ø	Sweet little sixteen/Reelin' and rockin'		HLM 8585	£ 9 - 12
58ø	Johnny B. Goode/Around and around		HLM 8629	£ 9 - 12
58	Beautiful Delilah/Vacation time		HL 8677	£ 9 - 12
58	Carol/Hey Pedro		HL 8712	£ 9 - 12
58	Sweet little rock and roller/Joe Joe Gun		HLM 8767	£ 9 - 12
59	Almost grown/Little Queenie		HLM 8853	£ 9 - 12
59	Back in the U.S.A./Memphis, Tennessee		HLM 8921	£ 9 - 12
60	Let it rock/Too pooped to pop		HLM 9069	£ 9 - 12
60	Bye bye Johnny/Mad lad		HLM 9159	£ 9 - 12

THE BEVERLEY SISTERS (qv VARIOUS ARTISTS)

53ø	I saw Mommy kissing Santa Claus/Triplets	PHILIPS	PB 188 º	£ 2 - 4
55	I remember Mama/I've been thinking	DECCA	F 10539	£ 4 - 6
55	Humming bird/Have you ever been lonely?		F 10603	£ 4 - 6
55	My heart goes a-sailing/Teddy bear		F 10641	£ 4 - 6
56ø	Willie can/I've started courtin'		F 10705	£ 6 - 9
56	Rickshaw boy/You ought to have a wife		F 10729	£ 2 - 4
56	Born to be with you/It's easy		F 10770	£ 4 - 6
56	Come home to my arms/Doodle-doo-doo		F 10813	£ 2 - 4
57ø	I dreamed/Mama from the train (A kiss, a kiss)		F 10832	£ 4 - 6
57	Greensleeves/I'll see you in my dreams		F 10853	£ 2 - 4
57	Mr. Wonderful/Blow the wind southerly		F 10893	£ 2 - 4
57	Bye, bye love/It's illegal, it's immoral, or it makes...		F 10909	£ 4 - 6
57	Riding down from Bangor/The young cavaliero		F 10943	£ 2 - 4
58	Long black nylons/Without you		F 10971	£ 6 - 9
58	Always and forever/Siesta		F 10999	£ 2 - 4
58	Left right out of my heart/I would (climb the highest..)		F 11042	£ 2 - 4
59ø	The little drummer boy/Strawberry Fair		F 11107	£ 2 - 4
59ø	Little donkey/And Kings came a-calling		F 11172	£ 2 - 4
60ø	Green fields/The Skye boat song	COLUMBIA	DB 4444	£ 2 - 4
60	The whole year round/I thought of you last night		DB 4523	£ 2 - 4

GENE BIANCO

53	Limehouse boogie/Harpin' boogie	LONDON	L 1209 º	£ 4 - 6
60	Alarm clock boogie/Harp rock boogie	VOGUE	V 9167	£ 4 - 6

THE BIG BEN ACCORDION BAND

56	"Rock 'N' Roll (No. 1)" medley	COLUMBIA	DB 3835	£ 6 - 9
57	"Rock 'N' Roll (No. 2)" medley		DB 3856	£ 6 - 9

THE BIG BEN BANJO BAND (qv BILLIE ANTHONY)

54ø	"Let's Get Together (No. 1)" medley	COLUMBIA	DB 3549 º	£ 2 - 4
55ø	"Let's Get Together Again (No. 1)" medley		DB 3676 º	£ 2 - 4

BIG BOB

59	Your line was busy/What am I	TOP RANK	JAR 185	£12 - 18

BIG BOPPER

58ø	Chantilly lace/Purple People Eater meets Witchdoctor ..	MERCURY	AMT 1002	£ 9 - 12
59	Big Bopper's wedding/Little Red Riding Hood		AMT 1017	£12 - 18
59	That's what I'm talking about/It's the truth Ruth		AMT 1046	£12 - 18

BIG DAVE (Cavanaugh) & HIS ORCH.

54	Rock, roll, ball and wail/The big goof	CAPITOL	CL 14156 º	£ 4 - 6
54	The cat from Coos Bay/Loosely with feeling		CL 14195	£ 6 - 9
55	Rock and roll party/Your kind of love		CL 14245	£ 9 - 12

BIG MAYBELLE

57	I don't want to cry/All of me	LONDON	HLC 8447	£18 – 25
59	Baby, won't you please come home/Say it isn't so		HLC 8854	£12 – 18

BIG MOE w. BOYD BENNETT & HIS ROCKETS

56	The groovy age/Hit that jive, Jack	PARLOPHONE	R 4214	£40 – 60
57	Rockin' up a storm/The most		R 4252	£40 – 60

THE BIKINIS

58	Bikini/Boogie rock and roll	COLUMBIA	DB 4149	£ 6 – 9

(Mr.) ACKER BILK & HIS PARAMOUNT JAZZ BAND

56	Gravier Street blues/My old Kentucky home	ESQUIRE	10–475 º	£ 2 – 4
56	Dippermouth blues/Where the River Shannon flows	TEMPO	A 134	£ 2 – 4
56	Gettysburg stomp/Over in Gloryland	ESQUIRE	10–483 º	£ 2 – 4
60ø	Summer set/Acker's away	COLUMBIA	DB 4382	£ 2 – 4
60	Delia gone/Marching through Georgia	PYE JAZZ	7NJ 2029	£ 2 – 4
60ø	Goodnight sweet Prince/East Coast trot	MELODISC	1547	£ 4 – 6
60ø	White cliffs of Dover/Fancy pants	COLUMBIA	DB 4492	£ 2 – 4
60	C.R.E. march/Willie the Weeper	PYE JAZZ	7NJ 2033	£ 2 – 4
60	Blaze away/Higher ground		7NJ 2034	£ 2 – 4
60	Under the Double Eagle/Easter Parade		7NJ 2035	£ 2 – 4
60	El Abanico/Carry me back		7NJ 2036	£ 2 – 4
60	Dardanella/Jump in the line		7NJ 2037	£ 2 – 4
60	Gladiolus rag/Louisian-i-ay		7NJ 2038	£ 2 – 4
60ø	Buona sera/Corrine Corrina	COLUMBIA	DB 4544	£ 2 – 4

BILLIE & EDDIE

59	The King is coming back/Come back, baby	TOP RANK	JAR 249	£ 9 – 12

BILLY & LILLIE (*& BILLY FORD & THE THUNDERBIRDS)

58	La dee dah/BILLY FORD'S THUNDERBIRDS: The monster	LONDON	HLU 8564	£ 9 – 12
58	Creepin', crawlin', cryin'/Happiness		*HLU 8630	£ 9 – 12
58	The greasy spoon/Hangin' on to you		*HLU 8689	£ 6 – 9
59	Lucky ladybug/I promise you		HLU 8795	£ 6 – 9
59	Bells, bells, bells/Honeymoonin'	TOP RANK	JAR 157	£ 4 – 6

UMBERTO BINDI & HIS ORCH.

60ø	Il nostro concerto/Un giorno, un mese, un anno	ORIOLE	CB 1577	£ 4 – 6

RONALD BINGE & HIS ORCH.

54	September in the rain/Holiday for bells	DECCA	F 10410	£ 2 – 4

STANLEY & JEFFREY BIRD

60	Johnny at the crossroads/Betty, Betty (go steady with..)	H.M.V.	POP 702	£ 4 – 6

DICKIE BISHOP (& THE SIDEKICKS) (qv CHRIS BARBER)

57	Cumberland Gap/No other baby	DECCA	F 10869	£ 6 – 9
57	The prisoner's song/Please remember me		F 10959	£ 4 – 6
58	No other baby/Skip to my Lou		F 10981	£ 4 – 6
58	Jumpin' Judy/They can't take that away from me		F 11028	£ 4 – 6

THE BLACK DYNAMITES

60	Brush those tears/Lonely cissy	TOP RANK	JAR 319	£ 9 – 12

BLACK MAMBAZO

58	Fuzzy night/Matshutshu	COLUMBIA	DB 4135	£ 2 – 4

BILL BLACK'S COMBO

59	Smokie – Parts 1 & 2	FELSTED	AF 129	£ 6 – 9
60ø	White silver sands/The wheel	LONDON	HLU 9090	£ 4 – 6
60	Josephine/Dry bones		HLU 9156	£ 4 – 6
60ø	Don't be cruel/Rollin'		HLU 9212	£ 4 – 6

REMEMBER! – THE SYMBOL º AFTER THE CATALOGUE NUMBER INDICATES A 78 rpm RECORD

"FLIP" BLACK & THE BOYS UPSTAIRS
59	For you my lover/Tell her Mister Moon	CAPITOL	CL 15037	£ 2 – 4

JEANNE BLACK (*or* JEANNE & JANIE)
60ø	He'll have to stay/Under your spell again*	CAPITOL	CL 15131	£ 4 – 6
60	Journey of love*/Lisa		CL 15146	£ 2 – 4
60	Sleep walkin'*/You'll find out		CL 15165	£ 2 – 4

STANLEY BLACK & HIS ORCH.
54	Gaviotta/Siciliano	DECCA	F 10195	£ 2 – 4
54	Beautiful spring/Tipica serenade		F 10354	£ 2 – 4
54	Midnight tango/Desire (Tango desiree)		F 10400	£ 2 – 4
55	Melody of love/Memory		F 10462	£ 2 – 4

OTIS BLACKWELL
58	Make ready for love/When you're around	LONDON	HLE 8616	£12 – 18

RORY BLACKWELL & HIS BLACKJACKS
57	Bye bye love/Such a shame	PARLOPHONE	R 4326	£ 9 – 12

THE BLACKWELLS
60	Unchained melody/Mansion on the hill	LONDON	HLW 9135	£ 4 – 6

VIVIAN BLAINE
53ø	A bushel and a peck/ROBERT ALDA: My time of day/Luck...	BRUNSWICK	05100 º	£ 2 – 4
54	Changing partners/Lonely	PARLOPHONE	MSP 6070	£ 2 – 4

BEVERLEY BLAIR
58	With love we live/Tony	MERCURY	7MT 209	£ 2 – 4

SALLY BLAIR
58	Whatever Lola wants (Lola gets)/Daddy	M–G–M	MGM 1000	£ 2 – 4

BLIND BLAKE
50	Hey hey Daddy blues/Brownskin Mama blues	TEMPO	R 23 º	£ 6 – 9

MEL BLANC
58	I taut I taw a puddy tat/K–K–K–Katy	CAPITOL	CL 14950	£ 4 – 6
60	Tweety's Twistmas twouble/I keep hearing those bells ..	WARNER–B	WB 26	£ 2 – 4

BILLY BLAND
60ø	Let the little girl dance/Sweet thing	LONDON	HL 9096	£ 4 – 6

ARCHIE BLEYER & HIS ORCH.
54	Amber/Julie's jump	LONDON	HL 8035	£12 – 18
54	The naughty lady of Shady Lane/While the vesper bells...		HL 8111	£12 – 18
55	Hernando's Hideaway/Sil vous plait		HLA 8176	£12 – 18
56	Nothin' to do/JANET BLEYER: 'Cause you're my lover		HLA 8243	£ 9 – 12
56	Bridge of Happiness/You tell me your dream, I'll tell...		HLA 8263	£ 9 – 12

THE BLOSSOMS
58	Move on/He promised me	CAPITOL	CL 14833	£ 6 – 9
58	Little Louie/Have faith in me		CL 14856	£ 6 – 9
58	Baby Daddy–O/No other love		CL 14947	£ 6 – 9

THE BLUE DIAMONDS
60	Ramona/All of me	DECCA	F 21292	£ 2 – 4

THE BLUENOTES (qv LITTLE BILL)
60	I don't know what it is/You can't get away from love ..	TOP RANK	JAR 291	£ 2 – 4

BOB & JERRY
58	Ghost satellite/Nothin'	PYE INT.	7N 25003	£ 6 – 9

BOBBEJAAN
60	I'm crying in my beer/A little bit of Heaven	PALETTE	PG 9009	£ 2 – 4

THE BOBBETTES
57	Mr. Lee/Look at the stars	LONDON	HLE 8477	£25 – 40
58	Come–a come–a/Speedy		HLE 8597	£18 – 25
60	I shot Mr. Lee/Untrue love		HLK 9173	£18 – 25
60	I shot Mr. Lee/Billy	PYE INT.	7N 25060	£12 – 18
60	Have mercy baby/Dance with me Georgie	LONDON	HLU 9248	£12 – 18

THE BOBBSEY TWINS
57	A change of heart/Part-time gal	LONDON	HLA 8474	£ 6 – 9

BOBBY & JIM
58	Carry my books/A lover can tell	CAPITOL	CL 14877	£ 2 – 4

SIMON BOLIVAR ORCH.
56	Merengue holiday/Shy	LONDON	HLG 8245	£ 9 – 12

THE BON-BONS
55	That's the way love goes/Make my dreams come true	LONDON	HL 8139	£18 – 25
56	Circle/Frog on a log		HLU 8262	£12 – 18

JOHNNY BOND
60	Hot rod jalopy/Five-minute love affair	LONDON	HLU 9189	£ 9 – 12

MARGARET BOND (qv MAE JONES)
55	You'll always be my lifetime sweet../Where is the one...	DECCA	F 10506	£ 2 – 4
55	Mirror, mirror/My love's a gentle man		F 10555	£ 2 – 4
55	There's always a first time/Dancing in my socks		F 10632	£ 2 – 4
57	Your love is my love/Goodnight my love, pleasant dreams	PARLOPHONE	R 4283	£ 2 – 4
57	The wind in the willow/Young and in love		R 4312	£ 2 – 4

(GARY) U.S. BONDS
60ø	New Orleans/Please forgive me	TOP RANK	JAR 527	£ 4 – 6

BROTHER BONES & HIS SHADOWS
60	Sweet Georgia Brown/Margie	ORIOLE	CB 1030	£ 2 – 4

PAT BOONE (qv THE FONTANE SISTERS)
55ø	Ain't that a shame/Tennessee Saturday night	LONDON	HLD 8172	£12 – 18
55	No arms can ever hold you/At my front door		HLD 8197	£12 – 18
56	Gee Whittakers/Take the time		HLD 8233	£12 – 18
56ø	I'll be home/Tutti frutti		HLD 8253	£ 9 – 12
56ø	Long tall Sally/Just as long as I'm with you		HLD 8291	£ 9 – 12
56ø	I almost lost my mind/I'm in love with you		HLD 8303	£ 9 – 12
56	Rich in love/Two hearts, two kisses		HLD 8316	£ 9 – 12
56ø	Friendly persuasion (Thee I love)/Chains of love		HLD 8346	£ 6 – 9
57ø	Don't forbid me/Anastasia		HLD 8370	£ 6 – 9
57ø	Why baby why/I'm just waiting for you		HLD 8404	£ 6 – 9
57ø	Love letters in the sand/Bernadine		HLD 8445	£ 4 – 6
57ø	Remember you're mine/There's a gold mine in the sky		HLD 8479	£ 4 – 6
57ø	April love/When the swallows come back to Capistrano		HLD 8512	£ 4 – 6
57ø	White Christmas/Jingle bells		HLD 8520	£ 4 – 6
58ø	A wonderful time up there/It's too soon to know		HLD 8574	£ 4 – 6
58ø	Sugar moon/Cherie, I love you		HLD 8640	£ 2 – 4
58ø	If dreams came true/That's how much I love you		HLD 8675	£ 2 – 4
58ø	Gee, but it's lonely/For my good fortune		HLD 8739	£ 2 – 4
59ø	I'll remember tonight/The Mardi Gras march		HLD 8775	£ 2 – 4
59ø	With the wind and rain in../There's good rockin' tonight		HLD 8824	£ 4 – 6
59ø	For a penny/Wang dang taffy-apple tango		HLD 8855	£ 2 – 4
59ø	Twixt twelve and twenty/Rock boll weevil		HLD 8910	£ 2 – 4
59	A fool's Hall of Fame/Brightest wishing star		HLD 8974	£ 2 – 4
60	Beyond the sunset/The faithful heart		HLD 9029	£ 2 – 4
60	(Welcome) New lovers/Words		HLD 9067	£ 2 – 4
60ø	Walking the floor over you/Spring rain		HLD 9138	£ 2 – 4
60	Candy sweet/Delia gone		HLD 9184	£ 2 – 4
60	Dear John/Alabam		HLD 9238	£ 2 – 4

BILLY BORLYNN

| 60 | Baby listens/Liebelei | PHILIPS | PB 1031 | £ 2 - 4 |
| 60 | Every step of the way/It takes time | | PB 1057 | £ 2 - 4 |

EARL BOSTIC & HIS ORCH. (& *BILL DOGGETT/+BILL JONES/qv SONNY CARTER)

52	Flamingo/Sleep	VOGUE	V 2145 ⍛	£ 2 - 4
52	Moonglow/Ain't misbehavin'		V 2148 ⍛	£ 2 - 4
54	Off shore/What! No pearls	PARLOPHONE	MSP 6075	£ 6 - 9
54	Deep purple/Smoke rings		MSP 6089	£ 6 - 9
54	Don't you do it/Melancholy serenade		MSP 6105	£ 6 - 9
54	Jungle drums/Danube waves		MSP 6110	£ 6 - 9
54	Mambolino/Blue skies		MSP 6119	£ 6 - 9
54	Mambostic/These foolish things		MSP 6131	£ 9 - 12
55	Melody of love/Sweet Lorraine		MSP 6162	£ 6 - 9
56	Flamingo/Sleep	VOGUE	V 2145	£ 9 - 12
56	Moonglow/Ain't misbehavin'		V 2148	£ 9 - 12
56	Ubangi stomp/Time on my hands	PARLOPHONE	R 4169 ⍛	£ 6 - 9
56	Steamwhistle jump/The hour of parting		R 4187 ⍛	£ 4 - 6
56	The bo-do rock/Mean to me		*R 4208	£ 9 - 12
56	Beyond the blue horizon/For all we know		R 4232	£ 6 - 9
57	Harlem nocturne/I hear a rhapsody		R 4263	£ 6 - 9
57	Bubbins rock/Indiana		*R 4278	£ 6 - 9
57	Too fine for crying+/Avalon		R 4305	£ 6 - 9
57	Temptation/September song		R 4370	£ 4 - 6
58	Over the waves rock/Twilight time		R 4460	£ 6 - 9

CONNEE BOSWELL

| 54 | If I give my heart to you/T-E-N-N-E-S-S-E-E (spells....) | BRUNSWICK | 05319 | £ 4 - 6 |
| 55 | How important can it be?/Fill my heart with happiness . | | 05397 | £ 4 - 6 |

EVE BOSWELL

53	Sugar bush/Moon above Malaya (China nights)	PARLOPHONE	MSP 6006	£ 9 - 12
55	Pam-poo-dey/Ready, willing and able		MSP 6158	£ 9 - 12
55	Tika tika tok/The heart you break (may be your own)		MSP 6160	£ 9 - 12
55ø	Pickin' a-chicken/Blue Star (The "Medic" theme)		R 4082 ⍛	£ 2 - 4
56	Young and foolish/Where you are		MSP 6208	£ 9 - 12
56	Cookie/It's almost tomorrow		MSP 6220	£ 9 - 12
56	Keeping cool with lemonade/Down by the sugar cane		MSP 6245	£ 6 - 9
56	Saries Marais/Come back my love		MSP 6250	£ 6 - 9
56	True love/Where in the world is Billy?		R 4230	£ 6 - 9
57	Tra la la/Rock bobbin' boats		R 4275	£ 9 - 12
57	Chantez, chantez/She said (Aunt Magnolia)		R 4299	£ 4 - 6
57	With all my heart/Sugar candy		R 4328	£ 4 - 6
57	The gypsy in my soul/Stop whistlin' wolf		R 4341	£ 4 - 6
57	Swedish polka (Chickadee)/Tell my love		R 4362	£ 4 - 6
58	Bobby/(I love you) For sentimental reasons		R 4401	£ 4 - 6
58	Love me again/I do		R 4414	£ 4 - 6
58	Left right out of your heart/Voom-ba-voom		R 4455	£ 4 - 6
58	More than ever (Come prima)/I know why		R 4479	£ 2 - 4
58	The Christmas tree/Christmas lullaby		R 4492	£ 2 - 4
59	Piccaninny/If I had a talking picture of you		R 4517	£ 2 - 4
59	Boegoeberg se dam/Wimoweh cha cha		R 4544	£ 2 - 4
59	You are never far away from me/Once again		R 4555	£ 2 - 4
59	Turnabout heart/Misty		R 4618	£ 2 - 4

PERRY BOTKIN

| 60 | The Executioner theme/Waltz of the hunter | BRUNSWICK | 05838 | £ 2 - 4 |

JIMMY BOWEN

57	I'm stickin' with you/Ever lovin' fingers	COLUMBIA	DB 3915	£18 - 25
57	Warm up to me, baby/I trusted you		DB 3984	£12 - 18
57	Cross over/It's shameful		DB 4027	£12 - 18
58	By the light of the silvery Moon/The two step		DB 4184	£ 9 - 12

REMEMBER! — THE SYMBOL ø AFTER THE YEAR OF ISSUE INDICATES A BRITISH CHART ENTRY

BEN BOWERS (*& HIS ROYAL JAMAICANS)
55	The Kentuckian song/The man from Laramie	COLUMBIA SCM 5192	£ 4 – 6
56	To you, my love/I'm still a King to you	SCM 5260	£ 2 – 4
57	Country boy/Rum and coconut water (Rum and coca–cola) .	*PARLOPHONE R 4317	£ 4 – 6

EL BOY
57	Jack, Jack, Jack/Tonight my heart she is crying	COLUMBIA DB 3927	£ 2 – 4

DENNY BOYCE & HIS ORCH./RHYTHM
57	One man went to rock/Thunderstorm	ORIOLE CB 1358 º	£ 4 – 6
58	Bad boy/When your hair has turned to silver	CB 1458	£ 2 – 4

JIMMY BOYD (qv FRANKIE LAINE)
53ø	I saw Mommy kissing Santa Claus/Little train a–chuggin'.	COLUMBIA DB 3365 º	£ 2 – 4
53ø	as above	SCM 5072	£ 9 – 12

JACQUELINE BOYER
60ø	Tom Pillibi/FRANCOIS DEGUELT: Ce soir–la	COLUMBIA DB 4452	£ 2 – 4

JANET BRACE
55	Teach me tonight/My old familiar heartache	BRUNSWICK 05272	£ 4 – 6

OWEN BRADLEY & HIS ORCH./QUINTET
56	Theme from "The Threepenny Opera"/Lights of Vienna	BRUNSWICK 05528	£ 2 – 4
57	White silver sands/Midnight blues	05700	£ 4 – 6
58	Big guitar/Sentimental dream	05736	£ 6 – 9

BUDDY BRADSHAW
59	Nothing you can say/Tonight I walk alone	CAPITOL CL 15036	£ 2 – 4

TINY BRADSHAW & HIS ORCH.
52	Breaking up the house/Walk that mess	VOGUE V 2146 º	£ 6 – 9
54	The gypsy/Spider web	PARLOPHONE MSP 6118	£ 6 – 9
55	Overflow/Don't worry 'bout me	MSP 6145	£ 9 – 12
55	Cat nap/Stomping room only	R 4062 º	£ 4 – 6
55	Pompton Turnpike/Come on	R 4084 º	£ 4 – 6

BILL BRAMWELL
58	My old man/Shoutin' in that Amen Corner	STARLITE ST.45 004	£ 4 – 6
60	Candid Camera theme/Frederika	DECCA F 11309	£ 2 – 4

JOHNNY BRANDON (qv VARIOUS ARTISTS)
54ø	Tomorrow/High as a mountain	POLYGON P 1131 º	£ 2 – 4
55ø	Don't worry/Strike it lucky	P 1163 º	£ 2 – 4
56	Tomorrow/Don't worry	PYE N 15025 º	£ 2 – 4
56	Rock–a–bye baby/Lonely lips	PARLOPHONE MSP 6238	£ 4 – 6
56	Shim sham shuffle/I didn't know	R 4207	£ 6 – 9
56	Glendora/Song for a Summer night	DECCA F 10778	£ 4 – 6
57	Nothing is too good for you/A sort–of–a–feeling	F 10858	£ 4 – 6
59	Santa Claus Jnr./I hear a bluebird sing	TOP RANK JAR 241	£ 2 – 4

JOHNNY BRANTLEY'S ALL STARS
58	The place/Pot luck	LONDON HLU 8606	£ 9 – 12

ROSSANO BRAZZI
57	Song for sweethearts/A place within my heart	COLUMBIA DB 3908	£ 2 – 4

JIMMY BREEDLOVE (qv THE CUES)
57	Over somebody else's shoulder/That's my baby	LONDON HLE 8490	£25 – 40

BUDDY BRENNAN QUARTET
60	Big river/The chase	LONDON HLU 9049	£ 2 – 4

REMEMBER! – THE SYMBOL º AFTER THE CATALOGUE NUMBER INDICATES A 78 rpm RECORD
REMEMBER! – THE SYMBOL ø AFTER THE YEAR OF ISSUE INDICATES A BRITISH CHART ENTRY

ROSE BRENNAN

55	Sincerely/Ding dong	H.M.V.	7M	299	£ 6 - 9
55	Ten little kisses/Wake the town and tell the people ...		7M	328	£ 4 - 6
56	You are my love/My Dublin Bay		7M	360	£ 4 - 6
56	Band of gold/My believing heart		7M	383	£ 6 - 9
56	Coortin' in the kitchen/Those who have loved		7M	392	£ 4 - 6
57	Tra la la/Without love (there is nothing)		POP	302	£ 6 - 9
58	Mean to me/Treasure of your love		POP	548	£ 2 - 4
59	Johnny let me go/My Summer diary	TOP RANK	JAR	152	£ 2 - 4

WALTER BRENNAN

60	Dutchman's gold/Back to the farm	LONDON	HLD	9148	£ 2 - 4

FRANKIE BRENT

57	Rockin' shoes/I ain't never gonna do you no good	PYE	N	15102 º	£ 6 - 9
57	Be my girl/Rang dang doo		N	15103 º	£ 4 - 6

TONY BRENT (& *JULIE DAWN/+ANNE WARREN/=THE CORONETS)

52ø	Walkin' to Missouri/I don't know what to do with my time	COLUMBIA	DB	3147 º	£ 2 - 4
52ø	Make it soon/Any old time		DB	3187 º	£ 2 - 4
53ø	Got you on my mind/My favourite song		DB	3226 º	£ 2 - 4
53	Ding dong boogie/When are we gonna get married?		*SCM	5029	£ 9 - 12
53	Have you heard?/Strange love		SCM	5042	£ 6 - 9
53	Which way the wind blows/My one and only heart		SCM	5057	£ 6 - 9
54	I understand just how you feel/The magic tango		SCM	5135	£ 6 - 9
54	Nicolette/Tell me, tell me		SCM	5146	£ 6 - 9
55	It's a woman's world/Give me the right to be wrong		SCM	5160	£ 6 - 9
55	Open up your heart+/Hearts of stone=		SCM	5170	£ 9 - 12
55	Mirror, mirror/Love and kisses		SCM	5188	£ 6 - 9
55	With your love/On a little balcony in Spain		SCM	5200	£ 6 - 9
56	Sooner or later (love comes along)/Pick yourself a star		SCM	5245	£ 6 - 9
56	My little angel/What a heavenly night for love		SCM	5272	£ 6 - 9
56ø	Cindy, oh Cindy/Two innocent hearts		DB	3844	£ 6 - 9
57	Amore/If wishes were horses		DB	3884	£ 4 - 6
57	Butterfly/How lonely can one be?		DB	3918	£ 6 - 9
57ø	Dark Moon/The game of love (A-one and a-two)		DB	3950	£ 6 - 9
57	Deep within me/Why ask for the Moon		DB	3987	£ 4 - 6
57	Love by the jukebox light/We belong together		DB	4043	£ 4 - 6
58ø	The clouds will soon roll by/Don't save your love (for..		DB	4066	£ 4 - 6
58	Chanson d'amour/Little serenade		DB	4128	£ 4 - 6
58ø	Girl of my dreams/Don't play that melody		DB	4177	£ 4 - 6
59	I surrender, dear/Call me		DB	4238	£ 2 - 4
59ø	Why should I be lonely?/My little room		DB	4304	£ 4 - 6
59	Forever, my darling (Pledging my love)/Worried mind ...		DB	4357	£ 2 - 4
60	Oh, so wunderbar/Just as much as ever		DB	4402	£ 2 - 4
60	Come on in/Your cheatin' heart		DB	4478	£ 2 - 4
60	Just a-wearyin' for you/I'm alone because I love you ..		DB	4514	£ 2 - 4

GERRY BRERETON (qv EDDIE CALVERT)

53	From here to eternity/If you've never been in love ..	PARLOPHONE	MSP	6056	£ 2 - 4
54	The book/Somewhere someone (is saying a prayer)		MSP	6081	£ 2 - 4
55	A million helping hands/Fair sets the wind for love ...	COLUMBIA	SCM	5195	£ 2 - 4

BERNARD BRESSLAW (qv MICHAEL MEDWIN)

58ø	Mad passionate love/You need feet	H.M.V.	POP	522	£ 4 - 6
59	Charlie Brown/The teenager's lament		POP	599	£ 4 - 6
59	Ivy will cling/I found a hole		POP	669	£ 2 - 4

TERESA BREWER (*& THE LANCERS)

50	Music! Music! Music!/Copenhagen	LONDON	L	604 º	£ 4 - 6
54	Jilted/Le grand tour de l'amour	V-CORAL	Q	2001 º	£ 6 - 9
54	Skinny Minnie (Fishtail)/I had someone else before I....		Q	2011	£ 9 - 12
54	Au revoir/Danger signs		Q	2029	£ 6 - 9
55ø	Let me go, lover*/Baby, baby, baby		Q	72043	£12 - 18
55	How important can it be?/What more is there to say? ...		Q	72065	£ 6 - 9
55	Rock love/Tweedlee dee		Q	72066	£12 - 18

55	Pledging my love/I gotta go get my baby		Q 72077	£ 9 – 12
55	You're telling our secret/Time		Q 72083	£ 6 – 9
55	The banjo's back in town/How to be very, very popular .		Q 72098	£ 6 – 9
56	A hard man is good to find/It's siesta time		Q 72130	£ 6 – 9
56	Rememb'ring/My sweetie went away		Q 72139	£ 6 – 9
56ø	A tear fell/Bo weevil		Q 72146	£ 9 – 12
56ø	A sweet old-fashioned girl/Goodbye, John		Q 72172	£ 9 – 12
56	Keep your cotton pickin' paddies offa./So doggone lonely		Q 72199	£ 4 – 6
56	Crazy with love/The Moon is on fire		Q 72213	£ 6 – 9
57ø	Nora Malone/When I leave the world behind		Q 72224	£ 6 – 9
57	I'm drowning my sorrows/How lonely can one be		Q 72239	£ 4 – 6
57	Empty arms/The ricky-tick song		Q 72251	£ 4 – 6
57	Lula rock-a-hula/Teardrops in my heart		Q 72278	£ 9 – 12
57	You send me/Born to love		Q 72292	£ 6 – 9
58	Mutual admiration society/Careless caresses	CORAL	Q 72301	£ 4 – 6
58	Saturday dance/I think the world of you		Q 72320	£ 4 – 6
58	Pickle up a doodle/The rain falls on ev'rybody		Q 72336	£ 4 – 6
58	The hula hoop song/So shy		Q 72340	£ 4 – 6
58	Jingle bell rock/I like Christmas		Q 72349	£ 4 – 6
59	The one rose (that's left in my heart)/Satellite		Q 72354	£ 2 – 4
59	Heavenly lover/Fair weather sweetheart		Q 72364	£ 4 – 6
59	Bye bye baby goodbye/Chain of friendship		Q 72375	£ 4 – 6
59	Mexicali Rose/Bill Bailey, won't you please come home .		Q 72383	£ 2 – 4
60	Peace of mind/Venetian sunset		Q 72386	£ 2 – 4
60ø	How do you know it's love/If there are stars in my eyes		Q 72396	£ 2 – 4
60	Anymore/That piano man		Q 72405	£ 2 – 4

BILLY BRIGGS
51	Chew tobacco rag (No. 2)/Alarm clock boogie	COLUMBIA	DB 2938 º	£ 9 – 12

LILLIAN BRIGGS
55	I want you to be my baby/Give me a band and my baby ...	PHILIPS	PB 522 º	£ 4 – 6
60	Not a soul (Blanket roll blues)/Smile for the people ..	CORAL	Q 72408	£ 4 – 6

MAY BRITT
59	Falling in love again/Lola-Lola	TOP RANK	JAR 230	£ 2 – 4

BOBBIE BRITTON (& *TED HEATH MUSIC/+THE KEYNOTES)
54	Wanted/Lost	DECCA	+F 10288	£ 2 – 4
54	Always you/When		F 10385	£ 2 – 4
55	Could it be/My eyes are wide open		F 10453	£ 2 – 4
55	Learnin' the blues/Strange lady in town		*F 10563	£ 2 – 4
56	Autumn concerto/The fool of the year		*F 10777	£ 2 – 4
56	True love/If you don't love me		*F 10807	£ 2 – 4
59	You, only you/Warm	ORIOLE	CB 1503	£ 2 – 4

NORAH BROCKSTEDT
60	Big boy/Tell me no lies	TOP RANK	JAR 353	£ 2 – 4

PATTI BROOK & THE DIAMONDS
60	Since you've been gone/That's the way it's gonna be ...	PYE	7N 15300	£ 2 – 4

THE BROOKS *or BROOK BROTHERS
60	Green fields/How will it end?	TOP RANK	JAR 349	£ 2 – 4
60ø	Please help me, I'm falling/When will I be loved		JAR 409	£ 4 – 6
60	Say the word/Everything but love	PYE	*7N 15298	£ 2 – 4

DONNIE BROOKS
60	Mission bell/Do it for me	LONDON	HLN 9168	£ 2 – 4
60	Doll house/Round Robin		HLN 9253	£ 2 – 4

NORMAN BROOKS
54	Hello sunshine/You're my baby	LONDON	L 1166	£12 – 18
54	You shouldn't have kissed me the.../Somebody wonderful		L 1202	£12 – 18
54ø	A sky-blue shirt and a rainbow tie/This waltz with you		L 1228	£12 – 18
54	I'd like to be in your shoes, baby/I'm kinda crazy		HL 8015	£12 – 18

54	I can't give you anything..../THE GO-BOYS: Johnny's tune		HL 8041	£12 – 18
54	My 3-D sweetie/Candy moon		HL 8051	£12 – 18
55	Back in circulation/Lou Lou Louisiana		HL 8115	£12 – 18

BIG BILL BROONZY (*as CHICAGO BILL)

51	Back water blues/Lonesome road blues	VOGUE	V 2068 ♀	£ 4 – 6
51	Keep your hands off/Stump blues	MELODISC	*1191 ♀	£ 6 – 9
51	In the evenin'/Low land blues	VOGUE	V 2073 ♀	£ 4 – 6
51	John Henry/Blues in 1890		V 2074 ♀	£ 4 – 6
51	Big Bill blues/Hey hey baby		V 2075 ♀	£ 4 – 6
51	House rent stomp/The moppin' blues		V 2076 ♀	£ 4 – 6
51	Black, brown and white/Feelin' low down		V 2077 ♀	£ 4 – 6
52	Five foot seven/Plough hand blues	MELODISC	*1203 ♀	£ 6 – 9
52	Make my getaway/What I used to do	VOGUE	V 2078 ♀	£ 4 – 6
56	Guitar shuffle/When did you leave Heaven?		V 2351 ♀	£ 2 – 4
56	When do I get to be called a man/Mindin' my own business	PYE JAZZ	NJ 2012 ♀	£ 4 – 6
57	Southbound train/It feels so good		NJ 2016 ♀	£ 4 – 6
58	Guitar shuffle/When did you leave Heaven?	VOGUE	V 2351	£ 6 – 9

THE BROTHERS FOUR
| 60ø | Greenfields/East Virginia .... | PHILIPS | PB 1009 | £ 2 – 4 |

THE BROWNS (qv JIM EDWARD BROWN)
59ø	The three bells/Heaven fell last night	R.C.A.	RCA 1140	£ 2 – 4
59	Scarlet ribbons (for her hair)/Blue bells ring		RCA 1157	£ 2 – 4
60	Teen-ex/The old lamplighter		RCA 1176	£ 2 – 4
60	Lonely little robin/Margo (The ninth of May)		RCA 1193	£ 2 – 4
60	Send me the pillow you dream on/You're so much a part...		RCA 1218	£ 2 – 4

THE BROWN BROTHERS
| 59 | Let the good times roll/You're right, I'm left .... | VOGUE | V 9131 | £25 – 40 |

AL BROWN'S TUNETOPPERS
| 60 | The Madison/Mo' Madison .... | TOP RANK | JAR 374 | £ 2 – 4 |

BOOTS BROWN & HIS BLOCKBUSTERS
| 58 | Cerveza/Juicy .... | R.C.A. | RCA 1078 | £ 4 – 6 |
| 59 | Trollin'/Jim Twangy .... | | RCA 1102 | £ 4 – 6 |

BUSTER BROWN
| 60 | Fannie Mae/Lost in a dream .... | MELODISC | 1559 | £12 – 18 |

CHARLES BROWN
| 56 | I'll always be in love with you/Soothe me .... | VOGUE | V 9061 | £40 – 60 |
| 57 | Confidential/Trouble blues .... | | V 9065 | £40 – 60 |

FAY BROWN
| 55 | Unchained melody/I was wrong .... | COLUMBIA | SCM 5185 | £ 6 – 9 |

GEORGIA BROWN
55	My crazy l'il mixed up heart/Before we know it	DECCA	F 10489	£ 2 – 4
55	I love to dance with you/That's all I need		F 10551	£ 2 – 4
55	I went to the village/Wrong again		F 10616	£ 2 – 4
60	As long as he needs me/Oom-pah-pah		F 11273	£ 2 – 4
60	Milord/Blue eyed boy		F 11286	£ 2 – 4

HYLO BROWN
| 59 | You can't relive the past/Thunder clouds of love ..... | CAPITOL | CL 15075 | £ 2 – 4 |
| 60 | I've waited as long as I can/Just any old love .... | | CL 15139 | £ 2 – 4 |

JAMES BROWN (& THE FAMOUS FLAMES)
| 60 | Think/You've got the power .... | PARLOPHONE | R 4667 | £ 9 – 12 |
| 60 | This old heart/Wonder when you're coming home .... | FONTANA | H 273 | £ 9 – 12 |

JERICHO BROWN
| 60 | Look for a star/Don'tcha know (that I love you) .... | WARNER-B | WB 14 | £ 4 – 6 |

JIM EDWARD BROWN & MAXINE BROWN (*& BONNIE/collectively became THE BROWNS)

55	Itsy witsy bitsy me/Why am I falling?	LONDON	HL 8123	£18 - 25
55	Your love is wild as the west wind/Draggin' Mainstreet		HLU 8166	£18 - 25
55	You thought I thought/Here today and gone tomorrow* ...		HLU 8200	£12 - 18

JOE BROWN (& THE BRUVVERS)

59	People gotta talk/Comes the day	DECCA	F 11185	£ 4 - 6
60ø	Darktown Strutters' Ball/Swagger		F 11207	£ 4 - 6
60	Jellied eels/Dinah		F 11246	£ 4 - 6

KAY BROWN

56	Me 'n' you 'n' the Moon/What do you think it does to me?	BRUNSWICK	05595	£ 2 - 4

LES BROWN & HIS BAND OF RENOWN (*& HOAGY CARMICHAEL)

54	Ramona/Hot point	V-CORAL	Q 2034	£ 2 - 4
54	St. Louis blues mambo/Moon song		Q 2042	£ 2 - 4
55	The man that got away/Doodle-doo-doo		Q 72049	£ 2 - 4
55	Frensi/Perfidia	CAPITOL	CL 14331	£ 4 - 6
55	He needs me/Simplicity		CL 14350	£ 4 - 6
55	Lullaby of Birdland/Bernie's tune	V-CORAL	Q 72107	£ 2 - 4
56	Hong Kong blues*/It's all right with me		Q 72123	£ 4 - 6
56	Sincerely yours/Take back your mink	CAPITOL	CL 14512	£ 2 - 4
56	Hit the road to Dreamland/That certain feeling		CL 14611	£ 2 - 4
56	Talk about a party/Ancient history		CL 14631	£ 2 - 4
56	Flamingo/Midnight Sun	V-CORAL	Q 72215	£ 2 - 4
57	Priscilla/The best years of my life	CAPITOL	CL 14675	£ 2 - 4
57	Original Joe/If I had the money		CL 14706	£ 2 - 4
57	Forty cups of coffee/I'm forever blowing bubbles	V-CORAL	Q 72242	£ 4 - 6
59	Boola/Say it with music	CORAL	Q 72367	£ 2 - 4

NAPPY BROWN

55	Don't be angry/It's really you	LONDON	HL 8145	£60 - 90
55	Pitter patter/There'll come a day		HLC 8182	£40 - 60
57	Little by little/I'm getting lonesome		HLC 8384	£40 - 60
58	It don't hurt no more/My baby		HLC 8760	£25 - 40

ROY BROWN

57	I'm sticking with you/Party doll	LONDON	HLP 8398	£60 - 90
57	Saturday night/Everybody		HLP 8448	£90 -120

RUTH BROWN

55	Mama (he treats your daughter mean)/Mambo baby	LONDON	HL 8153	£40 - 60
55	As long as I'm moving/R.B. blues		HLE 8210	£60 - 90
56	I want to do more/Sweet baby of mine		HLE 8310	£40 - 60
57	Mom oh Mom/I want to be loved (but only by you)		HLE 8401	£25 - 40
57	Lucky lips/My heart is breaking over you	COLUMBIA	DB 3913	£40 - 60
57	One more time/When I get you baby	LONDON	HLE 8483	£25 - 40
58	A new love/Look me up		HLE 8552	£18 - 25
58	Just too much/Book of lies		HLE 8645	£18 - 25
58	This little girl's gone rockin'/Why me		HLE 8757	£25 - 40
59	Jack O'Diamonds/I can't hear a word you say		HLE 8883	£18 - 25
59	I don't know/Papa Daddy		HLE 8946	£12 - 18
60	Don't deceive me/I burned your letter		HLE 9093	£12 - 18

SANDY BROWN'S JAZZ BAND (qv WALLY FAWKES)

58	African Queen/Special delivery	TEMPO	A 124	£ 2 - 4

TINY BROWN

50	No more blues/Slow-motion baby	CAPITOL	CL 13306 º	£ 6 - 9

GEORGE BROWNE (qv HUMPHREY LYTTELTON)

57	Sound barrier/Te-le-le	COLUMBIA	DB 3940	£ 2 - 4

LAIDMAN BROWNE & HIS BUDGERIGAR

58	Laidman Browne talking with his budgerigar "Mr. Browne"	PYE	7N 15111	£ 2 - 4

TEDD BROWNE
59	A corner in Paradise/The Everglades	CAPITOL	CL 15059	£ 2 – 4

DAVE BRUBECK QUARTET/TRIO
53	A foggy day/Lyons busy	VOGUE	45–2156	£ 4 – 6
53	Mam'selle/Me and my shadow		45–2157	£ 4 – 6
53	Frenesi/At a perfume counter		45–2158	£ 4 – 6
53	Body and soul/Let's fall in love		45–2159	£ 4 – 6
53	I'll remember April/Singin' in the rain		45–2160	£ 4 – 6
53	Lullaby in rhythm/You stepped out of a dream		45–2161	£ 4 – 6
56	Me and my shadow/At a perfume counter		V 2171	£ 2 – 4
56	Frenesi/Mam'selle		V 2206	£ 2 – 4
60	I'm in a dancing mood/Lover	PHILIPS	JAZ 106	£ 2 – 4

TOMMY BRUCE (& THE BRUISERS)
60ø	Ain't misbehavin'/Got the water boilin'	COLUMBIA	DB 4453	£ 4 – 6
60ø	Broken doll/I'm on fire		DB 4498	£ 6 – 9
60	My little girl/On the sunny side of the street		DB 4532	£ 4 – 6

WES BRYAN
58	Lonesome love/Tiny spaceman	LONDON	HLU 8607	£ 9 – 12
59	Honey baby/So blue over you		HLU 8978	£12 – 18

ANITA BRYANT
59	Six boys and seven girls/The blessings of love	LONDON	HLL 8983	£ 2 – 4
60	Little George (got the hiccoughs)/Love look away		HLL 9075	£ 2 – 4
60ø	Paper roses/Mixed emotions		HLL 9114	£ 2 – 4
60ø	In my little corner of the world/Anyone would love you		HLL 9171	£ 6 – 9
60ø	In my little corner of the world/Just in time		HLL 9171	£ 2 – 4
60	One of the lucky ones/The party's over		HLL 9219	£ 2 – 4
60	Wonderland by night/Pictures		HLL 9247	£ 2 – 4

BOOD & FILEECE (Boudleaux & Felice) BRYANT (*BOUDLEAUX only/+& SPARKS)
51	Overweight blues/I dreamed of a wedding	M–G–M	MGM 452 º	£ 4 – 6
60	Hot spot/Touche+	POLYDOR	*NH 66952	£ 2 – 4

LAURA K. BRYANT
58	Bobby/Angel tears	LONDON	HLU 8551	£ 6 – 9

MARIE BRYANT
52	Tomato/Rhumboogie Anna	LYRAGON	J 701 º	£ 4 – 6

RAY BRYANT TRIO/COMBO
60	Little Susie – Parts 2 & 4	PYE INT.	7N 25052	£ 2 – 4
60	Little Susie – Parts 1 & 3	PHILIPS	PB 1003	£ 2 – 4
60	The Madison time – Parts 1 & 2		PB 1014	£ 2 – 4

BERYL BRYDEN'S BACK-ROOM SKIFFLE
56	Casey Jones/Kansas City blues	DECCA	F 10823	£ 6 – 9

BETSY BRYE
59	Sleep walk/Daddy Daddy (gotta get a phone in my room) .	COLUMBIA	DB 4350	£ 4 – 6

TEDDY BUCKNER & HIS BAND
56	Oh, didn't he ramble/Battle Hymn of the Republic	VOGUE	V 2369	£ 2 – 4
56	When the Saints go marching in/West End blues		V 2375	£ 2 – 4
57	Sweet Georgia Brown/That's my home		V 2414	£ 2 – 4

BUD & HIS BUDDIES
58	June, July and August/Sing a little sweeter	STARLITE	ST.45 006	£ 2 – 4

BUD & TRAVIS
59	Bonsoir dame/Truly do	LONDON	HLU 8965	£ 2 – 4
60	Ballad of the Alamo/The green leaves of Summer		HLG 9211	£ 2 – 4

THE BULAWAYO SWEET RHYTHMS BAND

54	Skokiaan/In the mood	DECCA	F 10350	£ 4 – 6

DAVE BURGESS (TRIO)

55	I love Paris/Five foot two, eyes of blue	LONDON	HLB 8175	£12 – 18
57	I'm available/Who's gonna cry?	ORIOLE	CB 1413	£ 4 – 6

SONNY BURGESS

60	Sadie's back in town/A kiss tonight	LONDON	HLS 9064	£25 – 40

SONNY BURKE & HIS ORCH.

55	"Phffft" mambo/Long hair mambo	BRUNSWICK	O5361	£ 2 – 4

FRANCES BURNETT

59	Please remember me/How I miss you so	CORAL	Q 72374	£ 2 – 4

DORSEY BURNETTE

60	Juarez Town/(There was a) Tall oak tree	LONDON	HLN 9047	£ 6 – 9
60	Hey little one/Big Rock Candy Mountain		HLN 9160	£ 6 – 9

JOHNNY BURNETTE (*ROCK 'N' ROLL TRIO recordings)

56	Tear it up/You're undecided	V–CORAL	*Q 72177	£90 –120
57	Lonesome train/Honey hush		*Q 72227	£90 –120
57	Touch me/Eager beaver baby		*Q 72283	£60 – 90
60ø	Dreamin'/Cincinnati Fireball	LONDON	HLG 9172	£ 4 – 6
60ø	You're sixteen/I beg your pardon		HLG 9254	£ 2 – 4

SMILEY BURNETTE

50	Rudolph the red–nosed reindeer/Grandaddy Frog	CAPITOL	CL 13388 º	£ 6 – 9
54	Lazy locomotive/That long white line	LONDON	HL 8071	£25 – 40
54	Chuggin' on down "66"/Mucho gusto		HL 8085	£25 – 40

RAY BURNS (*& DIANA DECKER, RONNIE HARRIS, RUBY MURRAY & RAY MARTIN ORCH.)

53	Rags to riches/Begorrah	COLUMBIA	SCM 5077	£ 4 – 6
54	Helpless/The homecoming waltz		SCM 5115	£ 4 – 6
54	I can't tell a waltz from a tango/Lonely nightingale ..		SCM 5153	£ 4 – 6
55ø	Mobile/These are the things we'll share		DB 3563 º	£ 2 – 4
55	Spring, Spring, Spring/Goin' co'tin'		*SCM 5165	£ 4 – 6
55	Why?/A smile is worth a million tears		SCM 5179	£ 4 – 6
55ø	That's how a love song was born/The voice		DB 3640 º	£ 2 – 4
56	Stealin'/'Cause I'm sorry		SCM 5224	£ 4 – 6
56	Wild cherry/Give me another chance		SCM 5263	£ 4 – 6
56	Condemned for life (with a rock & roll wife)/The Mare...		DB 3811	£ 4 – 6
57	Whispering heart/Nashville		DB 3886	£ 2 – 4
57	Wonderful! Wonderful!/Bernadine		DB 3966	£ 2 – 4
57	The little hut/Dapper Dan		DB 3998	£ 2 – 4
58	Are you sincere/The best dream of all		DB 4107	£ 2 – 4
58	The better to love you/Meanwhile, back in my arms		DB 4157	£ 2 – 4

HAL BURTON (possibly NEVILLE TAYLOR)

58	Move it/Susie darling	EMBASSY	WB 308	£ 2 – 4

LOU BUSCH & HIS ORCH. (qv JOE "FINGERS" CARR)

56ø	Zambezi/Rainbow's end	CAPITOL	CL 14504	£ 6 – 9
57	The wild ones/Midnight melody		CL 14730	£ 2 – 4
57	Hot cappucchino/Cayo coco (Coconut rock)		CL 14751	£ 2 – 4
58	Cool/Street scene '58		CL 14957	£ 2 – 4

THE BUSH BOYS

59	A broken vow/Never before	CAPITOL	CL 15082	£ 2 – 4

RAY BUSH & THE AVON CITIES' SKIFFLE

56	Hey hey Daddy blues/Green corn	TEMPO	A 146	£ 4 – 6
56	Fisherman's blues/This little light of mine		A 149	£ 4 – 6
57	How long, how long, blues/Julian Johnson		A 156	£ 4 – 6
57	Lonesome day blues/I don't know		A 157	£ 4 – 6

SAM BUTERA (& THE WITNESSES) (qv LOUIS PRIMA)
58	Good gracious baby/It's better than nothing at all	H.M.V.	POP 476	£12 – 18
58	Bim bam/Twinkle in your eyes	CAPITOL	CL 14913	£25 – 40
59	French poodle/Handle with care		CL 14988	£ 9 – 12

CHAMP BUTLER
56	Someone on your mind/I want to love you	V-CORAL	Q 72119	£ 4 – 6
56	The Joshua tree/Down in Mexico		Q 72163	£ 4 – 6

JERRY BUTLER (& THE IMPRESSIONS)
58	For your precious love/Sweet was the wine	LONDON	HL 8697	£12 – 18
60	I found a love/A lonely soldier	TOP RANK	JAR 389	£ 6 – 9
60	He will break your heart/Thanks to you		JAR 531	£ 6 – 9

BILLY BUTTERFIELD & HIS ORCH.
51	Billy's boogie/Stardust	CAPITOL	CL 13514 º	£ 4 – 6
55	The magnificent matador/Sugar blues mambo	LONDON	HLF 8181	£12 – 18

SHEILA BUXTON (qv VARIOUS ARTISTS)
55	Thank you for the waltz/Just between friends	COLUMBIA	SCM 5193	£ 2 – 4
57	A perfect love/I love my baby (My baby loves me)		DB 3887	£ 2 – 4
57	The in-between age/Charm		DB 4051	£ 2 – 4
59	Soldier, won't you marry me?/Li per li	TOP RANK	JAR 113	£ 2 – 4
59	The wonder of you/The valley of love		JAR 144	£ 2 – 4
59	All I do is dream of you/Shakedown		JAR 240	£ 2 – 4
60	Sixteen reasons/Goodnight, God love you		JAR 356	£ 2 – 4

DON BYAS & HIS RHYTHM
56	On the way to your heart/The Portuguese washerwomen ...	VOGUE	V 2390	£ 2 – 4

MAX BYGRAVES (& *PETER BROUGH & ARCHIE ANDREWS/+TANNER SISTERS/=TED HEATH MUSIC/
qv JOAN REGAN/VARIOUS ARTISTS)
52ø	"Cowpuncher's Cantata"/True loves and false lovers	H.M.V.	B 10250 º	£ 1 – 2
53ø	as above		7M 112	£ 6 – 9
53	Bygraves boogie/Little Sir Echo		7M 113	£ 4 – 6
53	The travelling salesman/Ten bottles of gin		7M 114	£ 2 – 4
53	Lovely dollar lolly*/The Red Robin Cantata		7M 134	£ 4 – 6
53	Time to dream/The Queen of Ev'ryone's Heart		7M 145	£ 2 – 4
53	Big 'ead/Say "Si Si"*		7M 154	£ 4 – 6
53	You're a pink toothbrush/I wish I could sing like Jolson		B 10591 º	£ 2 – 4
54	She was a good girl (as good girls go)/The Jones boy ..		7M 180	£ 2 – 4
54ø	(The gang...) Heart of my heart/Once she's got you up+..		B 10654 º	£ 1 – 2
54ø	as above		7M 194	£ 6 – 9
54	Friends and neighbours+/Chip chopper Charlie		7M 220	£ 4 – 6
54ø	Gilly Gilly Ossenfeffer Katzenellen...../Third little...		B 10734 º	£ 1 – 2
54ø	as above		7M 237	£ 6 – 9
54	Bank of Sunshine/Little Johnny Rainbow		7M 238	£ 2 – 4
55ø	Mr. Sandman/He's a real tough guy		B 10821 º	£ 1 – 2
55ø	Meet me on the corner/The little Laplander		POP 116 º	£ 1 – 2
56ø	The ballad of Davy Crockett/A good idea – Son		POP 153 º	£ 1 – 2
56ø	as above		7M 357	£ 6 – 9
56ø	Out of town/Fingers crossed		POP 164 º	£ 1 – 2
56ø	as above		7M 368	£ 4 – 6
56	Nothin' to do/Lift boy		7M 388	£ 2 – 4
56	Try another cherry tree/Seventeen tons		7M 400	£ 2 – 4
57ø	Heart/In a shanty in old Shanty Town	DECCA	F 10862	£ 2 – 4
58ø	You need hands/Tulips from Amsterdam		F 11004	£ 2 – 4
58ø	Little train/Gotta have rain		F 11046	£ 2 – 4
58ø	(I love to play) My ukelele/Come to our coming out party		F 11077	£ 2 – 4
59ø	Jingle bell rock/Who made the morning		F 11176	£ 2 – 4
60ø	Fings ain't wot they used t'be/When the thrill has gone		F 11214	£ 2 – 4
60ø	Consider yourself/Tra-la-la I'm in love		=F 11251	£ 2 – 4
60	When you come to the end of a../Underneath the arches .		F 11308	£ 2 – 4

BOBBY BYRNE & THE ALL STAR ORCH.
59	Rhapsody in blue/Adios	TOP RANK	TR 5011	£ 2 – 4

EDWARD *or EDD BYRNES (+& CONNIE STEVENS)

60ø	Kookie, Kookie (lend me your comb)+/You're the top	WARNER-B	WB 5	£ 4 - 6
60	Yulesville/Lonely Christmas		*WB 27	£ 2 - 4

THE CADETS

56	Stranded in the jungle/I want you	LONDON	HLU 8313	£90 -120

EARL CADILLAC & HIS ORCH.

59	Zon, zon, zon/Il suffit d'une melodie	VOGUE	V 9133	£ 2 - 4
59	The fish seller/Tremendo cha cha cha (Plegaria)		V 9138	£ 2 - 4

THE CADILLACS

59	Peek-a-boo/Oh, oh, Lolita	LONDON	HLJ 8786	£12 - 18

AL CAIOLA

56	Flamenco love/From the heart	LONDON	HLC 8285	£12 - 18

JOHN CAIRNEY w. SAMMY SAN

57	Two strangers/A certain girl I know	H.M.V.	POP 424	£ 2 - 4

CAB CALLOWAY & HIS ORCH.

52	Minnie the Moocher/Kickin' the gong around	BRUNSWICK	05022 º	£ 6 - 9

EDDIE CALVERT (*& GERRY BRERETON)

53	Hora stacato/My Yiddisher Momme	COLUMBIA	SCM 5003	£ 4 - 6
53	Ave Maria/Just a-wearyin' for you		SCM 5004	£ 4 - 6
53ø	O mein Papa/Mystery St.		DB 3337 º	£ 1 - 2
54	Montparnasse/Tenderly		SCM 5084	£ 2 - 4
54	Midnight/Margot's minuet		SCM 5097	£ 2 - 4
54	Donna/Faraway		SCM 5109	£ 2 - 4
54	I speak to the stars/Caress		SCM 5125	£ 2 - 4
54	My son, my son/Sherpa song		SCM 5129	£ 4 - 6
55	Open your heart/Waiting for you		SCM 5163	£ 2 - 4
55ø	Cherry pink (and apple blossom white)/Roses of Picardy		DB 3581 º	£ 1 - 2
55ø	as above		SCM 5168	£ 9 - 12
55ø	Stranger in Paradise/Sincerely		DB 3594 º	£ 1 - 2
55ø	John and Julie/Heart of the sunset		DB 3624 º	£ 1 - 2
55	Love is a many splendored thing/Spellbound		SCM 5194	£ 4 - 6
56	The man with the golden arm/Memories of you		SCM 5237	£ 4 - 6
56ø	Zambesi/Trumpet tango		DB 3747 º	£ 2 - 4
56	The bells of St. Mary's/You above all		*SCM 5253	£ 4 - 6
56	Moonglow & Theme from "Picnic"/If I loved you		SCM 5277	£ 2 - 4
56	Goodnight Mother, goodnight/They didn't believe me		DB 3812	£ 2 - 4
56	Beyond Mombasa/Jungle Moon		DB 3837	£ 2 - 4
57	Trees/Let the rest of the world go by		*DB 3902	£ 4 - 6
57	Almost Paradise/Song of Corsica		DB 3917	£ 2 - 4
57ø	Mandy (La panse)/Never say goodbye		DB 3956	£ 4 - 6
58ø	Little serenade/Fanfare tango (The awakening)		DB 4105	£ 2 - 4

TABBY CALVIN & THE ROUNDERS

56	False alarm/I came back to say I'm sorry	CAPITOL	CL 14640	£ 4 - 6

JOHNNY CAMERON

60	I double dare you/Fantasy	TOP RANK	JAR 396	£ 2 - 4

JO-ANN CAMPBELL

58	Wait a minute/It's true	LONDON	HLU 8536	£12 - 18
60	A kookie little Paradise/Bobby, Bobby, Bobby	H.M.V.	POP 776	£ 4 - 6

PETE CANDOLI & HIS ORCH.

56	St. Louis blues - boogie/The big top (Entry of the ....)	CAPITOL	CL 14615	£ 4 - 6
60	77 Sunset Strip cha-cha/DON RALKE: 77 Sunset Strip	WARNER-B	WB 2	£ 2 - 4

PENNY CANDY

60	Come on over/They said	TOP RANK	JAR 328	£ 2 - 4

FREDDY CANNON

59ø	Tallahassee lassie/You know	TOP RANK	JAR 135	£ 4 –	6
59	Okefenokee/Kookie hat		JAR 207	£ 4 –	6
59ø	Way down yonder in New Orleans/Fractured		JAR 247	£ 2 –	4
60ø	California, here I come/Indiana		JAR 309	£ 4 –	6
60	Chatanoogie shoe shine boy/Boston (my home town)		JAR 334	£ 4 –	6
60ø	The urge/Jump over		JAR 369	£ 4 –	6
60	Happy shades of blue/Cuernavaca choo choo		JAR 407	£ 2 –	4
60	Humdinger/My blue Heaven		JAR 518	£ 2 –	4

THE CANNONS

60	I didn't know the gun was loaded/My guy's come back	DECCA	F 11269	£ 4 –	6

DANNY CAPRI

55	Desirable/I do, I do	CAPITOL	CL 14265	£ 4 –	6
55	Don't make a liar out of me/Angelica		CL 14302	£ 4 –	6

GUY CARAWAN

58	Michael row the boat../Old Man Atom (Talking atomic....)	PYE	7N 15132	£ 2 –	4

THE CARDIGANS

58	Poor boy/Each other	MERCURY	AMT 1007	£ 4 –	6

BILL CAREY

55	My fate is in your hands/Heavenly lover	V–CORAL	Q 72096	£ 2 –	4
56	Where walks my true love/Laughing boy		Q 72151	£ 2 –	4

DAVE CAREY JAZZ BAND (qv PAT HAWES)

56	Kater Street rag/Kansas City Kitty	TEMPO	A 122	£ 2 –	4
56	I've found a new baby/Brown skin Mama		A 133	£ 2 –	4
56	Sunset Cafe stomp/Sweet Georgia Brown		A 138	£ 2 –	4
56	Ida, sweet as apple cider/Button up your overcoat		A 150	£ 2 –	4

DAVID CAREY

53	Oh, happy day/Broken wings	COLUMBIA	SCM 5030	£ 2 –	4

THE CARIBS (qv LAUREL AITKEN/WILFRED EDWARDS)

60	Taboo/Matilda cha cha	STARLITE	ST.45 012	£ 4 –	6

BILL CARLISLE & THE CARLISLES

59	Down boy/Union suit	MERCURY	AMT 1063	£12 –	18

HOAGY CARMICHAEL (qv LES BROWN)

55	Crazy Otto rag/Happy Hoagy's medley	V–CORAL	Q 72078	£ 4 –	6
55	Lazy river/I'm just wild about Mary		Q 72095	£ 4 –	6
56	Flight to Hong Kong/I walk the line		Q 72206	£ 4 –	6

IAN CARMICHAEL

57	Lucky Jim (how I envy him)/Tomorrow, tomorrow	H.M.V.	POP 406	£ 2 –	4

CARMITA

58	The crowd/Waterwagon blues	FONTANA	H 160	£ 2 –	4

RENATO CAROSONE & HIS QUARTET/SEXTET

57	Ricordate Marcellino!/Lazzarella	PARLOPHONE	R 4366	£ 2 –	4
58ø	Torero – Cha cha cha/Il piccolo montanaro		R 4433	£ 4 –	6

CATHY CARR

56	Ivory tower/Please, please believe me	LONDON	HLH 8274	£12 –	18
56	Heartbroken/I'll cry at your wedding	V–CORAL	Q 72175	£ 4 –	6
59	First anniversary/With love	COLUMBIA	DB 4270	£ 2 –	4
59	I'm gonna change him/The little things you do		DB 4317	£ 2 –	4
60	Little sister/Dark river		DB 4408	£ 2 –	4

REMEMBER! – THE SYMBOL ø AFTER THE YEAR OF ISSUE INDICATES A BRITISH CHART ENTRY

JOE "FINGERS" CARR (actually LOU BUSCH/& *THE CARR-HOPS/+JOY-RIDERS/qv VICKI YOUNG)

54	Piccadilly rag/Fiddle-a-delphia	CAPITOL	CL 14169	£ 4 - 6
55	The barky-roll stomp/Deep in the heart of Texas		*CL 14359	£ 4 - 6
55	Give me a band and my baby/Zag-a-zig		+CL 14372	£ 4 - 6
56	Memories of you/Henderson stomp		*CL 14520	£ 2 - 4
56	Let me be your honey, honey/Ragtime Cowboy Joe		*CL 14535	£ 2 - 4
56ø	The Portuguese washerwoman/Stumbling		CL 14587	£ 4 - 6

VALERIE CARR

58	You're the greatest/Over the rainbow	COLUMBIA	DB 4083	£ 2 - 4
58ø	When the boys talk about the girls/Padre		DB 4131	£ 4 - 6
58	Bad girl/Look forward		DB 4225	£ 2 - 4
59	The way to my heart/I'm only asking		DB 4365	£ 2 - 4

BARBARA CARROLL

59	North by northwest/Far away	LONDON	HLR 8981	£ 2 - 4

BOB CARROLL

55	I love you so much it hurts/My dearest, my darling, my..	M-G-M	SP 1132	£ 4 - 6
56	Red confetti, pink balloons &.../Handwriting on the wall	LONDON	HLU 8299	£ 9 - 12
58	Hi yo Silver/Tonto the Brave		HLT 8724	£ 6 - 9
59	I can't get you out of my..../Since I'm out of your arms		HLT 8888	£ 4 - 6

DIAHANN CARROLL

59	The big country/Guiding light	LONDON	HLT 8788	£ 4 - 6

DON CARROLL

57	At your front door/The Gods were angry with me	CAPITOL	CL 14812	£ 2 - 4
58	In my arms/The things I might have been		CL 14823	£ 2 - 4

JOHNNY CARROLL & HIS HOT ROCKS

56	Corrine Corrina/Wild wild women	BRUNSWICK	05580	£90 -120
56	Crazy, crazy lovin'/Hot rock		05603	£90 -120

RONNIE CARROLL

56ø	Walk hand in hand/Sweet heartaches	PHILIPS	PB 605 ọ	£ 1 - 2
57ø	The wisdom of a fool/Without love		PB 667 ọ	£ 1 - 2
60ø	Footsteps/Where walks my true love		PB 1004	£ 2 - 4

TONI CARROLL

58	I've never felt this way before/Dreamsville	M-G-M	MGM 987	£ 2 - 4

DEL CARSON

59	I told myself a lie/Jean	DECCA	F 11135	£ 2 - 4

JOHNNY CARSON

60	Fraulein/I wish it were you	FONTANA	H 243	£ 2 - 4
60	The train of love/First proposal		H 259	£ 2 - 4
60	You talk too much/Now and always		H 277	£ 2 - 4

KAY CARSON

56	Those who have loved/The fellow over there	CAPITOL	CL 14565	£ 2 - 4
56	There's a shadow between us/This man		CL 14634	£ 2 - 4

KEN CARSON

55	Hawkeye/I've been working on the railroad	LONDON	HLF 8213	£12 - 18
56	Let her go, let her go/The song of Daniel Boone		HLF 8237	£12 - 18

KIT CARSON

56	Band of gold/Cast your bread upon the waters	CAPITOL	CL 14524	£ 4 - 6

MINDY CARSON (qv GUY MITCHELL)

58	The sentimental touch/I was born	PHILIPS	PB 822	£ 2 - 4

VINCE CARSON

55	Sweetie, sweet, sweet Sue/My possession	H.M.V.	7M 313	£ 2 - 4

ANITA CARTER
58	Blue doll/Go away Johnnie	LONDON	HLA 8693	£ 4 – 6
60	Moon girl/Mama don't cry at my wedding		HLW 9102	£ 2 – 4

BENNY CARTER & HIS ORCH. (qv HELEN HUMES)
54	Blue Mountain/Sunday afternoon	H.M.V.	7M 189	£ 2 – 4

SONNY CARTER w. EARL BOSTIC & HIS ORCH.
55	There is no greater love/Oh baby	PARLOPHONE	MSP 6167	£ 6 – 9

DICK CARUSO
60	Two long years/Yes sir, that's my baby	M-G-M	MGM 1077	£ 2 – 4
60	Pretty little dancin' doll/We've never met		MGM 1099	£ 2 – 4

MARIAN CARUSO
55	The dove/Before we know it	BRUNSWICK	05398	£ 2 – 4
55	A man called Peter/This is the thanks I get (for.......)		05442	£ 2 – 4
55	The Boston fancy/I keep telling myself		05462	£ 2 – 4

JOHNNY CASH
57	I walk the line/Get rhythm	LONDON	HL 8358	£25 – 40
57	Train of love/There you go		HLS 8427	£25 – 40
57	Next in line/Don't make me go		HLS 8461	£18 – 25
57	Home of the blues/Give my love to Rose		HLS 8514	£12 – 18
58	Ballad of a teenage queen/Big river		HLS 8586	£12 – 18
58	Guess things happen that way/Come in, stranger		HLS 8656	£ 9 – 12
58	The ways of a woman in.../You're the nearest thing to...		HLS 8709	£ 9 – 12
58	All over again/What do I care	PHILIPS	PB 874	£ 4 – 6
59	It's just about time/I just thought you'd like to know	LONDON	HLS 8789	£ 6 – 9
59	Don't take your guns to town/I still miss someone	PHILIPS	PB 897	£ 4 – 6
59	Luther played the boogie/Thanks a lot	LONDON	HLS 8847	£12 – 18
59	Frankie's man, Johnny/You dreamer you	PHILIPS	PB 928	£ 4 – 6
59	Katy too/I forgot to remember to forget	LONDON	HLS 8928	£ 6 – 9
59	I got stripes/Five feet high and rising	PHILIPS	PB 953	£ 4 – 6
59	You tell me/Goodbye, little darlin', goodbye	LONDON	HLS 8979	£ 6 – 9
59	Little drummer boy/I'll remember you	PHILIPS	PB 979	£ 2 – 4
60	Straight A's in love/I love you because	LONDON	HLS 9070	£ 9 – 12
60	Seasons of my heart/Smiling Bill McCall	PHILIPS	PB 1017	£ 2 – 4
60	Down the street to 301/Story of a broken heart	LONDON	HLS 9182	£ 6 – 9
60	Loading coal/Going to Memphis	PHILIPS	PB 1075	£ 2 – 4

JOEY CASTELL
57	Tryin' to get to you/I'm left, you're right, she's gone	DECCA	F 10966	£12 – 18

THE CASTLE SISTERS
59	Drifting and dreaming/Lucky girl	COLUMBIA	DB 4335	£ 2 – 4

ROY CASTLE
60ø	Little white berry/Crazy little horn	PHILIPS	PB 1087	£ 2 – 4

FRANKIE CASTRO
56	Goodbye, so long, I'm gone/Too much	MERCURY	MT 114 º	£ 6 – 9

GEORGE CATES & HIS ORCH. (*& STEVE ALLEN)
55	Autumn leaves*/High and dry	V-CORAL	Q 72106	£ 2 – 4

JIMMY CAVELLO & HIS HOUSE ROCKERS
57	Rock, rock, rock/The big beat	V-CORAL	Q 72226	£60 – 90
57	Ooh-wee/Foot stompin'		Q 72240	£60 – 90

FRANK CHACKSFIELD & HIS ORCH./*TUNESMITHS
53ø	Little red monkey/Roundabouts and swings	*PARLOPHONE	R 3658 º	£ 2 – 4
53	Quiet rhythm blues/Junior Miss		MSP 6018	£ 4 – 6
53ø	Terry's theme & Incidental music from "Limelight"	DECCA	F 10106 º	£ 1 – 2
53ø	Ebb tide/Waltzing bugle boy		F 10122 º	£ 2 – 4

54	Song of Canterbury/The Pied Piper		F 10255	£ 2 - 4
54	Fiddlers' boogie/Pizzicato rag		F 10284	£ 4 - 6
54	Smile (Theme from "Modern Times")/Piper in the heather		F 10354	£ 2 - 4
54	Sur le pave (Pavements of Paris)/Lonely nightingale ...		F 10387	£ 2 - 4
55	Blue mirage/Lady from Luxembourg		F 10467	£ 2 - 4
56ø	In old Lisbon (Lisboa antigua)/Memories of you		F 10689	£ 4 - 6
56ø	The donkey cart/The banks of the Seine		F 10743	£ 4 - 6
58	Rodeo/Souvenirs of love		F 11027	£ 2 - 4
59	Java boogie/A Paris Valentine		F 11146	£ 2 - 4

ERNIE CHAFFIN
57	Lonesome for my baby/Feelin' low	LONDON	HLS 8409	£25 - 40

LES CHAKACHAS
58	Ay! Mulata/Eso es el amor	R.C.A.	RCA 1097	£ 2 - 4

GEORGE CHAKIRIS
59	Cool/I got rhythm	SAGA	SAG 45-2905	£ 6 - 9
60ø	Heart of a teenage girl/I'm always chasing rainbows ...	TRIUMPH	RGM 1010	£ 6 - 9

EDDIE CHAMBLEE & HIS RHYTHM & BLUES BAND
53	All out/TOMMY DEAN R&B BAND: Scamon boogie	ESQUIRE	10-329 º	£ 6 - 9
53	Blues for Eddie/PINEY BROWN: That's right, little girl	»	10-330 º	£ 6 - 9
53	Cradle rock/Back street		10-340 º	£ 6 - 9

THE CHAMPS
58ø	Tequila/Train to nowhere	LONDON	HLU 8580	£ 6 - 9
58	El Rancho rock/Midnighter		HL 8655	£ 9 - 12
58	Chariot rock/Subway		HL 8715	£ 6 - 9
59	Beatnik/Gone train		HLH 8811	£ 6 - 9
59	Caramba/Moonlight Bay		HLH 8864	£ 6 - 9
60ø	Too much tequila/Twenty thousand leagues		HLH 9052	£ 4 - 6

JACQUI CHAN
60	But no one knows/Gentlemen please!	PYE	7N 15273	£ 2 - 4

JEFF CHANDLER
54	I should care/More than anyone	BRUNSWICK	05264	£ 2 - 4
55	Everything happens to me/Always		05380	£ 2 - 4
55	My prayer/When Spring comes		05417	£ 2 - 4
55	Foxfire/Shaner maidel		05441	£ 2 - 4
55	Only the very young/A little love can go a long, long...		05465	£ 2 - 4
57	Half of my heart/Hold me	LONDON	HLU 8484	£ 6 - 9

KAREN CHANDLER (*& JIMMY WAKELY)
55	The man in the raincoat/The price you pay for love	V-CORAL	Q 72091	£ 2 - 4
56	Love is the $64,000 question/(I'm just a) Beginner	BRUNSWICK	05570	£ 2 - 4
56	Tonight you belong to me/Crazy arms		*05596	£ 4 - 6
57	Your wild heart/It's an international language		05662	£ 2 - 4

THE CHANTELS (qv RICHARD BARRETT)
58	Maybe/Come my little baby	LONDON	HLU 8561	£18 - 25

THE CHANTS
58	Lost and found/Close friends	CAPITOL	CL 14876	£ 4 - 6

PAUL CHAPLAIN & HIS EMERALDS
60	Shortnin' bread/Nicotine	LONDON	HLU 9205	£ 9 - 12

CHARLES CHAPLIN cond. Orch.
57	The spring song/Mandolin serenade	H.M.V.	POP 370	£ 2 - 4

GRADY CHAPMAN
60	Sweet thing/I know what I want	MERCURY	AMT 1107	£ 2 - 4

CHAPPAQUA HIGH SCHOOL KIDS
55 Never mind the noise in.../It's time to say goodnight... V-CORAL   Q 72068   £ 2 - 4

CHAQUITO & HIS ORCH. (actually JOHNNY GREGORY)
60ø Never on Sunday/Song of Orpheus .... FONTANA   H 265   £ 2 - 4

BOBBY CHARLES
56 See you later, alligator/On bended knee .... LONDON   HLU 8247   £300 ++

JIMMY CHARLES
60 A million to one/Hop scotch hop .... LONDON   HLU 9206   £ 4 - 6

RAY CHARLES (& HIS ORCH.)
58 Rockhouse - Parts 1 & 2 .... LONDON   HLE 8768   £12 - 18
59 What'd I say - Parts 1 & 2 .... HLE 8917   £ 9 - 12
59 I'm movin' on/I believe to my soul .... HLE 9009   £ 6 - 9
60 Let the good times roll/Don't let the sun catch you..... HLE 9058   £ 6 - 9
60 Sticks and stones/Worried life blues .... H.M.V.   POP 774   £ 4 - 6
60 Tell the truth/You be my baby .... LONDON   HLK 9181   £ 6 - 9
60ø Georgia on my mind/Carry me back to old Virginny ...... H.M.V.   POP 792   £ 4 - 6
60 Come rain or come shine/Tell me you'll wait for me .... LONDON   HLK 9251   £ 4 - 6

THE CHARMERS
58 He's gone/Oh! Yes .... VOGUE   V 9095   £60 - 90

THE CHARMS (qv OTIS WILLIAMS/TINY TOPSY)
55 Hearts of stone/Ko Ko Mo (I love you so) .... PARLOPHONE MSP 6155   £60 - 90

LINCOLN CHASE
57 Johnny Klingeringding/You're driving me crazy .... LONDON   HLU 8495   £ 6 - 9

ROBERT CHAUVIGNY
59 The Bottle theme/French rockin' waltz (Eux) .... TOP RANK   JAR 142   £ 2 - 4

CHUBBY CHECKER
59 The class/Schooldays, oh, schooldays .... TOP RANK   JAR 154   £ 9 - 12
60ø The twist/Toot .... COLUMBIA   DB 4503   £ 4 - 6
60 The hucklebuck/Whole lotta shakin' goin' on .... DB 4541   £ 6 - 9

THE CHEERS
54 Bazoom (I need your lovin')/Arrivederci .... CAPITOL   CL 14189   £25 - 40
55 Bernie's tune/Whadaya want? .... CL 14248   £18 - 25
55 Blueberries/Can't we be more than friends .... CL 14280   £18 - 25
55 I must be dreaming/Fancy meeting you here .... CL 14337   £18 - 25
55 Black denim trousers and motorcycle.../Some night in.... CL 14377   £25 - 40
56 Chicken/Don't do anything .... CL 14561   £12 - 18
56 Que pasa muchacha/(by BERT CONVY) .... CL 14601   £ 9 - 12

DON CHERRY
56ø Band of gold/Rumble boogie .... PHILIPS   PB 549 º £ 6 - 9
56 Wanted someone to love me/The thrill is gone .... BRUNSWICK   05538   £ 2 - 4
57 The last dance/Don't you worry your pretty little head! PHILIPS   JK 1013   £ 6 - 9
58 Another time, another place/The golden age .... PB 816   £ 2 - 4
59 Hasty heart/I look for a love .... PB 911   £ 2 - 4

PETE CHESTER & THE CONSULATES
60 Ten swingin' bottles/Whole lotta shakin' on the range . PYE   7N 15305   £12 - 18

VIC CHESTER
57 Rock-a-billy/First date, first kiss, first love .... DECCA   F 10882   £ 9 - 12

MAURICE CHEVALIER
55 Mon p'tit moustique/Deux amoureux sur un banc .... DECCA   F 10429   £ 2 - 4

REMEMBER! - THE SYMBOL º AFTER THE CATALOGUE NUMBER INDICATES A 78 rpm RECORD

```
     THE CHEVRONS
60  Lullaby/Day after forever  ...........................  TOP RANK   JAR 308   £ 4 -  6

     CHICK w. TED CAMERON & THE D.J.'s
60  Early in the morning/Cool water  .......................  PYE        7N 15292  £ 9 - 12

     THE CHIEFS
58  Apache/Dee's dream  ....................................  LONDON     HLU 8624  £ 9 - 12
58  Enchiladas!/Moments to remember  .......................             HLU 8720  £ 9 - 12

     Dr. A.A. CHILDS & Congregation
60  The healing prayer (both sides)  ......................  STARLITE ST.45 009   £ 4 -  6

     TSAI CHIN
59  The ding dong song/The second Spring  ..................  DECCA      F 11192   £ 2 -  4

     THE CHIPMUNKS (qv DAVID SEVILLE)
58  The Chipmunk song/(by DAVID SEVILLE)  ..................  LONDON     HLU 8762  £ 2 -  4
60  Rudolph the red-nosed reindeer/Lily of Laguna  .........             HLG 9243  £ 2 -  4

     GEORGE CHISHOLM & THE BLUENOTES w. BERT WEEDON
56  Honky tonk/D.R. rock  ..................................  BELTONA    BL 2671   £ 6 -  9

     THE CHORDETTES
54ø  Mr. Sandman/I don't wanna see you cryin'  .............  COLUMBIA   DB 3553 ⁰ £ 4 -  6
54ø  as above  .............................................             SCM 5158  £25 - 40
55  Humming bird/Lonely lips  .............................  LONDON     HLA 8169  £12 - 18
56  Dudelsack polka/I told a lie  ..........................             HLA 8217  £12 - 18
56  Eddie my love/Our melody  ..............................             HLA 8264  £12 - 18
56ø  Born to be with you/Love never changes  ...............             HLA 8302  £18 - 25
56  Lay down your arms/Teenage goodnight  ..................             HLA 8323  £12 - 18
57  Just between you and me/Echo of love  ..................             HLA 8473  £ 9 - 12
57  Like a baby/Soft sands  ................................             HLA 8497  £ 9 - 12
58  Baby of mine/Photographs  ..............................             HLA 8566  £ 9 - 12
58ø  Lollipop/Baby, come-a-back-a  .........................             HLA 8584  £ 9 - 12
58  Love is a two-way street/I don't know, I don't care  ...             HLA 8654  £ 9 - 12
59  No other arms, no other lips/We should be together  ....             HLA 8809  £ 6 -  9
59  A girl's work is never done/No wheels  .................             HLA 8926  £ 9 - 12

     THE CHORDS
54  Sh-boom (Life could be a dream)/Little maiden  .........  COLUMBIA SCM 5133   £60 - 90

     BOBBY CHRISTIAN & HIS ORCH.
57  Crickets on parade/Enough man  ........................  ORIOLE     CB 1384   £ 4 -  6

     JUNE CHRISTY (qv STAN KENTON)
55  Pete Kelly's blues/Kicks  .............................  CAPITOL    CL 14355  £ 4 -  6
56  Look out up there/I never wanna look into those eyes....             CL 14554  £ 2 -  4
56  Intrigue/You took advantage of me  ....................             CL 14604  £ 2 -  4
57  Sing something simple/Maybe you'll be there  ..........             CL 14673  £ 2 -  4
57  The best thing for you/This year's kisses  ............             CL 14746  £ 2 -  4

     CHUCK & BETTY
59  Sissy britches/Come back little girl  .................  BRUNSWICK   05815   £ 9 - 12

     CHUCK & GARY
58  Teenie weenie Jeanie/Can't make up my mind  ...........  H.M.V.    POP  466   £ 9 - 12

     EUGENE CHURCH
59  I ain't goin' for that/Miami  .........................  LONDON    HL  8940   £12 - 18

     THE CINDERELLAS (qv GADDY WILSON)
59  Mister Dee-Jay/Yum yum yum  ...........................  BRUNSWICK   05794   £ 9 - 12
60  The trouble with boys/Puppy dog  ......................  PHILIPS   PB 1012   £ 6 -  9
```

CINDY & LINDY

57	Tell me something sweet/The language of love	H.M.V.	POP	409	£ 2 – 4
59	Saturday night in Tia Juana/The wonder that is you	CORAL	Q	72368	£ 4 – 6

CITY RAMBLERS SKIFFLE (GROUP)

57	Ella Speed/2.19 blues	TEMPO	A	158	£ 4 – 6
57	Mama don't allow/Tom Dooley		A	161	£ 4 – 6
57	Delia's gone/Boodle-am shake		A	165	£ 4 – 6

JIMMY CLANTON (& *HIS ROCKETS/+THE ACES)

58	Just a dream/You aim to please	LONDON	*HLS	8699	£ 9 – 12
59	A letter to an angel/A part of me		+HLS	8779	£ 9 – 12
59	My own true love/Little boy in love	TOP RANK	JAR	189	£ 4 – 6
60	Go, Jimmy, go/I trusted you		JAR	269	£ 4 – 6
60ø	Another sleepless night/I'm gonna try		JAR	382	£ 4 – 6
60	Come back/Wait		JAR	509	£ 4 – 6

THE CLARK SISTERS

59	Chicago/Opus 1	LONDON	HLD	8791	£ 4 – 6

DEE CLARK

59	When I call on you/Nobody but you	LONDON	HL	8802	£ 6 – 9
59ø	Just keep it up (and see what happens)/Whispering grass		HL	8915	£ 6 – 9
59	Hey, little girl/If it wasn't for love	TOP RANK	JAR	196	£ 4 – 6
60	How about that/Blues get off my shoulder		JAR	284	£ 4 – 6
60	At my front door/Cling-a-ling		JAR	373	£ 6 – 9
60	You're looking good/Gloria		JAR	501	£ 4 – 6

PETULA CLARK

54ø	The little shoemaker/Helpless	POLYGON	P	1117	º £ 2 – 4
54ø	Majorca/Fascinating rhythm		P	1146	º £ 2 – 4
55ø	Suddenly there's a valley/With your love	PYE	N	15013	º £ 2 – 4
56	The little shoemaker/Somebody		N	15024	º £ 2 – 4
56	Majorca/Fascinating rhythm		N	15026	º £ 2 – 4
56	Band of gold/Memories are made of this		N	15040	º £ 2 – 4
56	To you, my love/Fortune teller		N	15051	º £ 2 – 4
56	A million stars above/Another door opens		N	15073	º £ 2 – 4
57	Who needs you/The sky		N	15086	º £ 2 – 4
57ø	With all my heart/Gonna find me a bluebird		7N	15096	£ 4 – 6
57ø	Alone/Long before I knew you		7N	15112	£ 4 – 6
58ø	Baby lover/The little blue man		7N	15126	£ 4 – 6
58	Love me again/In a little moment		7N	15135	£ 2 – 4
58	St. Tropez (Sur la plage)/Devotion		7N	15152	£ 2 – 4
58	I wish I knew/Fibbin'		7N	15168	£ 2 – 4
59	Ever been in love/Lucky day		7N	15182	£ 2 – 4
59	Watch your heart/Suddenly		7N	15191	£ 2 – 4
59	Where do I go from here?/Mamma's talking soft		7N	15208	£ 2 – 4
59	Adonis/If I had my way		7N	15220	£ 2 – 4
59	Dear Daddy/Through the livelong day		7N	15230	£ 2 – 4
60	I love a violin/Guitare et tambourin		7N	15244	£ 2 – 4
60	Cinderella Jones/All over now		7N	15281	£ 2 – 4

ROY CLARK

59	Please Mr. Mayor/Puddin'	H.M.V.	POP	581	£25 – 40

SANFORD CLARK

56	The fool/Lonesome for a letter	LONDON	HLD	8320	£40 – 60
59	Run, boy run/New kind of fool		HLW	8959	£ 9 – 12
60	Son-of-a-gun/I can't help it		HLW	9026	£ 6 – 9
60	Pledging my love/Go on home		HLW	9095	£ 6 – 9

JEFFREY CLAY

55	No arms can ever hold you/Come back, come back	V-CORAL	Q	72093	£ 2 – 4
55	Sweet Kentucky rose/Unknown to me ....·.		Q	72113	£ 2 – 4
56	These hands/You'll be sorry (when someone else is glad)		Q	72143	£ 2 – 4

STEVE CLAYTON

56	Two different worlds/It happened again	V-CORAL	Q 72200	£ 2 - 4
57	The boy with the golden.../I wanna put my arms around...		Q 72253	£ 2 - 4
60	Let's tell them now/They say in time	LONDON	HLU 9033	£ 2 - 4

THE CLEFTONES

56	You baby, you/Little girl of mine	COLUMBIA	DB 3801	£40 - 60

JACK CLEMENT

58	Ten years/Your lover boy	LONDON	HLS 8691	£18 - 25

BILL CLIFTON

60	You don't think about me/Mail carrier's warning	MELODISC	1554	£ 4 - 6

PATSY CLINE

57	Walkin' after midnight/A poor man's roses (or a rich...)	BRUNSWICK	05660	£ 9 - 12

BUDDY CLINTON

60	Across the street from your house/How my prayers have...	TOP RANK	JAR 287	£ 2 - 4

BETTY CLOONEY (qv ROSEMARY CLOONEY)

55	I love you a mountain/Can't do without you	H.M.V.	7M 311	£ 4 - 6

ROSEMARY CLOONEY (& *MARLENE DIETRICH/+BETTY CLOONEY/=JOSE FERRER/qv BOB HOPE)

51	Come on-a my house/Kentucky waltz	COLUMBIA	DB 2895	ø £ 2 - 4
52ø	Half as much/Botch-a-me (Ba-ba-baciami piccina)		DB 3129	ø £ 2 - 4
53	Too old to cut the mustard/Good for nothin'		*SCM 5010	£ 9 - 12
53ø	Half as much/Botch-a-me (Ba-ba-baciami piccina)		SCM 5019	£12 - 18
53	If I had a penny/You're after my own heart		SCM 5027	£ 6 - 9
53	On the first warm day/If teardrops were pennies		SCM 5028	£ 6 - 9
53	(Remember me) I'm the one who loves you/Lovers' gold ..		SCM 5040	£ 6 - 9
53	Blues in the night/Who kissed me last night?		SCM 5049	£ 6 - 9
54ø	Man (uh-huh)/JOSE FERRER: Woman (uh-huh)	PHILIPS	PB 220	ø £ 2 - 4
54	I still feel the same about you+/Why fight the feeling?	COLUMBIA	SCM 5093	£ 6 - 9
54ø	This ole house/My baby sends me	PHILIPS	PB 336	ø £ 1 - 2
54ø	Mambo Italiano/We'll be together again		PB 382	ø £ 1 - 2
55ø	Where will the dimple be?/Brahms' lullaby		PB 428	ø £ 1 - 2
55ø	Hey there/It just happened to happen to me		PB 494	ø £ 1 - 2
57ø	Mangos/All the pretty little horses		PB 671	ø £ 1 - 2
57ø	*as above*		JK 1010	£ 9 - 12
58	I could have danced all night/I've grown accustomed to..		PB 800	£ 2 - 4
58	The Loudenboomer bird/It's a boy	M-G-M	MGM 990	£ 2 - 4
59	Tonight/Come rain or come shine	PHILIPS	PB 900	£ 2 - 4
59	Diga me (Deega may-tell me)/A touch of the blues	CORAL	Q 72357	£ 2 - 4
59	Love eyes/Flattery=	M-G-M	MGM 1010	£ 2 - 4
60	Love, look away/I wish I were in love again	CORAL	Q 72388	£ 2 - 4
60	For you/I wonder	M-G-M	MGM 1062	£ 2 - 4
60	Many a wonderful moment/Vaya. vaya	R.C.A.	RCA 1203	£ 2 - 4

CLAUDE CLOUD & HIS ORCH.

57	The beat/Around the Horn	M-G-M	MGM 946	£ 2 - 4

THE CLOVERLEAFS (qv ART MOONEY)

56	With plenty of money and you/Step right up and say howdy	M-G-M	MGM 933	£ 2 - 4

THE CLOVERS

56	Nip sip/If I could be loved by you	LONDON	HLE 8229	£90 -120
56	Love, love, love/Hey, doll baby		HLE 8314	£60 - 90
56	From the bottom of my heart/Your tender lips		HLE 8334	£60 - 90
58	Idaho/In the good old Summertime	H.M.V.	POP 542	£ 9 - 12
59	Love potion No. 9/Stay awhile	LONDON	HLT 8949	£12 - 18
60	Lovey/One mint julep		HLT 9122	£12 - 18
60	Easy lovin'/I'm confessin' (that I love you)		HLT 9154	£12 - 18

REMEMBER! - THE SYMBOL ø AFTER THE YEAR OF ISSUE INDICATES A BRITISH CHART ENTRY

THE CLYDE VALLEY STOMPERS (*w. MARY McGOWAN/qv IAN MENZIES)

56	Old time religion/Pearly gates	BELTONA	*BL 2650 º	£ 4 –	6
57	Milenberg joys/Bill Bailey won't you please come home*	DECCA	FJ 10897	£ 2 –	4

THE COACHMEN

59	Those brown eyes/Bald Mountain	VOGUE	V 9154	£ 4 –	6

THE COASTERS

57ø	Searchin'/Young blood	LONDON	HLE 8450	£ 9 –	12
58ø	Yakety yak/Zing! went the strings of my heart		HLE 8665	£ 6 –	9
58	The shadow knows/Sorry but I'm gonna have to pass		HLE 8729	£ 9 –	12
59ø	Charlie Brown/Three cool cats		HLE 8819	£ 6 –	9
59	Along came Jones/That is rock and roll		HLE 8882	£ 9 –	12
59ø	Poison Ivy/I'm a hog for you		HLE 8938	£ 6 –	9
60	What about us/Run Red run		HLE 9020	£ 6 –	9
60	Besame mucho – Parts 1 & 2		HLK 9111	£ 6 –	9
60	Wake me, shake me/Stewball		HLK 9151	£ 6 –	9
60	Shoppin' for clothes/The snake and the bookworm		HLK 9208	£ 6 –	9

JUNIE COBB'S HOMETOWN BAND

59	Chicago buzz/East Coast trot	COLLECTOR	JDL 38	£ 4 –	6

EDDIE COCHRAN

57	20 flight rock/Dark lonely street	LONDON	HLU 8386	£40 –	60
57	Sittin' in the balcony/Completely sweet		HLU 8433	£90 –	120
58ø	Summertime blues/Love again		HLU 8702	£ 9 –	12
59ø	C'mon everybody/Don't ever let me go		HLU 8792	£ 9 –	12
59	Teenage Heaven/I remember		HLU 8880	£12 –	18
59ø	Somethin' else/Boll weevil song		HLU 8944	£ 9 –	12
60ø	Hallelujah, I love her so/Little angel		HLW 9022	£ 6 –	9
60ø	Three steps to Heaven/Cut across Shorty		HLG 9115	£ 6 –	9
60ø	Sweetie pie/Lonely		HLG 9196	£ 9 –	12

JACKIE LEE COCHRAN

57	Mama don't you think I know/Ruby Pearl	BRUNSWICK	05669	£160–200

JAMIE COE

59	There's gonna be a day/Summertime symphony	PARLOPHONE	R 4600	£18 –	25
59	School day blues/I'll go on loving you		R 4621	£ 9 –	12

ALMA COGAN (& *LARRY DAY/+LES HOWARD/=FRANKIE VAUGHAN/qv RONNIE HILTON)

53	I went to your wedding/You belong to me	H.M.V.	7M 106	£12 –	18
53	To be loved by you/The homing waltz*		7M 107	£ 9 –	12
53	Isn't life wonderful (Mm....)/Over and over again		+7M 166	£ 9 –	12
54	Richochet (Rick–O–Shay)/The Moon is blue		7M 173	£ 9 –	12
54ø	Bell bottom blues/Love me again		B 10653 º	£ 2 –	4
54ø	*as above*		7M 188	£12 –	18
54	Make love to me/Said the little moment		7M 196	£ 9 –	12
54	The little shoemaker/Chiqui–Chaqui (Chick–ee Chock–ee)		7M 219	£12 –	18
54	Do, do, do, do, do, do, do it again/Jilted		=7M 226	£ 9 –	12
54ø	Little things mean a lot/Canoodlin' rag		B 10717 º	£ 2 –	4
54ø	*as above*		7M 228	£12 –	18
54	Skinnie Minnie (Fishtail)/What am I going to do, Ma ...		7M 239	£ 9 –	12
54	This ole house/Skokiaan		7M 269	£12 –	18
54ø	I can't tell a waltz from a tango/Christmas cards		B 10786 º	£ 2 –	4
54ø	*as above*		7M 271	£12 –	18
55	Paper kisses/Softly, softly		7M 286	£ 9 –	12
55	Tweedle–dee/More than ever now		7M 301	£12 –	18
55	Chee–chee–oo–chee (sang the little bird)/Tika tika tok		7M 293	£ 9 –	12
55ø	Dreamboat/(The diddle–ee–i) Irish mambo		B 10872 º	£ 2 –	4
55	Where will the dimple be?/Keep me in mind		B 10887 º	£ 2 –	4
55	Give a fool a chance/Got'n idea		7M 316	£ 9 –	12
55ø	Go on by/The banjo's back in town		B 10917 º	£ 2 –	4
55ø	Never do a tango with an Eskimo/Twenty tiny fingers ...		POP 129 º	£ 2 –	4
55ø	*as above*		7M 337	£12 –	18

56	Love and marriage/Sycamore tree		POP	163 º	£ 2 – 4
56	*as above*		7M	367	£ 9 – 12
56ø	Willie can/Lizzie Borden		POP	187 º	£ 2 – 4
56	Bluebell/Don't ring-a da bell (Don't knock at da door)		POP	189 º	£ 2 – 4
56ø	Why do fools fall in love/The birds and the bees		POP	223 º	£ 2 – 4
56ø	*as above*		7M	415	£12 – 18
56	I'm in love again/Mama teach me to dance		POP	239	£ 9 – 12
56ø	In the middle of the house/Two innocent hearts		POP	261	£ 9 – 12
57ø	You, me and us/Three brothers		POP	284	£ 9 – 12
57ø	Whatever Lola wants (Lola gets)/Lucky lips		POP	317	£ 9 – 12
57	Chantez, chantez/Funny, funny, funny		POP	336	£ 6 – 9
57	Fabulous/Summer love		POP	367	£ 9 – 12
57	That's happiness/What you've done to me		POP	392	£ 6 – 9
57	Party time/Please Mr. Brown (Mr. Jones, Mr. Smith)		POP	415	£ 6 – 9
58ø	The story of my life/Love is		POP	433	£ 9 – 12
58ø	Sugartime/Gettin' ready for Freddy		POP	450	£ 9 – 12
58	Stairway of love/Comes love		POP	482	£ 9 – 12
58	Fly away lovers/Sorry, sorry, sorry		POP	500	£ 4 – 6
58	There's never been a night/If this isn't love		POP	531	£ 6 – 9
59ø	Last night on the back porch/Mama says		POP	573	£ 6 – 9
59	Pink shoelaces/The Universe		POP	608	£ 6 – 9
59ø	We got love/I don't mind being all alone		POP	670	£ 4 – 6
60ø	Dream talk/O Dio mio		POP	728	£ 4 – 6
60ø	The train of love/The 'I love you' bit		POP	760	£ 4 – 6
60	Must be Santa/Just couldn't resist her with her pocket..		POP	815	£ 4 – 6

DON COGAN
58	The fountain of youth/I'm takin' over	M-G-M	MGM	984	£ 2 – 4

SHAYE COGAN (qv BUDDY MORROW)
58	Billy be sure/Doodle doodle doo	COLUMBIA	DB	4055	£ 2 – 4
60ø	Mean to me/They said it couldn't be done	M-G-M	MGM	1063	£ 4 – 6

ALVADEAN COKER
55	Do dee oodle de do I'm in love/We're gonna bop	LONDON	HLU	8191	£60 – 90

SANDY COKER & HIS BAND
54	Meadowlark melody/Toss over	LONDON	HL	8109	£18 – 25

MARION COLBY
58	A man could be a wonderful thing/He like it! She like...	CAPITOL	CL	14959	£ 2 – 4

BUDDY COLE & THE WOOD SISTERS
55	Plantation boogie/Foolishly	PHILIPS	PB	464 º	£ 4 – 6

COZY COLE
58ø	Topsy – Parts 1 & 2	LONDON	HL	8750	£ 6 – 9
58	Father co-operates/St. Louis blues	MERCURY	AMT	1015	£ 4 – 6
59	Turvy – Parts 1 & 2	LONDON	HL	8843	£ 4 – 6

NAT "KING" COLE (*TRIO/+QUINTET) (& =THE FOUR KNIGHTS/#STAN KENTON/qv DEAN MARTIN)
50	I almost lost my mind/Bang bang boogie	CAPITOL	*CL	13370 º	£ 6 – 9
52	(Get your kicks on) Route 66*/Wine, women and song		CL	13722 º	£ 4 – 6
52ø	Somewhere along the way/Walkin' my baby back home		CL	13774 º	£ 2 – 4
52ø	Because you're mine/Faith can move mountains		CL	13811 º	£ 2 – 4
53ø	Pretend/Funny (not much)		CL	13878 º	£ 2 – 4
53ø	Mother Nature and Father Time/My flaming heart		CL	13912 º	£ 2 – 4
53ø	Can't I/Small towns are smile towns		CL	13937 º	£ 2 – 4
54ø	Tenderly/Why		CL	14061 º	£ 2 – 4
54	Nat's kicks – Parts 1 & 2	VOGUE	+V	2214 º	£ 4 – 6
54ø	Smile (Theme from "Modern Times")/Make her mine	CAPITOL	CL	14149	£ 9 – 12
54	I am in love/There goes my heart		CL	14172	£ 6 – 9
54	If I give my heart to you/Hold my hand		CL	14203	£ 6 – 9
54	Teach me tonight/Papa loves mambo		CL	14207	£ 9 – 12
54	Hajji baba (Persian lament)/Unbelievable		CL	14155	£ 6 – 9

55ø	A blossom fell/Alone too long		CL 14235	£ 9 - 12
55	The sand and the sea/Darling, je vous aime beaucoup		CL 14251	£ 6 - 9
55	If I may=/I envy		CL 14295	£ 6 - 9
55	I'd rather have the blues/Annabelle		CL 14317	£ 6 - 9
55ø	My one sin/Don't hurt the girl		CL 14327	£ 9 - 12
55	Love is a many splendored thing/Autumn leaves		CL 14364	£ 6 - 9
55	Someone you love/Forgive my heart		CL 14378	£ 6 - 9
56ø	Dreams can tell a lie/Ask me		CL 14513	£ 6 - 9
56	Nothing ever changes (my love...)/I'm gonna laugh you...		CL 14529	£ 4 - 6
56ø	Too young to go steady/Never let me go		CL 14573	£ 6 - 9
56ø	Love me as though there were../That's all there is to..=		CL 14621	£ 6 - 9
56	My dream sonata/I just found out about love		CL 14632	£ 2 - 4
56	To the ends of the Earth/Toyland		CL 14661	£ 2 - 4
57	Night lights/Dame crazy		CL 14678	£ 2 - 4
57	You are my first love/Ballerina		CL 14688	£ 2 - 4
57ø	When I fall in love/Calypso blues		CL 14709	£ 4 - 6
57ø	When rock and roll come to Trinidad/It's all in the game		CL 14733	£ 6 - 9
57ø	My personal possession=/Send for me		CL 14765	£ 4 - 6
57ø	Stardust/Love letters		CL 14787	£ 4 - 6
58	Angel smile/Back in my arms		CL 14820	£ 2 - 4
58	With you on my mind/The song of Raintree County		CL 14853	£ 2 - 4
58	Looking back/Just for the fun of it		CL 14882	£ 2 - 4
58	Come closer to me/Nothing in the world		CL 14898	£ 2 - 4
58	Non dimenticar (Don't forget)/Bend a little my way		CL 14937	£ 2 - 4
59	Madrid/Give me your love		CL 14987	£ 2 - 4
59ø	You made me love you/I must be dreaming		CL 15017	£ 2 - 4
59ø	Midnight flyer/Sweet bird of youth		CL 15056	£ 2 - 4
59	Buon Natale/The happiest little Christmas tree		CL 15087	£ 2 - 4
60ø	Time and the river/Whatcha' gonna do		CL 15111	£ 2 - 4
60ø	That's you/Is it better to have loved and lost		CL 15129	£ 2 - 4
60	My love/Steady		#CL 15144	£ 2 - 4
60ø	Just as much as ever/I wish I knew the way to your heart		CL 15163	£ 2 - 4

LONNIE COLEMAN & JESSE ROBERTSON
56	Dolores Diane/Oh honey, why don'tcha	LONDON	HL 8335	£12 - 18

ROGER COLEMAN
60	Nobody's fool/Endlessly	TOP RANK	JAR 311	£ 2 - 4

AL "JAZZBO" COLLINS
56	Max/Sam	V-CORAL	Q 72160	£ 2 - 4

DOROTHY COLLINS
55	My boy - Flat Top/In love	V-CORAL	Q 72111	£18 - 25
56	Moments to remember/Love and marriage		Q 72116	£ 6 - 9
56	Seven days/Manuello		Q 72137	£ 9 - 12
56	Treasure of love/He's got me, hook, line and sinker		Q 72173	£12 - 18
56	Rock and roll train/Love me as though there were no.....		Q 72193	£18 - 25
56	Cool it, baby/The Italian theme		Q 72198	£18 - 25
56	The twelve gifts of Christmas/Mister Santa		Q 72208	£ 4 - 6
57	Baby can rock/Would you ever		Q 72232	£ 9 - 12
57	Mr. Wonderful/I miss you already		Q 72252	£ 4 - 6
57	Four walls/Big dreams		Q 72262	£ 4 - 6
57	Soft sands/Sing it, children, sing it		Q 72287	£ 4 - 6
59	Baciare, baciare (Kissing,...)/Everything I have is yours	TOP RANK	JAR 259	£ 2 - 4
60	Banjo boy/Tintarella di Luna		JAR 401	£ 2 - 4
60	Unlock those chains/I'll be yours, you'll be mine		JAR 523	£ 2 - 4

GLENDA COLLINS
60	Take a chance/Crazy guy	DECCA	F 11280	£ 2 - 4

TOMMY COLLINS
58	Think it over boys/All of the monkeys ain't in the zoo	CAPITOL	CL 14838	£ 4 - 6
58	Let down/It tickles		CL 14894	£ 4 - 6
59	Little June/A hundred years from now		CL 15076	£ 6 - 9
60	Wreck of the old '97/You belong in my arms		CL 15118	£ 4 - 6

JERRY COLONNA

54	Ebb tide/The velvet glove	BRUNSWICK	05243	£ 9 - 12
54	It might as well be Spring/Ja-da		05342	£ 4 - 6
55	Let me go, lover/I want to love you, cara mia	PARLOPHONE	MSP 6165	£ 4 - 6
55	Chicago style/Baffi	LONDON	HL 8143	£12 - 18
56	The shifting, whispering sands/Waltz me around	H.M.V.	7M 369	£ 4 - 6

KEN COLYER'S JAZZMEN

54	Goin' home/Isle of Capri	DECCA	F 10241 º	£ 2 - 4
54	La Harpe Street blues/Too busy		F 10332 º	£ 2 - 4
55	Early hours/Cataract rag		F 10504	£ 4 - 6
55	If I ever cease to love/The entertainer		F 10519	£ 4 - 6
55	Red Wing/It looks like a big time tonight		F 10565	£ 4 - 6
55	Gravier Street blues/Buddy Bolden's blues	VOGUE	V 2344 º	£ 2 - 4
55	How long blues, No. 2/Ciribiribin		V 2345 º	£ 2 - 4
56	Sheik of Araby/Just a closer walk with Thee	TEMPO	A 117	£ 4 - 6
56	Isle of Capri/If I ever cease to love		A 120	£ 4 - 6
56	Wabash blues/My bucket's got a hole in it		A 126	£ 4 - 6
56	Maryland my Maryland/The world is waiting for the sun-..		A 136	£ 4 - 6
56	Dippermouth blues/All the girls go crazy about the way..	DECCA	FJ 10755	£ 4 - 6

KEN COLYER'S SKIFFLE GROUP

55	Take this hammer/Down by the riverside	DECCA	F 10631	£ 6 - 9
56	Streamline train/Go down old Hannah		FJ 10711	£ 6 - 9
56	Down bound train/Mule skinner		FJ 10751	£ 6 - 9
56	Old Riley/Stack O'Lee blues		FJ 10772	£ 6 - 9
57	The grey goose/I can't sleep		FJ 10889	£ 6 - 9
57	Sporting life/House rent stomp		FJ 10926	£ 6 - 9
58	Ella Speed/Go down sunshine		F 10972	£ 6 - 9

THE COMMANDERS (qv LOUIS ARMSTRONG)

55	The elephants' tango/Commanders overture	BRUNSWICK	05366	£ 2 - 4
55	The cat from Coos Bay/Camptown boogie		05433	£ 4 - 6
55	The monster/Cornball No. 1		05467	£ 4 - 6

THE COMMODORES

55	Riding on a train/Uranium	LONDON	HLD 8209	£60 - 90
56	Speedo/Whole lotta shakin' goin' on		HLD 8251	£90 -120

PERRY COMO (& *THE FONTANE SISTERS/+BETTY HUTTON)

51	If/Zing zing - zoom zoom	H.M.V.	B 10042 º	£ 2 - 4
53ø	Don't let the stars get in your eyes/To know you (is..)*		B 10400 º	£ 2 - 4
53	The ruby and the pearl/My love and devotion		7M 102	£ 6 - 9
53	Some enchanted evening/Bali Ha'i		7M 110	£ 6 - 9
53ø	Don't let the stars get in your eyes/To know you (is..)*		7M 118	£12 - 18
53	Wild horses/Please believe me		7M 124	£ 6 - 9
53	A bushel and a peck+/My lady loves to dance		7M 138	£ 9 - 12
53	Say you're mine again/My one and only heart		7M 149	£ 6 - 9
53	Hello, young lovers/We kiss in a shadow		7M 155	£ 6 - 9
53	Why did you leave me?/Pa-Paya Mama		7M 163	£ 6 - 9
54	You alone/Surprising		7M 175	£ 6 - 9
54ø	Idle gossip/Look out the window		B 10667 º	£ 2 - 4
54ø	as above		7M 200	£ 9 - 12
54ø	Wanted/Give me your hand		B 10691 º	£ 2 - 4
54ø	as above		7M 215	£ 9 - 12
54	If you were only mine/Hit and run affair		7M 241	£ 6 - 9
54ø	Papa loves mambo/There never was a night so beautiful .		B 10776 º	£ 2 - 4
54ø	as above		7M 263	£ 9 - 12
54	Frosty the snowman/The twelve days of Christmas		7M 278	£ 6 - 9
55	Ko Ko Mo (I love you so)/You'll always be my lifetime...		7M 296	£ 9 - 12
55	Door of dreams/Nobody		7M 305	£ 6 - 9
55ø	Tina Marie/Home for the holidays		POP 103 º	£ 2 - 4
55ø	as above		7M 326	£ 9 - 12
56	The rose tattoo/Fooled		7M 366	£ 6 - 9
56ø	Juke box baby/The things I didn't do		POP 191 º	£ 4 - 6

56ø	Hot diggity (dog ziggity boom)/My funny Valentine		POP	212	ª £ 2 – 4
56ø	*as above*		7M	404	£ 9 – 12
56ø	Juke box baby/Hot diggity (dog ziggity boom)		7MC	39	£25 – 40
56ø	More/Glendora		POP	240	£ 9 – 12
56	Moonlight love/Chincherinchee		POP	271	£ 4 – 6
57	Somebody up there likes me/Dream along with me		POP	304	£ 4 – 6
57	Round and round/My house is your house		POP	328	£ 4 – 6
57	The girl with the golden braids/My little baby	R.C.A.	RCA	1001	£ 4 – 6
57	Silk stockings/Childhood is a meadow	H.M.V.	POP	369	£ 4 – 6
57	All at once you love her/As time goes by		POP	394	£ 4 – 6
57	Marching along to the blues/Dancin'	R.C.A.	RCA	1016	£ 2 – 4
57	Just born (to be your baby)/Ivy Rose		RCA	1027	£ 2 – 4
58ø	Magic moments/Catch a falling star		RCA	1036	£ 4 – 6
58ø	Kewpie doll/Dance only with me		RCA	1055	£ 4 – 6
58ø	I may never pass this way again/Prayer for peace		RCA	1062	£ 2 – 4
58ø	Moon talk/Beats there a heart so true		RCA	1071	£ 2 – 4
58ø	Love makes the world go 'round/Mandolins in the moon–...		RCA	1086	£ 2 – 4
59ø	Tomboy/Kiss me and kiss me and kiss me		RCA	1111	£ 2 – 4
59ø	I know/You are in love		RCA	1126	£ 2 – 4
59	A still small voice/No well on Earth		RCA	1156	£ 2 – 4
59	Ave Maria/The Lord's Prayer		RCA	1163	£ 2 – 4
60ø	Delaware/I know what God is		RCA	1170	£ 2 – 4
60	Gone is my love/Home for the holidays		RCA	1215	£ 2 – 4

LES COMPAGNONS DE LA CHANSON

53	The three bells (The Jimmy Brown song)/Ave Maria	COLUMBIA	SCM	5005	£ 6 – 9
53	The galley slave/Dreams never grow old		SCM	5056	£ 4 – 6
59ø	The three bells (The Jimmy Brown song)/Ave Maria		DB	4358	£ 4 – 6
60	Down by the riverside/Margoton		DB	4454	£ 2 – 4

BOBBY COMSTOCK & THE COUNTS

59	Tennessee waltz/Sweet talk	TOP RANK	JAR	223	£ 4 – 6
60	Jambalaya/Let's talk it over	LONDON	HLE	9080	£ 4 – 6

EDDIE CONDON & THE ALL-STARS

60	Heebie jeebies/What-cha-call-'em blues	PHILIPS	JAZ	115	£ 2 – 4

THE CONEY ISLAND KIDS

55	Baby, baby you/Moonlight beach	LONDON	HLJ	8207	£12 – 18

RAY CONNIFF & THE ROCKIN' RHYTHM BOYS

55	Piggy bank boogie/Short stuff	V-CORAL	QW	5001	£ 9 – 12

CHRIS CONNOR

59	Hallelujah I love him so/I won't cry anymore	LONDON	HLE	8869	£ 4 – 6
60	I only want some/That's my desire		HLK	9124	£ 4 – 6

KENNETH CONNOR

59	Rail road rock/Ramona	TOP RANK	JAR	138	£ 4 – 6

JESS CONRAD

60ø	Cherry pie/There's gonna be a day	DECCA	F	11236	£ 4 – 6
60	Unless you mean it/Out of luck		F	11259	£ 2 – 4

BERT CONVY (*& THE THUNDERBIRDS)

55	C'mon back/Hoo bop de bow	LONDON	*HLB	8190	£40 – 60
56	Heaven on Earth/(by THE CHEERS)	CAPITOL	CL	14601	£ 9 – 12

RUSS CONWAY (qv RONNIE HARRIS)

57	Roll the carpet up/The Westminster waltz	COLUMBIA	DB	3920	£ 2 – 4
57	Soho Fair/The spotlight waltz		DB	3971	£ 2 – 4
57	The red cat/Late extra		DB	3999	£ 2 – 4
57ø	"Party Pops" medley		DB	4031	£ 2 – 4
58ø	Got a match?/Toby's walk		DB	4166	£ 2 – 4
58ø	"More Party Pops" medley		DB	4204	£ 2 – 4
58ø	The world outside/Love like ours		DB	4234	£ 2 – 4

59ø Side saddle/Pixilated penguin		DB 4256	£ 2 - 4
59ø Roulette/Trampolina		DB 4298	£ 2 - 4
59ø China tea/The wee boy of Brussels		DB 4337	£ 2 - 4
59ø Snow coach/Time to celebrate		DB 4368	£ 2 - 4
59ø "More And More Party Pops" medley		DB 4373	£ 2 - 4
60ø Royal event/Rule Britannia!		DB 4418	£ 2 - 4
60ø "fings ain't wot they used t'be" medley		DB 4422	£ 2 - 4
60ø Lucky five/The birthday cakewalk		DB 4457	£ 2 - 4
60ø Passing breeze/The key to love		DB 4508	£ 2 - 4
60ø "Even More Party Pops" medley		DB 4535	£ 2 - 4

COO-COO RACHAS
59 Chili beans/Track down	CAPITOL	CL 15024	£ 4 - 6

SAM COOKE
57ø You send me/Summertime	LONDON	HLU 8506	£12 - 18
58 That's all I need to know/I don't want to cry		HLU 8615	£ 9 - 12
59 Love you most of all/Win your love for me	H.M.V.	POP 568	£ 6 - 9
59 Everybody likes to cha cha cha/Little things you do		POP 610	£ 6 - 9
59ø Only sixteen/Let's go steady again		POP 642	£ 6 - 9
59 There I've said it again/One hour ahead of the posse		POP 675	£ 4 - 6
60 Happy in love/I need you now	LONDON	HLU 9046	£ 6 - 9
60 Teenage sonata/If you were the only girl	R.C.A.	RCA 1184	£ 4 - 6
60ø Wonderful world/Along the Navajo Trail	H.M.V.	POP 754	£ 4 - 6
60ø Chain gang/I fall in love every day	R.C.A.	RCA 1202	£ 4 - 6

OLIVER COOL
60 I like girls/Oliver Cool	COLUMBIA	DB 4552	£ 2 - 4

EDDIE COOLEY & THE DIMPLES
57 Priscilla/Got a little woman	COLUMBIA	DB 3873	£40 - 60

SPADE COOLEY & HIS FIDDLIN' FRIENDS
51 Horse hair boogie/Down yonder	BRUNSWICK	04812 º	£ 4 - 6

COWBOY COPAS (*& GRANDPA JONES)
51 The feudin' boogie*/Strange little girl	VOGUE	V 9001 º	£ 6 - 9
53 It's no sin to love you/I've grown so used to you	PARLOPHONE	R 3708 º	£ 4 - 6
53 Doll of clay/If wishes were horses		R 3756 º	£ 4 - 6
54 Tennessee senorita/If you will let me be your love		MSP 6079	£12 - 18
54 A heartbreak ago/The blue waltz		MSP 6109	£12 - 18
55 I'll waltz with you in my dreams/Return to sender		MSP 6164	£12 - 18
60 Alabam/I can	MELODISC	1566	£ 6 - 9

ALAN or ALLAN COPELAND
57 Feeling happy/You don't know	V-CORAL	Q 72237	£ 6 - 9
57 How will I know?/Will you still be mine		Q 72277	£ 4 - 6
59 Flip flop/Lots more love	PYE INT.	7N 25007	£ 4 - 6

KEVIN CORCORAN *& JEROME COURTLAND
58 Old Yeller*/How much is that doggie in the window	PYE	7N 15145	£ 2 - 4

FRANK CORDELL & HIS ORCH.
56 Port-au-Prince/"Double Cross" TV theme	H.M.V.	7M 397	£ 2 - 4
56ø Sadie's shawl/Flamenco love		POP 229 º	£ 1 - 2
56ø as above		7M 419	£ 4 - 6

DON CORNELL
54ø Hold my hand/I'm blessed	V-CORAL	Q 2013	£12 - 18
54 S'posin'/I was lucky		Q 2037	£ 4 - 6
55 No man is an island/All at once		Q 72058	£ 4 - 6
55 When you are in love/Give me your love		Q 72070	£ 4 - 6
55 Size 12/Athena		Q 72071	£ 4 - 6
55ø Stranger in Paradise/The Devil's in your eyes		Q 72073	£ 9 - 12
55 Unchained melody/Most of all		Q 72080	£ 4 - 6
55 Love is a many splendored thing/The Bible tells me so		Q 72104	£ 4 - 6

56	There once was a beautiful/Make a wish		Q 72132	£ 4 – 6
56	Teenage meeting (Gonna rock it...)/I still have a prayer		Q 72144	£12 – 18
56	Rock Island line/Na–ne na–na		Q 72152	£ 9 – 12
56	But love me (Love but me)/Fort Knox		Q 72164	£ 4 – 6
56	Heaven only knows/All of you		Q 72203	£ 4 – 6
56	See–saw/From the bottom of my heart		Q 72218	£ 9 – 12
57	Let's be friends/Afternoon in Madrid		Q 72234	£ 4 – 6
57	Sittin' in the balcony/Let's get lost		Q 72257	£ 6 – 9
57	Mama Guitar/A face in the crowd		Q 72276	£ 4 – 6
57	Non dimenticar/There's only you		Q 72291	£ 2 – 4
58	Mailman, bring me no more.../Before it's time to say....	CORAL	Q 72308	£ 9 – 12
58	I've got bells on my heart/Keep God in the home		Q 72313	£ 2 – 4
59	This Earth is mine/The gang that sang Heart Of My Heart	LONDON	HLD 8937	£ 4 – 6
59	Sempre amore/Forever couldn't be long enough	PYE INT.	7N 25041	£ 2 – 4

JERRY CORNELL

55	Please don't talk about me when I'm gone/St. Louis blues	LONDON	HL 8157	£12 – 18

LYN CORNELL

60	Like love/Demon lover	DECCA	F 11227	£ 2 – 4
60	Teaser/What a feeling		F 11260	£ 2 – 4
60ø	Never on Sunday/Swain Kelly		F 11277	£ 2 – 4
60	The angel and the stranger/Xmas stocking		F 11301	£ 2 – 4

THE CORONETS (qv TONY BRENT/RONNIE HARRIS/BENNY HILL/ERIC JUPP/LEE LAWRENCE)

54	Do, do, do, (etc.) it again/I ain't gonna do it no more	COLUMBIA	SCM 5117	£ 6 – 9
55ø	Twenty tiny fingers/Meet me on the corner		DB 3671 º	£ 2 – 4
56	Lizzie Borden/My believing heart		SCM 5235	£ 6 – 9
56	The magic touch/There's no song like an old song		SCM 5261	£ 6 – 9
56	Someone to love/The rocking horse cowboy		DB 3827	£ 4 – 6

BOB CORT (SKIFFLE GROUP) (*& LIZ WINTERS)

57	Don't you rock me Daddy–o/It takes a worried man to.....	DECCA	FJ 10831	£ 6 – 9
57	Love is strange/Freight train		*F 10878	£ 6 – 9
57	Six–five Special/Roll Jen Jenkins		F 10892	£ 9 – 12
57	Maggie May/Jessamine		*F 10899	£ 4 – 6
57	School day (Ring! Ring! goes...)/Ain't it a shame (to..)		F 10905	£ 9 – 12
57	"Bob Cort Skiffle Party" medley		F 10951	£ 4 – 6
58	The ark (Noah found grace in the eyes of....)/Yes! Suh!		F 10989	£ 4 – 6
59	Foggy foggy dew/On top of Old Smokey		F 11109	£ 2 – 4
59	Waterloo/Battle of New Orleans		F 11145	£ 4 – 6
59	Kissin' time/I'm gonna get married		F 11160	£ 4 – 6
60	El Paso/A handful of gold		F 11197	£ 4 – 6
60	Mule skinner blues/The ballad of Walter Williams		F 11256	£ 4 – 6
60	Ballad of the Alamo/Five brothers		F 11285	£ 2 – 4

DAVE "BABY" CORTEZ

59	The happy organ/Love me as I love you	LONDON	HLU 8852	£ 4 – 6
59	The whistling organ/I'm happy		HLU 8919	£ 4 – 6
60	Dave's special/Piano shuffle	COLUMBIA	DB 4404	£ 6 – 9
60	Deep in the heart of Texas/You're just right	LONDON	HLU 9126	£ 4 – 6

DON COSTA & HIS ORCH. & CHORUS

55	Love is a many splendoured thing/Safe in the harbour ..	LONDON	HLF 8186	£12 – 18
59	I walk the line/Cat walk		HLT 8992	£ 4 – 6
60	"The Unforgiven" theme/Streets of Paris		HLT 9137	£ 2 – 4
60ø	Never on Sunday/The sound of love		HLT 9195	£ 2 – 4

DANNY COSTELLO

57	Like a brook gets lost in a river/That's where I shine	ORIOLE	CB 1393	£ 2 – 4

BILLY COTTON & HIS BAND (& THE BANDITS/etc./qv VARIOUS ARTISTS)

53ø	In a golden coach/Coronation bells march	DECCA	F 10058 º	£ 1 – 2
53ø	I saw Mommy kissing Santa Claus/The Queen's highway ...		F 10206 º	£ 1 – 2
54ø	Friends and neighbours/The Kid's last fight		F 10299	£ 6 – 9
54	This ole house/Somebody goofed		F 10377	£ 6 – 9

Do you love old Santa Claus?/When Santa got stuck up....		F 10405	£ 4 – 6
When you're home with the ones.../He's a real tough guy		F 10421	£ 4 – 6
The naughty lady of Shady Lane/Hearts of stone		F 10459	£ 4 – 6
Ready, willing and able/Bambino		F 10491	£ 4 – 6
Someone else I'd like to be/Where did the chickie lay...		F 10501	£ 2 – 4
Play me hearts and flowers/A present for Bob		F 10524	£ 2 – 4
Pals/Why did the chicken cross the road?		F 10546	£ 2 – 4
Yellow Rose of Texas/Domani		F 10602	£ 2 – 4
The Dam Busters march/Bring your smile along		F 10630	£ 4 – 6
Nuts in May/A-hunting we will go		F 10642	£ 2 – 4
Ballad of Davy Crockett/The one finger song		F 10664	£ 4 – 6
Robin Hood/Happy trails		F 10682	£ 4 – 6
Lizzie Borden/Little child		F 10702	£ 4 – 6
The March hare/Get neighbourly		F 10739	£ 2 – 4
Friends/The family's always around		F 10754	£ 2 – 4
Reach for the sky – March/Whatever will be, will be ...		F 10767	£ 2 – 4
Just walking in the rain/The rocking horse cowboy		F 10805	£ 2 – 4
Yaller yaller gold/Giant		F 10826	£ 2 – 4
The Garden of Eden/You don't owe me a thing		F 10841	£ 2 – 4
Amore/Commando patrol		F 10854	£ 2 – 4
The Amethyst march/Absent friends		F 10881	£ 2 – 4
Growing old/Ain't you got no 'omes to go to?	COLUMBIA	DB 4248	£ 2 – 4
fings ain't wot they used t'be/I'd rather be just me ..		DB 4430	£ 2 – 4

DIANA COUPLAND

Love him/I am loved	H.M.V.	POP 690	£ 2 – 4

BILL COURTNEY

Judy is/Without her love	R.C.A.	RCA 1142	£ 2 – 4
Petticoats fly/Blanket on the beach	COLUMBIA	DB 4512	£ 2 – 4

NOEL COWARD

Mad dogs and Englishmen/A room with a view	PHILIPS	BB 2001 º	£ 4 – 6
Poor little rich girl/Uncle Harry		BB 2002 º	£ 4 – 6

THE COWBOY CHURCH SUNDAY SCHOOL

Open up your heart/The Lord is counting on you	BRUNSWICK	05371	£ 2 – 4
Go on by/The little black sheep		05455	£ 2 – 4
Those bad bad kids/A handful of sunshine		05533	£ 2 – 4
It is no secret/Don't send those kids to Sunday School		05598	£ 2 – 4

MICHAEL COX

Boy meets girl/Teenage love	DECCA	F 11166	£ 6 – 9
Serious/Too hot to handle		F 11182	£ 6 – 9
Angela Jones/Don't want to know	TRIUMPH	RGM 1011	£ 6 – 9
as above	EMBER	EMB S103	£ 9 – 12
Along came Caroline/Lonely road	H.M.V.	POP 789	£ 4 – 6

BILLY "CRASH" CRADDOCK (*as CRASH CRADDOCK)

Don't destroy me/Boom boom baby	PHILIPS	*PB 966	£ 9 – 12
I want that/Since she turned seventeen		*PB 1006	£ 9 – 12
Good time Billy/Heavenly love		PB 1092	£ 6 – 9

FLOYD CRAMER

Fancy pants/Five foot two eyes of blue	LONDON	HL 8012	£12 – 18
Jolly cholly/Oh! Suzanna		HL 8062	£12 – 18
Rag-a-tag/Aunt Dinah's quiltin' party		HLU 8195	£12 – 18
Flip flop and bop/Sophisticated swing	R.C.A.	RCA 1050	£ 9 – 12
Last date/Sweetie baby		RCA 1211	£ 4 – 6

THE CRANE RIVER JAZZ BAND

Kentucky home/Moose march	DELTA	D 5 º	£ 6 – 9
If I ever cease to love/Gipsy lament		D 6 º	£ 6 – 9
Eh la bas!/(by CHRIS BARBER'S JAZZ BAND)	ESQUIRE	12–013 º	£ 6 – 9
Eh, la-bas/Just a closer walk with Thee	MELODISC	1027 º	£ 6 – 9

51	Dauphin St. blues/Just a little while to stay here			1030	º	£ 6
51	I'm travelling/(by SAINTS JAZZ BAND)	PARLOPHONE	R	3427	º	£ 6
51	Down by the river/Blanche Touquatoux	MELODISC		1165	º	£ 6
52	Sheik of Araby/Sobbin' blues			1202	º	£ 4
52	Slow drag blues/T'ain't nobody's biziness if I do	PARLOPHONE	R	3567	º	£ 4
52	Careless love/Spicy advice	MELODISC		1228	º	£ 4
53	Lily of the valley/Till we meet again	PARLOPHONE	MSP	6008		£ 4

THE CRANES SKIFFLE GROUP (actually CHAS McDEVITT SKIFFLE GROUP)

57	The banana boat song/Don't you rock me Daddy-O	EMBASSY	WB	223	º	£ 2
57	Freight train/Cumberland Gap		WB	238	º	£ 4

THE CRAWFORD BROTHERS

57	Midnight mover groover/Midnight happenins	VOGUE	V	9077	£40
59	It feels good/I ain't guilty		V	9140	£40

JIMMY CRAWFORD

60	Unkind/Long stringy baby	COLUMBIA	DB	4525	£ 6

THE CRESCENDOS

58	Oh Julie/My little girl	LONDON	HLU	8563	£25

THE CRESCENTS

58	Wrong/Baby, baby, baby	COLUMBIA	DB	4093	£12

THE CRESTS

59	16 candles/Beside you	LONDON	HL	8794	£12
59	Flower of love/Molly Mae	TOP RANK	JAR	150	£ 6
59	Six nights a week/I do		JAR	168	£ 6
59	The angels listened in/I thank the Moon	LONDON	HL	8954	£ 9
60	A year ago tonight/Paper crown	TOP RANK	JAR	302	£ 6
60	Step by step/Gee (but I'd give the world)		JAR	372	£ 6
60	Trouble in Paradise/Always you	H.M.V.	POP	768	£ 9
60	Isn't it amazing/Molly Mae		POP	808	£ 6

THE CREW CUTS

54ø	Sh-boom/I spoke too soon	MERCURY	MB	3140	º	£ 4
55ø	Earth angel/Ko Ko Mo		MB	3202	º	£ 4
56	Angels in the sky/Seven days		MT	100	º	£ 4
56	A story untold/Honey hair, sugar lips, eyes of blue ...		MT	108	º	£ 4
56	Rebel in town/Bei mir bist du schoen		MT	127	º	£ 4
57	Young love/Little by little		MT	140	º	£ 4
57	Susie-Q/Such a shame		MT	161	º	£ 6
57	I sit in my window/Hey, you face		MT	178	º	£ 4
58	Hey, Stella! (who zat down your...)/Forever, my darling	R.C.A.	RCA	1075		£18

BOB CREWE

60	Water boy/Voglio cantare	LONDON	HLI	9077	£ 2

BERNARD CRIBBINS (*& JOYCE BLAIR)

60	Folk song/My kind of someone*	PARLOPHONE	R	4712	£ 2

THE CRICKETS (*feat. BUDDY HOLLY/qv IVAN)

57ø	That'll be the day/I'm lookin' for someone to love	V-CORAL	*Q 72279	£ 9
58ø	*as above*	CORAL	*Q 72279	£ 6
57ø	Oh boy!/Not fade away		*Q 72298	£ 9
58ø	Maybe baby/Tell me how		*Q 72307	£ 6
58ø	Think it over/Fool's Paradise		*Q 72329	£ 6
58ø	It's so easy/Lonesome tears		*Q 72343	£ 6
59ø	Love's made a fool of you/Someone, someone		Q 72365	£ 6
59ø	When you ask about love/Deborah		Q 72382	£ 6
60ø	Baby my heart/More than I can say		Q 72395	£ 4

LINDA CRISTAL

59	A perfect romance/It's better in Spanish	CORAL	Q 72350	£ 2

TONY CROMBIE & HIS ORCH./*ROCKETS/etc. (+& ANNIE ROSS/qv RAY ELLINGTON)

54	Stop it/All of me	DECCA	F 10424	£ 6 - 9
55	Perdido/Love you madly		F 10454	£ 2 - 4
55	Flying home/Early one morning		F 10547	£ 4 - 6
55	Flying hickory/String of pearls		F 10592	£ 2 - 4
55	I want you to be my baby+/Three little words		F 10637	£ 9 - 12
56ø	Teach you to rock/Short'nin' bread rock	COLUMBIA	*DB 3822	£18 - 25
56	Sham rock/Let's you and I rock		*DB 3859	£12 - 18
57	Rock, rock, rock/The big beat		*DB 3880	£12 - 18
57	Lonesome train (on a lonesome.)/We're gonna rock tonight		*DB 3881	£12 - 18
57	Brighton rock/London rock		*DB 3921	£12 - 18
57	Sweet beat/Sweet Georgia Brown		DB 4000	£ 4 - 6
58	Dumplin's/Twon special		*DB 4076	£ 6 - 9
58	Ungaua/Piakukaungcung		DB 4145	£ 4 - 6
58	The gigglin' Gurgleburp/Rock-cha-cha		DB 4189	£ 4 - 6
59	"Man From Interpol" theme/Interpol cha cha cha & chase	TOP RANK	JAR 182	£ 2 - 4

BILL CROMPTON

58	A hoot an' a holler/The popocatepetl beetle	FONTANA	H 152	£ 4 - 6
59	Out of sight, out of mind/My lover		H 178	£ 2 - 4

BING CROSBY (& *GARY CROSBY/+DONALD O'CONNOR/=DANNY KAYE, PEGGY LEE, TRUDY STEVENS/ #PATTY ANDREWS/%GRACE KELLY/@FRANK SINATRA/qv LOUIS ARMSTRONG/BOB HOPE/JANE WYMAN)

47ø	Silent night, holy night/Adeste fideles	BRUNSWICK	03929 º	£ 1 - 2
52ø	The Isle of Innisfree/At last! At last!		04900 º	£ 2 - 4
54	What a little moonlight can do/Down by the riverside ..		*05224	£ 4 - 6
54ø	Changing partners/Y'all come		05244	£ 6 - 9
54	Secret love/My love, my love		05269	£ 4 - 6
54	Young at heart/I get so lonely		05277	£ 4 - 6
54	If there's anybody here (from..)/Back in the old routine		+05304	£ 4 - 6
54	Cornbelt symphony/The call of the South		*05315	£ 4 - 6
54ø	Count your blessings instead.../What can you do with a..		05339	£ 6 - 9
54	White Christmas/Snow		=05354	£ 4 - 6
54	White Christmas/Let's start the new year right		03384	£ 6 - 9
54ø	Silent night, holy night/Adeste fideles		03929	£ 6 - 9
55	The song from "Desiree" (We meet again)/I love Paris ..		05377	£ 2 - 4
55	Tobermory Bay/The river (Sciummo)		05385	£ 2 - 4
55	Dissertation on the state of bliss#/It's mine, it's.....		05403	£ 4 - 6
55	The search is through/The land around us		05404	£ 2 - 4
55ø	Stranger in Paradise/Who gave you the roses		05410	£ 6 - 9
55	Ohio/A quiet girl		05419	£ 2 - 4
55	Jim, Johnny and Jonas/Nobody		05430	£ 2 - 4
55	All she'd say was "Umh."/She is the sunshine of Virginia		05451	£ 2 - 4
55	Angel bells/There's music in you		05486	£ 2 - 4
55	Let's harmonize/Sleigh bell serenade		05501	£ 2 - 4
56	Farewell/Early American		05511	£ 2 - 4
56ø	In a little Spanish town/Ol' Man River		05543	£ 4 - 6
56	No other love/Sleepy time gal		05558	£ 2 - 4
56	Honeysuckle rose/Swanee		05585	£ 2 - 4
56	Christmas is a-comin'/Is Christmas only a tree		05620	£ 2 - 4
56ø	True love%/Well, did you evah?@	CAPITOL	CL 14645	£ 4 - 6
57ø	Around the world/VICTOR YOUNG ORCH.: Around the world .	BRUNSWICK	05674	£ 4 - 6
57	Man on fire/Seven nights a week	CAPITOL	CL 14761	£ 2 - 4
57	Never be afraid/I love you whoever you are	LONDON	HLR 8504	£ 4 - 6
57	How lovely is Christmas/My own individual star		HLR 8513	£ 4 - 6
57	Chicago/Alabamy bound	BRUNSWICK	05726	£ 2 - 4
58	Straight down the middle/Tomorrow's my lucky day	PHILIPS	PB 817	£ 4 - 6
58	Love in a home/In the good old Summer time	BRUNSWICK	05760	£ 2 - 4
58	It's beginning to look like Christmas/I heard the bells.		05764	£ 2 - 4
59	Gigi/The next time it happens		05770	£ 2 - 4
59	Rain/Church bells		05790	£ 2 - 4
59	Say one for me/I couldn't care less	PHILIPS	PB 921	£ 2 - 4
59	My own individual star/Never be afraid	GALA	GSP 801	£ 2 - 4
60	Happy birthday & Auld lang syne/Home sweet home	BRUNSWICK	05840	£ 2 - 4
60	The second time around/Incurably romantic	M-G-M	MGM 1098	£ 2 - 4

BOB CROSBY & HIS BOBCATS (qv THE MODERNAIRES)

59	Petite fleur/Such a long night	LONDON	HLD	8828	£ 4 – 6
60	The dark at the top of the stairs/Night theme		HLD	9228	£ 4 – 6

GARY CROSBY (*& THE PARIS SISTERS/qv LOUIS ARMSTRONG/BING CROSBY)

54	Mambo in the moonlight/Got my eyes on you	BRUNSWICK		05340	£ 6 – 9
55	Palsy walsy/Loop-de-loop mambo			05365	£ 6 – 9
55	Ready, willing and able/There's a small hotel			05378	£ 6 – 9
55	Ayuh ayuh/Mississippi pecan pie			05446	£ 6 – 9
55	Give me a band and my baby/Truly*			05496	£ 4 – 6
56	Yaller yaller gold/Noah found grace in the eyes of the..			05633	£ 4 – 6
58	Judy, Judy/Cheatin' on me	H.M.V.	POP	550	£ 9 – 12
59	The happy bachelor/This little girl of mine		POP	648	£ 4 – 6

THE CROWS

54	Gee/I love you so	COLUMBIA	SCM	5119	£120–160

SIMON CRUM (actually FERLIN HUSKY)

58	Stand up, sit down, shut your mouth/Country music is....	CAPITOL	CL	14965	£18 – 25
59	Morgan poisoned the waterhole/I fell out of love with...		CL	15077	£ 4 – 6

BARRY CRYER

58	The purple people eater/Hey! Eula	FONTANA	H	139	£ 4 – 6
58	Nothin' shakin'/Seven daughters		H	151	£ 4 – 6
59	Angelina/Kissin'		H	177	£ 2 – 4

CUDDLY DUDLEY (Heslop)

59	Lots more love/Later	H.M.V.	POP	586	£ 6 – 9
60	Too pooped to pop/Miss In–Between		POP	725	£ 4 – 6

THE CUES (*feat. JIMMY BREEDLOVE)

56	Burn that candle/Oh my darlin'	CAPITOL	CL	14501	£25 – 40
56	Crackerjack/The girl I love		*CL	14651	£25 – 40
57	Why/Prince or pauper		CL	14682	£25 – 40

THE CUMBERLAND THREE

60	Johnny Reb/Come along Julie	COLUMBIA	DB	4460	£ 2 – 4

THE CUPIDS

58	Now you tell me/Lillie Mae	VOGUE	V	9102	£60 – 90

MAC CURTIS

57	The low road/You ain't treatin' me right	PARLOPHONE	R	4279	£200 +

SONNY CURTIS

60	The red headed stranger/Talk about my baby	CORAL	Q	72400	£12 – 18

T. TOMMY CUTRER (*& GINNY WRIGHT)

54	Mexico gal/Wonderful world*	LONDON	HL	8093	£12 – 18

THE CUTTERS

59	I've had it/Rockaroo	DECCA	F	11110	£ 4 – 6

JOHNNY CYMBAL

60	It'll be me/Always, always	M–G–M	MGM	1106	£ 6 – 9

FRANK D'RONE

58	Little pixie/Our Summer love	MERCURY	7MT	228	£ 2 – 4
59	Fascinating rhythm/Yesterdays		AMT	1040	£ 2 – 4
60	Serenade in blue/I love you		AMT	1077	£ 2 – 4
60	Joey, Joey, Joey/The house and the old wisteria tree ..		AMT	1090	£ 2 – 4
60ø	Strawberry blonde (The band rocked on)/Time hurries by		AMT	1123	£ 2 – 4

THE DADDY–O'S

58	Got a match?/Have a cigar	ORIOLE	CB	1454	£ 4 – 6

JACK DAILEY
60 Please understand/Little charmer .... COLUMBIA DB 4487 £ 2 - 4

THE DALE SISTERS
60 The kiss/Billy boy, Billy boy .... H.M.V. POP 781 £ 4 - 6

ALAN DALE (*& BUDDY HACKETT/qv JOHNNY DESMOND)
55	Cherry pink and apple blossom white/I'm sincere	V-CORAL	Q 72072	£ 4 - 6
55	Sweet and gentle/You still mean the same to me		Q 72089	£ 2 - 4
55	Rockin' the cha-cha/Wham! (There I go in love again) ..		Q 72105	£ 4 - 6
56	Robin Hood/Lisbon antigua		Q 72121	£ 4 - 6
56	Dance on/Mr. Moon		Q 72156	£ 2 - 4
56	The birds and the bees/I promise		Q 72166	£ 2 - 4
56	Pardners/Be my guest		*Q 72191	£ 2 - 4
56	Test of time/I cry more		Q 72194	£ 4 - 6
57	Don't knock the rock/Your love is my love		Q 72225	£ 6 - 9
57	The girl can't help it/Lonesome road		Q 72231	£ 6 - 9
58	Volare/Weeping willow in the wind	M-G-M	MGM 986	£ 2 - 4

JIM DALE (qv VARIOUS ARTISTS)
57	Piccadilly Line/I didn't mean it	PARLOPHONE R 4329	£ 6 - 9
57ø	Be my girl/You shouldn't do that	R 4343	£ 4 - 6
57ø	Crazy dream/Just born (to be your baby)	R 4376	£ 4 - 6
58ø	Sugartime/Don't let go	R 4402	£ 4 - 6
58	Tread softly stranger/Jane Belinda	R 4424	£ 2 - 4
59	Gotta find a girl/The legend of Nellie D.	R 4522	£ 2 - 4

JIMMY DALEY & THE DING-A-LINGS
57 Rock, pretty baby/Can I steal a little love .... BRUNSWICK 05648 £40 - 60

THE FIVE DALLAS BOYS
57	Shangri-la/By the fireside	COLUMBIA DB 4005	£ 2 - 4
57	All the way/I never had the blues	DB 4041	£ 2 - 4
58	26 miles (Santa Catalina)/Sail along, silv'ry Moon	DB 4102	£ 2 - 4
58	Big man/Lonesome traveller	DB 4154	£ 4 - 6
58	Fatty Patty/Do you wanna jump children	DB 4231	£ 4 - 6
59	Morning papers/I'm aware	DB 4313	£ 2 - 4
60	Boston tea party/Ramona	DB 4445	£ 2 - 4

TADD DAMERON & HIS ORCH.
54 Focus/John's delight .... CAPITOL CL 14201 £ 4 - 6

VIC DAMONE (& *HOWARD KEEL/+ANN BLYTH/=THE EASY RIDERS/#MARTY MANNING)
57	And this is my beloved*+/Night of my nights	M-G-M	MGM 949	£ 2 - 4
57	Stranger in Paradise+/ANN BLYTH: Baubles, bangles and...		MGM 950	£ 2 - 4
57ø	An affair to remember/The legend of the bells	PHILIPS	PB 745	º £ 1 - 2
58ø	On the street where you live/Arrivederci, Roma		PB 819	£ 2 - 4
58ø	The only man on the island/When my love smiles		PB 837	£ 2 - 4
58	Ooooh, my love/Forever new=		PB 866	£ 2 - 4
58	Do I love you (because you're beautiful)/Unafraid		#PB 883	£ 2 - 4
59	Separate tables/Gigi		PB 889	£ 2 - 4
59	Penny serenade/As time goes by		PB 914	£ 2 - 4
59	A new romance in old Roma/My heart has many dreams		PB 942	£ 2 - 4
60	Never like this/What fools we mortals be		PB 1080	£ 2 - 4

DANCER, PRANCER & NERVOUS (qv THE SINGING REINDEER)
59 The happy reindeer/Dancer's waltz .... CAPITOL CL 15097 £ 2 - 4

CHRIS DANE
55 Cynthia's in love/My ideal .... LONDON HLA 8165 £12 - 18

JERRY DANE
60	You're my only girl/Nothing but the truth	DECCA F 11234	£ 2 - 4
60	Let's/Awhile in love	F 11284	£ 2 - 4

SHELLEY DANE
60	Hannah Lee/This is the time in my life	PYE INT. 7N 25064	£ 2 – 4	

BILLY DANIELS
56	I live for you/Medley: Easy to love, etc.	VOGUE	V	2386	£ 2 – 4
60	That old black magic/My Yiddishe Momme		V	9172	£ 2 – 4

JOE DANIELS' JAZZ GROUP/BAND/BIG DIXIE BAND
54	I wish I could shimmy like my sister Kate/Susie	PARLOPHONE MSP 6111	£ 4 – 6
54	Little brown jug/Mountain wine	MSP 6129	£ 4 – 6
54	Crazy rhythm/The champagne touch	MSP 6143	£ 4 – 6
56	"Dixieland Party (No. 2)" medley	R 4236	£ 2 – 4
57	When the Saints go marching in/Spanish shawl	R 4273	£ 2 – 4
57	Avalon/New Orleans parade	R 4324	£ 2 – 4
57	Oi! Oi! Oi!/Bottle beatin' blues	R 4330	£ 2 – 4
57	"Juke Box Jazz" medley	R 4378	£ 2 – 4

MAXINE DANIELS
57	Coffee–bar calypso/Cha–cha calypso	ORIOLE	CB 1366	£ 2 – 4
58	I never realised/Moonlight serenade	CB 1402	£ 2 – 4
58	Somebody else is taking my../You brought a new kind of..	CB 1440	£ 2 – 4
58	When it's Springtime in the Rockies/My Summer heart ...	CB 1449	£ 2 – 4
58	Passionate Summer/Lola's heart	CB 1462	£ 2 – 4

MIKE DANIELS & HIS BAND
57	Hiawatha/Don't you think I love you	PARLOPHONE R 4285	£ 2 – 4

JOHNNY DANKWORTH (SEVEN/ORCH.) (& *CLEO LAINE/+FRANK HOLDER/qv PHILIP GREEN/
TONY MANSELL)
53	Honeysuckle rose*/Swingin'	PARLOPHONE MSP 6026	£ 4 – 6
53	Two ticks/Moon flowers	MSP 6032	£ 4 – 6
53	Easy living*/I get a kick out of you+	MSP 6037	£ 4 – 6
54	'S wonderful/Younger every day	MSP 6067	£ 4 – 6
54	The slider/It's the talk of the town	MSP 6077	£ 4 – 6
54	My buddy/The jerky thing	MSP 6083	£ 4 – 6
54	Oo–be–doop/Runnin' wild	MSP 6092	£ 4 – 6
54	Perdido/Four of a kind	MSP 6113	£ 4 – 6
54	Bugle call rag/You go to my head	MSP 6139	£ 4 – 6
55	Singin' in the rain/Non–stop London	CAPITOL CL 14285	£ 4 – 6
56ø	Experiments with mice/Applecake	PARLOPHONE R 4185 º	£ 2 – 4
56ø	as above	MSP 6255	£ 6 – 9
57	All Clare/Melbourne marathon	R 4274	£ 2 – 4
57	Duke's joke/Coquette	R 4294	£ 2 – 4
57	Big jazz story/Firth of fourths	R 4321	£ 2 – 4
58	The Colonel's tune/Jim and Andy's	R 4456	£ 2 – 4
59	We are the Lambeth boys/Duet for 16	TOP RANK JAR 209	£ 2 – 4

THE DANLEERS
58	One Summer night/Wheelin' and a–dealin'	MERCURY AMT 1003	£18 – 25

DANNY & THE JUNIORS
58ø	At the hop/Sometimes (when I'm all alone)	H.M.V.	POP	436	£ 9 – 12
58	Rock and roll is here to stay/School boy romance	POP	467	£12 – 18
58	Dottie/In the meantime	POP	504	£ 9 – 12
60	Twistin' U.S.A./A thousand miles away	TOP RANK JAR 510	£ 4 – 6

DANTE & THE EVERGREENS
60	Alley–oop/The right time	TOP RANK JAR 402	£ 6 – 9

JOE DARENSBOURG & HIS DIXIE FLYERS
58	Yellow dog blues/Careless love	VOGUE	V 2409	£ 2 – 4

BOBBY DARIN (& *THE JAYBIRDS/+THE RINKY–DINKS)
56	Rock Island line/Timber	BRUNSWICK *05561	£12 – 18
58ø	Splish splash/Judy don't be moody	LONDON HLE 8666	£ 6 – 9
58	Early in the morning/Now we're one	+HLE 8679	£12 – 18

58ø	Queen of the hop/Lost love	HLE 8737	£ 6 - 9
59	Mighty mighty man/You're mine	+HLE 8793	£ 9 - 12
59	Plain Jane/While I'm gone	HLE 8815	£ 9 - 12
59ø	Dream lover/Bullmoose	HLE 8867	£ 4 - 6
59ø	Mack the knife/Was there a call for me	HLK 8939	£ 2 - 4
60ø	La mer (Beyond the sea)/That's the way love is	HLK 9034	£ 2 - 4
60ø	Clementine/Down with love	HLK 9086	£ 2 - 4
60ø	Bill Bailey won't you please come home/Tall story	HLK 9142	£ 2 - 4
60	Hear them bells/The greatest builder	BRUNSWICK 05831	£ 6 - 9
60	Beachcomber/Autumn blues	LONDON HLK 9197	£ 2 - 4
60	Somebody to love/I'll be there	HLK 9215	£ 2 - 4

BILL DARNEL
55	My little Mother/Bring me a bluebird	LONDON HLU 8204	£12 - 18
56	Rock a boogie baby/The last frontier	HLU 8234	£18 - 25
56	Guilty lips/Ain't misbehavin'	HLU 8267	£12 - 18
56	Tell me more/Satin doll	HLU 8292	£12 - 18

JAMES *or JIMMY DARREN
59	Gidget/There's no such thing	*PYE INT. 7N 25019	£ 4 - 6
59	Angel face/I don't wanna lose ya	*7N 25034	£ 4 - 6
60ø	Because they're young/Let there be love	7N 25059	£ 2 - 4

BARRY DARVELL
60	Geronimo stomp/How will it end?	LONDON HL 9191	£18 - 25

TOMMY DAVIDSON
56	Half past kissing time/I don't know yet but I'm learning	LONDON HLU 8219	£12 - 18

HUTCH DAVIE (& HIS HONKY TONKERS)
58	Honky tonk train blues/At the Woodchopper's Ball	LONDON HLE 8667	£ 9 - 12
60	Sweet Georgia Brown/Heartaches	HLE 9076	£ 2 - 4

JACKIE DAVIES & HIS QUARTET (became CHICO ARNEZ)
57	Land of Make Believe/Over the rainbow	PYE N 15115 º	£ 9 - 12

THE DAVIS SISTERS
53	Rock-a-bye boogie/I forgot more than you'll ever know .	H.M.V. B 10582 º	£ 9 - 12

BONNIE DAVIS
55	Pepper-hot baby/For always, darling	BRUNSWICK 05507	£12 - 18

DANNY DAVIS (U.K.)
60	You're my only girl/Love me	PARLOPHONE R 4657	£ 4 - 6

DANNY DAVIS ORCH. (U.S.)
58	Trumpet cha-cha-cha/Lonesome trumpet	LONDON HL 8766	£ 2 - 4

MILES DAVIS QUINTET
60	Budo/Tadd's delight	PHILIPS JAZ 100	£ 2 - 4

SAMMY DAVIS (JR.) (*& CARMEN McRAE)
54	Because of you - Parts 1 & 2	BRUNSWICK 05326	£ 4 - 6
55	The birth of the blues/Love (your magic spell is every-)	05383	£ 4 - 6
55	Six bridges to cross/Glad to be unhappy	05389	£ 4 - 6
55	And this is my beloved/The red grapes	05409	£ 4 - 6
55ø	Love me or leave me/Something's gotta give	05428	£ 9 - 12
55ø	That old black magic/Give a fool a chance	05450	£ 9 - 12
55ø	Hey there/My funny Valentine	05469	£ 9 - 12
55	It's bigger than you and me/Back track	05478	£ 2 - 4
56ø	In a Persian market/The man with the golden arm	05518	£ 6 - 9
56	Azure/Dedicated to you	CAPITOL CL 14562	£ 2 - 4
56	Adelaide/I'll know	BRUNSWICK 05583	£ 2 - 4
56	Earthbound/Five	05594	£ 2 - 4
56	Frankie and Johnny/Circus	05611	£ 2 - 4

Year	Title	Label	Catalogue No.	Price
56	You're sensational/Don't let her go		05617	£ 2 – 4
56ø	All of you/Just one of those things		05629	£ 4 – 6
57	The golden key/All about love		05637	£ 2 – 4
57	Dangerous/The world is mine tonight		05647	£ 2 – 4
57	Too close for comfort/Jacques D'Iraque		05668	£ 2 – 4
57	Goodbye, so long, I'm gone/French fried potaoes and.....		05694	£ 2 – 4
57	Mad ball/The nearness of you		05717	£ 2 – 4
57	Long before I knew you/Never like this		05724	£ 2 – 4
58	I'm comin' home/Hallelujah, I love her		05732	£ 2 – 4
58	No fool like an old fool/Unspoken		05747	£ 2 – 4
58	Song and dance man/I ain't gonna change (the way I.....)		05763	£ 2 – 4
59	That's Anna/I never got out of Paris		05778	£ 2 – 4
60ø	Happy to make your acquaintance/Baby, it's cold outside		*05830	£ 4 – 6
60	Eee-o eleven/Ain't that a kick in the head?	H.M.V.	POP 777	£ 2 – 4

SKEETER DAVIS
| 60 | (I can't help you) I'm falling too/No never | R.C.A. | RCA 1201 | £ 4 – 6 |

THE DAVISON BROTHERS
| 60 | Journey of love/Seven days a week | PHILIPS | PB 1053 | £ 2 – 4 |

JULIE DAWN (qv TONY BRENT/CYRIL STAPLETON)
| 53 | Wild horses/A whistling kettle and a dancing cat | COLUMBIA | SCM 5035 | £ 4 – 6 |

THE DAY BROTHERS
| 60 | Angel/Just one more kiss | ORIOLE | CB 1575 | £ 2 – 4 |

BING DAY
| 59 | I can't help it/Mama's place | MERCURY | AMT 1047 | £25 – 40 |

BOBBY DAY (*& THE SATELLITES)
57	Little bitty pretty one/When the swallows come back to..	H.M.V.	*POP 425	£18 – 25
58ø	Rockin' Robin/Over and over	LONDON	HL 8726	£ 9 – 12
59	The bluebird, the buzzard and the oriole/Alone too long		HL 8800	£12 – 18
59	Love is a one time affair/Ain't gonna cry no more		HL 8964	£ 6 – 9
60	My blue Heaven/I don't want to		HLY 9044	£ 6 – 9

DORIS DAY (& *FRANKIE LAINE/+JOHNNIE RAY/=THE FOUR LADS)
52ø	Sugarbush*/How it lies, how it lies, how it lies!	COLUMBIA	DB 3123 º	£ 2 – 4
52ø	My love and devotion/When I fall in love		DB 3157 º	£ 2 – 4
53ø	Ma says, Pa says/A full time job		+DB 3242 º	£ 2 – 4
53ø	as above		+SCM 5033	£ 9 – 12
53	April in Paris/Your Mother and mine=		SCM 5038	£ 6 – 9
53	That's what makes Paris Paree/I know a place		SCM 5039	£ 6 – 9
53ø	Let's walk that-a-way/Candy lips	PHILIPS	+PB 157 º	£ 2 – 4
53	A bushel and a peck/If I were a bell	COLUMBIA	SCM 5044	£ 9 – 12
53	The second star to the right=/I'm gonna ring the bell...		SCM 5045	£ 6 – 9
53	The cherries/Papa, won't you dance with me?		SCM 5059	£ 6 – 9
53	Mister Tap-Toe/Why should we both be lonely?		SCM 5062	£ 6 – 9
53	We kiss in a shadow/Something wonderful		SCM 5067	£ 6 – 9
53	That's the way he does it/Cuddle up a little closer		SCM 5075	£ 6 – 9
54	A load of hay/It had to be you		SCM 5087	£ 6 – 9
54ø	Secret love/The Deadwood stage	PHILIPS	PB 230 º	£ 1 – 2
54ø	The Black Hills of Dakota/Just blew in from the Windy...		PB 287 º	£ 2 – 4
54ø	If I give my heart to you/Anyone can fall in love		PB 325 º	£ 2 – 4
55ø	Ready, willing and able/You, my love		PB 402 º	£ 2 – 4
55	Just one of those things/Sometimes I'm happy	COLUMBIA	SCM 5171	£ 6 – 9
55ø	Love me or leave me/Sam, the accordion man	PHILIPS	PB 479 º	£ 2 – 4
55ø	I'll never stop loving you/Ten cents a dance		PB 497 º	£ 2 – 4
56ø	Whatever will be, will be (Que sera...)/We'll love again		PB 586 º	£ 1 – 2
57	Twelve o'clock tonight/Today will be yesterday tomorrow!		JK 1020	£ 6 – 9
57	The party's over/Rickety-rackety rendezvous		JK 1031	£ 6 – 9
58ø	A very precious love/Teacher's pet		PB 799	£ 2 – 4
58ø	Everybody loves a lover/Instant love		PB 843	£ 2 – 4
58	Love in a home/Blues in the night		PB 863	£ 2 – 4

59	Love me in the daytime/He's so married		PB	910	£ 2 – 4
59	Be prepared/It happened to Jane		PB	923	£ 2 – 4
59	The tunnel of love/Run away, skidaddle, skidoo		PB	949	£ 2 – 4
59	Possess me/Roly poly		PB	958	£ 2 – 4
60	I enjoy being a girl/Kissin' my honey		PB	987	£ 2 – 4
60	Anyway the wind blows/Soft as the starlight		PB	1007	£ 2 – 4
60	Please don't eat the daisies/Here we go again		PB	1018	£ 2 – 4
60	The blue train/A perfect understanding		PB	1043	£ 2 – 4

JILL DAY

55	Sincerely/Chee–chee–oo chee (sang the little bird)	PARLOPHONE	MSP	6169	£ 6 – 9
55	Promises/Whistlin' Willie		MSP	6177	£ 4 – 6
56	I hear you knocking/Far away from everybody	H.M.V.	7M	362	£ 9 – 12
56	A tear fell/Holiday affair		7M	391	£ 4 – 6
56	Happiness Street (corner.)/Somewhere in the great beyond		POP	254	£ 2 – 4
57	I dreamed/Give her my love when you see her		POP	288	£ 2 – 4
57	Mangos/Cinco robles (Five oaks)		POP	320	£ 4 – 6

KENNY DAY

60	Teenage sonata/My love doesn't love me at all	TOP RANK	JAR	339	£ 2 – 4

PETER DE ANGELIS ORCH. & CHORUS

58	The happy mandolin/Holiday in Naples	LONDON	HL	8743	£ 2 – 4

YVONNE DE CARLO

55	Take it or leave it/Three little stars	CAPITOL	CL	14380	£ 4 – 6

THE DE CASTRO SISTERS

54ø	Teach me tonight/It's love	LONDON	HL	8104	£18 – 25
55	Boom boom boomerang/Let your love walk in		HL	8137	£18 – 25
55	I'm bewildered/To say you're mine		HL	8158	£18 – 25
55	If I ever fall in love/Cuckoo in the clock		HLU	8189	£12 – 18
55	Christmas is a–comin'/Snowbound for Christmas		HLU	8212	£12 – 18
56	Give me time/Too late now		HLU	8228	£12 – 18
56	No one to blame but you/Cowboys don't cry		HLU	8296	£12 – 18
58	Who are they to say?/When you look at me	H.M.V.	POP	527	£ 4 – 6
59	Teach me tonight cha cha/The things I tell my pillow		POP	583	£ 4 – 6

GLORIA DE HAVEN

55	So this is Paris/The two of us	BRUNSWICK		05369	£ 2 – 4
55	Red hot pepper pot/Won't you save me?			05457	£ 4 – 6
59	Dearly beloved/Life	ORIOLE	CB	1524	£ 2 – 4

THE DE JOHN or DeJOHN SISTERS

56	Hotta chocolotta/I'm learnin' the Charleston	PHILIPS	PB	524 ♀	£ 4 – 6
60	Yes indeed!/Be anything (but be mine)	LONDON	HLT	9127	£ 2 – 4

LEO DE LYON

54	The band played on/Say it isn't so	M–G–M	SP	1087	£ 2 – 4
60	Rich in love/The blue train	ORIOLE	CB	1561	£ 2 – 4

THE (FIVE) DE MARCO or DeMARCO SISTERS

53	Bouillabasse/I'm never satisfied	M–G–M	SP	1043	£ 4 – 6
54	Love me/Just a girl that men forget	BRUNSWICK		05349	£ 4 – 6
55	Dreamboat/Two hearts, two kisses (make one love)			05425	£ 6 – 9
55	The hot barcarolle/Sailor boys have talk to me in			05474	£ 4 – 6
56	Romance me/This love of mine			05526	£ 2 – 4

RALPH DE MARCO

59	Old Shep/More than riches	LONDON	HLL	9010	£ 2 – 4

WILBUR DE PARIS' NEW ORLEANS BAND

59	Petite fleur/Over and over again	LONDON	HLE	8816	£ 2 – 4

FRANK DE ROSA or DeROSA & HIS ORCH.

58	Big guitar/Irish rock	LONDON	HLD	8576	£ 9 – 12

BARRY DE VORZON
58	Barbara Jean/JIMMY DELL: Teeny weeny	R.C.A.	RCA	1066	£18 – 25
60	Betty, Betty (go steady with..)/Across the street from..	PHILIPS	PB	993	£ 4 – 6

ALAN DEAN
55	The song from "Desiree"/Tonight, my love	M–G–M	SP	1116	£ 2 – 4
55	Remember me, wherever you go/Love is all that matters .		SP	1139	£ 2 – 4
56	Without you/Take a bow		SP	1173	£ 2 – 4
57	Rock 'n' roll tarantella/Life is but a dream	COLUMBIA	DB	3932	£ 6 – 9

JIMMY DEAN
59	Sing along/Weekend blue	PHILIPS	PB	940	£ 2 – 4
60	There's still time, brother/Thanks for the dream		PB	984	£ 2 – 4

TERRI DEAN
59	I'm confessin' (that I love you)/I blew out the flame .	TOP RANK	JAR	141	£ 2 – 4
59	Adonis/You treat me like a boy		JAR	179	£ 2 – 4

THE DEB–TONES
59	Knock, knock – who's there?/I'm in love again	R.C.A.	RCA	1137	£ 6 – 9

DIANA DECKER (qv RAY BURNS)
53ø	Poppa Piccolino/If I had a golden umbrella	COLUMBIA	DB	3325 º	£ 2 – 4
54	Oh, my Papa/Crystal ball		SCM	5083	£ 6 – 9
54	The happy wanderer/Till we two are one		SCM	5096	£ 4 – 6
54	The man with the banjo/Jilted		SCM	5120	£ 4 – 6
54	Kitty in the basket/Never Never Land		SCM	5123	£ 4 – 6
54	Mama mia/Percy the penguin		SCM	5130	£ 4 – 6
54	Abracadabra/Sisters		SCM	5145	£ 6 – 9
55	Open the window of your heart/The violin song		SCM	5166	£ 4 – 6
55	Apples, peaches and cherries/Paper Valentine		SCM	5173	£ 4 – 6
56	Rock-a-boogie baby/Willie can		SCM	5246	£12 – 18

DEE & THE DYNAMITES
60	South bound gasser/Blaze away	PHILIPS	PB	1081	£ 4 – 6

JOHNNY DEE (actually John D. Loudermilk)
57	Sittin' in the balcony/A–plus love	ORIOLE	CB	1367	£18 – 25

LENNY DEE
55	Plantation boogie/Birth of the blues	BRUNSWICK	05440		£ 4 – 6

TOMMY DEE
59	Three stars/TEEN JONES [TONES]: I'll never change	MELODISC	1516		£12 – 18

THE DEEP RIVER BOYS (*w. HARRY DOUGLASS/qv FATS WALLER)
54	Sweet Mama tree top tall/A kiss and cuddle polka	H.M.V.	7M	174	£12 – 18
54	Shake, rattle and roll/St. Louis blues		7M	280	£12 – 18
55	Rock around the clock/Adam never had a Mommy		POP	113 º	£ 4 – 6
56	Rock-a-beatin' boogie/Just a little bit more!		7M	361	£12 – 18
56ø	That's right/Honey honey		POP	263	£12 – 18
57	Whole lotta shakin' goin' on/There's a goldmine in the..		POP	395	£12 – 18
58	Not too old to rock and roll/Slow train to nowhere		POP	449	£ 9 – 12
58	Itchy twitchy feelng/I shall not be moved		POP	537	£ 9 – 12
59	Nola/Kissin'	TOP RANK	JAR	172	£ 2 – 4
59	I don't know why (I just do)/Timbers gotta roll		*JAR	174	£ 2 – 4
60	Go Galloway, go/Dum dum de dum		*JAR	352	£ 2 – 4

THE DEL–TONES
59	Rockin' blues/Moonlight party	TOP RANK	JAR	171	£18 – 25

ERIC DELANEY BAND
56	Rockin' the tymps/Ain't she sweet	PYE	N	15069 º	£ 4 – 6
57	Rock 'n' roll King Cole/Time for chimes		N	15079 º	£ 4 – 6
57	Fanfare jump/Jingle bells		7N	15113	£ 2 – 4
60	Bass drum boogie/Let's get organised	PARLOPHONE	R	4646	£ 4 – 6

THE DELICATES
59	Black and white Thunderbird/Ronnie is my lover	LONDON	HLT 8953	£25 – 40
60	Too young to date/The kiss		HLT 9176	£ 9 – 12

THE DELL-VIKINGS *or* DEL VIKINGS
57	Come go with me/How can I find true love	LONDON	HLD 8405	£18 – 25
57	Whispering bells/Little Billy boy		HLD 8464	£12 – 18
57	Cool shake/Jitterbug Mary	MERCURY	MT 169 ♀	£ 6 – 9
58	The voodoo man/Can't wait		7MT 199	£18 – 25
59	How could you/Flat tire		AMT 1027	£12 – 18

THE DELTA RHYTHM BOYS
54	Mood indigo/Have a hope, have a wish, have a prayer ...	BRUNSWICK	05353	£ 4 – 6

THE DELTA SKIFFLE GROUP
57	Skip to my Lou/John Brown's body	ESQUIRE	10–504 ♀	£ 4 – 6
57	Pick a bale of cotton/K.C. moan		10–507 ♀	£ 4 – 6
58	Ain't you glad?/Open up them pearly gates		10–517 ♀	£ 4 – 6

THE DEMENSIONS
60	Nursery rhyme rock/Over the rainbow	TOP RANK	JAR 505	£ 4 – 6

THE DENE BOYS *or* THE DENE FOUR
57	Bye bye love/Love is the thing	H.M.V.	POP 374	£ 4 – 6
58	I walk down the street/Skylark		POP 455	£ 2 – 4
59	Hush-a-bye/Something new		*POP 666	£ 4 – 6

TERRY DENE
57ø	A white sport coat/The man in the phone booth	DECCA	F 10895	£ 6 – 9
57ø	Start movin'/Green corn		F 10914	£ 6 – 9
57	Teenage dream/Come and get it		F 10938	£ 6 – 9
57	Baby, she's gone/Lucky lucky Bobby		F 10964	£ 9 – 12
58	C'min and be loved/The golden age		F 10977	£ 6 – 9
58ø	Stairway of love/Lover, lover!		F 11016	£ 4 – 6
58	Can I walk you home/Seven steps to love		F 11037	£ 4 – 6
58	Pretty little Pearly/Who baby who		F 11076	£ 6 – 9
59	Bimbombey/I've got a good thing going		F 11100	£ 4 – 6
59	There's no fool like a young fool/I've come of age		F 11136	£ 4 – 6
59	Thank you pretty baby/A boy without a girl		F 11154	£ 4 – 6
60	Geraldine/Love me or leave me	ORIOLE	CB 1562	£ 6 – 9

JACKIE DENNIS
58ø	La dee dah/You're the greatest	DECCA	F 10992	£ 6 – 9
58	My dream/Miss Valerie		F 11011	£ 4 – 6
58ø	The Purple People Eater/You-oo		F 11033	£ 6 – 9
58	More than ever (Come prima)/Linton Addie		F 11060	£ 2 – 4
58	Lucky ladybug/Gingerbread		F 11090	£ 4 – 6
59	Summer snow/Night bird	TOP RANK	JAR 129	£ 2 – 4

MARTIN DENNY
59	Quiet village/Llama serenade	LONDON	HLU 8860	£ 2 – 4
59	The enchanted sea/Martinique		HLU 8976	£ 2 – 4

JOHNNY DESMOND (*& ALAN DALE & BUDDY GRECO/+JIMMY SAUNDERS)
53	A bushel and a peck/ART LUND: If I were a bell	M-G-M	SP 1042	£ 4 – 6
54	The high and the mighty/Got no time	V-CORAL	Q 2019	£ 4 – 6
55	Don't/There's no happiness for me		*Q 72055	£ 4 – 6
55	Play me hearts and flowers/I'm so ashamed		Q 72076	£ 2 – 4
55	Togetherness/A straw hat and a cane		Q 72090	£ 2 – 4
55	Yellow Rose of Texas/You're in love with someone		Q 72099	£ 4 – 6
55	Land of the Pharaohs/This too shall pass		Q 72110	£ 2 – 4
56	Sixteen tons/Ballo Italiano		Q 72115	£ 4 – 6
56	Without you/I'll cry tomorrow		Q 72153	£ 2 – 4
56	A little love can go a long,../Please don't forget me,..		Q 72170	£ 2 – 4
56	"The Proud Ones" theme/I only know I love you		Q 72190	£ 2 – 4
56	A girl named Mary/"Run For The Sun" theme		Q 72207	£ 2 – 4

57	18th Century music box+/Where the river meets the sea .		Q 72235	£ 4 – 6
57	That's where I shine/I just want you to want me		Q 72246	£ 2 – 4
57	A white sport coat/Just lookin'		Q 72261	£ 4 – 6
57	Shenandoah Rose/Consideration		Q 72269	£ 2 – 4
58	Hot cha cha/I'll close my eyes	M–G–M	MGM 994	£ 2 – 4
59	Willingly/Apple (when ya gonna fall from the tree?) ...	PHILIPS	PB 890	£ 2 – 4
60	The most happy fella/(by THE LANCERS)	CORAL	Q 72398	£ 2 – 4
60	Hawk/Playing the field	PHILIPS	PB 1044	£ 2 – 4

LORRAE DESMOND (& *THE JOHNSTON BROTHERS/+THE REBELS)

54	Hold my hand/On the waterfront	DECCA	F 10375	£ 6 – 9
54	No one but you/Far away (My love is far away)		F 10398	£ 6 – 9
54	I can't tell a waltz from a tango/For better, for worse		*F 10404	£ 6 – 9
55	Why – oh why?/A boy on a Saturday night		F 10461	£ 6 – 9
55	Where will the dimple be?/Don't		F 10510	£ 6 – 9
55	Heartbroken*/Stowaway		F 10533	£ 6 – 9
55	Wake the town and tell the people/You should know		F 10612	£ 6 – 9
56	A house with love in it/Written on the wind	PARLOPHONE	R 4239	£ 4 – 6
57	You won't be around/Play the music		+R 4287	£ 4 – 6
57	Kansas City special/Preacher, preacher		+R 4320	£ 6 – 9
57	Ding–dong rock-a-billy weddin'/Cabin boy		+R 4361	£ 6 – 9
58	Two ships/Little David		R 4400	£ 4 – 6
58	The secret of happiness/Down by the river		R 4430	£ 4 – 6
58	Soda pop hop/Blue, blue day		R 4463	£ 4 – 6
59	Tall Paul/Wait for it		R 4534	£ 4 – 6
60	Get your Daddie's car tonight/Tell me again		R 4670	£ 2 – 4

MICHAEL DESMOND

57	Young and in love/Two loves	COLUMBIA	DB 3954	£ 2 – 4
57	Chances are/If you're not completely satisfied		DB 4018	£ 2 – 4

JIMMY DEUCHAR & HIS PALS

58	Bewitched/My funny Valentine	TEMPO	A 167	£ 2 – 4

EDDIE DEXTER & HIS BAND

55	The verse of Stardust/Moonlight	CAPITOL	CL 14371	£ 4 – 6

JERRY DIAMOND

57	Sunburned lips/Don't trust love	LONDON	HLE 8496	£ 6 – 9

THE DIAMONDS

55	Black denim trousers and motorcycle boots/Nip sip	V–CORAL	Q 72109	£18 – 25
56	Love, love, love/Ev'ry night about this time	MERCURY	MT 121 º	£ 6 – 9
57ø	Little darlin'/Faithful and true		MT 148 º	£ 4 – 6
57	Don't say goodbye/Words of love		MT 167 º	£ 4 – 6
57	Oh, how I wish/Zip zip		MT 179 º	£ 4 – 6
57	Silhouettes/Honey bird		7MT 187	£12 – 18
58	The stroll/Land of beauty		7MT 195	£12 – 18
58	Don't let me down/High sign		7MT 207	£12 – 18
58	Straight skirts/Patsy		7MT 208	£18 – 25
58	Where Mary go/Kathy-o		7MT 233	£ 4 – 6
58	Walking along/Eternal lovers		AMT 1004	£ 9 – 12
59	She say (oom dooby doom)/From the bottom of my heart ..		AMT 1024	£ 9 – 12
60	Tell the truth/Real true love		AMT 1086	£ 9 – 12

DOLES DICKEN'S BAND

58	Piakukaungcung/Our melody	LONDON	HLD 8639	£ 4 – 6

BO DIDDLEY

59	The Great Grandfather/Crackin' up	LONDON	HLM 8913	£25 – 40
59	Say man/The clock strikes twelve		HLM 8975	£18 – 25
60	Say man, back again/She's alright		HLM 9035	£18 – 25
60	Road runner/My story		HLM 9112	£25 – 40

MARLENE DIETRICH (qv ROSEMARY CLOONEY)

57	Near you/Another Spring, another love	LONDON	HLD 8492	£ 4 – 6

THE DINNING SISTERS (qv "TENNESSEE" ERNIE FORD)
55	Drifting and dreaming/Truly	LONDON	HLF 8179	£12 – 18
56	Hold me tight/Uncle Joe		HLF 8218	£12 – 18

MARK DINNING
60ø	Teen angel/Bye now baby	M–G–M	MGM 1053	£ 4 – 6
60	A star is born (A love is dead)/You win again		MGM 1069	£ 4 – 6
60	The lovin' touch/Come back to me (my love)		MGM 1101	£ 4 – 6

DION & THE BELMONTS (*DION only)
58	I wonder why/Teen angel	LONDON	HLH 8646	£12 – 18
58	I can't go on (Rosalie)/No one knows		HL 8718	£12 – 18
59	Don't pity me/Just you		HL 8799	£ 9 – 12
59ø	A teenager in love/I've cried before		HLU 8874	£ 9 – 12
59	A lover's prayer/Every little thing I do	PYE INT.	7N 25038	£ 9 – 12
60	Where or when/That's my desire	LONDON	HLU 9030	£ 9 – 12
60	When you wish upon a star/My private joy	TOP RANK	JAR 368	£ 6 – 9
60	In the still of the night/Swinging on a star		JAR 503	£ 6 – 9
60ø	Lonely teenager/Little Miss Blue		*JAR 521	£ 4 – 6

THE DIXIELAND JUG BLOWERS
54	Boodle–am–shake/Memphis shake	H.M.V.	7M 223	£ 4 – 6
54	Hen party blues/Carpet Alley breakdown		7M 233	£ 4 – 6

WILLIE DIXON & THE ALLSTARS
56	Walking the blues/Crazy for my baby	LONDON	HLU 8297	£160–200

THE DIXXY SISTERS
54	The game of broken hearts/Spin the bottle polka	COLUMBIA	SCM 5105	£ 4 – 6

CARL DOBKINS (JR.)
59	My heart is an open book/My pledge to you	BRUNSWICK	05804	£ 4 – 6
59	If you don't want my lovin'/Love is everything		05811	£ 9 – 12
60ø	Lucky devil/(There's a little song a–sing..) In my heart		05817	£ 4 – 6
60	Exclusively yours/One little girl		05832	£ 4 – 6

KEN DODD
60ø	Love is like a violin/The treasure in my heart	DECCA	F 11248	£ 1 – 2

MALCOLM DODDS
59	This is real (This is love)/I'll always be with you ...	BRUNSWICK	05774	£ 2 – 4
59	Tremble/Deep inside		05796	£ 2 – 4

THE DODGERS
60	Let's make a whole lot of love/You make me happy	DOWNBEAT	CHA 2	£12 – 18

BILL DOGGETT (qv EARL BOSTIC/ELLA FITZGERALD)
56	Honky tonk – Parts 1 & 2	PARLOPHONE	R 4231	£18 – 25
57	Slow walk/Peacock Alley		R 4265	£ 9 – 12
57	Ram–bunk–shush/Blue largo		R 4306	£ 9 – 12
57	Soft/Hot ginger		R 4379	£ 9 – 12
58	Leaps and bounds – Parts 1 & 2		R 4413	£ 6 – 9
60	Smokie/Evening dreams		R 4629	£ 4 – 6

FATS DOMINO
54	Rose Mary/You said you love me	LONDON	HL 8007 º	£12 – 18
54	Little school girl/You done me wrong		HL 8063 º	£12 – 18
54	Don't leave me this way/Something's wrong		HL 8096 º	£12 – 18
55	Love me/Don't you hear me calling you		HL 8124	£60 – 90
55	Thinking of you/I know		HL 8133	£40 – 60
55ø	Ain't that a shame/La la		HLU 8173	£18 – 25
56	Bo weevil/Don't blame it on me		HLU 8256	£25 – 40
56ø	I'm in love again/My blue Heaven		HLU 8280	£18 – 25
56	When my dream boat comes home/So long		HLU 8309	£18 – 25
56ø	Blueberry Hill/I can't go on		HLU 8330	£18 – 25

57ø Honey chile/Don't you know		HLU 8356	£18 – 25
57ø Blue Monday/What's the reason I'm not pleasing you		HLP 8377	£18 – 25
57ø I'm walkin'/I'm in the mood for love		HLP 8407	£12 – 18
57ø Valley of Tears/It's you I love		HLP 8449	£12 – 18
57 What will I tell my heart/When I see you		HLP 8471	£12 – 18
57 Wait and see/I still love you		HLP 8519	£12 – 18
58ø The big beat/I want you to know		HLP 8575	£ 9 – 12
58ø Sick and tired/No, no		HLP 8628	£ 9 – 12
58 Little Mary/The prisoner's song		HLP 8663	£ 9 – 12
58 It must be love/Young school girl		HLP 8727	£ 9 – 12
58 Whole lotta loving/Coquette		HLP 8759	£ 9 – 12
59 When the Saints go marching in/Telling lies		HLP 8822	£ 6 – 9
59ø Margie/I'm ready		HLP 8865	£ 6 – 9
59ø I want to walk you home/I'm gonna be a wheel someday ..		HLP 8942	£ 6 – 9
59ø Be my guest/I've been around		HLP 9005	£ 4 – 6
60ø Country boy/If you need me		HLP 9073	£ 4 – 6
60 Tell me that you love me/Before I grow too old		HLP 9133	£ 4 – 6
60ø Walking to New Orleans/Don't come knockin'		HLP 9163	£ 4 – 6
60ø Three nights a week/Put your arms around me, honey		HLP 9198	£ 4 – 6
60ø My girl Josephine/Natural born lover		HLP 9244	£ 4 – 6

THE DOMINOES (qv BILLY WARD)

51 Sixty minute man/I can't escape from you	VOGUE	V	9012	º	£12 – 18
52 Have mercy, baby/That's what you're doing to me		V	2135	º	£ 9 – 12

DON, DICK & JIMMY

54 Angela mia/Brand me with your kisses	COLUMBIA	SCM 5110		£ 4 – 6
55 You can't have your cake and eat.../That's what I like	LONDON	HL 8117		£12 – 18
55 Make yourself comfortable/((Whatever.....) Piano players		HL 8144		£12 – 18
56 Two voices in the night/That's the way I feel	H.M.V.	POP 280		£ 4 – 6

SAM DONAHUE & HIS ORCH.

55 Saxaboogie/September in the rain	CAPITOL	CL 14349	£ 9 – 12

LONNIE DONEGAN (& HIS SKIFFLE GROUP) (*& CHRIS BARBER)

55ø Rock Island line/John Henry	DECCA	F 10647			£ 9 – 12
56 Midnight Special/When the Sun goes down	PYE JAZZ	*NJ 2006	º		£ 2 – 4
56 Diggin' my potatoes/Bury my body	DECCA	FJ 10695			£ 9 – 12
56ø Lost John/Stewball	PYE	N 15036	º		£ 2 – 4
56 The passing stranger/TOMMY REILLY: The intimate stranger	ORIOLE	CB 1329	º		£ 9 – 12
56ø Bring a little water, Sylvie/Dead or alive	PYE	N 15071	º		£ 2 – 4
56 On a Christmas Day/Take my hand, precious Lord	COLUMBIA	*DB 3850			£ 9 – 12
57ø Don't you rock me Daddy–O/I'm Alabamy bound	PYE	N 15080	º		£ 2 – 4
57ø Cumberland Gap/Love is strange		N 15087	º		£ 2 – 4
57ø Putting on the style/Gamblin' man		N 15093	º		£ 2 – 4
57ø My Dixie darling/I'm just a rolling stone		N 15108	º		£ 2 – 4
58ø Jack o' Diamonds/Ham 'n' eggs		7N 15116			£ 4 – 6
58ø The Grand Coolie Dam/Nobody loves like an Irishman		7N 15129			£ 2 – 4
58 Midnight Special/When the Sun goes down	*PYE JAZZ	7NJ 2006			£ 6 – 9
58ø Sally don't you grieve/Betty, Betty, Betty	PYE	7N 15148			£ 4 – 6
58ø Lonesome traveller/Times are getting hard boys		7N 15158			£ 4 – 6
58ø "Lonnie's Skiffle Party" (both sides)		7N 15165			£ 4 – 6
58ø Tom Dooley/Rock o' my soul		7N 15172			£ 2 – 4
59ø Does your chewing gum lose its flavour/Aunt Rhody		7N 15181			£ 2 – 4
59ø Fort Worth Jail/Whoa buck		7N 15198			£ 2 – 4
59ø The Battle of New Orleans/Darling Corey		7N 15206			£ 2 – 4
59 Kevin Barry/My Laggan love		7N 15219			£ 9 – 12
59ø Sal's got a sugar lip/Chesapeake Bay		7N 15223			£ 2 – 4
59ø San Miguel/Talkng guitar blues		7N 15237			£ 2 – 4
60ø My old man's a dustman/The Golden Vanity		7N 15256			£ 2 – 4
60ø I wanna go home/Jimmy Brown the newsboy		7N 15267			£ 2 – 4
60ø Lorelei/In all my wildest dreams		7N 15275			£ 2 – 4
60ø Lively/Black cat (cross my path today)		7N 15312			£ 2 – 4
60ø Virgin Mary/Beyond the sunset		7N 15315			£ 2 – 4

JIMMY DONLEY
57	The trail of the lonesome pine/South of the border	BRUNSWICK 05715	£ 6 - 9
59	The shape you left me in/What must I do	05807	£18 - 25

DICKY DOO & THE DON'TS
58	Click clack/Did you cry	LONDON HLU 8589	£ 9 - 12
58	Leave me alone/Wild, wild party	HLU 8754	£ 9 - 12
60	Wabash Cannonball/WEST TEXAS MARCHING BAND: The drums...	TOP RANK JAR 318	£ 4 - 6

THE DOOLEY SISTERS
55	Ko Ko Mo (I love you so)/Heart throb	LONDON HL 8128	£12 - 18

HAROLD DORMAN
60	Mountain of love/To be with you	TOP RANK JAR 357	£ 4 - 6

DIANA DORS
60	Point of no return/April heart	PYE 7N 15242	£ 4 - 6

GERRY DORSEY (became Engelbert Humperdinck)
59	Crazy bells/Mister Music Man	DECCA F 11108	£ 4 - 6
59	I'll never fall in love again/Every day is a wonderful..	PARLOPHONE R 4595	£ 4 - 6

THE JIMMY DORSEY ORCHESTRA
57	So rare/Sophisticated swing	H.M.V. POP 324	£ 4 - 6
57	Jay-Dee's boogie woogie/June night	POP 383	£ 9 - 12

THE TOMMY DORSEY ORCH. (*starring WARREN COVINGTON)
58ø	Tea for two cha cha/My baby just cares for me	BRUNSWICK *05757	£ 2 - 4
59	Swing high/The minor goes muggin'	TOP RANK TR 5010	£ 2 - 4

THE DOUBLES w. THE GAY BLADES
59	Little Joe/Hey girl!	H.M.V. POP 613	£12 - 18

CHIC DOUGLAS
58	I'm not afraid anymore/Jo-Ann	FONTANA H 121	£ 4 - 6

CRAIG DOUGLAS (qv VARIOUS ARTISTS)
58	Sitting in a tree house/Nothin' shakin'	DECCA F 11055	£ 4 - 6
58	Are you really mine/Go chase a moonbeam	F 11075	£ 4 - 6
59	Come softly to me/Golden girl	TOP RANK JAR 110	£ 4 - 6
59ø	A teenager in love/The 39 steps	JAR 133	£ 4 - 6
59ø	Only sixteen/My first love affair	JAR 159	£ 4 - 6
59	Wish it were me/The riddle of love	JAR 204	£ 2 - 4
60ø	Pretty blue eyes/Sandy	JAR 268	£ 2 - 4
60ø	Heart of a teenage girl/New boy	JAR 340	£ 2 - 4
60ø	Oh, what a day/Why, why, why	JAR 406	£ 2 - 4
60	Where's the girl (I never met)/My hour of love	JAR 515	£ 2 - 4

JOHNNY DOUGLAS & HIS ORCH.
54	Ballet of the bells/Solfeggio	DECCA F 10276	£ 2 - 4

KIRK DOUGLAS & THE MELLOMEN
55	A whale of a tale/And the Moon grew brighter and........	BRUNSWICK 05408	£ 2 - 4

LEW DOUGLAS & HIS ORCH.
54	Caesar's boogie/Turn around boy	M-G-M SP 1093	£ 4 - 6

NORMA DOUGLAS
57	Be it resolved/Joe he gone	LONDON HLZ 8475	£ 6 - 9

CHARLIE DRAKE
58ø	Splish splash/Hello, my darlings	PARLOPHONE R 4461	£ 4 - 6
58ø	Volare/Itchy twitchy feeling	R 4478	£ 4 - 6
58	Tom Thumb's tune/Goggle Eye Ghee	R 4496	£ 4 - 6
59	Sea cruise/Starkle, starkle little twink	R 4552	£ 4 - 6
60	Naughty/Old Mr. Shadow	R 4675	£ 2 - 4
60ø	Mr. Custer/Glow worm	R 4701	£ 2 - 4

RUSTY DRAPER

53	Gambler's guitar/Free home demonstration	ORIOLE	CB 1214 º	£ 4 – 6
53	I love to jump/Lighthouse		CB 1220 º	£ 4 – 6
54	The train with the rhumba beat/Melancholy baby		CB 1277 º	£ 4 – 6
56	Are you satisfied?/Wabash Cannonball	MERCURY	MT 101 º	£ 4 – 6
56	Rock and roll Ruby/House of cards		MT 113 º	£ 9 – 12
57	Freight train/Seven come eleven		MT 155 º	£ 4 – 6
58	Buzz buzz buzz/I get the blues when it rains		MT 194 º	£ 4 – 6
58	Gamblin' gal/That's my doll		7MT 211	£ 6 – 9
58	June, July and August/Chicken-pickin' hawk		7MT 229	£ 6 – 9
59	Shoppin' around/With this ring		AMT 1019	£ 6 – 9
59	Hey Li Lee Li Lee Li/The Sun will always shine		AMT 1034	£ 4 – 6
60ø	Mule skinner blues/Please help me, I'm falling		AMT 1101	£ 6 – 9
60	Luck of the Irish/It's a little more like Heaven		AMT 1110	£ 2 – 4

THE DREAM WEAVERS

56ø	It's almost tomorrow/You've got me wondering	BRUNSWICK	05515	£ 9 – 12
56	A little love can go a long, long way/Into the night ..		05568	£ 4 – 6
56	You're mine/Is there somebody else?		05607	£ 4 – 6

THE DRIFTERS (U.K.) (became THE SHADOWS/qv CLIFF RICHARD)

59	Feelin' fine/Don't be a fool (with love)	COLUMBIA	DB 4263	£18 – 25
59	Driftin'/Jet black		DB 4325	£18 – 25

THE DRIFTERS (U.S.)

56	Soldier of fortune/I gotta get myself a woman	LONDON	HLE 8344	£90 –120
58	Drip-drop/Moonlight Bay		HLE 8686	£40 – 60
59	There goes my baby/Oh my love		HLE 8892	£ 9 – 12
59ø	Dance with me/True love, true love		HLE 8988	£ 4 – 6
60	This magic moment/Baltimore		HLE 9081	£ 4 – 6
60	Lonely winds/Hey senorita		HLK 9145	£ 4 – 6
60ø	Save the last dance for me/Nobody but me		HLK 9201	£ 2 – 4

ROY DRUSKY

59	Just about that time/Wait and see	BRUNSWICK	05785	£ 4 – 6

THE DUBS

57	Could this be magic/Such lovin'	LONDON	HLU 8526	£40 – 60
58	Gonna make a change/Beside my love		HL 8684	£40 – 60

DUDLEY

60	El pizza/Lone prairie rock	VOGUE	V 9171	£ 6 – 9

THE DUKE & DUCHESS w. SIR HUBERT PIMM

55	Borrowed sunshine/Get ready for love	LONDON	HLU 8206	£12 – 18

DUKES OF IRON

54	Last train to San Fernando/Big bamboo	MELODISC	1316 º	£ 4 – 6

AGGIE DUKES

58	John John/Well of loneliness	VOGUE	V 9090	£60 – 90

JOHNNY DUNCAN & THE BLUE GRASS BOYS (*without Group/qv CHRIS BARBER)

57	Kaw-Liga/Ella Speed	COLUMBIA	DB 3925	£ 6 – 9
57ø	Last train to San Fernando/Rock-a-billy baby		DB 3959	£ 6 – 9
57ø	Blue, blue heartache/Jig along home		DB 3996	£ 6 – 9
57ø	Footprints in the snow/Get along home, Cindy		DB 4029	£ 6 – 9
58	If you love me baby/Goodnight Irene		DB 4074	£ 9 – 12
58	Itching for my baby/I heard the bluebirds sing		DB 4118	£ 6 – 9
58	All of the monkeys ain't in the zoo/More and more		DB 4167	£ 4 – 6
58	My lucky love/Geisha girl		DB 4179	£ 4 – 6
59	This train/Rosalie		DB 4282	£ 4 – 6
59	Kansas City/That's all right darlin'		DB 4311	£ 4 – 6
60	Any time/Yellow yellow Moon		*DB 4415	£ 2 – 4

BLIND WILLIE DUNN'S GIN BOTTLE FOUR w. KING OLIVER
54 Jet black blues/Blue blood blues .... COLUMBIA SCM 5100   £ 4 - 6

TONY DUNNING
60 Seventeen tomorrow/Be my girl .... PALETTE   PG 9006   £ 2 - 4

CHAMPION JACK DUPREE
51 Fisherman's blues/County Jail special .... JAZZ PARADE B 16 º £ 6 - 9

JIMMY DURANTE (& *PATTY ANDREWS/+EDDIE JACKSON/=PETER LAWFORD/qv ETHEL MERMAN)
55 Pupalina (My little doll)/Little people .... BRUNSWICK   05395   £ 4 - 6
55 It's bigger than both of us*/When the circus leaves town   05445   £ 4 - 6
55 I love you, I do+/Swingin' with rhythm and blues=   05495   £ 4 - 6
60 The best things in life are free/Shine on harvest Moon   05829   £ 2 - 4

SLIM DUSTY
58ø A pub with no beer/Once when I was mustering .... COLUMBIA DB 4212   £ 4 - 6
59 The answer to a pub with no beer/Winter winds ....   DB 4294   £ 2 - 4

DUTCH SWING COLLEGE BAND
60 Milord/Marina .... PHILIPS   PB 1029   £ 2 - 4

JOSE DUVAL
57 Message of love/That's what you mean to me .... LONDON   HLR 8458   £ 6 - 9

THE DYNATONES
59 Steel guitar rag/The girl I'm searching for .... TOP RANK JAR 149   £ 6 - 9

VINCE EAGER
58 Five days, five days/No more .... PARLOPHONE R 4482   £ 9 - 12
59 The railroad song/When's your birthday, baby? ....   R 4531   £ 4 - 6
59 No other arms - no other lips/This should go on for ever   R 4550   £ 4 - 6
59 Makin' love/Primrose Lane .... TOP RANK JAR 191   £ 4 - 6
60 Why/El Paso ....   JAR 275   £ 4 - 6
60 Lonely blue boy/No love have I .... JAR 307   £ 4 - 6

JIM EANES
59 Christmas doll/It won't seem like Christmas .... MELODISC   1530   £ 4 - 6

ROBERT EARL
55ø With your love/He .... PHILIPS PB 517 º £ 1 - 2
56ø My September love/Now and forever ....   PB 552 º £ 1 - 2
58ø I may never pass this way again/Someone ....   PB 805   £ 2 - 4
58ø More than ever (Come prima)/No one but you (in my heart)   PB 867   £ 2 - 4
59ø The wonderful secret of love/The Boulevard of Broken....   PB 891   £ 2 - 4

KENNETH EARLE
60 The new Frankie and Johnny/40-30-40 .... DECCA F 11205   £ 2 - 4
60 Standing on the corner/Put your arms around me, honey .   F 11224   £ 2 - 4

THE EARTH BOYS
59 Space girl/Barbara Ann .... CAPITOL CL 14979   £ 6 - 9

THE EASY RIDERS (qv VIC DAMONE/TERRY GILKYSON/FRANKIE LAINE)
58 Kari waits for me/Salute to Windjammer .... PHILIPS PB 823   £ 2 - 4
60 Young in love/Saturday's child .... LONDON HLR 9204   £ 2 - 4

THE ECHOES
60 Born to be with you/My guiding light .... TOP RANK JAR 399   £ 4 - 6

BILLY ECKSTINE (& *THE METRONOME ALL STARS/+COUNT BASIE ORCH./qv SARAH VAUGHAN)
53 I apologise/Kiss of fire .... M-G-M   SP 1011   £ 4 - 6
53 Be fair/Come to the Mardi Gras ....   SP 1020   £ 2 - 4
53 Coquette/A fool in love ....   SP 1040   £ 2 - 4
53 I'll know/I've never been in love before ....   SP 1055   £ 2 - 4
53 St. Louis blues (both sides) ....   *SP 1060   £ 2 - 4

54	Fortune telling cards/Tenderly		SP	1082	£ 2 – 4
54	Rendezvous/Don't get around much anymore		SP	1084	£ 2 – 4
54	Seabreeze/Sophisticated lady		SP	1095	£ 2 – 4
54ø	No one but you/I let a song go out of my heart	MGM	763	º £ 1 – 2
54ø	as above		SP	1101	£ 6 – 9
54	Olay olay (The bullfighter's song)/Beloved		SP	1107	£ 2 – 4
55	Mood indigo/Do nothin' till you hear from me		SP	1117	£ 2 – 4
55	What more is there to say?/Prelude to a kiss		SP	1124	£ 2 – 4
55	The life of the party/Love me or leave me		SP	1136	£ 4 – 6
55	More than you know/La de do de do (Honey bug song)		SP	1140	£ 2 – 4
56	Lost in loveliness/Farewell to romance		SP	1153	£ 2 – 4
56	Good-bye/You've got me crying again		SP	1167	£ 2 – 4
56	You'll get yours/The show must go on		SP	1170	£ 2 – 4
56	Solitude/I got it bad (and that ain't good)		MGM	925	£ 2 – 4
57	A man doesn't know/My fickle heart		MGM	948	£ 2 – 4
57	Pretty, pretty/Blue illusion	H.M.V.	POP	341	£ 2 – 4
57	Bring back the thrill/Over the rainbow	M–G–M	MGM	970	£ 2 – 4
58	Boulevard of Broken Dreams/If I can help somebody	MERCURY	7MT	191	£ 2 – 4
58	Vertigo/In the rain		7MT	224	£ 2 – 4
58	Prisoner of love/Funny		AMT	1008	£ 2 – 4
59ø	Gigi/Trust in me		AMT	1018	£ 2 – 4
59	I want a little girl/Lonesome lover blues	COLUMBIA	+DB	4334	£ 2 – 4
60	Anything you wanna do (I wanna do with you)/Like wow		DB	4407	£ 2 – 4

DUANE EDDY (& THE REBELS) (qv LEE HAZLEWOOD)

58ø	Rebel–rouser/Stalkin'	LONDON	HL	8669	£ 6 – 9
58	Ramrod/The walker		HL	8723	£ 4 – 6
58ø	Cannonball/Mason Dixon lion		HL	8764	£ 4 – 6
59ø	The lonely one/Detour		HLW	8821	£ 4 – 6
59ø	Peter Gunn/Yep!		HLW	8879	£ 4 – 6
59ø	Forty miles of bad road/The quiet three		HLW	8929	£ 4 – 6
59ø	Some kind–a earthquake/First love, first tears		HLW	9007	£ 2 – 4
60ø	Bonnie came back/Movin' 'n' groovin'		HLW	9050	£ 4 – 6
60ø	Shazam!/The Secret Seven		HLW	9104	£ 2 – 4
60ø	Because they're young/Rebel walk		HLW	9162	£ 2 – 4
60ø	Kommotion/Theme for Moon children		HLW	9225	£ 2 – 4

PEARL EDDY

54	That's what a heart is for/Devil lips	H.M.V.	7M	262	£ 4 – 6

DAVID EDE & THE RABIN ROCK (qv OSCAR RABIN)

60	Easy go/The blue bird	PYE	7N	15280	£ 2 – 4

TONI EDEN

60	No one understands (my Johnny)/Teen Street	COLUMBIA	DB	4409	£ 2 – 4
60	Grown up dreams/Whad'ya gonna do		DB	4458	£ 2 – 4
60	Will I ever/The waiting game		DB	4527	£ 2 – 4

HARRY "SWEETS" EDISON SEXTET

60	Hollering at the Watkins/K.M. blues	H.M.V.	POP	720	£ 2 – 4

JIMMY EDWARDS (U.K.)

60	I've never seen a straight banana/Rhymes	FONTANA	H	260	£ 2 – 4

JIMMY EDWARDS (U.S.)

58	Love bug crawl/Honey lovin'	MERCURY	7MT	193	£60 – 90

TOM EDWARDS

57	What is a teen age girl?/What is a teen age boy?	V–CORAL	Q	72236	£ 4 – 6

TOMMY EDWARDS

52	It's all in the game/My concerto	M–G–M	MGM	466	º £ 4 – 6
53	A fool such as I/Take these chains from my heart		SP	1030	£ 4 – 6
56	Baby, let me take you../MARION SISTERS: Life could not..		SP	1168	£ 4 – 6
58ø	It's all in the game/Please love me forever		MGM	989	£ 4 – 6
58	Love is all we need/Mr. Music Man		MGM	995	£ 2 – 4

59	Please, Mr. Sun/The morning side of the mountain	MGM	1006	£ 2 – 4
59ø	My melancholy baby/It's only the good times	MGM	1020	£ 4 – 6
59	I've been there/I looked at Heaven	MGM	1032	£ 2 – 4
59	(New in) The ways of love/Honestly and truly	MGM	1045	£ 2 – 4
60	Don't fence me in/I'm building castles again	MGM	1065	£ 2 – 4
60	I really don't want to know/Unloved	MGM	1080	£ 2 – 4
60	Blue heartaches/It's not the end of everything	MGM	1097	£ 2 – 4

VINCE EDWARDS

58	Widget/Lollipop	CAPITOL	CL 14825	£ 2 – 4

WILFRED EDWARDS (*& THE CARIBS)

60	We're gonna love/Your eyes are dreaming .... *STARLITE	ST.45 016	£ 9 – 12
60	Tell me darling/I know	ST.45 026	£ 4 – 6

DONNIE ELBERT

58	Wild child/Let's do the stroll	PARLOPHONE R 4403	£18 – 25

ROY ELDRIDGE & CLAUDE BOLLING

56	Wild man blues/Fireworks	VOGUE	V 2373	£ 2 – 4

THE ELEGANTS

58ø	Little star/Getting dizzy	H.M.V.	POP 520	£ 6 – 9
58	Please believe me/Goodnight	POP 551	£ 9 – 12

ELIAS & HIS ZIG-ZAG JIVE FLUTES

58ø	Tom Hark/Ry–Ry	COLUMBIA	DB 4109	£ 6 – 9
58	Zeph boogie/Vucka' magcwabeni (Back from the dead)	DB 4146	£ 4 – 6

THE ELIGIBLES

59	24 hours (till my date with you)/Faker, faker	CAPITOL	CL 15067	£ 2 – 4
59	My first Christmas with you/The little engine	CL 15098	£ 2 – 4

DUKE ELLINGTON & HIS (FAMOUS) ORCH.

53	Time's a–wastin'/Otto make that riff staccato	H.M.V.	7M 156	£ 4 – 6
53	The flaming sword/BARNEY BIGARD ORCH.: A lull at dawn .	7M 170	£ 4 – 6
54ø	Skin deep – Parts 1 & 2	PHILIPS	PB 243 º	£ 2 – 4
54	Smile/If I give my heart to you	CAPITOL	CL 14186	£ 4 – 6
55	Twelfth Street rag (Mambo)/Chile bowl	CL 14229	£ 4 – 6
55	Tyrolean tango/All day long	CL 14260	£ 4 – 6
55	Ting–a–ling/Brown Betty	COLUMBIA SCM 5182	£ 4 – 6
59	Anatomy of a murder/Flirtibird	PHILIPS	PB 946	£ 2 – 4
59ø	Skin deep – Parts 1 & 2	PB 243	£ 4 – 6
60	Malletoba spank/All of me	JAZ 101	£ 2 – 4
60	Duke's place/Jones	JAZ 117	£ 2 – 4

RAY ELLINGTON (QUARTET) (*& MARION RYAN/+TONY CROMBIE ORCH.)

53	The little red monkey/Kaw–Liga	COLUMBIA SCM 5050	£ 4 – 6
54	All's going well (my Lady Montmorency)*/Ol' Man River .	SCM 5088	£ 4 – 6
54	The owl song/Rub–a–dub–dub	SCM 5104	£ 4 – 6
54	A.B.C. boogie/Christmas cards	SCM 5147	£ 9 – 12
55	Ko Ko Mo (I love you so)/Woodpecker	SCM 5177	£ 9 – 12
55	Play it boy, play/The Irish were Egyptians long ago ...	SCM 5187	£ 4 – 6
55	Cloudburst/Pet	SCM 5199	£ 4 – 6
56	Who's got the money?/Hold him tight	SCM 5250	£ 4 – 6
56	Keep that coffee hot/Lucky 13	SCM 5274	£ 4 – 6
56	Stranded in the jungle/Left hand boogie	DB 3821	£ 9 – 12
56	Giddy–up–a ding dong/The green door	DB 3838	£ 9 – 12
57	That rock 'n' rollin' man/Marianne	DB 3905	£ 9 – 12
57	Swaller–tail coat/Don't burn me up	DB 4013	£ 4 – 6
58	Long black nylons/Living doll	DB 4057	£ 9 – 12
58	The Sultan of Bezaaz/You gotta love everybody	PYE	7N 15159	£ 2 – 4
59	Charlie Brown/Chip off the old block	7N 15189	£ 4 – 6
59	Carina/I was a little too lonely	ORIOLE	CB 1512	£ 2 – 4
60ø	The Madison/Jump over	EMBER	+EMB S102	£ 4 – 6
60	Tres jolie/Dracula's three daughters	EMB S114	£ 2 – 4

PETER ELLIOTT
57	All at once (you love her)/To the aisle	PARLOPHONE	R 4355	£ 2 – 4
58	Devotion/No fool like an old fool		R 4457	£ 2 – 4
59	Call me/Flamingo		R 4514	£ 2 – 4
59	The young have no time/Over and over		R 4529	£ 2 – 4

HERB ELLIS–JIMMY GIUFFRE ALL STARS
60	Goose grease/My old flame	H.M.V.	POP 721	£ 2 – 4

LARRY ELLIS
58	Nothing you can do/Buzz goes the bee	FELSTED	AF 110	£ 6 – 9

LEE & JAY ELVIN (JERRY LORDAN & Another)
59	So the story goes/When you see her	FONTANA	H 191	£ 4 – 6

MELVIN ENDSLEY
57	I like your kind of love/Is it true	R.C.A.	RCA 1004	£ 9 – 12
58	I got a feelin'/There's bound to be		RCA 1051	£ 9 – 12

SCOTT ENGEL (became Scott Walker)
58	Blue bell/Paper doll	VOGUE	V 9125	£ 9 – 12
59	The livin' end/Good for nothin'		V 9145	£60 – 90
59	Charlie bop/All I do is dream of you		V 9150	£ 9 – 12

THE ENGLAND SISTERS
60ø	Heartbeat/Little child	H.M.V.	POP 710	£ 4 – 6

THE ENJAYS
59	All my love, all my life/Cross my heart	TOP RANK	JAR 145	£ 6 – 9

PRESTON EPPS
59	Bongo rock/Bongo party	TOP RANK	JAR 140	£ 4 – 6
59	Bongo in pastel/Doin' the cha cha cha		JAR 180	£ 2 – 4
60	Bongo boogie/Flamenco boogie		JAR 345	£ 4 – 6
60	Bongo bongo bongo/Hully gully bongo		JAR 413	£ 4 – 6
60	Bongola/Blue bongo		JAR 522	£ 2 – 4

NORMAN ERSKINE
57	Till we meet again/What's to become of me	CAPITOL	CL 14784	£ 2 – 4

BLUEGRASS ERWIN
59	I won't cry alone/I can't love you	TOP RANK	JAR 252	£ 4 – 6

THE ESCORTS & KAY JUSTICE
54	If you took your love from me/Yes, indeed	COLUMBIA	SCM 5132	£ 4 – 6

ESQUERITA
58	Rockin' the joint/Esquerita and the Voola	CAPITOL	CL 14938	£40 – 60

THE ETERNALS
59	Rockin' in the jungle/Rock 'n' roll cha–cha	LONDON	HL 8995	£12 – 18

ETTA & HARVEY (ETTA JAMES & HARVEY Fuqua of THE MOONGLOWS)
60	If I can't have you/My heart cries	LONDON	HLM 9180	£ 9 – 12

LARRY EVANS
56	Crazy 'bout my baby/Henpecked	LONDON	HLU 8269	£60 – 90

MAUREEN EVANS
58	Stupid Cupid/Carolina Moon	EMBASSY	WB 300	£ 2 – 4
58	Fever/Born too late		WB 303	£ 2 – 4
58	The hula hoop song/Hoopa hoola		WB 309	£ 2 – 4
59	I'll get by/Someday (you'll want me to want you)		WB 313	£ 2 – 4
59	The day the rains came/You always hurt the one you love		WB 316	£ 2 – 4
59	To know him is to love him/Kiss me, honey honey, kiss me		WB 319	£ 2 – 4

59	Goodbye Jimmy, goodbye/May you always		WB 344	£ 2 - 4
59	Lipstick on your collar/What a diff'rence a day made ..		WB 348	£ 2 - 4
59	Broken-hearted melody/Plenty good lovin'		WB 356	£ 2 - 4
59	Don't want the moonlight/The years between	ORIOLE	CB 1517	£ 2 - 4
59	Among my souvenirs/Happy anniversary	EMBASSY WB 371		£ 2 - 4
60ø	The big hurt/I can't begin to tell you	ORIOLE	CB 1533	£ 4 - 6
60ø	Love, kisses and heartaches/We just couldn't say goodbye		CB 1540	£ 4 - 6
60	Paper roses/Please understand		CB 1550	£ 4 - 6
60	My little corner of the world/Mama wouldn't like it ...		CB 1563	£ 2 - 4
60	As long as he needs me/Where is love?		CB 1578	£ 2 - 4
60	Till/Why don't you believe me		CB 1581	£ 2 - 4

PAUL EVANS (*& THE CURLS)

59ø	Seven little girls sitting in the../Worshipping an idol	LONDON	*HLL 8968	£ 4 - 6
60ø	Midnite Special/Since I met you, baby		HLL 9045	£ 6 - 9
60	Happy-go-lucky me/Fish in the ocean		HLL 9129	£ 4 - 6
60	Brigade of broken hearts/Twins		HLL 9183	£ 4 - 6
60	Hushabye little guitar/Blind boy		HLL 9239	£ 4 - 6

THE EVERLY BROTHERS

57ø	Bye bye, love/I wonder if I care as much	LONDON	HLA 8440	£ 6 - 9
57ø	Wake up little Susie/Maybe tomorrow		HLA 8498	£ 6 - 9
58	Should we tell him/This little girl of mine		HLA 8554	£ 9 - 12
58ø	All I have to do is dream/Claudette		HLA 8618	£ 4 - 6
58ø	Bird dog/Devoted to you		HLA 8685	£ 4 - 6
59ø	Problems/Love of my life		HLA 8781	£ 4 - 6
59ø	Poor Jenny/Take a message to Mary		HLA 8863	£ 4 - 6
59ø	('Til) I kissed you/Oh, what a feeling		HLA 8934	£ 4 - 6
60ø	Let it be me/Since you broke my heart		HLA 9039	£ 2 - 4
60ø	as above		HLA 9039 º	£ 9 - 12
60ø	Cathy's clown/Always it's you	WARNER-B	WB 1	£ 2 - 4
60ø	as above		WB 1 º	£ 9 - 12
60ø	When will I be loved/Be-bop-a-lula	LONDON	HLA 9157	£ 2 - 4
60ø	as above		HLA 9157 º	£ 9 - 12
60ø	Lucille/So sad (to watch good love go bad)	WARNER-B	WB 19	£ 2 - 4
60ø	as above		WB 19 º	£12 - 18
60ø	Like strangers/Leave my woman alone	LONDON	HLA 9250	£ 2 - 4

LENY EVERSONG

57	Jezebel/Jealousy	V-CORAL	Q 72255	£ 2 - 4

FABIAN

59	I'm a man/Hypnotized	H.M.V.	POP 587	£ 9 - 12
59	Turn me loose/Stop thief!		POP 612	£ 9 - 12
59	Tiger/Mighty cold (to a warm, warm heart)		POP 643	£ 9 - 12
59	Come on and get me/Got the feeling		POP 659	£ 9 - 12
60ø	Hound dog man/This friendly world		POP 695	£ 6 - 9
60	String along/About this thing called love		POP 724	£ 4 - 6
60	Strollin' in the Springtime/I'm gonna sit right down....		POP 778	£ 4 - 6
60	King of love/Tomorrow		POP 800	£ 4 - 6
60	Long before/Kissin' and twistin'		POP 810	£ 4 - 6

BRIAN FAHEY & HIS ORCH.

60	At the sign of the Swingin' Cymbals/The clanger	PARLOPHONE R 4686		£ 4 - 6

WERLY FAIRBURN & THE DELTA BOYS

56	I'm a fool about your love/All the time	LONDON	HLC 8349	£90 -120

JOHNNY FAIRE

58	Bertha Lou/Till the law says stop	LONDON	HLU 8569	£60 - 90

ADAM FAITH

58	(Got a) Heartsick feeling/Brother Heartache and Sister..	H.M.V.	POP 438	£12 - 18
58	High school confidential/Country music holiday		POP 557	£18 - 25
59	Runk bunk/Ah, poor little baby!	TOP RANK	JAR 126	£ 9 - 12
59ø	What do you want?/From now until forever	PARLOPHONE R 4591		£ 2 - 4

60ø	Poor me/The reason		R 4623	£ 2 – 4
60ø	Someone else's baby/Big time		R 4643	£ 2 – 4
60ø	Johnny comes marching home/Made you		R 4665	£ 2 – 4
60ø	How about that!/With open arms		R 4689	£ 2 – 4
60ø	Lonely pup (in a Christmas shop)/Greenfinger		R 4708	£ 2 – 4

PERCY FAITH & HIS ORCH.
60ø	Theme from "A Summer Place"/Go–go–po–go	PHILIPS	PB 989	£ 2 – 4

THE FALCONS
59	You're so fine/Goddess of angels	LONDON	HLT 8876	£18 – 25

JOHNNY FALLIN
59	Party kiss/The creation of love	CAPITOL	CL 15043	£12 – 18
59	Wild streak/If I could write a love song		CL 15091	£12 – 18

JULES FARMER
59	Love me now/Part of me (is still with you)	LONDON	HLP 8967	£ 4 – 6

BILLY FARRELL
58	Yeah yeah/Someday (you'll want me to want you)	PHILIPS	PB 828	£ 2 – 4

DO & DENA FARRELL
57	Young magic/New love tonight	H.M.V.	POP 427	£ 2 – 4

THE FASCINATORS
58	Chapel bells/I wonder who	CAPITOL	CL 14942	£ 9 – 12
59	Oh, Rose Marie/Fried chicken and macaroni		CL 15062	£ 9 – 12

FATTY GEORGE & HIS ORCH.
60	Mambo jambo/Black eyes cha cha	QUALITON	PSP 7104	£ 2 – 4

WALLY FAWKES & HIS TROGLODYTES (*or –SANDY BROWN QUINTET)
57	Petite fleur/Baby Brown	DECCA	*FJ 10855	£ 2 – 4
57	Sent for you yesterday and here.../Why can't you behave		FJ 10936	£ 2 – 4
58	The pilot fish and the whale/Pale blues		F 11002	£ 2 – 4

Little RITA FAYE
53	Rock City boogie/Wait a little longer	M–G–M	MGM 671 º	£ 6 – 9
53	I fell out of the Christmas tree/I'm a problem child ..		MGM 697 º	£ 4 – 6

VICTOR FELDMAN BIG BAND/QUARTET
56	Big top/Cabaletto	TEMPO	A 142	£ 2 – 4
57	Jackpot/You are my heart's delight		A 154	£ 2 – 4

FELIX & His Guitar
59	Chili beans/Puerto Rican riot	LONDON	HLU 8875	£ 4 – 6

THE FENDERMEN
60ø	Mule skinner blues/Torture	TOP RANK	JAR 395	£ 4 – 6
60	Don't you just know it/Beach party		JAR 513	£ 4 – 6

H–BOMB FERGUSON
54	Feel like I do/My love	ESQUIRE	10–372 º	£ 6 – 9

JOHNNY FERGUSON
60	Angela Jones/Blue serge and white lace	M–G–M	MGM 1059	£ 4 – 6

FERKO STRING BAND
55ø	Alabama jubilee/Sing a little melody	LONDON	HL 8140	£12 – 18
55	Ma (she's making eyes at me)/You are my sunshine		HLF 8183	£12 – 18
55	Happy days are here again/Deep in the heart of Texas ..		HLF 8215	£12 – 18

PHIL FERNANDO
58	Make ready for love/Blonde bombshell	PYE	7N 15142	£ 6 – 9

FERRANTE & TEICHER
| 50ø | Theme from "The Apartment"/Lonely room | LONDON | HLT 9164 | £ 2 – 4 |

ALAN FIELDING
| 58 | Just remember/Don't say goodbye | FONTANA | H 124 | £ 2 – 4 |
| 60 | I'll never understand/I love Suzie Brown | DECCA | F 11261 | £ 2 – 4 |

JERRY FIELDING & HIS ORCH.
| 54 | When I grow too old to dream/Button up your overcoat | LONDON | HL 8017 | £12 – 18 |

BILLY FIELDS
| 55 | Sincerely/Thrilled | M-G-M | SP 1126 | £ 2 – 4 |
| 59 | The greatest love in the world/No other love | MERCURY | AMT 1067 | £ 2 – 4 |

ERNIE FIELDS & HIS ORCH.
59ø	In the mood/Christopher Columbus	LONDON	HL 8985	£ 4 – 6
60	Chattanooga choo choo/Workin' out		HL 9100	£ 4 – 6
60	Raunchy/My prayer		HL 9227	£ 4 – 6

GRACIE FIELDS
55	Twenty/Summertime in Venice	DECCA	F 10614	£ 2 – 4
56	A letter to a soldier/The sweetest prayer in all the....		F 10824	£ 2 – 4
57ø	Around the world/Far away	COLUMBIA	DB 3953	£ 4 – 6
57	Mary's boy child/Scarlet ribbons (for her hair)		DB 4047	£ 2 – 4
58	The little clockmaker/Belonging to someone		DB 4200	£ 2 – 4
59ø	Little donkey/The carefree heart		DB 4360	£ 2 – 4
60	In Jerusalem/The twelfth of Never		DB 4537	£ 2 – 4

IRVING FIELDS TRIO & ORCH.
| 58 | Ragtime rock/Syncopated Sadie | ORIOLE | CB 1436 | £ 2 – 4 |

THE FIESTAS
| 59 | So fine/Last night I dreamed | LONDON | HL 8870 | £ 9 – 12 |

THE FIREBALLS
59	Torquay/Cry baby	TOP RANK	JAR 218	£ 4 – 6
60	Bulldog/Nearly sunrise		JAR 276	£ 4 – 6
60	Foot-patter/Kissin'		JAR 354	£ 4 – 6
60	Vaquero (Cowboy)/Chief Whoopin-Koff		JAR 507	£ 4 – 6

THE FIREFLIES
| 59 | Stella got a fella/You were mine | TOP RANK | JAR 198 | £ 6 – 9 |
| 60 | I can't say goodbye/What did I do wrong | LONDON | HLU 9057 | £ 4 – 6 |

FIREHOUSE FIVE plus TWO
| 56 | Runnin' wild/Lonesome railroad blues | G.T.J. | GV 2192 | £ 2 – 4 |

CHIP FISHER
| 59 | Poor me/No one | PARLOPHONE | R 4604 | £ 4 – 6 |

EDDIE FISHER (*& SALLY SWEETLAND)
52ø	Outside of Heaven/Lady of Spain	H.M.V.	B 10362 º	£ 2 – 4
52ø	Everything I have is yours/You'll never know		B 10398 º	£ 2 – 4
53	I'm yours/That's the chance you take		7M 101	£ 9 – 12
53ø	Downhearted/Am I wasting my time on you?		B 10450 º	£ 2 – 4
53ø	Everything I have is yours/You'll never know		7M 115	£ 9 – 12
53	Trust in me/Forgive me		7M 116	£ 6 – 9
53ø	Outside of Heaven/Lady of Spain		7M 117	£ 9 – 12
53	Even now/If it were up to me		7M 125	£ 6 – 9
53ø	Downhearted/Am I wasting my time on you		7M 126	£ 9 – 12
53ø	I'm walking behind you*/Hold me		B 10489 º	£ 2 – 4
53	*as above*		7M 133	£ 9 – 12
53	Just another polka/When I was young (Yes, very young) .		7M 146	£ 6 – 9
53ø	Wish you were here/A fool was I		B 10564 º	£ 2 – 4
53ø	*as above*		7M 159	£ 9 – 12

Year	Title	Label	Cat. No.	Price
53	Many times/With these hands		7M 168	£ 6 -
53ø	Oh my Papa/(I never missed...) Until you said "Goodbye"		B 10614 º	£ 2 -
54ø	as above		7M 172	£ 9 - 1
54	How deep is the ocean/That old feeling		7M 185	£ 6 -
54	Just to be with you/April showers		7M 201	£ 6 -
54	A girl, a girl/I'm in the mood for love		7M 212	£ 6 -
54	My friend/May I sing to you		7M 235	£ 6 -
54	How do you speak to an angel?/My arms, my heart, my love		7M 242	£ 6 -
54ø	I need you now/Heaven was never like this		B 10755 º	£ 2 -
54ø	as above		7M 251	£ 9 - 1
54	Green years/They say it's wonderful		7M 257	£ 6 -
54	Count your blessings instead of sheep/White Christmas		7M 266	£ 6 -
55ø	(I'm always hearing) Wedding bells/A man chases a girl		B 10839 º	£ 2 -
55ø	as above		7M 294	£ 9 - 1
56	Magic fingers/My one and only love		7M 353	£ 4 -
56	Dungaree doll/If it hadn't been for you		7M 374	£ 6 -
56	No other one/Without you		7M 402	£ 6 -
56	Sweet heartaches/What is this thing called love?		7M 421	£ 4 -
56ø	Cindy, oh Cindy/Fanny		POP 273	£ 9 - 1
57	Some day soon/All about love		POP 296	£ 2 -
57	Tonight my heart she is crying/Blues for me		POP 342	£ 2 -
57	A second chance/Slow burning love	R.C.A.	RCA 1009	£ 2 -
58	Sayonara/That's the way it goes		RCA 1030	£ 2 -
58	Kari waits for me/I don't hurt anymore		RCA 1061	£ 2 -
59	The last mile home/I'd sail a thousand seas		RCA 1147	£ 2 -

TONI FISHER

Year	Title	Label	Cat. No.	Price
59ø	The big hurt/Memphis belle	TOP RANK	JAR 261	£ 4 -
60	How deep is the ocean/Blue, blue, blue		JAR 341	£ 2 -

ELLA FITZGERALD (& *LOUIS JORDAN/+BILL DOGGETT/=OSCAR PETERSON/qv COUNT BASIE)

Year	Title	Label	Cat. No.	Price
50	Ain't nobody's business if I do/I'll never be free	BRUNSWICK	*04617 º	£ 4 -
54	Who's afraid (Not I, not I, not I)/I wished on the Moon		05324	£ 4 -
55	Lullaby of Birdland/Later		05392	£ 4 -
55	Moanin' low/Taking a chance on love		05427	£ 4 -
55	Lover, come back to me/Old devil Moon		05468	£ 4 -
55	Pete Kelly's blues/Hard hearted Hannah		05473	£ 4 -
55	Soldier boy/Air mail special+		05477	£ 4 -
56	(Love is) The tender trap/My one and only love		05514	£ 4 -
56	Ella's contribution to the blues/Early Autumn		05539	£ 4 -
56	You'll never know/But not like mine		05584	£ 4 -
56	The silent treatment/The Sun forgot to shine this	H.M.V.	POP 266	£ 4 - 6
57	A beautiful friendship/Too young for the blues		POP 290	£ 4 - 6
57	Hotta chocolatta/Stay there		POP 316	£ 4 - 6
57	Johnny One Note/To keep my love alive		POP 348	£ 4 - 6
57	Manhattan/Ev'ry time we say goodbye		POP 373	£ 4 - 6
57	Goody goody/A tisket, a tasket		POP 380	£ 4 - 6
58ø	The swingin' shepherd blues/Midnight Sun		POP 486	£ 4 - 6
58	Beale Street blues/St. Louis blues		POP 499	£ 2 - 4
58	Your red wagon/Trav'lin light		POP 518	£ 2 - 4
59	My happiness/A satisfied mind	BRUNSWICK	05783	£ 2 - 4
59ø	But not for me/You make me feel so young	H.M.V.	POP 657	£ 4 - 6
59	The Christmas song/The secret of Christmas		POP 686	£ 2 - 4
60	Beat me Daddy eight to the bar/Like young		POP 701	£ 4 - 6
60	It's all right with me/Don'cha go way mad		=POP 719	£ 2 - 4
60ø	Mack the knife/Lorelei		POP 736	£ 4 - 6
60ø	How high the Moon - Parts 1 & 2		POP 782	£ 4 - 6
60	Jingle bells/Good morning blues		POP 809	£ 2 - 4
60	We three Kings of Orient are etc./White Christmas		POP 817	£ 2 - 4

THE FIVE BLOBS

Year	Title	Label	Cat. No.	Price
58	The blob/Saturday night in Tiajuana	PHILIPS	PB 881	£ 4 - 6

REMEMBER! - THE SYMBOL º AFTER THE CATALOGUE NUMBER INDICATES A 78 rpm RECORD
REMEMBER! - THE SYMBOL ø AFTER THE YEAR OF ISSUE INDICATES A BRITISH CHART ENTRY

THE FIVE CHESTERNUTS
58	Teenage love/Jean Dorothy	COLUMBIA	DB 4165	£40 – 60

THE FIVE FLEETS
58	Oh what a feeling/I been cryin'	FELSTED	AF 103	£60 – 90

THE FIVE KEYS
54	Ling, ting, tong/I'm alone	CAPITOL	CL 14184 º	£12 – 18
55	The verdict/Me make um pow pow		CL 14313	£60 – 90
55	Doggone it, you did it/(Close your..) Take a deep breath		CL 14325	£40 – 60
56	Gee Whittakers!/'Cause you're my lover		CL 14545	£25 – 40
56	She's the most/I dreamt I dwelt in Heaven		CL 14582	£25 – 40
56	That's right/Out of sight, out of mind		CL 14639	£40 – 60
57	The wisdom of a fool/Now don't that prove I love you? .		CL 14686	£25 – 40
57	Four walls/Let there be you		CL 14736	£12 – 18
57	The blues don't care/This I promise you		CL 14756	£18 – 25
58	From me to you/Whippety whirl		CL 14829	£18 – 25
58	Really-o truly-o/One great love		CL 14967	£18 – 25

THE FIVE SATINS
57	To the aisle/Wish I had my baby	LONDON	HL 8501	£60 – 90
59	Wonderful girl/Weeping willow	TOP RANK	JAR 199	£12 – 18
59	Shadows/Toni my love		JAR 239	£ 9 – 12
60	Your memory/I didn't know	M–G–M	MGM 1087	£ 9 – 12

THE FLAIRS
57	Swing pretty Mama/I'd climb the hills and mountains ...	ORIOLE	CB 1392	£90 –120

JOHNNY FLAMINGO
58	My teen-age girl/When I lost you	VOGUE	V 9089	£18 – 25
58	So long/Make me a present of you		V 9100	£18 – 25

THE FLAMINGOS
57	Would I be crying/Just for a kick	LONDON	HLN 8373	£120–160
57	The ladder of love/Let's make up	BRUNSWICK	05696	£90 –120
59	Love walked in/Yours	TOP RANK	JAR 213	£ 6 – 9
60	I only have eyes for you/I was such a fool		JAR 263	£ 9 – 12
60	Nobody loves me like you/You, me and the sea		JAR 367	£ 6 – 9
60	Mio amore/At night		JAR 519	£ 6 – 9

THE FLANAGAN BROTHERS
58	Salton City/Early one evening	V–CORAL	Q 72342	£ 9 – 12

BUD FLANAGAN
59	Strollin'/Home is where your heart is	COLUMBIA	DB 4265	£ 2 – 4

MICHAEL FLANDERS (*& DONALD SWANN)
57	A Gnu/Misalliance	*PARLOPHONE	R 4354	£ 2 – 4
59ø	The little drummer boy/D. SWANN: The youth of the heart		R 4528	£ 2 – 4

LORD FLEA & HIS CALYPSONIANS
57	The naughty little flea/Shake shake Sonora	CAPITOL	CL 14704	£ 2 – 4

THE (FABULOUS) FLEE–RAKKERS (qv RICKY WAYNE)
60ø	Green jeans/You are my sunshine	TRIUMPH	RGM 1008	£18 – 25
60	*as above*	TOP RANK	JAR 431	£ 9 – 12
60	Sunday date/Shiftless Sam	PYE	7N 15288	£ 6 – 9

THE FLEETWOODS
59ø	Come softly to me/I care so much	LONDON	HLU 8841	£ 6 – 9
59	Graduation's here/Oh Lord let it be me		HLU 8895	£ 4 – 6
59	Mr. Blue/You mean everything to me	TOP RANK	JAR 202	£ 6 – 9
60	Outside my window/Magic star		JAR 294	£ 4 – 6
60	Runaround/Truly do		JAR 383	£ 4 – 6

WADE FLEMONS
59	Slow motion/Walkin' by the river	TOP RANK	JAR 206	£ 4 – 6
60	What's happening/Goodnight, it's time to go		JAR 327	£ 4 – 6
60	Easy lovin'/Woops now		JAR 371	£ 4 – 6

SAM FLETCHER
59	Time has a way/No such luck	M–G–M	MGM 1024	£ 2 – 4

DICK FLOOD
59	The three bells/Far away	FELSTED	AF 125	£ 4 – 6

ERROL FLYNN (*& PATRICE WYMORE)
55	Lily of Laguna/We'll gather lilacs*	PHILIPS	PB 380 º	£ 4 – 6

RED FOLEY (& *ERNEST TUBB/+BETTY FOLEY)
51	Hot rod race/The chicken song*	BRUNSWICK	04679 º	£ 4 – 6
53	Hot toddy/(by ROBERTA LEE)		05076 º	£ 6 – 9
54	Pin ball boogie/Jilted		05307 º	£ 6 – 9
54	Skinnie Minnie (Fishtail)/Thank you for calling		05321	£ 6 – 9
55	Hearts of stone/Never+		05363	£ 9 – 12
55	Croce di oro (Cross of gold)+/The night watch		05508	£ 6 – 9

EDDIE FONTAINE
55	Rock love/All my love belongs to you	H.M.V.	B 10852 º	£ 9 – 12
55	*as above*		7M 304	£40 – 60
56	Cool it, baby/Into each life some rain must fall	BRUNSWICK	05624	£40 – 60
58	Nothin' shakin'/Don't ya know	LONDON	HLM 8711	£12 – 18

ARLENE FONTANA
59	I'm in love/Easy	PYE INT.	7N 25010	£ 4 – 6

THE FONTANE SISTERS (*& PAT BOONE/qv PERRY COMO)
54	Happy days and lonely nights/If I didn't have you	LONDON	HL 8099	£18 – 25
55	Hearts of stone/Bless your heart		HL 8113	£25 – 40
55	Rock love/You're mine		HL 8126	£18 – 25
55	Seventeen/If I could be with you		HLD 8177	£25 – 40
55	Rolling stone/Daddy–O		HLD 8211	£18 – 25
56	Adorable/Playmates		HLD 8225	£12 – 18
56	Eddie my love/Yum yum		HLD 8265	£18 – 25
56	I'm in love again/You always hurt the one you love		HLD 8289	£18 – 25
56	Voices*/Willow weep for me		HLD 8318	£12 – 18
56	Silver bells/Nuttin' for Christmas		HLD 8343	£12 – 18
57	The banana boat song/Lonesome lover blues		HLD 8378	£12 – 18
57	Please don't leave me/Still		HLD 8415	£12 – 18
57	Fool around/Which way to your heart		HLD 8488	£ 9 – 12
58	Chanson d'amour/Cocoanut grove		HLD 8621	£ 6 – 9
59	Billy boy/Encore d'amour		HLD 8861	£ 6 – 9
60	Listen to your heart/Please be kind		HLD 9037	£ 4 – 6
60	Theme from "A Summer Place"/Darling, it's wonderful		HLD 9078	£ 2 – 4

BILL FORBES
58	God's little acre/My cherie	COLUMBIA	DB 4232	£ 2 – 4
59	Once more/Believe in me		DB 4269	£ 2 – 4
59ø	Too young/It's not the end of the world		DB 4386	£ 2 – 4

CLINTON FORD (*& THE HALLELUJAH SKIFFLE GROUP)
58	Sweet sixteen/Eleven more months and ten more days	ORIOLE	CB 1425	£ 2 – 4
58	Jesus remembered me/In the sweet bye and bye		*CB 1427 º	£ 4 – 6
59	I cried a tear/(You were only) Teasin'		CB 1483	£ 2 – 4
59ø	Old Shep/Nellie Dean rock		CB 1500	£ 4 – 6
59	Lovesick blues/Give a little, take a little		CB 1516	£ 2 – 4

DEE DEE FORD
60	Good–morning blues/I just can't believe	LONDON	HLU 9245	£ 9 – 12

EMILE FORD (& THE CHECKMATES)

59ø	What do you want to make those eyes.../Don't tell me....	PYE	7N 15225	£ 2 – 4
60ø	On a slow boat to China/That lucky old Sun		7N 15245	£ 2 – 4
60ø	You'll never know what you're missin' 'til you try/Still		7N 15268	£ 2 – 4
60	Red sails in the sunset/Afraid		7N 15279	£ 2 – 4
60ø	Them there eyes/Question		7N 15282	£ 2 – 4
60ø	Counting teardrops/White Christmas		7N 15314	£ 2 – 4

"TENNESSEE" ERNIE FORD (& *EDDIE KIRK/+THE DINNING SISTERS/=BETTY HUTTON)

49	Smokey Mountain boogie/Country Junction	CAPITOL	CL 13211 º	£ 6 – 9
50	Mule train/Milk 'em in the morning blues		CL 13237 º	£ 4 – 6
50	The cry of the wild goose/Anticipation blues		CL 13271 º	£ 4 – 6
51	The shot gun boogie/My hobby		CL 13447 º	£ 6 – 9
51	Kissin' bug boogie/Woman is a five letter word		CL 13604 º	£ 4 – 6
51	Leetle Juan Pedro*/Feed 'em in the mornin' blues		CL 13599 º	£ 4 – 6
52	Rock City boogie/Streamlined Cannon Ball		+CL 13682 º	£ 4 – 6
52	Blackberry boogie/Tennessee local		CL 13797 º	£ 4 – 6
53	Catfish boogie/Kiss me big		CL 14006 º	£ 4 – 6
54	as above		CL 14006	£18 – 25
54ø	Give me your word/River of no return		CL 14005	£ 9 – 12
54	This must be the place/The honeymoon's over		=CL 14133	£ 6 – 9
55	His hands/I am a pilgrim		CL 14261	£ 4 – 6
55	There is beauty in everything/Losing you		CL 14273	£ 4 – 6
56ø	Sixteen tons/You don't have to be a baby to cry		CL 14500	£ 9 – 12
56ø	The ballad of Davy Crockett/Farewell		CL 14506	£ 9 – 12
56	That's all/Bright lights and blonde-haired women		CL 14557	£ 6 – 9
56	Who will shoe your pretty little.../Gaily the troubadour		CL 14616	£ 2 – 4
56	Have you seen her?/First born		CL 14657	£ 2 – 4
57	The watermelon song/One suit		CL 14691	£ 2 – 4
57	The lonely man/False hearted girl		CL 14734	£ 2 – 4
57	In the middle of an island/Ivy league		CL 14759	£ 4 – 6
58	Bless your pea pickin' heart/Down deep		CL 14846	£ 2 – 4
58	Sunday barbecue/Love makes the world go 'round		CL 14896	£ 2 – 4
59	Sleepin' at the foot of the bed/Glad rags		CL 14972	£ 2 – 4
59	Blackeyed Susie/Code of the mountains		CL 15010	£ 4 – 6
59	Love is the only thing/Sunny side of Heaven		CL 15100	£ 2 – 4
60	Joshua fit the battle of Jericho/O Mary, don't you weep		CL 15148	£ 2 – 4
60	Little Klinker/Jingle-o-the-Brownie		CL 15171	£ 2 – 4

FRANKIE FORD (*& HUEY "PIANO" SMITH)

59	Sea crusie/Roberta	LONDON	*HL 8850	£12 – 18
59	Alimony/Can't tell my heart (what to do)	TOP RANK	*JAR 186	£ 6 – 9
60	Cheatin' woman/(by HUEY "PIANO" SMITH)		JAR 282	£ 9 – 12
60	Time after time/I want to be your man		JAR 299	£ 6 – 9
60	You talk too much/If you've got troubles	LONDON	HLP 9222	£ 6 – 9

PERRY FORD

59	Bye, bye baby, goodbye/She came as a stranger	PARLOPHONE	R 4573	£ 4 – 6
60	Crazy over you/Garden of happiness		R 4633	£ 4 – 6
60	Don't weep (Little lady)/Little grown-up		R 4683	£ 2 – 4

GEORGE FORMBY

60ø	Banjo boy/Happy go lucky me	PYE	7N 15269	£ 2 – 4

HELEN FORREST

56	Taking a chance on love/I love you much too much	CAPITOL	CL 14594	£ 2 – 4

JANE FORREST

56	Sincerely yours/A girl can't say	COLUMBIA	SCM 5213	£ 2 – 4

LANCE FORTUNE

60ø	Be mine/Action	PYE	7N 15240	£ 6 – 9
60ø	This love I have for you/All on my own		7N 15260	£ 4 – 6
60	I wonder/Will you still be my girl?		7N 15297	£ 2 – 4

SHIRLEY FORWOOD
57 Juke box lovers/Two hearts (with an arrow between) .... LONDON HLD 8402 £ 9 - 1

PETE FOUNTAIN
60 A closer walk/Do you know what it means to miss New..... CORAL Q 72389 £ 2 -
60 Columbus Stockade blues/Sentimental journey .... Q 72404 £ 2 -

THE FOUR ACES (feat. AL ALBERTS)
54 The gang that sang "Heart Of My Heart"/Heaven can wait BRUNSWICK 05256 £ 4 -
54ø Three coins in the fountain/Wedding bells (are break-..) 05308 £ 9 - 1
54 It shall come to pass/Dream .... 05322 £ 4 -
54 It's a woman's world/The cuckoo bird in the pickle tree 05348 £ 4 -
54ø Mister Sandman/(I'll be with you) In apple blossom time 05355 £ 9 - 1
55 Melody of love/There is a tavern in the town .... 05379 £ 4 -
55 There goes my heart/Take me in your arms .... 05401 £ 4 -
55ø Stranger in Paradise/You'll always be the one .... 05418 £ 9 - 1
55 Sluefoot/I'm in the mood for love .... 05429 £ 4 -
55ø Love is a many splendored thing/Shine on harvest Moon . 05480 £ 9 - 1
55 Jingle bells/The Christmas song (Merry Christmas to you) 05504 £ 2 -
56 To love again/Charlie was a boxer .... 05562 £ 4 -
56 The gal with the yaller shoes/Of this I'm sure .... 05566 £ 4 -
56 If you can dream/It's the talk of the town .... 05573 £ 4 -
56ø A woman in love/I only know I love you .... 05589 £ 6 -
56 Dreamer/Let's fall in love .... 05601 £ 2 -
56 You can't run away from it/Written on the wind .... 05613 £ 2 -
56ø Friendly persuasion (Thee I love)/Someone to love ..... 05623 £ 6 -
57 Heart/What a difference a day made .... 05651 £ 2 -
57 Bahama Mama/You're mine .... 05663 £ 2 -
57 Three sheets to the wind/Yes, sir, that's my baby .... 05695 £ 2 -
57 Half of my heart/When my sugar walks down the street .. 05712 £ 2 -
58 Rock and roll rhapsody/I wish I may, I wish I might ... 05743 £ 4 -
58 Hangin' up a horseshoe/Two arms. two lips, one heart! . 05758 £ 4 -
58 The world outside/The Christmas tree .... 05767 £ 2 -
59ø The world outside/The Inn of the Sixth Happiness ...... 05773 £ 2 -
59 Waltzing Matilda/Roses of Rio .... 05812 £ 2 -

THE FOUR COINS
58 The world outside/Be still my heart .... FONTANA H 168 £ 2 -

THE FOUR DOLLS
57 Three on a date/Proud of you .... CAPITOL CL 14778 £ 2 -
58 Whoop-a-lala/I'm following you! .... CL 14845 £ 2 -

THE FOUR ESCORTS
54 Love me/Loop de loop mambo .... H.M.V. 7M 277 £ 4 -

THE FOUR ESQUIRES
55 The Sphinx won't tell/Three things (a man must do) .... LONDON HL 8152 £12 - 18
56 Adorable/Thunderbolt .... HLA 8224 £ 9 - 12
57 Look homeward angel/Santo Domingo .... HL 8376 £18 - 25
58ø Love me forever/I ain't been right since you left ..... HLO 8533 £ 9 - 12
58 Always and forever/I walk down the street .... HLO 8579 £ 6 - 9
58 Hideaway/Repeat after me .... HL 8746 £ 4 - 6
59 Non e cosi/Land of you and me .... PYE INT. 7N 25012 £ 2 - 4
59 Act your age/So ends the night .... 7N 25027 £ 2 - 4
60 Wouldn't it be wonderful/Wonderful one .... 7N 25049 £ 2 - 4

THE FOUR FRESHMEN
54 Love turns Winter to Spring/Mood indigo .... CAPITOL CL 14196 £ 4 - 6
55 Day by day/How can I tell her .... CL 14338 £ 4 - 6
56 Love is just around the corner/Angel eyes .... CL 14580 £ 2 - 4
56 Graduation day/Lonely night in Paris .... CL 14610 £ 2 - 4
56 You're so far above me/He who loves and runs away .... CL 14633 £ 2 - 4

THE FOUR GUYS (Of THE MODERNAIRES)
55 Mine/Half-hearted kisses .... V-CORAL Q 72054 £ 4 - 6

THE FOUR JACKS
58	Hey! Baby/The prayer of love	DECCA	F 10984	£ 6 – 9

THE FOUR KNIGHTS (qv NAT "KING" COLE)
54ø	I get so lonely/Till then	CAPITOL	CL 14076	£ 9 – 12
54	In the chapel in the moonlight/Easy street		CL 14154	£ 6 – 9
54	Saw your eyes/I don't wanna see you cryin'		CL 14204	£ 6 – 9
55	Honey bunch/Write me, baby		CL 14244	£ 6 – 9
55	Foolishly yours/Inside out		CL 14290	£ 6 – 9
56	You/Guilty		CL 14516	£ 4 – 6
59	O' falling star/Foolish tears	CORAL	Q 72355	£ 2 – 4

THE FOUR LADS (qv DORIS DAY/FRANKIE LAINE/JOHNNIE RAY)
57	Golly/I just don't know	PHILIPS	JK 1021	£ 6 – 9
58	Enchanted island/Guess what the neighbours'll say		PB 839	£ 2 – 4
59	The girl on page 44/The mocking bird		PB 894	£ 2 – 4
60ø	Standing on the corner/Sunday		PB 1000	£ 2 – 4
60	Goona Goona/You're nobody 'til somebody loves you		PB 1020	£ 2 – 4

THE FOUR PALMS
58	Jeanie, Joanie, Shirley, Toni/Consideration	VOGUE	V 9116	£40 – 60

THE FOUR PREPS
57	Falling star/Where wuz you	CAPITOL	CL 14727	£ 2 – 4
57	Moonstruck in Madrid/I cried a million tears		CL 14747	£ 2 – 4
57	Again 'n' again 'n' again/Promise me baby		CL 14768	£ 2 – 4
57	Band of angels/How about that?		CL 14783	£ 2 – 4
58	Fools will be fools/26 miles (Santa Catalina)		CL 14815	£ 2 – 4
58ø	Big man/Stop, baby		CL 14873	£ 4 – 6
58	Summertime lies/Lazy Summer night		CL 14914	£ 2 – 4
59	The riddle of love/She was five and he was ten		CL 14992	£ 2 – 4
59	Gidget/Cinderella		CL 15032	£ 2 – 4
59	The big surprise/Try my arms		CL 15044	£ 2 – 4
59	Memories, memories/I ain't never		CL 15065	£ 2 – 4
60	Down by the station/Listen honey (I'll be home)		CL 15110	£ 2 – 4
60ø	Got a girl/(Wait till you) Hear it from me		CL 15128	£ 2 – 4

4 SAXOPHONES IN 12 TONES
56	Frantastic/Frankly speaking	VOGUE	V 2355	£ 2 – 4

THE FOUR SPICES
57	Fire engine boogie/Armen's theme (Yesterday and you) ..	M-G-M	MGM 944	£ 6 – 9

THE FOUR TONES
58	Rickshaw boy/Voom ba voom	DECCA	F 11074	£ 2 – 4

THE FOUR TOPHATTERS
55	Leave-a my gal alone/Go baby go	LONDON	HLA 8163	£60 – 90
55	Forty five men in a telephone booth/Wild Rosie		HLA 8198	£60 – 90

THE FOUR TUNES
55	I sold my heart to a junkman/The greatest feeling in....	LONDON	HL 8151	£18 – 25
55	Tired of waitin'/L'amour toujours l'amour		HLJ 8164	£18 – 25

THE FOUR VOICES
58	Tell me you're mine/Tight spot	PHILIPS	PB 864	£ 2 – 4

THE FOUR WINDS
58	Short shorts/Five minutes more	LONDON	HLU 8556	£12 – 18

DON FOX
57	Be my girl/You'll never go to Heaven	DECCA	F 10927	£ 4 – 6
57	Majesty of love/Party time		F 10955	£ 4 – 6
58	Pretend you don't see her/Wasteland		F 10983	£ 2 – 4
58	She was only seventeen/When you're a long, long way.....		F 11057	£ 2 – 4
60	Out there/'Tain't what you do	TRIUMPH	RGM 1022	£ 9 – 12

CONNIE FRANCIS (& *MARVIN RAINWATER)

56	My first real love/Believe in me (Credimi)	M-G-M	MGM 902 º	£ 6 - 9
56	*as above*		SP 1169	£18 - 25
56	My sailor boy/Everyone needs someone		MGM 932	£ 9 - 12
57	I never had a sweetheart/Little blue wren		MGM 945	£ 9 - 12
57	Eighteen/Faded orchid		MGM 962	£ 6 - 9
57	The majesty of love/You, my darlin', you		*MGM 969	£ 9 - 12
58ø	Who's sorry now/You were only fooling (while I was.....)		MGM 975	£ 4 - 6
58ø	I'm sorry I made you cry/Lock up your heart		MGM 982	£ 4 - 6
58ø	Stupid Cupid/Carolina moon		MGM 985	£ 4 - 6
58ø	I'll get by/Fallin'		MGM 993	£ 4 - 6
58ø	You always hurt the one you love/In the Valley of Love		MGM 998	£ 4 - 6
59ø	My happiness/Happy days and lonely nights		MGM 1001	£ 2 - 4
59	If I didn't care/Toward the end of the day		MGM 1012	£ 4 - 6
59ø	Lipstick on your collar/Frankie		MGM 1018	£ 4 - 6
59ø	Plenty good lovin'/You're gonna miss me		MGM 1036	£ 2 - 4
59ø	Among my souvenirs/Do you love me like you kiss me? ...		MGM 1046	£ 2 - 4
60ø	Valentino/It would be worth it		MGM 1060	£ 2 - 4
60	Mama/Teddy		MGM 1070	£ 6 - 9
60ø	Robot man/Mama		MGM 1076	£ 4 - 6
60ø	Everybody's somebody's fool/Jealous of you		MGM 1086	£ 2 - 4
60ø	My heart has a mind of its own/Malaguena		MGM 1100	£ 2 - 4

JOHNNIE FRANCIS

55	Funny thing/Give me the right	DECCA	F 10440	£ 2 - 4

FRANKIE & LARRY

60	Not yet/A fool for you	CAPITOL	CL 15153	£ 2 - 4

JOHNNY FRANKS & HIS QUARTET/RHYTHM

55	Tweedle dee/Shake, rattle and roll	MELODISC	P 230 º	£ 4 - 6
56	Rock candy baby/Sing-ing-ing		1355 º	£ 4 - 6
58	Good old country music/Cheatin' on me		1459	£ 4 - 6

JOHN FRASER

58	Trolley stop/Don't take your love from me	PYE	7N 15118	£ 2 - 4
59	Bye, bye baby, goodbye/Golden cage		7N 15212	£ 2 - 4

THE FRATERNITY BROTHERS (*& GIL FIELDS)

59	Passion flower/A nobody like me*	H.M.V.	POP 582	£ 2 - 4

STAN FREBERG (& *DAWS BUTLER/+JUNE FORAY/=JUD CONLON CHORALE/#JESSE WHITE)

51	John and Marsha/Ragtime Dan	CAPITOL	CL 13465 º	£ 4 - 6
52	Try/Maggie		CL 13747 º	£ 4 - 6
52	The boogie-woogie banjo man from.../The world is wait-..		CL 13846 º	£ 4 - 6
53	St. George and the dragonet*+/Little Blue Riding Hood .		CL 14025 º	£ 6 - 9
54	Christmas Dragnet (both sides)		*CL 14019 º	£ 4 - 6
54ø	Sh-boom (Life could be a dream)/C'est si bon		CL 14187	£12 - 18
55	The lone psychiatrist/The honey-earthers		*CL 14316	£ 6 - 9
56ø	The yellow rose of Texas/Rock around Stephen Foster ...		CL 14509	£ 9 - 12
56	The great pretender/The quest for Bridey Hammerschlaugen+		CL 14571	£ 9 - 12
56ø	Heartbreak Hotel/Rock Island line		CL 14608	£ 9 - 12
57	Banana boat (Day-o)/Tele-vee-shun		CL 14712	£ 6 - 9
58	Green Chritma*/The meaning of Christmas=		CL 14966	£ 4 - 6
60ø	The old payola roll blues#/Sh-boom (Life could be a....)		CL 15122	£ 9 - 12

DOTTY FREDERICK

59	Ricky/Just wait	TOP RANK	JAR 106	£ 6 - 9

TOMMY FREDERICK & THE HI-NOTES

58	Prince of players/I'm not pretending	LONDON	HLU 8555	£ 9 - 12

DOLORES FREDERICKS

56	Whole lotta shakin' goin' on/Cha Cha Joe	BRUNSWICK	05540	£ 9 - 12

MARC FREDERICKS
56 Mystic midnight/Symphony to Anne .... LONDON   HLD 8281   £ 9 – 12

ALAN FREED & HIS ROCK 'N' ROLL BAND
56 Teen rock/Right now, right now .... V–CORAL   Q 72219   £25 – 40
57 Rock 'n' roll boogie/Teener's canteen ....   Q 72230   £25 – 40

BOBBY FREEMAN
58 Do you want to dance/Big fat woman .... LONDON   HLJ 8644   £12 – 18
58 Betty Lou got a new pair of shoes/Starlight ....   HLJ 8721   £12 – 18
59 Need your love/Shame on you Miss Johnson ....   HLJ 8782   £12 – 18
59 Mary Ann Thomas/Love me ....   HLJ 8898   £ 9 – 12
60 Sinbad/Ebb tide (The sea) ....   HLJ 9031   £ 4 – 6
60 (I do the) Shimmy shimmy/You don't understand me ...... PARLOPHONE R 4684   £ 6 – 9

ERNIE FREEMAN
57 Raunchy/Puddin' .... LONDON   HLP 8523   £ 9 – 12
58 Dumplin's/Beautiful weekend ....   HLP 8558   £ 6 – 9
58 Indian love call/Summer serenade ....   HLP 8660   £ 4 – 6
60 Big river/Night sounds ....   HLP 9041   £ 4 – 6

DON FRENCH
59 Lonely Saturday night/Goldilocks .... LONDON   HLW 8884   £25 – 40
59 Little blonde girl/I look into my heart ....   HLW 8989   £25 – 40

THE FRIDAY KNIGHTS
60 Poor man's roses/Don't open that door .... ORIOLE   CB 1579   £ 2 – 4

VONNIE FRITCHIE
55 Sugar Booger Avenue/There I stood (to throw old shoes..) LONDON   HLU 8178   £18 – 25

JANE FROMAN
54 The finger of suspicion points at you/My shining hour . CAPITOL   CL 14209   £ 6 – 9
54 The song from "Desiree" (We meet again)/Mine ....   CL 14208   £ 4 – 6
55ø I wonder/I'll never be the same ....   CL 14254   £ 9 – 12
56 A sound foundation/Summertime in Venice ....   CL 14530   £ 2 – 4
56 You'll never walk alone/One little candle ....   CL 14658   £ 2 – 4

DOM FRONTIERE & HIS ORCH.
57 Jet Rink ballad/Uno mas .... LONDON   HLU 8385   £12 – 18

JERRY FULLER
59 Tennessee waltz/Charlene .... LONDON   HLH 8982   £ 4 – 6

LOWELL FULSON
53 I love my baby/The blues come rollin' in .... LONDON   L 1199 º £ 6 – 9

TOMMY FURTADO
57 Sun Tan Sam/Isabella .... LONDON   HLA 8418   £ 9 – 12

BILLY FURY
59ø Maybe tomorrow/Gonna type a letter .... DECCA   F 11102   £ 9 – 12
59ø Margo, don't go/Don't knock upon my door ....   F 11128   £ 9 – 12
59 Angel face/Time has come ....   F 11158   £ 6 – 9
59 My Christmas prayer/Last kiss ....   F 11189   £ 9 – 12
60ø Colette/Baby how I cried ....   F 11200   £ 4 – 6
60ø That's love/You don't know ....   F 11237   £ 6 – 9
60ø Wondrous place/Alright, goodbye ....   F 11267   £ 4 – 6
60ø A thousand stars/Push push ....   F 11311   £ 4 – 6

THE G–CLEFS
56 Ka–ding dong/Darla, my darlin' .... COLUMBIA   DB 3851   £40 – 60

THE G—NOTES
58 I would/Ronnie .... ORIOLE   CB 1456   £ 4 – 6

MEL GADSON
60 Comin' down with love/I'm gettin' sentimental over you   LONDON   HLX 9105   £ 4 — 6

SLIM GAILLARD QUARTET/TRIO
50 Jam man/(by JOHNNY OTIS) .... PARLOPHONE R 3291 º £ 6 — 9
51 Voot boogie/Queen's boogie .... VOGUE   V 2029 º £ 6 — 9
51 Central Avenue boogie/Sighing boogie ....   V 2044 º £ 6 — 9

THE GAINORS
58 Gonna rock tonite/The secret .... LONDON   HLU 8734   £25 — 40

THE GALAXIES
60 The big triangle/Until the next time .... CAPITOL CL 15158 £ 2 — 4

DAVID GALBRAITH
57 Heartbreak is new to me/Miracle in Milan .... COLUMBIA DB 3947 £ 2 — 4

SUNNY GALE
53 Send my baby back to me/Teardrops on my pillow .... H.M.V.   7M 147 £ 4 — 6
54 Goodnight, well it's time to go/Close to me ....   7M 243 £ 4 — 6
55 C'est la vie/Looking glass ....   7M 344 £ 4 — 6
57 Two hearts (with an arrow between)/Maybe you'll be there BRUNSWICK 05659 £ 4 — 6
57 Come go with me/Please go ....   05661 £ 4 — 6
58 A certain smile/Just friends ....   05753 £ 2 — 4

THE GALLAHADS
55 Ooh-ah/Careless .... CAPITOL CL 14282 £ 4 — 6

BOB GALLION
59 You take the table and I'll take..../Out of a honky tonk M—G—M   MGM 1028 £ 4 — 6
60 Froggy went a courtin'/Hey! Joe ....   MGM 1057 £ 4 — 6

FRANK GALLUP
58 Got a match?/I beg your pardon .... H.M.V.   POP 509 £ 2 — 4

LORD GANDA
57 Everybody is rockin' & rollin'/Landlady don't steal my.. MELODISC   1417 º £ 4 — 6

GANIM'S ASIA MINORS
58 Daddy Lolo/Halvah .... LONDON   HLE 8637 £ 4 — 6

CLENTT GANT
60 I'm just a lucky so-and-so/I need you so .... STARLITE ST.45 023 £ 4 — 6

REGINALD GARDINER
60 Trains (both sides) .... DECCA   F 5278 £ 2 — 4

AVA GARDNER
53 Bill/Can't help lovin' dat man .... M—G—M   SP 1005 £ 2 — 4

DAVE GARDNER
58 Hop along rock/All by myself .... BRUNSWICK   05740 £18 — 25

JUDY GARLAND (*& FRED ASTAIRE)
53 A couple of swells/I love a piano, etc. .... M—G—M   *SP 1001 £ 4 — 6
55ø The man that got away/Here's what I'm here for .... PHILIPS PB 366 º £ 2 — 4
56 Look for the silver lining/Who? .... M—G—M   SP 1157 £ 4 — 6
57 After you've gone/Rock-a-bye your baby with a Dixie..... CAPITOL CL 14789 £ 2 — 4
57 I feel a song coming on/Just imagine ....   CL 14790 £ 2 — 4
57 It's lovely to be back in London/By myself ....   CL 14791 £ 2 — 4

ERROLL GARNER
60 Cheek to cheek/The way you look tonight .... PHILIPS JAZ 103 £ 2 — 4
60 Lullaby of Birdland/Easy to love ....   JAZ 105 £ 2 — 4

JOHN GARY
59	Let them talk/Tell my love	TOP RANK	JAR 177	£ 2 – 4
60	Little things mean a lot/Ever since I met Lucy		JAR 392	£ 2 – 4

DAVID GATES
60	The happiest man alive/The road that leads to love	TOP RANK	JAR 504	£ 9 – 12

JIMMY GAVIN
57	I sit in my window/Lonely chair	LONDON	HLU 8478	£12 – 18

JOHNNY GAVOTTE
60	It's not too late/Can't forget	PARLOPHONE R 4631	£ 2 – 4

ELAINE GAY
54	Love/Instantly	PARLOPHONE MSP 6140	£ 2 – 4

THE GAYLORDS
55	Mambo rock/Plantation boogie	MERCURY	MB 3226 º	£ 6 – 9
58	Flamingo l'amore/I'm longin' for love		AMT 1006	£ 2 – 4
59	Again/How about me		AMT 1023	£ 2 – 4
59	Sweeter than you/Homin' pigeon		AMT 1049	£ 2 – 4

MEL GAYNOR (qv OSCAR RABIN)
55	Just a man/How important can it be?	DECCA	F 10497	£ 2 – 4
55	Oh, my love/With you beside me		F 10542	£ 2 – 4
55	Bella notte/Sweet Kentucky rose		F 10618	£ 2 – 4

MITZI GAYNOR
59	Happy anniversary/Play for keeps	TOP RANK	JAR 258	£ 2 – 4
60	I don't regret a thing/The touch of time		JAR 289	£ 2 – 4

ROSEMARY GAYNOR
55	Ain't that a shame/A happy song	COLUMBIA SCM 5196	£ 4 – 6

PAUL GAYTEN
57	Yo, yo, walk/THE TUNE WEAVERS: Happy happy birthday baby	LONDON	HL 8503	£18 – 25
59	The hunch/Hot cross buns		HLM 8998	£18 – 25

GENE & EUNICE
56	I gotta go home/Have you changed your mind?	VOGUE	V 9062	£18 – 25
57	Move it over, baby/This is my story		V 9066	£25 – 40
57	I'm so in love with you/Let's get together		V 9071	£18 – 25
57	Don't treat me this way/Doodle doodle doo		V 9083	£18 – 25
58	The angels gave you to me/I mean love		V 9106	£12 – 18
58	Strange world/The vow		V 9126	£12 – 18
59	Bom bom Lulu/Hi diddle diddle		V 9136	£18 – 25
59	Poco-loco/Go-on Kokomo	LONDON	HL 8956	£12 – 18

JOHNNY GENTLE
59	Wendy/Boys and girls (were meant for each other)	PHILIPS	PB 908	£ 2 – 4
59	Milk from the coconut/I like the way		PB 945	£ 2 – 4
60	Darlin' won't you wait/This friendly world		PB 988	£ 2 – 4
60	After my laughter came tears/Sonja		PB 1069	£ 2 – 4

THE GEORGETTES
58	Love like a fool/Oh tonight	LONDON	HL 8548	£ 9 – 12
60	Down by the river/A pair of eyes	PYE INT.	7N 25058	£ 4 – 6

GERALDO & HIS (DANCE) ORCH.
56	Rockin' through Dixie/Stranger than fiction	ORIOLE	CB 1323 º	£ 4 – 6
57	Laughing rock 'n' roll/Thunderstorm	POLYDOR	BM 6070 º	£ 4 – 6

STAN GETZ QUARTET
60	I hadn't anyone till you/With the wind and the rain in..	H.M.V.	POP 735	£ 2 – 4

GEORGIA GIBBS

55ø	Tweedle dee/You're wrong, all wrong	MERCURY	MB 3196 º	£ 6 – 9
55	Dance with me Henry/Ballin' the Jack		MB 3223 º	£ 4 – 6
55	Ballin' the Jack/I still feel the same about you	V–CORAL	Q 72088	£ 6 – 9
56ø	Kiss me another/Rock right	MERCURY	MT 110 º	£ 4 – 6
56	I'll know/If I were a bell	V–CORAL	Q 72182	£ 4 – 6
57	Tra la la/Morning, noon and night	MERCURY	MT 133 º	£ 4 – 6
57	Sugar candy/I'm walking the floor over you	R.C.A.	RCA 1011	£ 4 – 6
57	Great balls of fire/I miss you		RCA 1029	£ 9 – 12
58	Arrivederci Roma/24 hours a day	MERCURY	7MT 210	£ 6 – 9
58	The hula hoop song/Keep in touch	COLUMBIA	DB 4201	£ 4 – 6
59	The hucklebuck/Better loved you'll never be		DB 4259	£ 6 – 9
60	The stroll that stole my heart/Seven lonely days	LONDON	HLP 9098	£ 4 – 6

THE FOUR GIBSON GIRLS

58	June, July and August/No school tomorrow	ORIOLE	CB 1447	£ 4 – 6
58	Safety Sue (both sides)		CB 1453	£ 2 – 4

DON GIBSON

56	Sweet dreams/The road of life alone	M–G–M	SP 1177	£ 6 – 9
58	Oh lonesome me/I can't stop lovin' you	R.C.A.	RCA 1056	£ 4 – 6
58	Blue blue day/Too soon		RCA 1073	£ 4 – 6
58	Give myself a party/Look who's blue		RCA 1098	£ 4 – 6
59	Who cares/A stranger to me		RCA 1110	£ 2 – 4
59	Don't tell me your troubles/Heartbreak Avenue		RCA 1150	£ 2 – 4
59	I'm movin' on/Big hearted me		RCA 1158	£ 2 – 4
60	Just one time/I may never get to Heaven		RCA 1183	£ 2 – 4
60	Far far away/A legend in my time		RCA 1200	£ 2 – 4
60	Sweet dreams/The same street		RCA 1217	£ 2 – 4

GINNY GIBSON

55	Like ma-a-ad/Once there was a little girl	M–G–M	SP 1121	£ 2 – 4
57	Whatever Lola wants (Lola..)/If anything should happen..		MGM 953	£ 2 – 4

JODY GIBSON & THE MULESKINNERS

59	Kissin' time/Man on my trail	PARLOPHONE	R 4579	£ 4 – 6
60	So you think you've got troubles/If you don't know		R 4645	£ 4 – 6

STEVE GIBSON & THE RED CAPS

57	Silhouettes/Flamingo	H.M.V.	POP 417	£ 9 – 12

TERRY GILKYSON & THE EASY RIDERS

57	Marianne/Goodbye Chiquita	PHILIPS	JK 1007	£ 9 – 12

DIZZY GILLESPIE SEXTET/ORCH.

56	The champ (both sides)	VOGUE	V 2116	£ 2 – 4
60	Doddlin'/Dizzy's blues	H.M.V.	POP 705	£ 2 – 4

PETER GILMORE

60	Follow that girl/Come away	H.M.V.	POP 740	£ 2 – 4

HERMIONE GINGOLD & GILBERT HARDING

53	Oh, Grandma/Takes two to tango	PHILIPS	PB 104 º	£ 4 – 6

GINO & GINA

58	Pretty baby/Love's a carousel	MERCURY	7MT 230	£ 9 – 12

THE GLADIOLAS

57	Little darlin'/Sweetheart, please don't go	LONDON	HLO 8435	£40 – 60

JACKIE GLEASON (& HIS ORCH.) (*as CAPT. GLEASON'S GARDEN BAND)

55	Rain/I'll never be the same	CAPITOL	CL 14289	£ 4 – 6
55	In the good old summertime/The band played on		*CL 14323	£ 4 – 6
55	Autumn leaves/Oo! What you do to me		CL 14363	£ 4 – 6
56	Capri in May/You're my greatest lover		CL 14549	£ 2 – 4
60	What is a boy?/What is a girl?	BRUNSWICK	04775	£ 6 – 9

HARRY GOLD w. NORRIE PARAMOR ORCH.
Be good to me/Frou Frou .... COLUMBIA SCM 5144 £ 2 - 4

THE GOLDEN GATE QUARTET
Moses smote the waters/Bones, bones, bones .... COLUMBIA SCM 5054 £ 4 - 6

THE GOLLYWOGS
Parade of the Jelly Babies/The Teddy Bears' picnic .... PARLOPHONE R 4647 £ 2 - 4

THE GONDOLIERS
God's green acres/Fly, seagull, fly .... STARLITE ST.45 001 £ 6 - 9

NAT GONELLA & HIS GEORGIA JAZZ BAND
Show me the way to go home/My gal Sal .... COLUMBIA DB 4465 £ 2 - 4

"THE GOOD COMPANIONS" film soundtrack (actually Janette Scott)
This kind of love/If only .... PARLOPHONE R 4282 £ 2 - 4

JACK GOOD'S FAT NOISE
The fat washerwoman/The fat noise .... DECCA   F 11233 £ 4 - 6

BENNY GOODMAN & HIS ORCH./SEXTET/COMBOS
Temptation rag/Bugle call rag .... COLUMBIA SCM 5053 £ 4 - 6
Let's dance/Jumpin' at the Woodside .... CAPITOL CL 14258 £ 4 - 6
Memories of you/King Porter stomp .... COLUMBIA SCM 5239 £ 4 - 6
Down South camp meeting/Don't be that way .... H.M.V.   7M 380 £ 4 - 6
Goody goody/Sometimes I'm happy .... CAPITOL CL 14531 £ 2 - 4
And the angels sing/Don't be that way ....   CL 14570 £ 2 - 4
Liza/Slipped disc .... PHILIPS JAZ 107 £ 2 - 4

RON GOODWIN & HIS ORCH./*PARLOPHONE POPS ORCH.
Limelight/The song from Moulin Rouge .... PARLOPHONE R 3686 º £ 1 - 2
Jet journey/When I fall in love ....   MSP 6020 £ 2 - 4
Limelight/The song from Moulin Rouge ....   MSP 6035 £ 6 - 9
Shane (Call of the far-away hills)/The Melba waltz ....   MSP 6044 £ 2 - 4
"The Man Between" theme/Tropical mirage ....   MSP 6055 £ 2 - 4
The song of the high seas/Guadalcanal march ....   MSP 6103 £ 2 - 4
Three coins in the fountain/Cara mia ....   MSP 6115 £ 2 - 4
Theme from "Modern Times" (Smile)/The messenger boy ...   MSP 6116 £ 2 - 4
Blue Star (The "Medic" theme)/Lonely heart ....   R 4074 º £ 1 - 2
Rock around the clock/Giddy-up-a ding dong ....   *R 4250 º £ 4 - 6
Elizabethan serenade/Red cloak ....   R 4272 £ 2 - 4
Skiffling strings/I'll find you ....   R 4297 £ 2 - 4
Colonel Bogey & The River Kwai March/Laughing sailor ..   R 4391 £ 2 - 4

THE GOOFERS
Hearts of stone/You're the one .... V-CORAL Q 72051 £18 - 25
Flip, flop and fly/My babe ....   Q 72074 £18 - 25
Goofie drybones/Nare ....   Q 72094 £ 9 - 12
Sick! Sick! Sick!/Twenty one ....   Q 72124 £12 - 18
Tear Drop Motel/Tennessee rock and roll ....   Q 72171 £18 - 25
Wow!/Push, push, push cart ....   Q 72267 £ 9 - 12
The dipsy doodle/Take this heart ....   Q 72289 £12 - 18

THE GOONS (*& ERIC SYKES/qv SPIKE MILLIGAN/HARRY SECOMBE/PETER SELLERS)
I'm walking backwards for Christmas/Bluebottle blues .. DECCA   F 10756 £ 6 - 9
The ying tong song/Bloodnok's rock 'n' roll call ......   F 10780 £ 6 - 9
My September love*/You gotta go oww! .... PARLOPHONE R 4251 £ 6 - 9
I love you/Eeh! Ah! Oh! Ooh! .... DECCA   F 10885 £ 4 - 6
A Russian love song/Whistle your cares away ....   F 10945 £ 4 - 6

ANITA GORDON
Lonesome like nobody knows/His hands .... BRUNSWICK   05456 £ 2 - 4

REMEMBER! - THE SYMBOL º AFTER THE CATALOGUE NUMBER INDICATES A 78 rpm RECORD

BARRY GORDON
56	I can't whistle/The milkman's polka	M—G—M	MGM	928	£ 2 – 4
56	Nuttin' for Christmas/Rock around Mother Goose		MGM	935	£ 4 – 6

CURTIS GORDON
57	Sixteen/Cry, cry	MERCURY	MT	163 º	£ 9 – 12

JOE GORDON (FOLK FOUR)
59	Gotta travel on/Ho ro my nutbrown maiden	H.M.V.	POP	600	£ 2 – 4
59	Dream lover/Dance to your Daddy		POP	634	£ 2 – 4
60	Football crazy/By the bright shining light of the Moon		POP	737	£ 2 – 4

PHIL GORDON
55	Get a load of that crazy walk/Strip polka	BRUNSWICK		05481	£ 2 – 4
56	Down the road apiece/I'm gonna move to the outskirts....			05545	£ 6 – 9

ROSCO GORDON
60	Just a little bit/Goin' home	TOP RANK	JAR 332	£ 6 – 9

EYDIE GORME (*& STEVE LAWRENCE)
54	Climb up the wall/Frenesi	V—CORAL	Q	2014	£ 4 – 6
54	Sure/Tea for two		Q	2027	£ 4 – 6
55	Make yourself comfortable*/Chain reaction		Q 72044	£ 4 – 6
55	Take a deep breath/Besame mucho		*Q 72085	£ 4 – 6
55	Give a girl a chance/A girl can't say		Q 72092	£ 4 – 6
55	Soldier boy/What is the secret of your success?		Q 72103	£ 4 – 6
56	Sincerely yours/Come home	LONDON	HL 8227	£ 9 – 12
57	Kiss in your eyes/Your kisses kill me	H.M.V.	POP	400	£ 4 – 6
58ø	Love me forever/Until they sail		POP	432	£ 6 – 9
58	You need hands/The gentleman is a dope		POP	493	£ 2 – 4
58	Gotta have rain/To you, from me		POP	513	£ 2 – 4
58	Dormi, dormi, dormi/Be careful, it's my heart		POP	529	£ 2 – 4
59	Separate tables/The voice in my heart		POP	577	£ 2 – 4
59	I'm yours/Don't take your love from me		POP	616	£ 2 – 4
60	The dance is over/Too young to know		POP	767	£ 2 – 4

CHARLIE GRACIE
57ø	Butterfly/Ninety—nine ways	PARLOPHONE	R 4290	£12 – 18
57ø	Fabulous/Just lookin'		R 4313	£12 – 18
57ø	Wandering eyes/I love you so much it hurts	LONDON	HL 8467	£ 9 – 12
57ø	Cool baby/You got a heart like a rock		HLU 8521	£12 – 18
58	Crazy girl/Dressin' up		HLU 8596	£12 – 18
59	Hurry up, Buttercup/Doodlebug	CORAL	Q 72362	£ 9 – 12
59	Angel of love/I'm a fool, that's why		Q 72373	£ 9 – 12
59	Oh—well—a/Because I love you so		Q 72381	£ 9 – 12
60	The race/I look for you	COLUMBIA	DB 4477	£ 9 – 12

KENNY GRAHAM'S AFRO—CUBISTS
60	Bongo chant/Beguine	STARLITE	ST.45 013	£ 2 – 4

LOU GRAHAM
58	Wee Willie Brown/You were mean baby	CORAL	Q 72322	£60 – 90

RON GRAINER & HIS MUSIC
60	The Maigret theme/Along the boulevards	WARNER—B	WB 24	£ 2 – 4

BILLY GRAMMER
58	Gotta travel on/Chasing a dream	LONDON	HLU 8752	£ 6 – 9
59	Bonaparte's retreat/The kissing tree	FELSTED	AF 121	£ 6 – 9
59	Willy, quit your playing/It takes you		AF 128	£ 4 – 6

GERRY GRANAHAN
58	No chemise, please/Girl of my dreams	LONDON	HL 8668	£12 – 18
60	It hurts/RICHIE ROBIN: Strange dreams	TOP RANK	JAR 262	£ 4 – 6

EARL GRANT

58	The end/Hunky dunky doo	BRUNSWICK	05762	£ 2 — 4
59	Evening rain/Kathy-O		05779	£ 2 — 4
59	Imitation of life/Last night (I went out of my mind) ..		05792	£ 2 — 4
60	House of bamboo/Two loves have I		05824	£12 — 18
60	Building castles/Not one minute more		05841	£ 2 — 4

GOGI GRANT

55	Suddenly there's a valley/Love is	LONDON	HLB 8192	£12 — 18
56	Who are we/We believe in love		HLB 8257	£12 — 18
56ø	Wayward wind/No more than forever		HLB 8282	£12 — 18
57	You're in love/When the tide is high		HLB 8364	£ 9 — 12
58	It's a wonderful thing to../What a beautiful combination	R.C.A.	RCA 1038	£ 2 — 4
58	The golden ladder/All of me	LONDON	HLB 8550	£ 6 — 9
58	Bonjour tristesse/Johnny's dream	R.C.A.	RCA 1047	£ 2 — 4
59	Say a prayer for me tonight/(by TONY MARTIN)		RCA 1101	£ 2 — 4
59	Kiss me Honey, Honey kiss me/Two dreams		RCA 1105	£ 4 — 6
60	Goin' home/I'm going to live the life	LONDON	HLG 9185	£ 2 — 4

DOLORES GRAY

55	After you get what you want, you don't want it/Heat wave	BRUNSWICK	05382	£ 4 — 6
55	Rock love/One		05407	£ 6 — 9
57	There'll be some changes made/Fool's errand	CAPITOL	CL 14732	£ 4 — 6
57	I'm innocent/My Mama likes you		CL 14770	£ 2 — 4

JERRY GRAY & HIS ORCH.

54	The ooh and ah mambo/Kettle drum hop	BRUNSWICK	05351	£ 2 — 4

JOHNNIE (The Gash) GRAY

58	Tequila/Big guitar	FONTANA	H 123	£ 4 — 6
58	Apache/Zach's tune		H 134	£ 4 — 6

OWEN GRAY

60	Far love/Please let me go	STARLITE	ST.45 015	£ 4 — 6
60	Jenny Lee/The plea		ST.45 019	£ 6 — 9

KATHRYN GRAYSON (*& HOWARD KEEL/+ANN MILLER & TOMMY RALL)

53	(All of a sudden) My heart sings/Jealousy	M-G-M	SP 1002	£ 2 — 4
53	Why do I love you/Make believe		*SP 1003	£ 2 — 4
53	Smoke gets in your eyes/The touch of your hand*/etc. ..		SP 1014	£ 2 — 4
54	So in love*/ANN MILLER: Too darn hot		SP 1076	£ 2 — 4
54	We open in Venice*+/Wunderbar*/HOWARD KEEL: Were thine..		SP 1077	£ 2 — 4
54	I hate men/A.MILLER & T.RALL: Always true to you in my..		SP 1078	£ 2 — 4
54	So kiss me Kate*/(by ANN MILLER/KEENAN WYNN/etc.)		SP 1079	£ 2 — 4

MILTON GRAYSON

60	Forget you/The puppet	LONDON	HLU 9068	£ 2 — 4

RUDY GRAYZELL

54	Looking at the Moon and wishing../The heart that once...	LONDON	HL 8094	£12 — 18

BUDDY GRECO (qv JOHNNY DESMOND)

56	They didn't believe me/Here I am in love again	V-CORAL	Q 72192	£ 2 — 4
57	Paris loves lovers/Ain't no in between		Q 72268	£ 2 — 4
57	With all my heart/Game of love	LONDON	HLR 8452	£ 4 — 6
58	I've grown accustomed to her face/On the street where...		HLR 8613	£ 2 — 4
60ø	The lady is a tramp/Like young	FONTANA	H 255	£ 2 — 4

BERNIE GREEN & HIS MIS-LED ORCH.

60	Clinkerated chimes/Give me that good old progressive....	R.C.A.	RCA 1173	£ 2 — 4

PHILIP GREEN & THE PINEWOOD STUDIO ORCH. (*& JOHNNY DANKWORTH)

59	Sapphire*/Tiger Bay	TOP RANK	JAR 112	£ 2 — 4
60	"League Of Gentlemen" march/"Golden Fleece" theme		JAR 355	£ 2 — 4

LEE GREENLEE
59 Starlight/Cherry, I'm in love with you .... TOP RANK JAR 226   £ 2 - 4

GINNY GREER
57 Five oranges, four apples/Kiss me hello (but never.....) BRUNSWICK   05673   £ 2 - 4

IAN GREGORY
60ø Time will tell/The night you told a lie .... PYE   7N 15295 £ 6 - 9

JOHNNY GREGORY & HIS ORCH./*CASCADING STRINGS (qv CHAQUITO)
60 Honky tonk train blues/"Sons And Lovers" theme .... FONTANA   *H 251   £ 2 - 4
60 Bonanza/Maverick ....   H 286   £ 2 - 4

JOEL GREY
57 Everytime I ask my heart/Moonlight swim .... CAPITOL CL 14779 £ 2 - 4
58 Shoppin' around/Be my next .... CL 14832 £ 2 - 4

RONNIE GREY & THE JETS
55 Run, Manny, run/Sweet baby .... CAPITOL CL 14329 £ 6 - 9

THE GRIFFIN BROTHERS' ORCH. (*& TOMMY BROWN)
52 Weepin' and cryin'*/The teaser boogie .... VOGUE   V 2139 º £ 9 - 12

ANDY GRIFFITH
55 Ko Ko Mo (I love you so)/Make yourself comfortable .... CAPITOL CL 14263 £ 6 - 9
56 No time for Sergeants/Make yourself comfortable .... CL 14619 £ 4 - 6
57 Mama Guitar/A face in the crowd .... CL 14766 £ 6 - 9
58 Midnight Special/She's bad, bad business .... CL 14936 £ 4 - 6
59 Hamlet (both sides) .... CL 15003 £ 2 - 4

TINY GRIMES & HIS R&B QUINTET
54 Annie Laurie/Hot in Harlem .... ESQUIRE   10-349 º £ 6 - 9

GROUP ONE
58 She's neat/Made for each other .... H.M.V.   POP 463 £ 6 - 9
58 Chanson d'amour/Londonderry air .... POP 492 £ 2 - 4

GROUP SIX
59 Rock-a-boogie/Rockin' the blues .... ORIOLE   CB 1488 £ 4 - 6

HARRY GROVE & HIS MUSIC
54 Song of "The Maggie"/Wanderlust .... DECCA   F 10267 £ 2 - 4

BONNIE GUITAR
58 A very precious love/Johnny Vagabond .... LONDON   HLD 8591 £ 4 - 6
59 Candy apple red/Come to me, I love you .... TOP RANK JAR 260 £ 2 - 4

JIM GUNNER & THE ECHOES
60 Hoolee jump/Footloose .... DECCA   F 11276 £ 4 - 6

HARDROCK GUNTER (qv ROBERTA LEE)
52 Silver and gold/The Senator from Tennessee .... BRUNSWICK 04907 º £ 9 - 12

WOODY GUTHRIE
51 Ramblin' blues/Talkin' Columbia blues .... MELODISC   1141 º £ 4 - 6

JOAN HAGER
57 Happy is a girl named me/Run darlin', don't walk ...... BRUNSWICK   05650   £ 2 - 4

JOYCE HAHN
57 Gonna find me a bluebird/I saw you, I saw you .... LONDON   HLA 8453 £ 6 - 9

. **THE HAL HOPPERS**
54 More love/Do nothin' blues .... LONDON   HL 8107 £12 - 18
55 Mother of pearl/Baby I've had it .... HL 8129 £12 - 18

- 90 -

DENNIS HALE (qv JACK PARNELL)

55	The butterscotch mop/S'posin'	PARLOPHONE	MSP 6153	£ 2 - 4
55	Sweet and gentle/Walk with me forever	DECCA	F 10554	£ 2 - 4
55	The longest walk/Tina Marie		F 10623	£ 2 - 4
56	It's almost tomorrow/Stealin'		F 10674	£ 2 - 4

TERENCE HOLDERWAY HALE

60	My New Year's Eve/Beauty and the beast	FONTANA	H 285	£ 2 - 4

BILL HALEY & HIS COMETS (qv THE KINGSMEN)

53	Crazy man, crazy/Whatcha gonna do	LONDON	L 1190 ª	£18 - 25
53	Pat-a-cake/Fractured		L 1216 ª	£18 - 25
54ø	Rock around the clock/Thirteen women	BRUNSWICK	05317 ª	£ 4 - 6
54ø	Shake, rattle and roll/A.B.C. boogie		05338	£25 - 40
55ø	Rock around the clock/Thirteen women		05317	£25 - 40
55	Happy baby/Dim, dim the lights		05373	£18 - 25
55ø	Mambo rock/Birth of the boogie		05405	£18 - 25
55	Green tree boogie/Sundown boogie	LONDON HL	8142	£60 - 90
55ø	Razzle dazzle/Two hound dogs	BRUNSWICK	05453	£18 - 25
55	Farewell, so long, goodbye/I'll be true	LONDON HLF	8161	£60 - 90
55	Rocking chair on the Moon/Ten little Indians	HLF	8194	£60 - 90
55ø	Rock-a-beatin' boogie/Burn that candle	BRUNSWICK	05509	£12 - 18
56ø	See you later, alligator/The paper boy		05530	£12 - 18
56ø	The Saints rock 'n roll/R-O-C-K		05565	£12 - 18
56ø	Rockin' through the rye/Hot dog buddy buddy		05582	£12 - 18
56	I'm gonna dry every tear with a.../Why do I cry over you	MELODISC	1376 ª	£12 - 18
56ø	Rip it up/Teenagers' Mother	BRUNSWICK	05615	£12 - 18
56ø	Rudy's rock/Blue Comet blues		05616	£12 - 18
57ø	Rock the joint/Yes indeed!	LONDON HLF	8371	£40 - 60
57ø	Don't knock the rock/Calling all Comets	BRUNSWICK	05640	£12 - 18
57	Hook, line and sinker/Goofin' around		05641	£12 - 18
57	Forty cups of coffee/Choo choo ch'boogie		05658	£12 - 18
57	(You hit the wrong....) Billy goat/Rockin' rollin' Rover		05688	£12 - 18
57	Miss you/The dipsy doodle		05719	£18 - 25
58	It's a sin/Mary, Mary Lou		05735	£ 9 - 12
58	Skinny Minnie/How many		05742	£ 9 - 12
58	Lean Jean/Don't nobody move		05752	£ 6 - 9
58	Whoa Mabel!/Chiquita Linda		05766	£ 6 - 9
59	I got a woman/Charmaine		05788	£ 6 - 9
59	Shaky/Caldonia		05805	£ 6 - 9
59	Joey's song/Ooh looka there, ain't she pretty		05810	£ 6 - 9
60	Puerto Rican peddler/Skokiaan		05818	£ 6 - 9
60	Tamiami/Candy kisses	WARNER-B	WB 6	£ 4 - 6

EDMOND HALL

60	Lover/African fu-fu	TOP RANK	TR 5019	£ 2 - 4

LARRY HALL

60	Sandy/Lovin' tree	PARLOPHONE	R 4625	£ 2 - 4

RENE HALL'S ORCHESTRA

58	Twitchy/Flippin'	LONDON	HLU 8581	£12 - 18

ROBIN HALL & JIMMIE MACGREGOR

60	Football crazy/Rosin the beau	COLLECTOR	JDS 3	£ 2 - 4
60	*as above*	DECCA	F 11266	£ 2 - 4

ROY HALL

56	See you later, alligator/Don't stop now	BRUNSWICK	05531	£90 -120
56	Blue suede shoes/Luscious		05555	£60 - 90
56	Three alley cats/Diggin' the boogie		05627	£90 -120

THE HALLELUJAH SKIFFLE GROUP (qv CLINTON FORD)

58	I saw the light/A closer walk with Thee	ORIOLE	CB 1429	£ 4 - 6

STUART HAMBLEN
56	Hell train/A few things to remember	H.M.V.	7M	394	£ 4 — 6

CHICO HAMILTON QUINTET
57	The sage/The morning after	VOGUE	V	2407	£ 2 — 4

GEORGE HAMILTON IV
57	A rose and a candy bar/If you don't know	LONDON	HL	8361	£40 — 60
57ø	Why don't they understand/Even tho'	H.M.V.	POP	429	£ 4 — 6
58	Now and for always/One heart		POP	474	£ 2 — 4
58ø	I know where I'm goin'/Who's taking you to the Prom? ..		POP	505	£ 2 — 4
58	When will I know?/Your cheatin' heart		POP	534	£ 2 — 4
60	Before this day ends/Loneliness all around us		POP	813	£ 4 — 6

ROY HAMILTON
55	You'll never walk alone/If I loved you	PHILIPS	PB	368 º	£ 4 — 6
55	Unchained melody/From here to eternity		PB	448 º	£ 4 — 6
55	Forgive this fool/You wanted to change me		PB	515 º	£ 4 — 6
56	Without a song/Cuban love song		PB	551 º	£ 4 — 6
56	Walk along with Kings/There goes my heart		PB	583 º	£ 4 — 6
58	Don't let go/All of a sudden my heart sings	FONTANA	H	113	£ 9 — 12
58	Crazy feelin'/In a dream		H	143	£ 9 — 12
59	Pledging my love/My one and only love		H	180	£ 9 — 12
59	I need your lovin'/Somewhere along the way		H	193	£ 6 — 9

RUSS HAMILTON
57ø	We will make love/Rainbow	ORIOLE	CB	1359	£ 4 — 6
57ø	Wedding ring/I still belong to you		CB	1388	£ 4 — 6
57	I don't know why/My Mother's eyes		CB	1406	£ 2 — 4
58	Little one/I had a dream		CB	1404	£ 2 — 4
58	Tip—toe through the tulips/Drifting and dreaming		CB	1451	£ 2 — 4
58	I wonder who's kissing her now/September in the rain ..		CB	1459	£ 2 — 4
58	Strange are the ways of love/Things I didn't say		CB	1465	£ 2 — 4
59	The reprieve of Tom Dooley/Dreaming of you		CB	1492	£ 2 — 4
59	My unbreakable heart/I found you		CB	1506	£ 2 — 4
59	Smile, smile, smile and sing, sing, sing/Shadow		CB	1508	£ 2 — 4
60	Things no money can buy/Mama		CB	1527	£ 2 — 4
60	Folks get married in the Spring/It's a sin to tell a lie		CB	1531	£ 2 — 4
60	Gonna find me a bluebird/Choir girl	M—G—M	MGM	1096	£ 2 — 4

CURLEY HAMNER
59	Twistin' and turnin'/King and Queen	FELSTED	SD	80061	£ 4 — 6

LIONEL HAMPTON & HIS HAMP—TONES/*JUST JAZZ ALL STARS (+& SONNIE PARKER)
52	Samson's boogie/Helpless+	M—G—M	MGM	468 º	£ 6 — 9
57	Perdido/Flying home	VOGUE	*V	2405	£ 4 — 6
57	Hamp's boogie woogie/Blues		*V	2406	£ 9 — 12

WAYNE HANDY (*& THE KING SISTERS)
58	Say yeah/Could it be*	LONDON	HL	8547	£60 — 90

PAUL HANFORD
60	Itsy bitsy teenie weenie yellow../Why have you changed..	PARLOPHONE	R	4680	£ 2 — 4
60	Ev'ry little girl/If you ain't got love			R 4694	£ 2 — 4

PETER HANLEY
56	I love you, Samantha/I wanna see you when you weep	H.M.V.	POP	279	£ 2 — 4

THE HAPPY WANDERERS
60	White Christmas/Jingle bells	STARLITE	ST.45 027		£ 2 — 4

RON HARGRAVE
57	Latch on/Only a daydream	M—G—M	MGM	956	£200 +

REMEMBER! — THE SYMBOL ø AFTER THE YEAR OF ISSUE INDICATES A BRITISH CHART ENTRY

DON HARPER SEXTET
58 Hi-diddle-fiddle/It's the bluest kind of blues .... PYE JAZZ 7NJ 2024 £ 2 - 4

JANICE HARPER
57 Bon voyage/Tell me that you love me tonight .... H.M.V. POP 376 £ 2 - 4
58 Devotion/In time .... CAPITOL CL 14899 £ 2 - 4
59 I was hoping you'd ask me/I'm making love to you ...... CL 14977 £ 2 - 4
59 Let me call you sweetheart/Just whistle .... CL 15026 £ 2 - 4
60 Forever, forever/Just say I love him .... CL 15125 £ 2 - 4
60 Only once/Love me now, love me never .... CL 15159 £ 2 - 4

JOE "HARMONICA" HARPER
58 Lazy train/Her lips were like velvet .... M-G-M MGM 983 £ 2 - 4

THE HARRIS SISTERS
55 We've been walkin' all night/Kissin' bug .... CAPITOL CL 14232 £ 9 - 12

MAX HARRIS & HIS GROUP
60ø Gurney Slade/Hat and cane .... FONTANA H 282 £ 2 - 4

PHIL HARRIS
51 Southern fried boogie/Oh, what a face .... H.M.V. B 10067 º £ 4 - 6
54 Take your girlie to the movies/I know an old lady ..... 7M 199 £ 4 - 6
54 I guess I'll have to change my plan/The Persian kitten 7M 231 £ 4 - 6
55 I wouldn't touch you with a ten-.../There's a lot more.. 7M 289 £ 4 - 6

ROLF HARRIS
60ø Tie me kangaroo down sport/Nick Teen and Al K. Hall ... COLUMBIA DB 4483 £ 2 - 4
60 Tame Eagle/Uncomfortable Yogi .... DB 4556 £ 2 - 4

RONNIE HARRIS (& *THE CORONETS/+RUSS CONWAY/qv RAY BURNS)
54ø The story of Tina/Guiding star .... COLUMBIA DB 3499 º £ 2 - 4
54 Hold my hand/No one can change destiny .... SCM 5138 £ 4 - 6
54 I love Paris/I still believe .... SCM 5139 £ 4 - 6
55 Don't go to strangers/Surprisngly .... *SCM 5159 £ 4 - 6
55 Stranger in Paradise/I wonder .... SCM 5176 £ 4 - 6
55 Hello, Mrs. Jones (is Mary there?)/I know you love me . SCM 5178 £ 4 - 6
55 On the way to your heart/Maria, Maria, Maria .... SCM 5189 £ 4 - 6
55 Cabaret/United .... SCM 5206 £ 4 - 6
56 I've changed my mind a thousand times/Come to me* ..... SCM 5242 £ 4 - 6
56 What is the reason?/Aurora .... SCM 5266 £ 4 - 6
56 Cry upon my shoulder/Tell me why .... DB 3814 £ 2 - 4
56 That's right/A house with love in it .... DB 3836 £ 4 - 6
57 Armen's theme (Yesterday and you)/Dancing chandelier .. DB 3877 £ 2 - 4
57 Dear to me/It's not for me to say+ .... DB 3934 £ 2 - 4
57 Let me be loved/Day by day .... DB 4007 £ 2 - 4

THURSTON HARRIS (& *THE SHARPS/+THE MASTERS)
57 Little bitty pretty one/I hope you won't hold it........ VOGUE *V 9092 £40 - 60
58 Do what you did/I'm asking forgiveness .... *V 9098 £60 - 90
58 Be Baba Leba/I'm out to getcha .... V 9108 £60 - 90
58 Smokey Joe's/Only one love is blessed .... V 9122 £18 - 25
58 Over somebody else's shoulder/Tears from my heart ..... V 9127 £18 - 25
59 Purple stew+/I hear a rhapsody .... V 9139 £18 - 25
59 You don't know how much I...../In the bottom of my heart V 9144 £18 - 25
59 Hey little girl/My love will last .... V 9146 £25 - 40
59 Runk bunk/Bless your heart .... V 9149 £40 - 60
59 Slip-slop/Paradise Hill .... V 9151 £40 - 60

WEE WILLIE HARRIS
57 Back to school again/Rockin' at the Two I's .... DECCA F 10970 £12 - 18
58 Love bug crawl/Rosie Lee .... F 10980 £12 - 18
58 Got a match/No chemise, please .... F 11044 £ 9 - 12
60 Wild one/Little bitty girl .... F 11217 £ 9 - 12

WYNONIE "Mr. Blues" HARRIS (& HIS ORCH.)

51	All she wants to do is rock/Drinking wine, spo-dee-o-dee	VOGUE	V	2006	º	£12 – 18
52	Lovin' machine/Luscious woman		V	2111	º	£12 – 18
52	Bloodshot eyes/Lollipop Mama		V	2127	º	£ 9 – 12
52	Good morning Judge/Just like two drops of water		V	2128	º	£ 9 – 12
52	Do it again please/Night train		V	2133	º	£ 9 – 12
52	Put it back/Rock, Mr. Blues		V	2134	º	£ 9 – 12
52	Teardrops from my eyes/Keep on churnin'		V	2144	º	£ 9 – 12
53	Adam, come and get your rib!/I like my baby's pudding .		V	2166	º	£12 – 18
56	Bloodshot eyes/Lollipop Mama		V	2127		£25 – 40

WILBERT HARRISON

59	Kansas City/Listen, my darling	TOP RANK	JAR 132	£ 9 – 12

DERRY HART & THE HARTBEATS

59	Nowhere in this world/Come on baby	DECCA	F 11138	£ 9 – 12

HARVEY (Fuqua) & THE MOONGLOWS (qv ETTA & HARVEY)

58	Ten commandments of love/Mean old blues	LONDON	HLM 8730	£40 – 60

THE HARVEY BOYS

57	Nothing is too good for you/Marina girl	LONDON	HLA 8397	£12 – 18

JACK HASKELL (*& THE HONEY-DREAMERS)

57	Around the world/Away out West	LONDON	HL 8426	£ 6 – 9
58	The night of the Senior Prom/Hungry for love	ORIOLE	*CB 1442	£ 2 – 4

PAT HAWES w. DAVE CAREY'S RHYTHM

56	Snowy morning blues/Sheik of Araby	TEMPO	A 141	£ 2 – 4

TOMMY HAWKE

60	Good gravy (I'm in love again)/Umpteen years (and a....)	TOP RANK	JAR 348	£ 4 – 6

THE HAWKEYES

57	Someone someday/Who is he?	CAPITOL	CL 14764	£ 2 – 4

COLEMAN HAWKINS

55	Lucky duck/Bye 'n' bye	BRUNSWICK	05459	£ 4 – 6

DALE HAWKINS

57	Susie-Q/Don't treat me that way	LONDON	HL 8482	£60 – 90
58	La-do-dada/Cross ties		HLM 8728	£12 – 18
59	Yea-yea/Lonely nights		HLM 8842	£12 – 18
59	Liza Jane/Back to school blues		HLM 9016	£12 – 18
60	Hot dog/Our turn		HLM 9060	£12 – 18

HAWKSHAW HAWKINS

51	Doghouse boogie/Yesterday's kisses	VOGUE	V 9003 º	£ 6 – 9
51	Slow coach/Two roads		V 9027 º	£ 4 – 6

SCREAMIN' JAY HAWKINS

58	Little demon/I put a spell on you	FONTANA	H 107 º	£12 – 18

RONNIE HAWKINS & THE HAWKS

59	Forty days/One of these days	COLUMBIA	DB 4319	£12 – 18
59	Mary Lou/Need your lovin' (Oh so bad)		DB 4345	£12 – 18
60	Southern love (What-cha-gonna' do)/Love me like you can		DB 4412	£ 9 – 12
60	Clara/Lonely hours		DB 4442	£12 – 18

SAM HAWKINS

60	No time for tears/Let me be	BRUNSWICK	05834	£ 2 – 4

(Johnny) HAWKSWORTH - (Ronnie) VERRELL JAZZ GROUP (qv JOHNNY'S JAZZ)

56	Ring dem bells/Always	DECCA	FJ 10726	£ 2 – 4

BILL HAYES

53	The donkey song/My ever-lovin'	M-G-M	SP 1036	£ 4 - 6
55	The berry tree/Blue black hair	LONDON	HL 8149	£12 - 18
56ø	Ballad of Davy Crockett/Farewell		HLA 8220	£12 - 18
56	Kwela kwela/The white buffalo		HLA 8239	£ 9 - 12
56	Das ist musik/I know an old lady		HLA 8300	£ 9 - 12
56	The legend of Wyatt Earp/That do make it nice		HLA 8325	£ 9 - 12
57	Wringle wrangle/Westward ho the wagons		HL 8430	£ 9 - 12
59	Wimoweh/Goin' down the road feelin' bad		HLR 8833	£ 6 - 9

BRUCE HAYES w. MARY MAYO & JERRY GRAFF SINGERS

60	"Gather Round Eva'body And Sing" medley	TOP RANK	TR 5016	£ 2 - 4

LINDA HAYES (& *THE PLATTERS/+TONY WILLIAMS)

55	Please have mercy*/Oochi pachi+	PARLOPHONE	MSP 6174	£60 - 90

PETER LIND HAYES

60	Life gets tee-jus, don't it?/Sing me a happy song	BRUNSWICK	05821	£ 2 - 4

TUBBY HAYES QUINTET

57	Ode to Ernie/No, I Woodyn't	TEMPO	A 148	£ 2 - 4

DICK HAYMES

56	You'll never know/Love walked in	CAPITOL	CL 14618	£ 2 - 4
56	Two different worlds/Love is a great big nothin'		CL 14659	£ 2 - 4
57	Never leave me/New York's my home		CL 14674	£ 2 - 4
57	C'est la vie/Now at last		CL 14720	£ 2 - 4

LEE HAZLEWOOD w. DUANE EDDY

60	Words mean nothing/The girl on Death Row	LONDON	HLW 9223	£ 6 - 9

THE HEADLINERS

59	The bubble car song/Andy's theme	PARLOPHONE	R 4593	£ 2 - 4

TED HEATH & HIS MUSIC (qv W. ATWELL/B. BRITTON/M. BYGRAVES/JOHNSTON BROS./ANNETTE
KLOOGER/KATHY LLOYD/D. LOTIS/J. REGAN/LITA ROZA/MEL TORME/VARIOUS ARTISTS)

52ø	Vanessa/The pipers' patrol	DECCA	F 9983 º	£ 2 - 4
53ø	Hot toddy/Strike up the band		F 10093 º	£ 2 - 4
53ø	Dragnet/Sloppy Joe		F 10176 º	£ 2 - 4
54	Seven eleven/Lullaby of Birdland		F 10200	£ 4 - 6
54	The creep/Slim Jim - Creep		F 10222	£ 4 - 6
54ø	Skin deep/Walking shoes		F 10246	£ 6 - 9
54	Viva Verrell/Holiday for strings		F 10272	£ 4 - 6
54	Lush slide/Fascinating rhythm		F 10273	£ 4 - 6
54	Dig deep/Asia Minor		F 10425	£ 4 - 6
55	Peg o' my heart (Mambo)/In the mood (for mambo)		F 10447	£ 4 - 6
55	Haitian ritual/Late night final		F 10477	£ 4 - 6
55	Bell bell boogie/Amethyst		F 10540	£ 4 - 6
55	Barber shop jump/Look for the silver lining		F 10590	£ 2 - 4
55	Malaguena/Cloudburst		F 10624	£ 2 - 4
56	The man with the golden arm/Paris by night		F 10683	£ 2 - 4
56ø	The faithful Hussar/Siboney		F 10746	£ 4 - 6
58ø	Swingin' shepherd blues/Raunchy		F 11000	£ 2 - 4
58ø	Tequila/Little serenade		F 11003	£ 2 - 4
58ø	Tom Hark/Cha cha baby		F 11025	£ 2 - 4

RONNIE HEIGHT

59	Come softly to me/So young, so wise	DECCA	F 11126	£ 2 - 4
60	The one finger symphony/Mem'ries and habits	LONDON	HLN 9144	£ 2 - 4

BOBBY HELMS

57	Fraulein/(Got a) Heartsick feeling	BRUNSWICK	05711	£ 4 - 6
57ø	My special angel/Standing at the end of my world		05721	£ 6 - 9
58ø	No other baby/The magic song		05730	£ 6 - 9
58	Love my lady/Just a little lonesome		05741	£ 4 - 6
58ø	Jacqueline/Living in the shadow of the past		05748	£ 4 - 6

58	Schoolboy crush/Borrowed dreams			05754	£ 6 - 9
58	Jingle bell rock/Captain Santa Claus			05765	£ 9 - 12
59	New River train/Miss Memory			05786	£ 2 - 4
59	I guess I'll miss the prom/Soon it can be told			05801	£ 2 - 4
59	My lucky day/Hurry baby			05813	£ 2 - 4

BILL HENDERSON

60	Sweet pumpkin/Joey, Joey, Joey	TOP RANK	JAR 412	£ 4 - 6

JOE "MR. PIANO" HENDERSON

55ø	"Sing It With Joe" medley	POLYGON	P 1167 º	£ 2 - 4
55ø	"Sing It Again With Joe" medley		P 1184 º	£ 2 - 4
57	Coffee bar jive/Forgotten dreams	PYE	*N 15099 º	£ 4 - 6
58ø	Trudie/Love is the sweetest thing		7N 15147	£ 2 - 4
59ø	Treble chance/Flirtation waltz		7N 15224	£ 1 - 2
60ø	Ooh! la! la!/Mitzi		7N 15257	£ 1 - 2

LORNA HENDERSON

60	Lollipops to lipstick/Steady Eddy	ORIOLE	CB 1549	£ 2 - 4
60	A thousand stars/Murray, what's your hurry?		CB 1590	£ 2 - 4

RUSS HENDERSON & HIS CALYPSO BAND

57	Waiting for the coconuts to fall/Nobody's business	H.M.V.	POP 333	£ 2 - 4

BOBBY HENDRICKS

58	Itchy twitchy feeling/A thousand dreams	LONDON	HL 8714	£12 - 18
59	Little John Green/Sincerely, your lover	TOP RANK	JAR 193	£ 4 - 6

JON HENDRICKS

56	Four brothers/Cloudburst	BRUNSWICK	05521	£ 2 - 4

ANN HENRY

60	Sugar blues/Like young	TOP RANK	JAR 292	£ 2 - 4

CLARENCE HENRY

57	Ain't got no home/Troubles troubles	LONDON	HLN 8389	£60 - 90

HERB & KAY

54	This ole house/Angels in the sky	PARLOPHONE	MSP 6127	£ 6 - 9

WOODY HERMAN & HIS ORCH./THIRD HERD/etc. (*& THE ALLEN SISTERS/qv DAVID ROSE)

54	Wooftie/Moten stomp	LONDON	HL 8013	£12 - 18
54	Fancy woman/Eight babies to mind		HL 8031	£12 - 18
54	Woodchopper's mambo/Muskrat ramble	CAPITOL	CL 14183	£ 4 - 6
55	Sorry 'bout the whole darned thing/Love's a dog	LONDON	HL 8122	£12 - 18
55	Mexican hat trick/Sleepy serenade	CAPITOL	CL 14231	£ 4 - 6
55	My sin is you/Have it your way		*CL 14278	£ 4 - 6
55	Kiss the baby/Long, long night		CL 14299	£ 4 - 6
55	The girl upstairs/You're here, my love		CL 14333	£ 4 - 6
55	Love is a many splendored thing/House of bamboo		CL 14366	£ 4 - 6
56	Skinned/Skinned again		CL 14522	£ 2 - 4
56	To love again/For all we know		CL 14578	£ 2 - 4
57	Comes love/Makin' whoopee	H.M.V.	POP 371	£ 2 - 4
59	Blowin' up a storm/It's coolin' time	TOP RANK	TR 5012	£ 2 - 4
60	The Third Herd/Keen and peachy	PHILIPS	JAZ 113	£ 2 - 4

EVERIT HERTER

60	Don't get serious/Boys were made for girls	CAPITOL	CL 15142	£ 2 - 4

THE HEWETT SISTERS

59	Baby-O/Jerri-Lee (I love him so)	H.M.V.	POP 567	£ 4 - 6

BEN HEWITT

59	I ain't givin' up nothin'/You break me up	MERCURY	AMT 1041	£12 - 18
59	Patricia June/For quite a while		AMT 1055	£ 9 - 12
60	I want a new girl now/My search		AMT 1084	£18 - 25

ANNE HEYWOOD
59 Love is/I'd rather have roses (than riches) .... TOP RANK JAR 130 £ 2 - 4

EDDIE HEYWOOD
58 Soft Summer breeze/Heywood's bounce .... MERCURY 7MT 131 £ 4 - 6

JIMMY HEYWORTH & HIS ASTORIA ORCH.
54 I get a kick out of you/April in Paris .... DECCA F 10433 £ 2 - 4

THE HI-FI FOUR
56 Band of gold/Davy, you upset my life .... PARLOPHONE MSP 6210 £40 - 60

THE HI-LITERS
58 Dance me to death/Cha cha rock .... MERCURY AMT 1011 £25 - 40

THE HI-SPOTS
58 Lend me your comb/I don't hurt anymore .... MELODISC 1457 £ 6 - 9
58 Secretly/I got .... 1473 £ 4 - 6

AL HIBBLER
55ø Unchained melody/Daybreak .... BRUNSWICK 05420 £ 9 - 12
55 They say you're laughing at me/I can't put my arms...... 05454 £ 2 - 4
55 Now I lay me down to dream/Danny boy .... LONDON HL 8184 £12 - 18
55 He/Breeze (blow my baby back to me) .... BRUNSWICK 05492 £ 2 - 4
56 The eleventh hour melody/Let's try again .... 05523 £ 2 - 4
56 After the lights go down low/Stella by starlight ...... 05552 £ 2 - 4
56 Away all boats/Never turn back .... 05590 £ 2 - 4
56 Nightfall/I'm free .... 05619 £ 2 - 4
57 The town crier/Trees .... 05653 £ 2 - 4
57 I complain/Around the corner from the blues .... 05703 £ 2 - 4
58 When will I forget you/My heart tells me .... 05739 £ 2 - 4
58 Honeysuckle rose/Ain't nothing wrong with that baby ... 05749 £ 2 - 4
58 Love me long, hold me close, kiss me warm...../Love land 05768 £ 2 - 4

EDDIE HICKEY
59 Lady May/Cap and gown .... DECCA F 11153 £ 2 - 4
60 Who could be bluer/Plain Jane .... F 11204 £ 2 - 4
60 Another sleepless night/Barbara .... F 11241 £ 2 - 4

ERSEL HICKEY
59 You threw a dart/Don't be afraid of love .... FONTANA H 198 £12 - 18

DWAYNE HICKMAN
60 I'm a lover, not a fighter/I pass your house .... CAPITOL CL 15164 £ 4 - 6

COLIN HICKS (& HIS CABIN BOYS)
57 Wild eyes and tender lips/Empty arms blues .... PYE 7N 15114 £ 6 - 9
58 La dee dah/Wasteland .... 7N 15125 £ 6 - 9
58 Little boy blue/Jambalaya .... 7N 15163 £ 4 - 6

HIGGS & WILSON
60 Manny, ho/When you tell my baby .... BLUE BEAT BB 3 £ 6 - 9

DONNA HIGHTOWER
59 Lover, come back to me/Because of you .... CAPITOL CL 15048 £ 2 - 4
59 Ain't that love/Forgive them .... CL 15049 £ 2 - 4

BENNY HILL (*& THE CORONETS)
55 I can't tell a waltz from a tango/Teach me tonight .... DECCA F 10442 £ 6 - 9
56 Who done it/Memories are made of this .... *COLUMBIA SCM 5238 £ 4 - 6

DAVID HILL
57 All shook up/Melody for lovers .... VOGUE V 9076 £18 - 25
58 That's love/Keep me in mind .... R.C.A. RCA 1041 £60 - 90

JESSIE HILL
60	Ooh poo pah doo – Parts 1 & 2	LONDON	HLU 9117	£ 6 –

MICHAEL HILL
60	Joey's song/Juke's jingle	PARLOPHONE	R 4671	£ 2 –
60	Mike's tune/Beatnik boogie		R 4700	£ 2 –

THE HILLTOPPERS
52	Trying/You made up my mind	VOGUE	V 9045 º	£ 4 –
54	From the vine came the grape/Time will tell	LONDON	HL 8026	£18 – 2
54	Poor butterfly/Wrapped up in a dream		HL 8070	£12 – 1
54	Will you remember/The old cabaret		HL 8081	£12 – 1
54	If I didn't care/Bettina		HL 8092	£12 – 1
55	Time waits for no one/You try somebody else		HL 8116	£12 – 1
55	The Kentuckian song/I must be dreaming		HLD 8168	£12 – 1
55	Searching/All I need is you		HLD 8208	£12 – 1
56ø	Only you (and you alone)/Until the real thing comes.....		HLD 8221	£12 – 1
56	My treasure/Last word in love		HLD 8255	£12 – 1
56	Do the bop/When you're alone		HLD 8278	£18 – 2
56ø	Trying/D–A–R–L–I–N'		HLD 8298	£12 – 1
56	So tired/Faded rose		HLD 8333	£12 – 1
57ø	Marianne/You're wasting your time		HLD 8381	£12 – 1
57	I'm serious/I love my girl		HLD 8441	£ 9 – 1
57	A fallen star/Footsteps		HLD 8455	£ 9 – 1
57	The joker/Chicken, chicken		HLD 8528	£12 – 1
58	You sure look good to me/Starry eyes		HLD 8603	£ 6 – 9
60	Alone/The prisoner's song		HLD 9038	£ 4 – 6

RONNIE HILTON (*& ALMA COGAN)
54ø	I still believe/Veni–vedi–vici	H.M.V.	B 10785 º	£ 2 – 4
55ø	A blossom fell/Prize of gold		B 10808 º	£ 2 – 4
55ø	as above		7M 285	£ 9 – 12
55	My loving hands/Just say you love her		7M 303	£ 4 – 6
55ø	Stars shine in your eyes/We'll go a long, long way......		B 10901 º	£ 2 – 4
55ø	The yellow rose of Texas/Have you ever been lonely? ...		B 10924 º	£ 2 – 4
55	He/Bella notte		7M 336	£ 4 – 6
56ø	Young and foolish/Moments to remember		POP 154 º	£ 2 – 4
56ø	as above		7M 358	£ 9 – 12
56	Here comes my love/The last frontier		7M 382	£ 4 – 6
56ø	No other love/It's all been done before*		POP 198 º	£ 2 – 4
56ø	as above		7M 390	£ 9 – 12
56ø	Who are we/Give me my ranch		POP 221 º	£ 2 – 4
56ø	as above		7M 413	£ 9 – 12
56ø	A woman in love/I just found out about love		POP 248	£ 9 – 12
56ø	Two different worlds/Constant and true		POP 274	£ 9 – 12
57	Amore/The wisdom of a fool		POP 291	£ 2 – 4
57	For your love/Once		POP 307	£ 2 – 4
57	Heart/Penny serenade		POP 318	£ 2 – 4
57ø	Around the world/I'd give you the world		POP 338	£ 4 – 6
57ø	Wonderful! Wonderful!/The miracle of love		POP 364	£ 4 – 6
57	Marching along to the blues/She		POP 393	£ 2 – 4
57	That's why I was born/The moonraker's song		POP 422	£ 2 – 4
58	I'll buy you a star/You should belong to me		POP 437	£ 2 – 4
58ø	Magic moments/One blade of grass (in a meadow)		POP 446	£ 4 – 6
58ø	I may never pass this way again/Love walked in		POP 468	£ 4 – 6
58	On the street where you live/I've grown accustomed to...		POP 479	£ 2 – 4
58	Her hair was yellow/Let me stay with you		POP 497	£ 2 – 4
58	The day the rains came/Do I love you (because you're...)		POP 556	£ 2 – 4
58ø	The world outside/As I love you		POP 559	£ 2 – 4
59	Gigi (Gaston's soliloquy)/Keep your kisses		POP 560	£ 2 – 4
59ø	The wonder of you/A hundred miles from everywhere		POP 638	£ 2 – 4
59	Happy anniversary/The most wonderful thing in the world		POP 684	£ 2 – 4
60	I don't know what it is/A simple love		POP 711	£ 2 – 4
60	Mission bell/I'd do anything		POP 770	£ 2 – 4

AL HIRT'S JAZZ BAND

60	Tin roof blues/The original Dixieland one step	H.M.V.	POP 749	£ 2 – 4

LES HOBEAUX

57	Toll the bell easy/Oh, Mary don't you weep	H.M.V.	POP 377	£ 6 – 9
57	Mama don't allow/Hey, hey, Daddy blues		POP 403	£ 6 – 9
58	Dynamo/Two ships		POP 444	£ 9 – 12

EDMUND HOCKRIDGE

53	Luck be a lady/I'll know	PARLOPHONE	MSP 6027	£ 2 – 4
53	I've never been in love before/My time of day		MSP 6028	£ 2 – 4
56ø	Young and foolish/Sixteen tons	PYE	N 15039 º	£ 1 – 2
56ø	No other love/This same heart		N 15048 º	£ 1 – 2
56ø	By the fountains of Rome/I'll need your love		N 15063 º	£ 1 – 2

JOHNNY HODGES & HIS ORCH./*THE ELLINGTON MEN

58	All of me/On the sunny side of the street	H.M.V.	POP 546	£ 2 – 4
60	Waiting for Duke/Don't call me, I'll call you		*POP 748	£ 2 – 4

RON HOLDEN

60	Love you so/My babe	LONDON	HLU 9116	£12 – 18

FRANK HOLDER (qv JOHNNY DANKWORTH)

57	The caterpillar bush/Red beans and rice	DECCA	F 10880	£ 2 – 4
57	Battle of the Century/Chinese cricket match		F 10908	£ 2 – 4
57	Champion calypso/Sweetie Charlie		F 10919	£ 2 – 4

BILLIE HOLIDAY

56	Detour ahead/Blue, turning grey over you	VOGUE	V 2408	£ 4 – 6
59	Don't worry 'bout me/Just one more chance	M-G-M	MGM 1033	£ 4 – 6

CHICO HOLIDAY

59	Young ideas/Cuckoo girl	R.C.A.	RCA 1117	£ 4 – 6

JUDY HOLLIDAY

57	"Full Of Life" theme/These will be the good old days ..	BRUNSWICK	05667	£ 2 – 4

MICHAEL HOLLIDAY

56	Sixteen tons/The rose tattoo	COLUMBIA	SCM 5221	£ 9 – 12
56ø	Nothin' to do/Perfume, candy and flowers		SCM 5252	£ 9 – 12
56ø	The gal with the yaller shoes/Hot diggity (dog ziggity.)		SCM 5273	£ 9 – 12
56ø	Ten thousand miles/The runaway train		DB 3813	£ 9 – 12
57	Yaller yaller gold/I saw Esau		DB 3871	£ 4 – 6
57	My house is your house/Love is strange		DB 3919	£ 4 – 6
57	Wringle wrangle/Four walls		DB 3948	£ 4 – 6
57	All of you/It's the good things we remember		DB 3973	£ 4 – 6
57	Old Cape Cod/Love you darlin'		DB 3992	£ 4 – 6
58ø	The story of my life/Keep your heart		DB 4058	£ 4 – 6
58ø	In love/Rooney		DB 4087	£ 4 – 6
58ø	Stairway of love/May I?		DB 4121	£ 4 – 6
58	I'll always be in love with you/I'll be lovin' you, too		DB 4155	£ 4 – 6
58	She was only seventeen/The gay vagabond		DB 4188	£ 2 – 4
58	My heart is an open book/Careless hands		DB 4216	£ 2 – 4
59	Palace of love/The girls from the County Armagh		DB 4255	£ 2 – 4
59	Moments of love/Dearest		DB 4307	£ 2 – 4
59	For you, for you/Life is a circus		DB 4336	£ 2 – 4
59ø	Starry eyed/The steady game		DB 4378	£ 2 – 4
60ø	Skylark/Dream talk		DB 4437	£ 2 – 4
60ø	Little boy lost/The one-finger symphony		DB 4475	£ 2 – 4
60	Stay in love/Catch me a kiss		DB 4548	£ 2 – 4

STANLEY HOLLOWAY

59	Dark girl dressed in blue/Growing old	DECCA	F 11140	£ 2 – 4
60	Petticoat Lane/Sing a song of London	COLUMBIA	DB 4517	£ 2 – 4
60	Lily of Laguna/A bachelor gay	PYE	7N 15302	£ 2 – 4

BUDDY HOLLY (qv THE CRICKETS)

56	Love me/Blue days – black nights	BRUNSWICK	05581	£90	–120
57ø	Peggy Sue/Everyday	V–CORAL	Q 72293	£12	– 18
58ø	as above	CORAL	Q 72293	£ 6	– 9
58ø	Listen to me/I'm gonna love you too		Q 72288	£ 6	– 9
58ø	Rave on/Take your time		Q 72325	£ 6	– 9
58ø	Early in the morning/Now we're one		Q 72333	£ 6	– 9
58ø	Heartbeat/Well ... all right		Q 72346	£ 6	– 9
59ø	It doesn't matter anymore/Raining in my heart		Q 72360	£ 4	– 6
59ø	Midnight shift/Rock around with Ollie Vee	BRUNSWICK	05800	£12	– 18
59ø	Peggy Sue got married/Crying, waiting, hoping	CORAL	Q 72376	£ 6	– 9
60ø	Heartbeat/Everyday		Q 72392	£ 6	– 9
60ø	as above		Q 72392 ⍾	£ 9	– 12
60ø	True love ways/Moonbeams		Q 72397	£ 4	– 6
60ø	as above		Q 72397 ⍾	£ 9	– 12
60ø	Learning the game/That makes it tough		Q 72411	£ 6	– 9

THE HOLLYWOOD ARGYLES

60ø	Alley–oop/Sho' know a lot about love	LONDON	HLU 9146	£ 9	– 12
60	Gun totin' critter called Jack/GARY PAXTON: Bug–eye	TOP RANK	JAR 530	£ 6	– 9

THE HOLLYWOOD FLAMES

58	Buzz buzz buzz/Crazy	LONDON	HL 8545	£18	– 25
59	Much too much/In the dark		HLW 8955	£12	– 18
60	If I thought you needed me/Every day every way		HLE 9071	£12	– 18

BILL HOLMAN OCTET

54	Cousin Jack/Plain folks	CAPITOL	KC 65000	£ 4	– 6

HOMER & JETHRO

54	Swappin' partners/Crazy mix up song	H.M.V.	7M 211	£ 4	– 6
59	Waterloo/The battle of Kookamonga	R.C.A.	RCA 1148	£ 2	– 4

THE HONEYTONES

58	Don't look now, but –/I know, I know	LONDON	HLX 8671	£12	– 18

ROBBIN HOOD

56	The rock-a-bye blues/Beautiful, beautiful love	M–G–M	SP 1178	£ 2	– 4

JOHN LEE HOOKER

52	Whistlin' and moanin' blues/Hoogie boogie	VOGUE	V 2102 ⍾	£ 9	– 12
54	Need somebody/Too much boogie	LONDON	HL 8037 ⍾	£ 9	– 12

BOB HOPE (& *BING CROSBY/+ROSEMARY CLOONEY)

58	Paris holiday/Nothing in common	LONDON	*HLU 8593	£ 4	– 6
59	Ain't a-hankerin'/Protection	R.C.A.	+RCA 1139	£ 2	– 4

LYN HOPE

57	Blue moon/Blues for Anna Bacoa	VOGUE	V 9081	£ 6	– 9
57	Eleven till two/Blues for Mary		V 9082	£ 6	– 9
58	Temptation/The scrunch		V 9115	£ 6	– 9

THE HOPLITES

58	The stranger/Proud as a peacock	PARLOPHONE	R 4436	£ 2	– 4

LENA HORNE

55	I love to love/Love me or leave me	H.M.V.	7M 309	£ 4	– 6
55	It's love/It's all right with me		7M 319	£ 4	– 6
56	If you can dream/What's right for you (is right for me)		7M 423	£ 2	– 4
56	Can't help lovin' dat man/The man I love	M–G–M	MGM 917	£ 2	– 4
59	A new fangled tango/Honeysuckle rose	R.C.A.	RCA 1120	£ 4	– 6

HANK HORNSBY

57	Pots and pans/Cotton	M–G–M	MGM 955	£ 2	– 4
58	The legend of the birds and the bees/Girls, girls, girls		MGM 972	£ 2	– 4

JOHNNY HORTON

59ø	The Battle of New Orleans/All for the love of a girl ..	PHILIPS	PB 932	£ 4 – 6
59	Johnny Reb/Sal's got a sugar lip		PB 951	£ 6 – 9
59	Take me like I am/I'm ready if you're willing		PB 976	£ 4 – 6
60	Sink the Bismarck!/The same old tale the crow told me .		PB 995	£ 6 – 9
60ø	North to Alaska/The mansion you stole		PB 1062	£ 4 – 6

HOT-TODDYS

59	Rockin' crickets/Shakin' and stompin'	PYE INT.	7N 25020	£12 – 18

DAVID HOUSTON

55	Blue prelude/I'm sorry I made you cry	LONDON	HL 8147	£12 – 18

LARRY HOVIS

58	Do I love you/We could have lots of fun	CAPITOL	CL 14843	£ 2 – 4
59	My heart belongs to only you/I want to fall in love ...		CL 15083	£ 2 – 4

JOHNNY HOWARD BAND

60	Up the wall/Orbit	DECCA	F 11298	£ 2 – 4

LES HOWARD (qv ALMA COGAN)

53	Love evermore/I lived when I met you	H.M.V.	7M 127	£ 2 – 4
53	Rags to riches/From here to eternity		7M 171	£ 2 – 4
57	Singin' the blues/Priscilla	CONQUEST	CP 103 ọ	£ 2 – 4
59	To Him we're all the same/I'll be there	COLUMBIA	DB 4391	£ 2 – 4
60	Sweet tooth/Auf wiedersehen my dear		DB 4476	£ 2 – 4

FRANKIE HOWERD

54	(Don't let the) Kiddy geddin/Abracadabra	DECCA	F 10420	£ 6 – 9
58	It's all right with me/Song and dance man	COLUMBIA	DB 4230	£ 4 – 6

CHRIS HOWLAND

58	Fraulein/Mama (Ma, he's making eyes at me)	COLUMBIA	DB 4114	£ 2 – 4
58	Susie darlin'/The rain falls on ev'rybody		DB 4194	£ 2 – 4

ROCK HUDSON

59	Pillow talk/Roly poly	BRUNSWICK	05816	£ 2 – 4

CAROL HUGHES

58	Lend me your comb/First date	COLUMBIA	DB 4094	£ 2 – 4

DAVID HUGHES

56ø	By the fountains of Rome/Tombolee, tombola	PHILIPS	PB 606 ọ	£ 1 – 2

"FRIDAY" HUGHES

51	Lazy morning/The Devil ain't lazy	M-G-M	MGM 422 ọ	£ 6 – 9

HUGO & LUIGI

57	Rockabilly party/Shenandoah Rose	COLUMBIA	DB 3978	£ 4 – 6
58	Cha-hua-hua/Twilight in Tennessee		DB 4156	£ 2 – 4
59ø	La plume de ma tante/Honolulu Lu	R.C.A.	RCA 1127	£ 2 – 4
60	Just come home/Lonesome stranger		RCA 1169	£ 2 – 4

HELEN HUMES (*& BENNY CARTER'S ALL-STARS)

56	If I could be with you one hour.../Million dollar secret	VOGUE	V 2048	£ 4 – 6
59	Bill Bailey, won't you please..../When the Saints go....	*CONTEMP.	CV 2415	£ 4 – 6

PEE WEE HUNT & HIS ORCH.

55	It's never too late to fall in love/A room in Bloomsbury	CAPITOL	CL 14225	£ 4 – 6
55	Save your love for me/My extraordinary gal		CL 14286	£ 4 – 6

DANNY HUNTER (& THE GIANTS)

60	Make it up/Little girl	H.M.V.	POP 722	£ 4 – 6
60	Who's gonna walk ya home?/Lonely and blue		POP 775	£ 2 – 4

IVORY JOE HUNTER (& HIS ORCH.)

50	I almost lost my mind/S.P. blues	M-G-M	MGM 271 º	£12 - 18	
56	A tear fell/I need you by my side	LONDON	HLE 8261	£60 - 90	
57	Since I met you, baby/You can't stop this rocking and...	COLUMBIA	DB 3872	£40 - 60	
57	Love's a hurting game/Empty arms	LONDON	HLE 8486	£40 - 60	

SUSAN HUNTER

55	Not yet/Was that the right thing to do?	BRUNSWICK	05458	£ 2 - 4	

TAB HUNTER

57ø	Young love/Red sails in the sunset	LONDON	HLD 8380	£ 9 - 12	
57ø	Ninety-nine ways/Don't get around much anymore		HLD 8410	£ 6 - 9	
58	Don't let it get around/I'm alone because I love you		HLD 8535	£ 6 - 9	
60	I'll be with you in apple.../(What can I..) My only love	WARNER-B	WB 8	£ 2 - 4	
60	Waitin' for Fall/Our love		WB 20	£ 2 - 4	

THE HUNTERS (qv DAVE SAMPSON)

60	Teen scene/Santa Monica Flyer	FONTANA	H 276	£ 4 - 6	

FERLIN HUSKY (& HIS HUSH PUPPIES) (qv SIMON CRUM)

57	Gone/Missing persons	CAPITOL	CL 14702	£ 4 - 6	
57	Prize possession/A fallen star		CL 14753	£ 4 - 6	
57	This moment of love/Make me live again		CL 14785	£ 2 - 4	
58	Wang dang doo/What'cha doin' after school		CL 14824	£ 9 - 12	
58	The drunken driver/Slow down brother		CL 14883	£ 9 - 12	
58	I saw God/I feel that old heartache again		CL 14916	£ 2 - 4	
58	Terrific together/The kingdom of love		CL 14922	£ 2 - 4	
58	I will/All of the time		CL 14954	£ 2 - 4	
59	Wrong/My reason for living		CL 14995	£ 2 - 4	
59	Draggin' the river/Sea sand		CL 15027	£ 2 - 4	
59	Black sheep/I'll always return		CL 15094	£ 2 - 4	
60	Wings of a dove/Next to Jimmy		CL 15160	£ 2 - 4	

"HUTCH" (Leslie Hutchinson)

54	I love Paris/It's all right with me	DECCA	F 10388	£ 2 - 4	
55	Surprisingly/Wait till Spring		F 10436	£ 2 - 4	

THE HUTTON SISTERS (Betty & Marion)

55	Ko Ko Mo (I love you so)/Heart throb	CAPITOL	CL 14250	£ 9 - 12	

BETTY HUTTON (*& PAT MORGAN/qv PERRY COMO/"TENNESSEE" ERNIE FORD/HUTTON SISTERS)

53	Somebody loves me/Jealous*	H.M.V.	7M 103	£ 4 - 6	
56	Sleepy head/Hit the road to Dreamland	CAPITOL	CL 14568	£ 2 - 4	

JUNE HUTTON

53ø	Say you're mine again/The song from Moulin Rouge	CAPITOL	CL 13918 º	£ 2 - 4	

BRIAN HYLAND

60	Rosemary/Library love affair	LONDON	HLR 9113	£ 2 - 4	
60ø	Itsy bitsy teenie weenie yellow.../Don't dilly dally,...		HLR 9161	£ 4 - 6	
60ø	Four little heels/That's how much		HLR 9203	£ 2 - 4	

DICK HYMAN TRIO

56ø	"The Threepenny Opera" theme/Baubles, bangles and beads	M-G-M	MGM 890 º	£ 1 - 2	
56ø	as above		SP 1164	£ 6 - 9	

FRANK IFIELD

60ø	Lucky devil/Nobody else but you	COLUMBIA	DB 4399	£ 2 - 4	
60	Happy-go-lucky me/Unchained melody		DB 4464	£ 2 - 4	
60ø	Gotta get a date/No love tonight		DB 4496	£ 2 - 4	

THE IMPALAS

59ø	Sorry (I ran all the way home)/Fool, fool, fool	M-G-M	MGM 1015	£ 9 - 12	
59	Oh, what a fool/Sandy went away		MGM 1031	£ 6 - 9	
60	Peggy darling/'Bye everybody		MGM 1068	£ 4 - 6	

THE IMPS
58 Dim dumb blonde/Let me lie .... PARLOPHONE R 4398 £ 4 - 6

THE INADEQUATES
59 Audie/Pretty face .... CAPITOL CL 15051 £ 4 - 6

RED INGLE & THE NATURAL SEVEN
51 Chew tobacco rag/Let me in .... CAPITOL CL 13485 º £ 6 - 9

THE INK SPOTS
54 Here in my lonely room/Flowers, Mister Florist, please PARLOPHONE MSP 6063 £ 9 - 12
54 Ebb tide/If you should say goodbye .... MSP 6074 £ 9 - 12
54 Planting rice/Yesterdays .... MSP 6126 £ 9 - 12
55ø Melody of love/Am I too late? .... R 3977 º £ 2 - 4
55ø *as above* .... MSP 6152 £ 9 - 12

THE INNOCENTS
60 Honest I do/My baby hully gullys .... TOP RANK JAR 508 £ 6 - 9

THE INTRUDERS
59 Frankfurters and sauerkraut/Creepin' .... TOP RANK JAR 158 £ 2 - 4

LORD INVADER & HIS CALYPSO RHYTHM BOYS
59 Teddy boy calypso/Reincarnation (The bed bug) .... PYE N 15162 º £ 4 - 6

LONNIE IRVING
60 Pin-ball machine/I got blues on my mind .... MELODISC 1546 £ 6 - 9

THE ISLANDERS
59 The enchanted sea/Pollyanna .... TOP RANK JAR 215 £ 2 - 4
60 Blue rain/Tornado .... JAR 305 £ 2 - 4

JIMMY ISLE
59 Diamond ring/I've been waiting .... LONDON HLS 8832 £ 9 - 12
60 Billy boy/Oh Judy .... TOP RANK JAR 274 £ 4 - 6

THE ISLEY BROTHERS
59 Shout - Parts 1 & 2 .... R.C.A. RCA 1149 £ 9 - 12
60 Respectable/I'm gonna knock on your door .... RCA 1172 £ 9 - 12
60 How deep is the ocean/He's got the whole world in His... RCA 1190 £ 6 - 9
60 Tell me who/Say you love me too .... RCA 1213 £ 6 - 9

IVAN (Jerry Allison of THE CRICKETS)
58 Real wild child/Oh, you beautiful doll .... CORAL Q 72341 £60 - 90

BURL IVES
56 Ballad of Davy Crockett/Goober peas .... BRUNSWICK 05510 £ 4 - 6
56 Dying stockman/Click go the shears .... 05551 £ 2 - 4
56 The bus stop song/That's my heartstrings .... 05604 £ 2 - 4

THE IVY THREE
60 Yogi/Was Judy there .... LONDON HLW 9178 £ 4 - 6

BOBBY JACK
59 Tempting me/Early mornin' .... TOP RANK JAR 190 £ 2 - 4

JACKIE & ROY
58 You smell so good/Let's take a walk around the block .. VOGUE V 9101 £ 4 - 6

THE JACKSON BROTHERS
59 Tell him no/Love me .... LONDON HLX 8845 £ 9 - 12

BO WEAVIL JACKSON
59 Why do you moan?/Some scream high yellow .... COLLECTOR JDL 127 £ 4 - 6

BULL MOOSE JACKSON & HIS ORCH.
52 Nosey Joe/I know who threw the whiskey in the well .... VOGUE V 2129 º £ 9 – 1?

PAPA CHARLIE JACKSON
50 Long gone Lost John/Looking for a woman .... TEMPO R 30 º £ 9 – 1?

CHUBBY JACKSON'S BIG BAND
60 A ballad for Jai/Hail, hail, The Herd's all here ...... TOP RANK TR 5015 £ 2 – ?

HAROLD JACKSON & THE TORNADOES
58 Move it on down the line – Parts 1 & 2 .... VOGUE V 9105 £25 – 4?

JIMMY JACKSON('S ROCK 'N' SKIFFLE)
57 California zephyr/I shall not be moved .... COLUMBIA DB 3898 £ 9 – 1?
57 Sittin' in the balcony/Good morning blues .... DB 3937 £ 9 – 1?
57 River line/Lonely road .... DB 3957 £ 6 – ?
57 White silver sands/Build your love (on a strong........) DB 3988 £ 6 – ?
58 Photographs/Love–a love–a love .... DB 4085 £ 6 – ?
58 Swing down, sweet chariot/This little light of mine ... DB 4153 £ 6 – ?

MAHALIA JACKSON
58 For my good fortune/Have you any rivers .... PHILIPS PB 869 £ 2 – ?
59 Trouble of the world/Tell the world about this .... PB 933 £ 2 – 4
60 Onward, Christian soldiers/The Lord's Prayer .... PB 1070 £ 2 – 4
60 The Lord's prayer/Bless this house .... VOGUE V 2418 £ 2 – 4

STONEWALL JACKSON
59ø Waterloo/Smoke along the track .... PHILIPS PB 941 £ 4 – 6
60 I'm gonna find you/A little guy called Joe .... PB 1073 £ 4 – 6

WANDA JACKSON
59 You're the one for me/A date with Jerry .... CAPITOL CL 15033 £ 6 – ?
59 Reaching/I'd rather have you .... CL 15090 £ 4 – 6
60ø Let's have a party/Cool love .... CL 15147 £ 9 – 12

DICK JACOBS & HIS ORCH.
56 "The Man With The Golden Arm" themes/Butternut .... V–CORAL Q 72154 £ 2 – 4
57 The big beat/The tower trot .... Q 72245 £ 6 – 9
57 Rock–a–billy gal/The golden strings .... Q 72260 £ 4 – 6

ILLINOIS JACQUET & HIS ORCH.
56 Blow Illinois blow/Destination Moon .... VOGUE V 2387 £ 4 – 6

MAX JAFFA (& HIS ORCH.) (& *ERIC JUPP ORCH.)
54 My gypsy heart/Camille .... DECCA F 10426 £ 2 – 4
56 China boogie/Slap happy .... *COLUMBIA SCM 5226 £ 2 – 4
59 Cha–cha–boogie/Gipsy cha cha .... DB 4280 £ 2 – 4

DICK JAMES
53 Mother Nature and Father Time/Don't you care .... PARLOPHONE MSP 6039 £ 4 – 6
53 The joker/Guessing .... MSP 6047 £ 4 – 6
55 Unchained melody/Come back (come back to me) .... MSP 6170 £ 4 – 6
55 He/So must I love you .... MSP 6190 £ 2 – 4
56ø Robin Hood/The ballad of Davy Crockett .... R 4117 º £ 2 – 4
56ø as above .... MSP 6199 £ 9 – 12
56 "Summer Sing–Song" medley .... MSP 6230 £ 2 – 4
56 Mirabelle/I only know I love you .... R 4220 £ 2 – 4
56 "Sing Song Time (No. 3)" medley .... R 4241 £ 2 – 4
57ø The Garden of Eden/I accuse .... R 4255 £ 6 – 9
57 Westward ho the wagons!/The gay Cavalier .... R 4314 £ 2 – 4
57 "Skiffling Sing Song" medley .... R 4375 £ 4 – 6
58 Daddy's little girl/When you're young .... R 4498 £ 2 – 4
59 There but for your love go I/Minus one heart .... R 4606 £ 2 – 4

REMEMBER! – THE SYMBOL º AFTER THE CATALOGUE NUMBER INDICATES A 78 rpm RECORD

ETTA JAMES (qv ETTA & HARVEY)

⊃	All I could do was cry/Tough Mary .... LONDON	HLM 9139	£ 9 – 12
⊃	My dearest darling/Girl of my dreams	HLM 9234	£ 9 – 12

HARRY JAMES & HIS ORCH.

9	Ballad for beatniks/The blues about Manhattan .... M–G–M	MGM 1038	£ 2 – 4
⊃	Doodlin'/I'll take care of your cares	MGM 1071	£ 2 – 4

JESSE JAMES

4	Lonesome day blues/Southern Casey Jones .... VOCALION	V 1037 º	£ 6 – 9

JONI JAMES

3ø	Why don't you believe me?/Wishing ring .... M–G–M	MGM 582 º	£ 2 – 4
3ø	*as above*	SP 1013	£ 9 – 12
3	Have you heart/Purple shades	SP 1025	£ 4 – 6
3	Your cheatin' heart/I'll be waiting for you	SP 1026	£ 4 – 6
3	Almost always/Is it any wonder?	SP 1041	£ 4 – 6
4	I'll never stand in your way/Why can't I	SP 1064	£ 4 – 6
4	I need you now/You're nearer	SP 1081	£ 4 – 6
4	Am I in love/I'll be seeing you	SP 1089	£ 4 – 6
4	You're my everything/Maybe next time	SP 1094	£ 4 – 6
4	In a garden of roses/Every day	SP 1100	£ 4 – 6
4	Mama, don't cry at my wedding/Pa pa pa	SP 1105	£ 4 – 6
5	How important can it be?/This is my confession	SP 1125	£ 4 – 6
5	Is this the end of the line?/When you wish upon a star	SP 1135	£ 4 – 6
6	You are my love/My believing heart	SP 1149	£ 4 – 6
6	Give us this day/How lucky you are	MGM 918	£ 2 – 4
7	Only trust your heart/I need you so	MGM 954	£ 2 – 4
8	My funny Valentine/My darling, my darling	MGM 973	£ 2 – 4
8	Love works miracles/Never 'till now	MGM 978	£ 2 – 4
8	There goes my heart/Funny	MGM 991	£ 2 – 4
9ø	There must be a way/I'm sorry for you, my friend	MGM 1002	£ 4 – 6
9	I still get a thrill (thinking of you)/Perhaps	MGM 1022	£ 2 – 4
9	I still get jealous/Prayer of love	MGM 1034	£ 2 – 4
9	Are you sorry?/What I don't know won't hurt me	MGM 1041	£ 2 – 4
⊃0	Little things mean a lot/I laughed at love	MGM 1050	£ 2 – 4
50	You belong to me/I need you now	MGM 1064	£ 2 – 4
50	We know/They really don't know you	MGM 1089	£ 2 – 4
60	Be my love/Tall a tree	MGM 1105	£ 2 – 4

RICKY JAMES

57	Knee deep in the blues/Bluer than blue .... H.M.V.	POP 306	£ 9 – 12
57	Ninety–nine ways/Party doll	POP 334	£ 9 – 12

SONNY JAMES

56ø	The cat came back/Hello old broken heart .... CAPITOL	CL 14635	£ 9 – 12
56	Twenty feet of muddy water/For rent (One empty heart)	CL 14664	£ 4 – 6
57ø	Young love/You're the reason I'm in love	CL 14683	£ 6 – 9
57	First date, first kiss, first love/Speak to me	CL 14708	£ 4 – 6
57	Dear love/Lovesick blues	CL 14742	£ 4 – 6
57	A mighty lovable man/(Love came, love...) Love conquered	CL 14788	£ 9 – 12
57	UH–HUH–mm/Why can't they remember?	CL 14814	£ 9 – 12
58	Kathaleen/Walk to the dance	CL 14848	£ 4 – 6
58	Are you mine/Let's play love	CL 14879	£ 2 – 4
58	I can see it in your eyes/You got that touch	CL 14915	£ 4 – 6
58	Let me be the one to love you/I can't stay away from you	CL 14952	£ 2 – 4
59	Yo–yo/Dream big	CL 14991	£ 6 – 9
59	Talk of the school/The table	CL 15022	£ 2 – 4
59	Pure love/This love of mine	CL 15046	£ 2 – 4
59	Red mud/Who's next in line	CL 15079	£ 2 – 4
60	Jenny Lou/Passin' through .... LONDON	HL 9132	£ 4 – 6

THE JAMIES

58	Summertime, Summertime/Searching for you .... FONTANA	H 153	£ 9 – 12

JAN & ARNIE
58	Jennie Lee/Gotta getta date	LONDON	HL 8653	£18 – 2

JAN & DEAN
59	Baby talk/Jeanette, get your hair done	LONDON	HLN 8936	£ 9 – 1
59	There's a girl/My heart sings		HLU 8990	£ 6 –
60	Clementine/You're on my mind		HLU 9063	£ 6 –

JAN & KJELD
59	Buona sera/Tiger rag	PYE INT.	7N 25013	£ 2 –
60ø	Banjo boy/Don't raise a storm	EMBER	EMB S101	£ 2 –

LADY JANE & VERITY
59	The slow look/Cry baby	PYE INT.	7N 25036	£ 2 –

JOHNNY JANIS
58	The better to love you/Can this be love	LONDON	HLU 8650	£ 6 –
60	Gina/If the good Lord's willin'	PHILIPS	PB 1090	£ 2 –

BOB JAXON (*& THE HI-TONES)
55	Ali Baba/Why does a woman cry	LONDON	*HL 8156	£18 – 2
57	(Gotta have something in the) Bank Frank/Beach party ..	R.C.A.	RCA 1019	£40 – 6

PETER JAY (*& THE BLUE MEN)
60	Just too late/Friendship	TRIUMPH	*RGM 1000	£ 9 – 1
60	Who's that girl?/Paradise Garden	PYE	7N 15290	£ 9 – 1

THE JAYE SISTERS
59	Sure fire love/G-3	LONDON	HLT 9011	£12 – 1

THE JAYHAWKS
56	Stranded in the jungle/My only darling	PARLOPHONE	R 4228	£90 –12

THE JEAN-ETTES
59	May you always/I saw a light	PYE	7N 15185	£ 2 –

AUDREY JEANS
56	Ticky ticky tick (I'm gonna tell on..)/Will you, Willyum	DECCA	F 10768	£ 4 –
56	It's better in the dark/The bus stop song		F 10788	£ 2 –
58	Send a letter to Jeanette – yet!/Bad pianna rag		F 11035	£ 2 –

BLIND LEMON JEFFERSON
50	Weary dogs blues/Change my luck blues	TEMPO	R 38 º	£ 6 –
50	Hangman's blues/Lockstep blues		R 39 º	£ 6 –
51	Shuckin' sugar blues/Rabbit foot blues		R 46 º	£ 6 –
52	Gone dead on you blues/One dime blues		R 54 º	£ 6 –

JOHNNY JENENE
59	No matter where/Shame, shame, Johnny, shame	PYE	7N 15210	£ 2 – 4

BILL JENNINGS QUARTET (*or –LEO PARKER QUINTET)
55	Stuffy/Solitude	*PARLOPHONE	MSP 6146	£ 2 – 4
55	What's new?/Soft winds		MSP 6156	£ 2 – 4

THE JETSTREAMS
59	Bongo rock/Tiger	DECCA	F 11149	£ 4 – 6

JIMMIE & THE NIGHT HOPPERS
59	Cruising/Night hop	LONDON	HLP 8830	£12 – 18

THE JIV-A-TONES
58	Flirty Gertie/Fire engine baby	FELSTED	AF 101	£40 – 60

THE JIVERS
56	Little Mama/Cherie	VOGUE	V 9060	£40 – 60
57	Dear little one/Ray pearl		V 9068	£60 – 90

THE JIVING JUNIORS
60	Lollipop girl/Dearest darling	....	BLUE BEAT	BB 4	£ 6 – 9
60	My heart's desire/I love you	....		BB 5	£ 6 – 9
60	Tu-woo-up-tu-woo/Lovers line	....	STARLITE	ST.45 028	£ 6 – 9

DAMITA JO
60	The widow walk/What would you do (if you were in my....)	MERCURY	AMT 1085	£ 2 – 4
60	I'll save the last dance for you/Forgive	....		AMT 1116	£ 2 – 4

THE JODIMARS
56	Let's all rock together/Well now, dig this	....	CAPITOL	CL 14518	£18 – 25
56	Rattle my bones/Lotsa love	....		CL 14627	£18 – 25
56	Rattle shakin' Daddy/Eat your heart out Annie	....		CL 14641	£18 – 25
56	Dance the bop/Boom, boom my Bayou baby	....		CL 14642	£18 – 25
56	Clarabella/Midnight	....		CL 14663	£18 – 25
57	Cloud 99/Later	....		CL 14700	£18 – 25

JOE & EDDIE
59	Green grass/And I believed	....	CAPITOL	CL 15038	£ 2 – 4

LITTLE WILLIE JOHN
56	Fever/Letter from my darling	....	PARLOPHONE	R 4209	£18 – 25
58	Dinner date (with his girl friend)/Uh, uh, baby	....		R 4396	£ 9 – 12
58	Talk to me, talk to me/Spasms	....		R 4432	£ 9 – 12
58	Let's rock while the rockin's good/You're a sweetheart		R 4472	£18 – 25
59	Leave my kitten alone/Let nobody love you	....		R 4571	£ 9 – 12
60	Heartbreak (It's hurtin' me)/Do you love me	....		R 4674	£ 6 – 9
60	Sleep/There's a difference	....		R 4699	£ 6 – 9

JOHNNIE & JACK
59	Sailor man/Wild and wicked world	....	R.C.A.	RCA 1145	£ 2 – 4

JOHNNIE & JOE
58	Over the mountain, across the sea/My baby's gone, on, on	LONDON	HLM 8682	£40 – 60

JOHNNY & JUDY
59	Bother me baby/Who's to say	....	VOGUE	V 9128	£40 – 60

JOHNNY & THE HURRICANES
59	Crossfire/Lazy	....	LONDON	HL 8899	£ 6 – 9
59ø	Red River rock/Buckeye	....		HL 8948	£ 4 – 6
59ø	Reveille rock/Time bomb	....		HL 9017	£ 4 – 6
60ø	Beatnik fly/Sand storm	....		HLI 9072	£ 4 – 6
60ø	*as above*	....		HLI 9072 º	£ 9 – 12
60ø	Down yonder/Sheba	....		HLX 9134	£ 4 – 6
60ø	*as above*	....		HLX 9134 º	£ 9 – 12
60ø	Rocking goose/Revival	....		HLX 9190	£ 4 – 6
60ø	*as above*	....		HLX 9190 º	£ 9 – 12

JOHNNY'S BOYS
59	Sleepwalk/Ciao ciao bambina	....	DECCA	F 11156	£ 4 – 6

JOHNNY'S JAZZ feat. JOHNNY HAWKSWORTH
56	R.J. boogie/Get happy	....	DECCA	FJ 10663	£ 4 – 6

BARRY JOHNS
58	Locked in the arms of love/Are you sincere	....	H.M.V.	POP 472	£ 2 – 4

GLYNIS JOHNS
54	I can't resist men/Always you	....	COLUMBIA	SCM 5149	£ 4 – 6

BETTY JOHNSON
56	I'll wait/Please tell me why	....	LONDON	HLU 8307	£12 – 18
56	Honky tonk rock/Say it isn't so, Joe	....		HLU 8326	£40 – 60
57	I dreamed/If it's wrong to love you	....		HLU 8365	£12 – 18
57	1492/Little white lies	....		HLU 8432	£12 – 18

58	Little blue man/Song you heard when you fell in love ..		HLE 8557	£12 – 18
58	Dream/How much		HLE 8678	£ 9 – 12
58	There's never been a night/Mr. Brown is out of town ...		HLE 8701	£18 – 25
58	Hoopa hoola/One more time		HLE 8725	£12 – 18
59	Does your heart beat for me?/You and only you		HLE 8839	£ 9 – 12

BRYAN JOHNSON
60ø	Looking high, high, high/Each tomorrow	DECCA	F 11213	£ 2 – 4

BUBBER JOHNSON
57	Confidential/Have a little faith in me	PARLOPHONE	R 4259	£ 9 – 12

BUNK JOHNSON & HIS NEW ORLEANS BAND
53	When the Saints go marching in/Darktown Strutters' Ball	H.M.V.	7M 141	£ 2 – 4

JAMES P. JOHNSON
54	Feeling blues/Riffs	COLUMBIA	SCM 5127	£ 4 – 6

LONNIE JOHNSON
51	Solid blues/Rocks in my bed	MELODISC	1138 º	£ 9 – 12
51	Jelly Roll Baker/Drunk again	VOGUE	V 2015 º	£ 9 – 12
51	Blues for everybody/In love again	MELODISC	1186 º	£ 9 – 12
51	Little rockin' chair/Happy New Year, darling	VOGUE	V 2079 º	£ 9 – 12
52	Keep what you got/Blues in my soul	MELODISC	1221 º	£ 9 – 12

MARV JOHNSON
59	Come to me/Whisper	LONDON	HLT 8856	£ 9 – 12
59ø	You got what it takes/Don't leave me		HLT 9013	£ 4 – 6
60ø	I love the way you love/Let me love you		HLT 9109	£ 4 – 6
60ø	Ain't gonna be that way/All the love I've got		HLT 9165	£ 4 – 6
60	(You've got to) Move two mountains/I need you		HLT 9187	£ 4 – 6

PETE JOHNSON
56	J.J. boogie/Yancey special	VOGUE	V 2007	£12 – 18
56	Swanee River boogie/St. Louis boogie		V 2008	£12 – 18

PLAS JOHNSON (& HIS ORCH.)
57	The big twist/Come rain or come shine	CAPITOL	CL 14772	£ 9 – 12
57	You send me/Swanee River rock		CL 14816	£ 9 – 12
58	Popcorn/Hoppin' mad		CL 14836	£ 9 – 12
58	Little rockin' Deacon/Dinah		CL 14903	£ 9 – 12
59	Robbins Nest cha cha/Plaz jazz		CL 14973	£ 4 – 6

RAY JOHNSON
57	If you don't want me baby/Calypso Joe	VOGUE	V 9073	£18 – 25
58	Calypso blues/Are you there		V 9093	£ 9 – 12

TEDDY JOHNSON (*& PEARL CARR) (+& THE POLKA DOTS/qv VARIOUS ARTISTS)
54	Promise me/Love me	COLUMBIA	SCM 5098	£ 2 – 4
57	Tomorrow, tomorrow/Mandolin serenade	PYE	*7N 15110	£ 2 – 4
58	Sweet Elizabeth/Never let me go		*7N 15123	£ 2 – 4
58	Merci beaucoup/A great big piece of chalk		+7N 15153	£ 2 – 4
59	Petite fleur/Missouri waltz	COLUMBIA	*DB 4260	£ 2 – 4
59ø	Sing little birdie/If only I could live my life again .		*DB 4275	£ 2 – 4
59	Tell me, tell me/Viva viva amor		*DB 4318	£ 2 – 4
60	Pazzo pazzo (Crazy crazy)/The Five Pennies		*DB 4397	£ 2 – 4
60	When the tide turns/Pickin' petals	H.M.V.	*POP 697	£ 2 – 4

THE JOHNSTON BROTHERS (& *TED HEATH MUSIC/+THE KEYNOTES/qv LYS ASSIA/L. DESMOND/ D. LOTIS/V. LYNN/S. MILLER/J. REGAN/E. ROS/L. ROZA/VARIOUS ARTISTS)
53ø	Oh, happy day/Downhearted	DECCA	F 10071 º	£ 6 – 9
54	The creep/Crystal ball		F 10234	£ 6 – 9
54	I get so lonely/My love, my life, my own		F 10286	£ 4 – 6
54	The bandit/(by THE KEYNOTES)		F 10302	£ 4 – 6
54	Sh-boom (Life could be a dream)/Crazy 'bout ya baby ...		F 10364	£ 9 – 12
54	Mambo in the moonlight/Papa loves mambo		*F 10401	£ 4 – 6

54	"Join In And Sing" medley		F 10414	£ 4 – 6
55	Majorca/Heartbroken		F 10451	£ 4 – 6
55	The right to be wrong/Hot potato mambo		F 10490	£ 4 – 6
55	Chee chee–oo chee (sang the little bird)/Hubble bubble		F 10513	£ 4 – 6
55	Dreamboat/Jim, Johnny and Jonas		F 10526	£ 4 – 6
55ø	Hernando's Hideaway/Hey there		F 10608	£ 9 – 12
55ø	"Join In And Sing Again" medley		F 10636	£ 6 – 9
56ø	No other love/Flowers mean forgiveness		F 10721	£ 6 – 9
56	How little we know/The street musician		F 10747	£ 4 – 6
56ø	In the middle of the house+/Stranded in the jungle		F 10781	£ 9 – 12
56ø	"Join In And Sing, No. 3" medley		F 10814	£ 6 – 9
56ø	Give her my love (when you......)/A rose and a candy bar		F 10828	£ 6 – 9
57ø	Heart/Whatever Lola wants (Lola gets)		F 10860	£ 4 – 6
57	I like music – you like music/Seven bar blues		F 10939	£ 2 – 4
57	"Join In And Sing, No. 4" medley		F 10962	£ 2 – 4
58	A very precious love/Yours, yours, yours		F 10996	£ 2 – 4
58	Scratch, scratch/Little serenade		F 11021	£ 2 – 4
58	Love is all we need/Clementine cha–cha		F 11083	£ 2 – 4

JOINER, ARKANSAS, JUNIOR HIGH SCHOOL BAND
60	National City/Big Ben	LONDON	HLG 9147	£ 4 – 6

THE (*FOUR) JONES BOYS (qv ANNETTE KLOOGER)
55	When I let you go/A real romance	DECCA	*F 10568	£ 2 – 4
56	Moments to remember/Sing–ing–ing–ing		*F 10671	£ 2 – 4
56	Tutti frutti/Are you satisfied?		*F 10717	£ 6 – 9
56	Happiness Street (Corner of Sunshine...)/Someone to love		*F 10789	£ 2 – 4
56	Priscilla/It isn't right		*F 10829	£ 4 – 6
57	Rock–a–hula baby (Ukelele lady)/Cool baby	COLUMBIA	DB 4046	£ 6 – 9
58	A certain smile/Kathy–O		DB 4170	£ 2 – 4
58	The day the rains came/Hideaway		DB 4217	£ 2 – 4
59	Dream girl/Straight as an arrow		DB 4278	£ 2 – 4

AL JONES
58	Mad, mad world/Lonely traveller	H.M.V.	POP 451	£40 – 60

ALLAN JONES
53	Why do I love you/Make believe	H.M.V.	7M 111	£ 2 – 4
53	I believe/I talk to the trees		7M 135	£ 2 – 4
53	Poppa Piccolino/Why?		7M 161	£ 2 – 4

CAROL JONES
60	I gave him back his ring/The boy with the eyes of blue	TRIUMPH	RGM 1012	£ 9 – 12

DAVY JONES
60	Amapola/Mighty man	PYE	7N 15254	£ 2 – 4

DILL JONES TRIO (qv TONY KINSEY)
58	Little Rock getaway/Carolina shout	PYE JAZZ	7NJ 2021	£ 2 – 4

GEORGE JONES
59	Treasure of love/If I don't love you (grits ain't......)	MERCURY	AMT 1021	£ 6 – 9
59	White lightning/Long time to forget		AMT 1036	£12 – 18
59	Who shot Sam/Into my arms again		AMT 1058	£ 9 – 12
60	Money to burn/Big Harlan Taylor		AMT 1078	£ 4 – 6
60	Accidentally on purpose/Sparkling brown eyes		AMT 1100	£ 4 – 6

GRANDPA JONES (qv COWBOY COPAS)
57	Eight more miles to Louisville/Dark as a dungeon	BRUNSWICK	05676	£ 9 – 12

JACK JONES
57	Good luck, good buddy/Baby, come home	CAPITOL	CL 14798	£ 2 – 4
58	A very precious love/What's the use?		CL 14871	£ 2 – 4
58	Come on baby, let's go/You laugh		CL 14895	£ 2 – 4
58	Laffin' at me/Deeply devoted		CL 14969	£ 2 – 4
59	Make room for the joy/When I love I'll love forever ...		CL 15011	£ 2 – 4

JIMMY JONES
60ø	Handy man/The search is over	M-G-M	MGM 1051	£ 4 – 6
60ø	Good timin'/Too long will be too late		MGM 1078	£ 4 – 6
60ø	I just go for you/That's when I cried		MGM 1091	£ 4 – 6
60ø	Ready for love/For you		MGM 1103	£ 4 – 6

JOE JONES
60	You talk too much/I love you still	COLUMBIA	DB 4533	£ 6 – 9

JONAH JONES QUARTET
58	Slowly but surely/Ballin' the Jack	CAPITOL	CL 14901	£ 2 – 4
58	Night train/Lots of luck, Charley		CL 14939	£ 2 – 4
59	High hopes/Hit me again		CL 15060	£ 2 – 4
59	I dig chicks!/Cherry		CL 15085	£ 2 – 4

MAE JONES ENSEMBLE w. MARGARET BOND
55	I walked into the garden/Tenderly He watches	DECCA	F 10486	£ 2 – 4

QUINCY JONES & HIS ORCH.
59	Tuxedo Junction/The syncopated clock	MERCURY	AMT 1037	£ 2 – 4
60	Love is here to stay/Moonglow		AMT 1111	£ 2 – 4

SPIKE JONES & HIS CITY SLICKERS/*COUNTRY COUSINS
53	I went to your wedding/Lulu had a baby	H.M.V.	B 10482 º	£ 4 – 6
53	Hot lips/Hotter than a pistol		*7M 121	£ 6 – 9
53	I saw Mommy kissing Santa Claus/Winter		7M 160	£ 6 – 9
55	Secret love/I'm in the mood for love		7M 324	£ 6 – 9

THUNDERCLAP JONES
56	Hurricane boogie/The laughing rag	ORIOLE	CB 1320 º	£ 4 – 6
56	Sound barrier boogie/Ask for Joe		CB 1328 º	£ 4 – 6

JOHNNY JORDAAN
57	It's grand to be in love/Home at last	H.M.V.	POP 349	£ 2 – 4

THE JORDAN BROTHERS
60	Never, never/Please tell me now	LONDON	HLW 8908	£ 9 – 12
60	Things I didn't say/Polly plays her kettle drum		HLW 9235	£ 4 – 6

DICK JORDAN
60ø	Hallelujah, I love her so/Sandy	ORIOLE	CB 1534	£ 4 – 6
60ø	Little Christine/I'll love you forever		CB 1548	£ 4 – 6
60	Alive, alive oh!/Garden of Eden		CB 1566	£ 2 – 4
60	Angel on my shoulder/The next train home		CB 1591	£ 2 – 4

LOUIS JORDAN (& HIS TYMPANY FIVE/ORCH.) (qv LOUIS ARMSTRONG/ELLA FITZGERALD)
50	Saturday night fish fry (both sides)	BRUNSWICK	04402 º	£ 9 – 12
50	Push ka pee shee pie/Hungry man		04519 º	£ 6 – 9
51	Three-handed woman/Is my Pop in there?		04770 º	£ 6 – 9
54	Dad gum ya hide boy/Whiskey do your stuff	MELODISC	1031 º	£ 9 – 12
56	Messy Bessy/I seen what'cha done		1349 º	£ 9 – 12
60	Ooo-wee/I'll die happy	DOWNBEAT	CHA 3	£12 – 18

THE JORDANAIRES
57	Sugaree/Baby, won't you please come home?	CAPITOL	CL 14687	£12 – 18
57	Summer vacation/Each day		CL 14773	£ 6 – 9
58	Little Miss Ruby/All I need is you		CL 14921	£ 9 – 12

JOY & DAVID *or JOY & DAVE
58	Whoopee!/My oh my!	PARLOPHONE	R 4477	£ 9 – 12
59	If you pass me by/Rocking away the blues	DECCA	F 11123	£ 9 – 12
60	Let's go see Gran'ma/Believe me	TRIUMPH	*RGM 1002	£ 9 – 12
60	My very good friend the milkman/Doopey darling	DECCA	*F 11291	£ 6 – 9

REMEMBER! – THE SYMBOL ø AFTER THE YEAR OF ISSUE INDICATES A BRITISH CHART ENTRY

COL JOYE & THE JOY BOYS
59	(Rockin' rollin') Clementine/Bye bye baby goodbye	BRUNSWICK	05806	£ 6 –	9
60	Yes sir, that's my baby/Be my girl	TOP RANK	JAR 529	£ 4 –	6

JULIAN (Scott)
59	Sue Saturday/Can't wait	PYE	7N 15236	£ 6 –	9

THE JUMPIN' JACKS
58	My girl, my girl/Tried and tested	H.M.V.	POP 440	£ 6 –	9

THE JUMPING JACKS
56	About a quarter to nine/Lady, play your mandolin	CAPITOL	CL 14597	£ 4 –	6

ROSANNE JUNE
56	The Charge of the Light Brigade/Broken windows	LONDON	HLU 8352	£12 –	18
58	When a woman cries/The great Chicago fire	ORIOLE	CB 1430	£ 2 –	4

ROSEMARY JUNE
58	I'll always be in love with you/Person to person	FONTANA	H 141	£ 2 –	4
59ø	I'll be with you in apple blossom.../Always a bridesmaid	PYE INT.	7N 25005	£ 4 –	6
59	With you beside me/I used to love you, but it's all.....		7N 25015	£ 2 –	4
59	The village of St. Bernadette/But not for me	LONDON	HLT 9014	£ 2 –	4

ERIC JUPP & HIS ORCH. (+& THE CORONETS/qv MAX JAFFA)
53	Jog trot/Doina voda	COLUMBIA	SCM 5070	£ 2 –	4
54	Oop dee ooh (Lazy mambo)/Footsteps in the fog		SCM 5081	£ 4 –	6
54	Rock, rock, rock/Catwalk		DB 3465 º	£ 4 –	6
54	They were doin' the mambo/Skokiaan		+SCM 5140	£ 4 –	6
57	Bleep! Bleep!/Three–two–one–zero!		DB 4030	£ 2 –	4

CURT JURGENS
59	Ferry to Hong Kong/Live for love	TOP RANK	JAR 151	£ 2 –	4

JIMMY JUSTICE & THE JURY
60	I understand just how you feel/Bloodshot eyes	PYE	7N 15301	£ 4 –	6

JAY JUSTIN
60	Nobody's darlin' but mine/Sweet sensation	H.M.V.	POP 801	£ 2 –	4

BILL JUSTIS & HIS ORCHESTRA
57ø	Raunchy/The midnight man	LONDON	HLS 8517	£ 6 –	9
58	College man/The stranger		HLS 8614	£ 6 –	9

KALASANDRO!
60	Chi Chi/Forbidden city	WARNER–B	WB 13	£ 4 –	6

THE KALIN TWINS
58ø	When/Three o'clock thrill	BRUNSWICK	05751	£ 4 –	6
58	Forget me not/Dream of me		05759	£ 4 –	6
59	Oh! My goodness/It's only the beginning		05775	£ 9 –	12
59	Cool/When I look in the mirror		05797	£ 4 –	6
59	Sweet sugar lips/Moody		05803	£ 4 –	6
59	The meaning of the blues/Why don't you believe me?		05814	£ 2 –	4
60	Chicken thief/Loneliness		05826	£ 2 –	4
60	Zing! went the strings of my heart/No money can buy ...		05844	£ 4 –	6

KITTY KALLEN (*& GEORGIE SHAW)
54	In the chapel in the moonlight/Are you looking for a....	BRUNSWICK	05261	£ 6 –	9
54ø	Little things mean a lot/I don't think you love me any..		05287	£ 9 –	12
54	The spirit of Christmas/Heartless heart		05357	£ 4 –	6
54	(Don't let the) Kiddy geddin/I want you all to myself .		05359	£ 4 –	6
55	A little lie/Take everything but you		05394	£ 4 –	6
55	I'm a lonely little petunia/Polly Pigtails		05402	£ 4 –	6
55	Kitty who?/By Bayou Bay		05431	£ 4 –	6
55	Forgive me/Lonely		05447	£ 4 –	6

55	Let's make the most of tonight/Just between friends ...		05475	£ 4 – 6
55	How lonely can I get?/Sweet Kentucky rose		05494	£ 4 – 6
56	Go on with the wedding*/Only forever		05536	£ 6 – 9
56	True love/Will I always be your sweetheart?		05612	£ 2 – 4
57	Long lonely nights/Lasting love		05705	£ 4 – 6
58	Crying roses/I never was the one		05734	£ 2 – 4
59	If I give my heart to you/The door that won't open	PHILIPS	PB 971	£ 2 – 4
60	Make love to me/Heaven help me		PB 1028	£ 2 – 4

DICK KALLMAN

56	Two different worlds/Love me as though there were no....	BRUNSWICK	05608	£ 2 – 4
60	Born to be loved/Just squeeze me but don't teeze me ...	VOGUE	V 9162	£ 2 – 4

EDEN KANE

60	You make love so well/Hot chocolate crazy	PYE	7N 15284	£ 4 – 6

LEE KANE

55	Ev'ry day/How would you have me?	CAPITOL	CL 14297	£ 4 – 6
55	Around and around/Merci beaucoup		CL 14328	£ 4 – 6

ANTON KARAS

60	The "Harry Lime" theme/The Cafe Mozart waltz	DECCA	F 9235	£ 2 – 4

AL KASHA

60	Teardrops are falling/No matter where you are	CORAL	Q 72410	£ 2 – 4

MICKEY KATZ & HIS ORCH.

56	Duvid Crockett (The ballad of Davy Crockett)/Keneh hora	CAPITOL	CL 14579	£ 4 – 6
58	The poiple kishke eater/Knish doctor		CL 14926	£ 4 – 6

KATHIE KAY or KAYE

55	Suddenly there's a valley/Teddy bear	H.M.V.	7M 335	£ 2 – 4
56	Jimmy Unknown/Dreams can tell a lie		7M 363	£ 2 – 4
56	Old Scotch Mother/There is somebody waiting for me		7M 370	£ 2 – 4
56	Bonnie Scotland/The wee hoose 'mang the heather		7M 412	£ 2 – 4
56	A house with love in it/To be sure		POP 265	£ 2 – 4
57	Every day is Mother's Day/From the first hello – to the.		POP 315	£ 2 – 4
57	We will make love/Wind in the willow		POP 352	£ 2 – 4
57	Tammy/Away from you		POP 385	£ 2 – 4
57	Be content/My last love		POP 410	£ 2 – 4
58	The secret of happiness/Summer is a'coming in		POP 485	£ 2 – 4
58	Hillside in Scotland/Tomorrow is my birthday		POP 498	£ 2 – 4
59	Goodbye Jimmy, goodbye/Come home to Loch Lomond and me		POP 625	£ 2 – 4

THE (+THREE) KAYE SISTERS (*as THE THREE KAYES/qv FRANKIE VAUGHAN)

56ø	Ivory tower/Mister Cuckoo (sing your song)	H.M.V.	*POP 209 º	£ 2 – 4
56ø	as above		*7M 401	£ 9 – 12
56	Lay down your arms/First. row balcony		+POP 251	£ 6 – 9
57ø	Alone/Shake me I rattle	PHILIPS	PB 752 º	£ 2 – 4
58	Are you ready, Freddy?/The pansy		PB 806	£ 6 – 9
58	Stroll me/Torero		PB 832	£ 4 – 6
58	Calla, calla (The bride, the bride)/Oho–aha		PB 877	£ 2 – 4
59	Jerri–Lee (I love him so)/Deeply devoted		PB 892	£ 2 – 4
59	Goodbye Jimmy, goodbye/Dancing with my shadow		PB 925	£ 2 – 4
59	True love, true love/Too young to marry		PB 970	£ 2 – 4
60ø	Paper roses/If only you'd be mine		PB 1024	£ 2 – 4
60	Come to me/A whole lot of lovin'		PB 1088	£ 2 – 4

DANNY KAYE (*& DENA KAYE/qv BING CROSBY)

52ø	Wonderful Copenhagen/Anywhere I wander	BRUNSWICK	05023 º	£ 1 – 2
54	Knock on wood/All about you		05296	£ 2 – 4
54	The best things happen while you're dancing/Choreography		05344	£ 2 – 4
55	Not since Ninevah/Night of my nights		05414	£ 2 – 4
55	In my neck o' the woods/Manhattan mambo		05424	£ 2 – 4
55	I love you fair dinkum (Dinky di I do)/Happy ending ...		05499	£ 2 – 4

56	Life could not better be/I'll take you dreaming			05524	£ 2 - 4
56	Outfox the Fox/Pass the basket			05525	£ 2 - 4
56	Little child (Daddy dear)/Laugh it off upsy daisey			*05532	£ 2 - 4
56	Delilah Jones/Molly-O			05559	£ 2 - 4
57	Love me do/Ciu ciu bella	CAPITOL	CL 14672		£ 2 - 4
58	Everything is ticketty-boo/The square of the hypotenuse		CL 14907		£ 2 - 4
59	Mommy, gimme a drinka water!/Crazy Barbara		CL 15061		£ 2 - 4
59ø	Wonderful Copenhagen/Anywhere I wander	BRUNSWICK	05023		£ 2 - 4
59	The ugly duckling/The King's new clothes		05031		£ 2 - 4

MARION KEENE

56	Fortune teller/A dangerous age	H.M.V.	7M 395	£ 2 - 4
57	In the middle of an island/It's not for me to say		POP 375	£ 2 - 4

NELSON KEENE

60ø	Image of a girl/Ocean of love	H.M.V.	POP 771	£ 2 - 4
60	Teenage troubles/Keep loving me		POP 814	£ 2 - 4

REX KEENE

56	Happy Texas Ranger/Rebel in town	COLUMBIA	DB 3831	£ 4 - 6

GRETA KELLER

56	Goodbye lieber Johnny/Apollo Umberto Silvano Roberto....	DECCA	F 10649	£ 2 - 4

JERRY KELLER

59ø	Here comes Summer/Time has a way	LONDON	HLR 8890	£ 2 - 4
59	If I had a girl/Lovable		HLR 8980	£ 2 - 4
60	Now, now, now/Lonesome lullaby		HLR 9106	£ 2 - 4

GENE KELLY (*& GEORGES GUETARY)

53	Singin' in the rain/All I do is dream of you	M-G-M	SP 1012	£ 6 - 9
53	'S wonderful*/I got rhythm		SP 1015	£ 4 - 6
57	The happy road (Ca ca c'est..)/My baby just cares for me		MGM 965	£ 2 - 4
58	A very precious love/Uncle Samson	R.C.A.	RCA 1068	£ 2 - 4

KEITH KELLY

60ø	(Must you always) Tease me/Ooh-la-la	PARLOPHONE	R 4640	£ 6 - 9
60ø	Listen little girl/Uh-huh		R 4676	£ 6 - 9
60	With you/You'll break my heart		R 4713	£ 4 - 6

SALLY KELLY

59	Little cutie/Come back to me	DECCA	F 11175	£ 2 - 4
60	He'll have to stay/Honey that's alright		F 11238	£ 2 - 4

Rev. (Samuel) KELSEY & Congregation (*& Sister ROSETTA THARPE)

52	Little boy/Low down the chariot	VOCALION	V 1020 º	£ 4 - 6
53	I'm a royal child/Where is the Lion in the tribe of.....		V 1028 º	£ 4 - 6
52	Wedding Ceremony of Sister R.Tharpe & Russell Morrison		*V 1014 º	£ 9 - 12

THE KEN-TONES (qv BENNY LEE)

56	Get with it/In Port Afrique	PARLOPHONE	MSP 6229	£ 4 - 6
57	I saw Esau/Yaller, yaller gold		R 4257	£ 4 - 6

THE KENDALL SISTERS

58	Won't you be my baby/Yea. yea	LONDON	HLM 8622	£18 - 25

NAT KENDRICK & THE SWANS

60	Mashed potatoes - Parts 1 & 2	TOP RANK	JAR 351	£ 4 - 6
60	Dish rag - Parts 1 & 2		JAR 387	£ 4 - 6

LOU KENNEDY

55	The Kentuckian song/Stars shine in your eyes	COLUMBIA	SCM 5198	£ 2 - 4
56	Sincerely yours/Whisper		SCM 5216	£ 2 - 4

REMEMBER! - THE SYMBOL º AFTER THE CATALOGUE NUMBER INDICATES A 78 rpm RECORD

JAMES KENNEY
58 The shrine on the second floor/Expresso party .... PYE   7N 15150   £ 2 – 4

KENNY & CORKY
59 Nuttin' for Christmas/Suzy Snowflake .... LONDON   HLX 9002   £ 4 – 6

BILL KENT
58 The prettiest girl in school/Hasty words .... DECCA   F 10975   £ 2 – 4
58 Oh–oh, I'm falling in love again/In love ....   F 10997   £ 2 – 4

STAN KENTON & HIS ORCH. (& *ANN RICHARDS/+JUNE CHRISTY/qv NAT "KING" COLE)
54 The lady in red/Skoot .... CAPITOL   CL 14191   £ 4 – 6
55 Alone too long/Don't take your love from me ....   CL 14247   £ 4 – 6
55 A–ting–a–ling/Malaguena ....   *CL 14259   £ 6 – 9
55 Lover man/I've got you under my skin ....   CL 14287   £ 4 – 6
55 Casanova/Dark eyes ....   *CL 14301   £ 4 – 6
55 23 degrees North – 82 degrees West/Falling* ....   CL 14269   £ 4 – 6
55 Freddy/The handwriting's on the wall ....   *CL 14319   £ 4 – 6
56 Winter in Madrid*/Baa–too–kee ....   CL 14537   £ 2 – 4
56 Sunset tower/Opus in chartreuse ....   CL 14539   £ 2 – 4
56 My lady/Frank speaking ....   CL 14540   £ 2 – 4
56 Portrait of a Count/Invention for guitar and trumpet ..   CL 14541   £ 2 – 4
56 Cherokee/Limelight ....   CL 14542   £ 2 – 4
57 His feet too big for de bed+/Stardust – boogie ....   CL 14707   £ 2 – 4
57 Lemon twist/Baby you're tough ....   CL 14806   £ 2 – 4
58 Tequila/Cuban mumble ....   CL 14847   £ 2 – 4
58 Reverie/More love than your love ....   CL 14866   £ 2 – 4
59 Whistle walk/Tamer–lane ....   CL 15029   £ 2 – 4

THE KENTUCKY BOYS
55 Don't fetch it/A little feller like me .... H.M.V.   7M 312   £ 4 – 6

JOHN KESTON
53 Mardi Gras/There was a time .... M–G–M   SP 1058   £ 2 – 4

THE KESTRELS
59 In the chapel in the moonlight/There comes a time ..... PYE   7N 15234   £ 2 – 4
60 I can't say goodbye/We were wrong ....   7N 15248   £ 2 – 4

THE KEYBOARD KINGS
56 Rhapsody in boogie/Rainbow rag .... ORIOLE   CB 1331 ² £ 4 – 6

THE KEYMEN
59 Gazackstahagen/Miss you .... H.M.V.   POP 584   £ 4 – 6

THE KEYNOTES (qv BOBBIE BRITTON/JOHNSTON BROTHERS/DAVE KING/SUZI MILLER)
54 A dime and a dollar/(by JOHNSTON BROTHERS) .... DECCA   F 10302   £ 4 – 6
55 Steam heat/Relax–ay–vous ....   F 10643   £ 4 – 6
56 Let's go steady/Chincherinchee ....   F 10745   £ 2 – 4

JOHNNY KIDD & THE PIRATES
59ø Please don't touch/Growl .... H.M.V.   POP 615   £ 6 – 9
59 If you were the only girl in the world/Feelin' ....   POP 674   £ 4 – 6
60ø You got what it takes/Longin' lips ....   POP 698   £ 4 – 6
60ø Shakin' all over/Yes sir, that's my baby ....   POP 753   £ 4 – 6
60ø Restless/Magic of love ....   POP 790   £ 4 – 6

JUDY KILEEN
56 Just walking in the rain/A heart without a sweetheart . LONDON   HLU 8328   £12 – 18

MERLE KILGORE
54 It can't rain all the time/Seeing double, feeling single LONDON   HL 8103   £18 – 25
57 Ernie/Trying to find (someone like you) ....   HLP 8392 · £40 – 60
60 Dear Mama/Jimmie bring sunshine .... MELODISC   1545   £ 6 – 9

THE KILTIES
56	Teach you to rock/Giddy-up-a ding dong	BELTONA	·BL 2666	£ 9 - 12

THE KING BROTHERS (qv VARIOUS ARTISTS)
57	The cradle rock/Crazy little palace	CONQUEST CP 104 º	£ 6 - 9
57	Marianne/Little by little	PARLOPHONE R 4288	£ 4 - 6
57	Steamboat railroad/Heart	CONQUEST CP 109 º	£ 4 - 6
57ø	A white sport coat (and a pink........)/Minne-Minnehaha!	PARLOPHONE R 4310	£ 4 - 6
57ø	In the middle of an island/Rockin' shoes	R 4338	£ 4 - 6
57ø	Wake up little Susie/Winter wonderland	R 4367	£ 4 - 6
58ø	Put a light in the window/Miss Otis regrets	R 4389	£ 4 - 6
58	6-5 jive/Hand me down my walking cane	R 4410	£ 4 - 6
58	Torero/Moonlight and roses	R 4438	£ 2 - 4
58	Sitting in a tree house/Father Time	R 4469	£ 2 - 4
59	Leaning on a lamp-post/Thank Heaven for little girls .. ,	R 4513	£ 2 - 4
59	Hop, skip and jump/Civilization (Bongo, bongo, bongo) .	R 4554	£ 2 - 4
59	Makin' love/Caribbean	R 4577	£ 2 - 4
60ø	Standing on the corner/The waiter and the porter and....	R 4639	£ 2 - 4
60ø	Mais oui/Gotta feeling	R 4672	£ 2 - 4
60ø	Doll house/Si si si	R 4715	£ 2 - 4

THE KING SISTERS (qv WAYNE HANDY)
57	In Hamburg (when the nights...)/While the lights are low	CAPITOL CL 14711	£ 2 - 4
57	Imagination/You're my thrill	CL 14729	£ 2 - 4
57	Easy to love/That old feeling	CL 14777	£ 2 - 4
58	Unbelievable/Deep purple	CL 14865	£ 2 - 4
58	What's new?/The thrill was new	CL 14893	£ 2 - 4
58	The guy in the foreign sports../Autumn time in Pleasant.	CL 14934	£ 2 - 4
59	Keep smiling (keep laughin', be...)/The maids of Cadiz	CL 15012	£ 2 - 4
59	Lovin' up a storm/What would I do without you	CL 15069	£ 2 - 4
59	Over the river (and through the woods)/Holiday of love	CL 15096	£ 2 - 4

BOB KING & THE COUNTRY KINGS
59	Hey Honey/My petite Marie	ORIOLE	CB 1497	£18 - 25

BUZZY KING
60	Schoolboy blues/Your picture	TOP RANK	JAR 278	£ 4 - 6

DAVE KING (*& THE KEYNOTES/qv VARIOUS ARTISTS)
56ø	Memories are made of this*I've changed my mind a........	DECCA	F 10684	£ 6 - 9
56ø	You can't be true to two/A little bit independent	F 10720	£ 6 - 9
56	The birds and the bees/Hotta chocolotta	*F 10741	£ 4 - 6
56ø	Christmas and you/You make nice	F 10791	£ 6 - 9
57	Love is a golden ring/If your heart wants to dance	F 10865	£ 2 - 4
57	With all my heart/Red shutters	F 10910	£ 2 - 4
57	Shake me I rattle/Chances are	F 10947	£ 4 - 6
58ø	The story of my life/I'll buy you a star	F 10973	£ 4 - 6
58	I suddenly/There's only one of you	F 11012	£ 2 - 4
58	The story/Home	F 11061	£ 2 - 4
59	High hopes/Night and day	PYE INT. 7N 25032	£ 2 - 4
60	Many a wonderful moment/Goody goody	PYE 7N 15283	£ 2 - 4

PEE WEE KING & HIS BAND/*GOLDEN WEST COWBOYS
52	Bull fiddle boogie*/Silver and gold	H.M.V.	B 10229 º	£ 6 - 9

SID KING & THE FIVE STRINGS
56	Booger Red/Oobie-doobie	PHILIPS	PB 589 º	£25 - 40

TEDDI KING (qv GEORGE SHEARING)
56	My funny little lover/I'll never be the same	V-CORAL	Q 72142	£ 2 - 4

THE KINGPINS
58	Ungaua - Parts 1 & 2	LONDON	HLU 8658	£ 6 - 9

REMEMBER! - THE SYMBOL ø AFTER THE YEAR OF ISSUE INDICATES A BRITISH CHART ENTRY

THE KINGS IV
59	Some like it hot/The world goes on	LONDON	HLT 8914	£ 4 – 6

KINGS OF THE CARIBBEAN STEEL BAND
57	Rock 'n' roll Susie/Down in Soho	MELODISC	1429 º	£ 4 – 6

THE KINGSMEN (actually BILL HALEY'S COMETS)
58	Week-end/Better believe it	LONDON	HLE 8735	£12 – 18
59	Conga rock/The cat walk		HLE 8812	£12 – 18

THE KINGSTON TRIO
58ø	Tom Dooley/Ruby red	CAPITOL	CL 14951	£ 2 – 4
59ø	San Miguel/A worried man		CL 15073	£ 2 – 4

THE TONY KINSEY QUARTET/QUINTET (*& DILL JONES)
55	She's funny that way/Fascinatin' rhythm	DECCA	F 10548	£ 2 – 4
55	Close your eyes/Pierrot		F 10606	£ 2 – 4
55	Hey! There/Ballet		F 10648	£ 2 – 4
56	Stompin' at the Savoy/China boy		*F 10708	£ 2 – 4
56	Moonglow/One o'clock jump		*F 10709	£ 2 – 4
56	Starboard bow/Body and soul		FJ 10725	£ 2 – 4
56	Lullaby of the leaves/Isolation		FJ 10760	£ 2 – 4
56	In a ditch/A smooth one		FJ 10773	£ 2 – 4
57	Mean to me/Supper party		FJ 10851	£ 2 – 4
57	The midgets/Blue eyes		FJ 10952	£ 2 – 4

KATHY KIRBY
60	Love can be/Crush me	PYE	7N 15313	£ 4 – 6

LARRY KIRBY & THE ENCORES
59	My baby don't love me/My Rose of Kentucky	TOP RANK	JAR 143	£ 2 – 4

PAT KIRBY
56	Happiness is a thing called Joe/Don't tell me not to....	BRUNSWICK	05560	£ 2 – 4
56	What a heavenly night for love/Greensleeves		05575	£ 2 – 4
57	Tammy/Don't keep silent (tell me so)		05697	£ 2 – 4
58	Sayonara/Please be gentle with me		05731	£ 2 – 4

THE (IVOR & BASIL) KIRCHIN BAND (*& SHANI WALLIS)
54	Mambo Macoco/Tangerine	PARLOPHONE	MSP 6144	£ 4 – 6
55	Mother Goose jumps/Minor mambo	DECCA	F 10434	£ 9 – 12
55	Mambo rock/Tweedlee-dee	PARLOPHONE	R 4010 º	£ 6 – 9
56	Rock-a-beatin' boogie/Stone age mambo		R 4140 º	£ 6 – 9
56	The roller/St. Louis blues		R 4222	£ 4 – 6
56	Rockin' & rollin' thru the Darktown Strutters'..:/Ambush		R 4237	£ 6 – 9
57	"Rock Around The World" medley		*R 4266	£ 6 – 9
57	Calypso!!/Jungle fire dance		R 4284	£ 2 – 4
57	The high life/Blues and the happy times		R 4302	£ 2 – 4
57	So rare/Teenage world		R 4335	£ 2 – 4

THE BASIL KIRCHIN BAND
59	Rock-a-conga/Skin tight	PARLOPHONE	R 4527	£ 2 – 4

KEN KIRKHAM
56	It's almost tomorrow/No, not much	COLUMBIA	SCM 5244	£ 2 – 4
58	Now and for always/Cathy		DB 4116	£ 2 – 4

LORD KITCHENER
56	Rock 'n' roll calypso/Life begins at forty	MELODISC	1400 º	£ 4 – 6

EARTHA KITT
53	I want to be evil/Annie doesn't live here any more	H.M.V.	B 10584 º	£ 4 – 6
54ø	Under the bridges of Paris/Lovin' spree		B 10647 º	£ 2 – 4
54ø	as above		7M 191	£ 9 – 12
54	Somebody bad stole de wedding bell/Sandy's tune		7M 198	£ 6 – 9

54	Santa baby/Let's do it (let's fall in love)		7M	234	£ 6 – 9
54	Easy does it/Mink shmink		7M	246	£ 6 – 9
55	Monotonous/African lullaby		7M	282	£ 6 – 9
55	C'est si bon/Senor		7M	288	£ 6 – 9
55	The day that the circus left town/I've got that lovin'..		B	10922 ọ	£ 4 – 6
56	Honolulu rock-a-roll-a/Je cherche un homme (I want a...)		7M	422	£12 – 18
57	Just an old-fashioned girl/If I can't take it with me...		POP	309	£ 6 – 9
57	There is no cure for l'amour/Hey Jacque		POP	346	£ 4 – 6
58	Take my love/Proceed with caution	R.C.A.	RCA	1037	£ 2 – 4
58	Just an old-fashioned girl/If I can't take it with me...		RCA	1087	£ 4 – 6
58	I want to be evil/Oh John!		RCA	1093	£ 4 – 6
59	Love is a gamble/Sholem	LONDON	HLR	8969	£ 4 – 6
60	There's no cure for l'amour/Let's do it	R.C.A.	RCA	1180	£ 2 – 4

ANNETTE KLOOGER (& *TED HEATH MUSIC/+FOUR JONES BOYS/=EDMUNDO ROS ORCH.)

56	The rock and roll waltz/Rock around the island	DECCA	*F	10701	£ 6 – 9
56	The magic touch/We'll love again		+F	10733	£ 4 – 6
56	Why do fools fall in love?/Lovely one		+F	10738	£ 6 – 9
56	Mama, teach me to dance/Mama, I long for a sweetheart .		=F	10776	£ 4 – 6
57	The wisdom of a fool/Tra la la		*F	10844	£ 4 – 6

SONNY KNIGHT

57	Confidential/Jail bird	LONDON	HLD	8362	£40 – 60
59	But officer/Dear wonderful God	VOGUE	V	9134	£40 – 60

THE KNIGHTSBRIDGE STRINGS

59	Cry/The windows of Paris	TOP RANK	JAR	170	£ 2 – 4
59	Wheel of fortune/Cow-cow boogie		JAR	216	£ 2 – 4

THE KNOCKOUTS

60	Riot in Room 3c/Darling Lorraine	TOP RANK	JAR	279	£ 9 – 12

BUDDY KNOX

57ø	Party doll/My baby's gone	COLUMBIA	DB	3914	£18 – 25
57	Rock your little baby to sleep/Don't make me cry		DB	3952	£18 – 25
57	Hula love/Devil woman		DB	4014	£12 – 18
58	Whenever I'm lonely/Swingin' daddy		DB	4077	£12 – 18
58	C'mon baby/Somebody touched me		DB	4180	£12 – 18
59	I think I'm gonna kill myself/To be with you		DB	4302	£12 – 18

MOE KOFFMAN QUARTET

58ø	Swingin' shepherd blues/Hambourg bound	LONDON	HLJ	8549	£ 4 – 6
58	Little pixie/Koko-mamey		HLJ	8633	£ 2 – 4
59	Shepherd's cha-cha/The great healer		HLJ	8813	£ 2 – 4

JIMMIE KOMACK

54	Nic-name song/Cold Summer blues	V-CORAL	Q	2031	£ 2 – 4
55	Wabash 4-7473/An old beer bottle		Q	72061	£ 2 – 4
55	Rock-a-bye your baby with a Dixie...../This is the place		Q	72087	£ 2 – 4

ALEXIS KORNER SKIFFLE GROUP

58	I ain't gonna worry no more/County jail	TEMPO	A	166	£ 9 – 12

BILL KRENZ & HIS RAGTIMERS

56	There'll be no new tunes on this old piano/Goofus	LONDON	HLU	8258	£ 9 – 12

HARDY KRUGER

59	Blind date (I'm a lonely man)/PINEWOOD ORCH.: Blind date	TOP RANK	TR	5005	£ 2 – 4

GENE KRUPA

60	Cherokee/Indiana "Montage"	H.M.V.	POP	750	£ 2 – 4

THE KUF-LINX

58	So tough/What'cha gonna do	LONDON	HLU	8583	£40 – 60

CHARLIE KUNZ

54ø	"Charlie Kunz Piano Medley, No. 114" .... DECCA	F 10419	£ 4 - 6
55	"Charlie Kunz Piano Medley, No. 115"	F 10441	£ 2 - 4
55	"Charlie Kunz Piano Medley, No. 116"	F 10481	£ 2 - 4

JULIUS LA ROSA or LaROSA

55	Mobile/Pass it on .... LONDON	HL 8154	£12 - 18
55	Domani/Mama Rosa	HLA 8170	£12 - 18
55	Suddenly there's a valley/Every time that I kiss Carrie	HLA 8193	£12 - 18
56	Lipstick and candy and rubber-..../Winter in New England H.M.V.	7M 384	£ 4 - 6
56	No other love/Rosanne .... LONDON	HLA 8272	£ 9 - 12
56	Jingle bells (Campanelle)/Jingle dingle	HLA 8353	£ 9 - 12
58ø	Torero/Milano .... R.C.A.	RCA 1063	£ 4 - 6
58	Let nature take its course/Until he gets a girl .... COLUMBIA	DB 4218	£ 2 - 4
59	Where's the girl/Protect me	DB 4287	£ 2 - 4
60	Green fields/Caress me .... LONDON	HLR 9092	£ 2 - 4

CLEO LAINE (*& JOHNNY DANKWORTH ORCH.)

54	I know you're mine/I got rhythm .... *PARLOPHONE	MSP 6107	£ 2 - 4
55	I got it bad and that ain't good/Ain't misbehavin' ...	*MSP 6147	£ 2 - 4
58	Hand me down love/They were right .... PYE	7N 15143	£ 2 - 4
60ø	Let's slip away/Thieving boy .... FONTANA	H 269	£ 2 - 4

FRANKIE LAINE (& *JIMMY BOYD/+JOHNNIE RAY/=THE FOUR LADS/#THE EASY RIDERS/qv DORIS DAY/JO STAFFORD)

51	Jezebel/Rose, Rose, I love you .... COLUMBIA	DB 2876 º	£ 4 - 6
51ø	The girl in the wood/Wonderful, wasn't it?	DB 2907 º	£ 2 - 4
52ø	High noon/Rock of Gibraltar	DB 3113 º	£ 2 - 4
53	The ruby and the pearl/The mermaid	SCM 5016	£ 9 - 12
53	Jealousy/The Gandy Dancers' Ball	SCM 5017	£ 9 - 12
53ø	I believe/Your cheatin' heart .... PHILIPS	PB 117 º	£ 2 - 4
53ø	Tell me a story/The little boy and the old man	*PB 126 º	£ 2 - 4
53	I'm just a poor bachelor/Tonight you belong to me ..... COLUMBIA	SCM 5031	£ 9 - 12
53ø	Where the winds blow/I let her go .... PHILIPS	PB 167 º	£ 2 - 4
53ø	Hey Joe!/Sittin' in the sun (countin' my money)	PB 172 º	£ 2 - 4
53ø	Answer me/Ramblin' man	PB 196 º	£ 2 - 4
53ø	Blowing wild/Te amo	PB 207 º	£ 2 - 4
53	The swan song/My Ohio home .... COLUMBIA	SCM 5073	£ 6 - 9
54	I'd give my life/Tomorrow Mountain	SCM 5085	£ 6 - 9
54ø	Granada/New Orleans .... PHILIPS	PB 242 º	£ 2 - 4
54ø	The Kid's last fight/Long distance love	PB 258 º	£ 2 - 4
54ø	There must be a reason/Some day	PB 306 º	£ 2 - 4
54ø	My friend/The Lord don't treat his children that way ..	PB 316 º	£ 2 - 4
54ø	Rain, rain, rain=/Your heart, my heart	PB 311 º	£ 2 - 4
55ø	In the beginning/Old shoes	PB 404 º	£ 2 - 4
55ø	Cool water/Bubbles	PB 465 º	£ 1 - 2
55ø	Strange lady in town/The tarrier song	PB 478 º	£ 2 - 4
55ø	Hummingbird/My little one	PB 498 º	£ 2 - 4
55ø	Hawk-Eye/Your love	PB 519 º	£ 2 - 4
56ø	Sixteen tons/Walking the night away	PB 539 º	£ 2 - 4
56ø	Hell hath no fury/I heard the angels singing	=PB 585 º	£ 2 - 4
56	The cry of the wild goose/Mule train .... MERCURY	MT 109 º	£ 4 - 6
56	Champion, the Wonder Horse/Ticky ticky tick (I'm gonna.) PHILIPS	PB 607 º	£ 4 - 6
56ø	A woman in love/Make me a child again	PB 617 º	£ 1 - 2
56ø	Moonlight gambler/Only if we love	PB 638 º	£ 2 - 4
56ø	*as above*	JK 1000	£ 9 - 12
57ø	Love is a golden ring#/There's not a moment to spare ..	PB 676 º	£ 2 - 4
57ø	*as above*	JK 1009	£ 9 - 12
57	Without him/Lonely man	JK 1017	£ 6 - 9
57ø	Good evening friends/Up above my head, I hear music in..	+PB 708 º	£ 2 - 4
57ø	*as above*	+JK 1026	£ 9 - 12
57	The greater sin/East is east	JK 1032	£ 6 - 9
58	Annabel Lee/Shine	PB 797	£ 4 - 6
58	My gal and a prayer/The lonesome road	PB 821	£ 4 - 6
58	Lovin' up a storm/A kiss can change the world	PB 836	£ 4 - 6

58	I have to cry/Choombala Bay	PB 848	£ 2 – 4
58	When I speak your name/Cottage for sale	PB 886	£ 2 – 4
59	That's my desire/In my wildest dreams	PB 905	£ 2 – 4
59ø	Rawhide/Journey's end	PB 965	£ 4 – 6
60	Rocks and gravel/Jelly coal man	PB 997	£ 2 – 4
60	Et voila/St. James Infirmary	PB 1011	£ 2 – 4
60	Seven women/And doesn't she roll	PB 1064	£ 2 – 4

BONNIE LAKE & HER BEAUX (qv JACK PLEIS)
56	Miracle of love/Thirteen black cats	BRUNSWICK	05622	£ 9 – 12

LEE LAMAR & HIS ORCH.
57	Teenage pedal pushers/Sophia	LONDON	HLB 8508	£ 9 – 12

THE LANA SISTERS (*& AL SAXON)
58	Ring-a my phone/Chimes of Arcady	.FONTANA	H 148	£ 6 – 9
59	Buzzin'/Cry, cry, baby		H 176	£ 6 – 9
59	Mister Dee-Jay/Tell him no		H 190	£ 6 – 9
59	(Seven little girls) Sitting in the...*/Sitting on the..		H 221	£ 4 – 6
60	You've got what it takes/My Mother's eyes		H 235	£ 4 – 6
60	Someone loves you, Joe/Tinatarella di Luna		H 252	£ 2 – 4
60	Two-some/Down South		H 283	£ 2 – 4

CYNTHIA LANAGAN *or LANIGAN
57	Jamie boy/Silent lips	*PARLOPHONE	R 4316	£ 2 – 4
57	I'm available/(Don't stop, don't stop) Tell me more		R 4383	£ 2 – 4

THE LANCERS (*& GEORGIE AULD/qv TERESA BREWER)
54	Stop chasin' me baby/Peggy O'Neil	LONDON	HL 8027	£12 – 18
54	So high, so low, so wide/It's you, it's you I love		HL 8079	£12 – 18
54	Mister Sandman/The little white light	V-CORAL	Q 2038	£ 6 – 9
55	Timberjack/C-r-a-z-y music		Q 72062	£ 6 – 9
55	Get out of the car*/Close your eyes		Q 72081	£ 6 – 9
55	Jo-Ann/The bonnie banks of Loch Lomond		Q 72100	£ 6 – 9
56	Rock around the island/Alphabet rock		Q 72128	£ 9 – 12
56	A man is as good as his word/Little fool		Q 72157	£ 6 – 9
56	The first travelling saleslady/Free		Q 72183	£ 4 – 6
56	Never leave me/I came back to say I'm sorry		Q 72220	£ 2 – 4
57	It happened in Monterey/Ramona//Freckled-face Sara Jane		Q 72254	£ 2 – 4
57	Charm bracelet/And it don't feel bad		Q 72282	£ 2 – 4
58	The stroll/Don't go near the water	CORAL	Q 72300	£ 4 – 6
60	Joey, Joey, Joey/(by JOHNNY DESMOND)		Q 72398	£ 2 – 4

BILL & BRETT LANDIS
59	Bright eyes/Since you've gone	PARLOPHONE	R 4516	£ 2 – 4
59	Forgive me/By you, by you		R 4551	£ 2 – 4
59	Baby talk/Love me true		R 4570	£ 2 – 4

THE LANE BROTHERS
60	Mimi/Two dozen and a half	LONDON	HLR 9150	£ 6 – 9

DESMOND or DES LANE (*w. JOHN BARRY/qv CYRIL STAPLETON)
56	Penny-whistle rock/Penny-whistle polka	DECCA	F 10821	£ 4 – 6
57	Rock Mister Piper/Plymouth Rock		F 10847	£ 4 – 6
59	Moonbird/The clanger march	TOP RANK	*JAR 203	£ 2 – 4

ROSEMARY LANE
60	Down by the river/My first love letter	PHILIPS	PB 1041	£ 2 – 4

DON LANG (& HIS FRANTIC FIVE/+SKIFFLERS) (qv GORDON LANGHORN)
55ø	Cloudburst/Seventeen	H.M.V.	POP 115 ª	£ 2 – 4
56	I want you to be my baby/Four brothers		7M 354	£12 – 18
56	Rock around the island/Jumpin' to conclusions		7M 381	£12 – 18
56	Rock and roll blues/Stop the world I wanna get off		7M 416	£12 – 18
56	Sweet Sue – just you/Lazy Latin		POP 260	£ 6 – 9

57	Rock around the cookhouse/Rock Mister Piper	POP	289	£12 – 18
57	Rock-a-billy/Come go with me+	POP	335	£12 – 18
57ø	School day (Ring! Ring! goes the bell)/Six-five Special	POP	350	£12 – 18
57	White silver sands/Again 'n' again 'n' again	POP	382	£ 6 – 9
57	Texas tambourine/Red planet rock	POP	414	£12 – 18
58	6-5 hand jive/Ramshackle Daddy	POP	434	£12 – 18
58	Tequila/Junior hand jive	POP	465	£ 9 – 12
58ø	Witch doctor/Cool baby cool	POP	488	£ 4 – 6
58	The bird on my head/Hey Daddy!	POP	510	£ 4 – 6
58	Queen of the hop/La-do-da-da	POP	547	£ 6 – 9
59	Wiggle wiggle/(You were only) Teasin'	POP	585	£ 4 – 6
59	Phineas McCoy/Percy Green	POP	623	£ 2 – 4
59	A hoot an' a holler/See you Friday	POP	649	£ 4 – 6
59	Reveille rock/Frankie and Johnny	POP	682	£ 4 – 6
60ø	Sink the Bismarck!/They call him Cliff	POP	714	£ 6 – 9
60	Time machine/Don't open that door	POP	805	£ 4 – 6

RAY LANG
57	Last train (Biddi-biddi bum bum)/Keetch (Hey! Bernice)	BRUNSWICK	05683	£ 4 – 6

GORDON LANGHORN (became DON LANG/qv CYRIL STAPLETON)
55	Give a fool a chance/Don't stay away too long	DECCA	F 10591	£ 4 – 6

SNOOKY LANSON
56	It's almost tomorrow/Why don't you write	LONDON	HLD 8223	£18 – 25
56	Stop (Let me off the bus)/Last minute love		HLD 8236	£40 – 60
56	Seven days/Tippity top		HLD 8249	£40 – 60

MARIO LANZA
52ø	Because you're mine/The song angels sing	H.M.V.	DA 2017 º	£ 1 – 2
52ø	*as above*		7R 144	£ 4 – 6
54ø	I'll walk with God/Beloved		DA 2062 º	£ 1 – 2
54ø	Drinking song/Serenade [Romberg]		DA 2065 º	£ 1 – 2
56ø	Serenade [Brodszky]/My destiny		DA 2085 º	£ 1 – 2
58	Drinking song/Serenade [Romberg]	R.C.A.	RCA 1090	£ 2 – 4
58	I'll walk with God/The Lord's Prayer		RCA 1094	£ 2 – 4
60	Because you're mine/The donkey serenade		RCA 1166	£ 2 – 4

THE LASSIES
56	Sleepy head/This I offer you	BRUNSWICK	05571	£ 4 – 6

ROD LAUREN
59	If I had a girl/No wonder	R.C.A.	RCA 1165	£ 2 – 4

JOHN LAURENZ
55	Goodbye, stranger, goodbye/Red roses	LONDON	HL 8138	£12 – 18

THE LAURIE SISTERS.
60	Don't forget (to sign your name with..)/I surrender dear	M-G-M	MGM 1083	£ 2 – 4

LINDA LAURIE
59	Ambrose/Ooh, what a lover	LONDON	HL 8807	£ 4 – 6
60	All winter long/Stay with me	TOP RANK	JAR 277	£ 4 – 6

AZIE LAWRENCE & THE CARIB SERENADERS
60	West Indians in England/Jump up	STARLITE	ST.45 022	£ 4 – 6

EDDIE LAWRENCE
59	The salesman's philosopher/Mother Philosopher	CORAL	Q 72361	£ 2 – 4

ELLIOT LAWRENCE & HIS ORCH.
51	Sixty minute man/Quick	VOGUE	V 9024 º	£ 4 – 6
52	Lovin' machine/Don't leave my poor heart breakin'		V 9032 º	£ 4 – 6

REMEMBER! – THE SYMBOL º AFTER THE CATALOGUE NUMBER INDICATES A 78 rpm RECORD

LARRY LAWRENCE (& *THE BAND OF GOLD/+THE BEATNIKS)

59	Goofin' off/Bongo boogie	*PYE INT. 7N 25042	£ 4 - 6
60	Jug-a-roo/Squad Car theme	EMBER +EMB S106	£ 4 - 6

LEE LAWRENCE (*& THE CORONETS)

53ø	Crying in the chapel/To live my life with you	DECCA	F 10177 º	£ 2 - 4
54	The little mustard seed/My love for you		F 10285	£ 4 - 6
54	The story of Tina/For you my love		F 10367	£ 4 - 6
54	The things I didn't do/You still mean the same to me ..		F 10408	£ 4 - 6
55	My own true love (Tara's theme)/Beware now!		F 10422	£ 4 - 6
55	Lights of Paris/A love like ours		F 10438	£ 4 - 6
55	Will you be mine alone?/Wedding bells and silver horse..		F 10485	£ 4 - 6
55	Beyond the stars/Give me your word	COLUMBIA SCM 5175	£ 4 - 6
55	My world stood still/Don't worry		SCM 5181	£ 4 - 6
55	More than a millionaire/Overnight		SCM 5190	£ 4 - 6
55ø	Suddenly there's a valley/Mi muchacha (Little girl) ...		DB 3681 º	£ 2 - 4
55ø	as above		SCM 5201	£ 9 - 12
56	Don't tell me not to love you/Young and foolish		SCM 5228	£ 4 - 6
56	We believe in love/Welcome to my heart		SCM 5254	£ 4 - 6
56	Valley Valparaiso/Come back, my love		SCM 5283	£ 4 - 6
56	High upon a mountain/From the candy store on the corner.		DB 3830	£ 4 - 6
56	Rock'n roll opera/Don't nobody move		DB 3855	£12 - 18
57	By you, by you, by you/Your love is my love		*DB 3885	£ 4 - 6
57	Chapel of the Roses/Sold to the man with the broken.....		DB 3922	£ 4 - 6
57	Lonely ballerina/His servant		DB 3981	£ 4 - 6
59	Be my love/The man I could be	TOP RANK JAR 175	£ 2 - 4

STEVE LAWRENCE (*& BERNIE LAWRENCE/+GUINEVERE/qv EYDIE GORME)

53	This night (Madalena)/Say it isn't true	*PARLOPHONE MSP 6038	£ 6 - 9
54	Too little time/Remember me (You taught me to love) ..		MSP 6080	£ 6 - 9
54	You can't hold a memory in your arms/King for a day ..		MSP 6106	£ 6 - 9
55	Open up the gates of mercy/My impression of Janie	V-CORAL Q 72114	£ 4 - 6
56	Speedoo/The chicken and the hawk		Q 72133	£ 9 - 12
57	The banana boat song/If you would say you're mine		Q 72228	£ 4 - 6
57	Party doll/Pum-pa-lum (The bad donkey)		Q 72243	£ 6 - 9
57	Fabulous/Can't wait for the Summer		Q 72264	£ 6 - 9
57	Fraulein/Blue rememberin' you		Q 72281	£ 4 - 6
57	Never mind/Long before I knew you		Q 72286	£ 2 - 4
58	Geisha girl/I don't know	CORAL Q 72304	£ 2 - 4
58	Those nights at the Round Table+/Stranger in Mexico ...		Q 72335	£ 2 - 4
59	These things are free/I only have eyes for you		Q 72353	£ 2 - 4
59	Only love me (Angelina)/Loving is a way of living	H.M.V. POP 604	£ 2 - 4
60	Pretty blue eyes/You're nearer		POP 689	£ 4 - 6
60ø	Footsteps/You don't know		POP 726	£ 4 - 6
60	Say it isn't true/My shawl	TOP RANK JAR 416	£ 2 - 4
60	Why, why, why/You're everything wonderful	H.M.V. POP 763	£ 2 - 4
60ø	Girls, girls, girls/Little Boy Blue	LONDON HLT 9166	£ 2 - 4
60	Going steady/Come back, silly girl	H.M.V. POP 795	£ 2 - 4

YANK LAWSON & THE YANKEE CLIPPERS

60	The party's over/The march of the Siamese children	PYE INT. 7N 25054	£ 2 - 4

THE LAY-A-BAHTS

60	fings ain't wot they used t'be/layin' abaht/etc.	PARLOPHONE R 4641	£ 2 - 4

EDDIE LAYTON

58	Bright lights of Brussels/Over the waves	MERCURY 7MT 221	£ 2 - 4
59	Doodles/Duck walk		AMT 1064	£ 4 - 6

TEDDY LAYTON JAZZ BAND

58	Down by the riverside/Wooden Joe's weary blues	PARLOPHONE R 4411	£ 2 - 4

THE LEA VALLEY SKIFFLE GROUP

57	Streamline train/Railroad Bill	ESQUIRE 10-508 º	£ 4 - 6
58	I'm gonna walk and talk with Jesus/Oh Mary, don't you...		10-518 º	£ 4 - 6

BILL LEATHERWOOD

60	The long walk/My foolish heart	TOP RANK	JAR 506	£ 2 – 4

LORD LEBBY

60	Caldonia/One kiss from my baby	STARLITE ST.45 018	£12 – 18

HUDDIE LEDBETTER (*as LEADBELLY)

50	Becky Deem, she was a gamblin' gal/Pig meat Papa	TEMPO	R 11 º £ 6 – 9
50	Four day worry blues/New black snake moan		R 13 º £ 6 – 9
51	How long/Good morning blues	MELODISC	*1140 º £ 6 – 9
51	Goodnight Irene/Ain't you glad		*1151 º £ 6 – 9
51	On a Monday/John Henry		*1187 º £ 6 – 9

LEE & PAUL

59	The chick/Valentina, my Valentina	PHILIPS	PB 912	£ 2 – 4

BENNY LEE (*& THE KEN–TONES)

56	Love plays the strings of my banjo*/Born to sing the..	PARLOPHONE	MSP 6214	£ 4 – 6
56	Sweet heartaches/How long has this been going on?		MSP 6252	£ 4 – 6
56	Rock 'n rollin' Santa Claus/Life was made for livin' ..		*R 4245	£ 4 – 6

BRENDA LEE

56	I'm gonna lasso Santa Claus/Christy Christmas	BRUNSWICK	05628	£40 – 60
57	Love you till I die/Dynamite		05685	£40 – 60
57	Ain't that love/One teenager to another		05720	£25 – 40
58	Ring–a–my–phone/(Rock on your little......) Little Jonah		05755	£40 – 60
59	Bill Bailey, won't you please../Hummin' the blues over..		05780	£ 9 – 12
60ø	Sweet nuthin's/Weep no more my baby		05819	£ 6 – 9
60ø	I'm sorry/That's all you gotta do		05833	£ 4 – 6
60ø	I want to be wanted/Just a little		05839	£ 4 – 6
61ø	Let's jump the broomstick/Rock–a–bye baby blues		05823	£ 6 – 9

BYRON LEE & THE DRAGONAIRES

60	Dumplin's/Kissin' gal	BLUE BEAT	BB 2	£ 4 – 6

CURTIS LEE

60	With all my heart (I love you)/Pure love	TOP RANK	JAR 317	£ 9 – 12

DICK LEE

53	All I want is a chance/The show has ended	COLUMBIA	SCM 5066	£ 2 – 4
53	Happy bells/I thought you might be lonely		SCM 5078	£ 2 – 4
54	The Book/Stay in my arms, Cinderella		SCM 5094	£ 2 – 4
59	A penny a kiss – a penny a hug/Bermuda	M–G–M	MGM 1013	£18 – 25

JACKIE LEE (U.K.)

55	I was wrong/For as long as I live	DECCA	F 10550	£ 2 – 4

JACKIE LEE (U.S.)

60	Rancho/Like sunset	TOP RANK	JAR 286	£ 4 – 6

JOHNNIE LEE

59	It's–a me, it's–a me, it's–a me my love/Echo	PYE	7N 15201	£ 2 – 4
59	I'm finally free/I fell		7N 15233	£ 2 – 4
60	They're wrong/Cindy Lou	FONTANA	H 257	£ 2 – 4
60	Poetry in motion/Let it come true		H 280	£ 2 – 4

LAURA LEE

60	Tell Tommy I miss him/I'm sending back your roses	TRIUMPH	RGM 1030	£ 9 – 12

PEGGY LEE (*& MILLS BROTHERS/+OLIVER WALLACE/=THE POUND HOUNDS/#JIM BACKUS/%GEORGE
SHEARING QUINTET/qv BING CROSBY)

54	Johnny Guitar/I didn't know what time it was	BRUNSWICK	05286	£ 4 – 6
54	Sisters/Love, you didn't do right by me		05345.	£ 4 – 6
55	Let me go, lover/Bouquet of blues		05360	£ 4 – 6
55	Straight ahead/It must be so		*05368	£ 4 – 6

55	Baubles, bangles and beads/Summer vacation		05421	£ 2 -	4
55	I belong to you/How bitter, my sweet		05435	£ 2 -	4
55	Ooh that kiss/Oh! No! (Please don't go)		05461	£ 2 -	4
55	Sugar/What can I say after I say I'm sorry		05471	£ 2 -	4
55	He needs me/Sing a rainbow		05472	£ 2 -	4
55	He's a tramp=/The Siamese cat song+		05482	£ 4 -	6
55	Bella notte/La La Lu		05483	£ 2 -	4
56	Three cheers for Mister Magoo/Mister Magoo does the.....		#05549	£ 4 -	6
56	The come back/You've got to see Mama every night		05554	£ 2 -	4
56	That's all right honey/Love you so		05593	£ 2 -	4
56	We laughed at love/They can't take that away from me ..		05625	£ 2 -	4
57ø	Mr. Wonderful/The gyspy with fire in his shoes		05671	£ 4 -	6
57	Baby, baby wait for me/Every night	CAPITOL	CL 14741	£ 2 -	4
57	I don't know enough about you/Where flamingos fly	BRUNSWICK	05714	£ 2 -	4
57	Listen to the rockin' bird/Uninvited dreams	CAPITOL	CL 14795	£ 2 -	4
58ø	Fever/You don't know		CL 14902	£ 4 -	6
58	Light of love/Sweetheart		CL 14955	£ 2 -	4
59	My man/Alright, okay, you win		CL 14984	£ 2 -	4
59	It ain't necessarily so/Swing low, sweet chariot	BRUNSWICK	05798	£ 2 -	4
59	Hallelujah, I love him so/I'm lookin out the window ...	CAPITOL	CL 15025	£ 2 -	4
59	You came a long way from St. Louis/I lost my sugar in...		%CL 15058	£ 2 -	4
59	You deserve/Things are swingin'		CL 15103	£ 2 -	4

ROBERTA LEE (*& HARDROCK GUNTER)

53	Sixty minute man*/(by RED FOLEY)	BRUNSWICK	05076 ℚ	£ 6 -	9
54	When the organ played at twilight/True love and tender..	H.M.V.	7M 261	£ 2 -	4
55	Ridin' to Tennessee/I'll be there if you ever want me .	BRUNSWICK	05388	£ 4 -	6

BRAD LEEDS

60	I'm walking behind you/A teenage love is born	PYE INT. 7N 25050		£ 2 -	4

TOM LEHRER

60	Poisoning pigeons in the park/Masochism tango	DECCA	F 11243	£ 4 -	6

GLENDA LEIGH

58	Crying roses/Lingering lovers	FONTANA	H 116	£ 2 -	4

JACK LEMMON

60	Theme from "The Apartment"/Lemmon-flavoured blues	FONTANA	H 262	£ 2 -	4

THE LENNON SISTERS

56	Graduation day/Toy tiger	V-CORAL	Q 72176	£ 4 -	6
57	Young and in love/Teenage waltz		Q 72259	£ 4 -	6
57	Shake me I rattle/Pocohontas		Q 72285	£ 6 -	9

ANN LEONARDO

57	Straws in the wind/Travelling stranger	CAPITOL	CL 14723	£ 2 -	4
57	Lottery/One and only		CL 14755	£ 2 -	4
57	Three time loser/I'll wait till Monday		CL 14797	£ 2 -	4

TOMMY LEONETTI

54	That's what you made me/I love my Mama	CAPITOL	CL 14199	£ 4 -	6
55	Ever since you went away/Untied		CL 14272	£ 4 -	6
56	Heartless/Sometime		CL 14556	£ 2 -	4
56	It's wild/Free		CL 14598	£ 2 -	4
56	Too proud/Wrong		CL 14654	£ 2 -	4
59	Dream lover/Moonlight serenade	R.C.A.	RCA 1107	£ 4 -	6

LORNE LESLEY

59	Some of these days/When love has let you down	PARLOPHONE R 4518		£ 2 -	4
59	Warm/You ought to be mine		R 4567	£ 2 -	4
59	So high, so low/I don't know		R 4581	£ 4 -	6
60	Take all my love/Ritroviamoci (Till we meet again)	POLYDOR	NH 66928	£ 2 -	4
60	We're gonna dance/Bloodshot eyes		NH 66956	£ 4 -	6

BOB LEWIS
57	The Mayflower song/Far away	PARLOPHONE	R 4309	£ 2 – 4

GEORGE LEWIS & HIS NEW ORLEANS STOMPERS/BAND
56	Climax rag/Deep Bayou blues	VOGUE	V 2051	£ 2 – 4
56	Milenberg joys/Two Jim blues		V 2052	£ 2 – 4
56	Just a closer walk with Thee/Just a little while to.....		V 2053	£ 2 – 4
56	Fidgety feet/Dauphine Street blues		V 2054	£ 2 – 4
56	Don't go 'way nobody/Careless love blues		V 2055	£ 2 – 4
60	South Rampart Street Parade/Chinatown my Chinatown	H.M.V.	POP 707	£ 2 – 4

JERRY LEWIS (*& DEAN MARTIN)
56	I love a murder mystery/I keep her picture hanging up–..	CAPITOL	CL 14559	£ 2 – 4
56	Buckskin beauty/Pardners*		CL 14626	£ 2 – 4
57ø	Rock-a-bye your baby with a Dixie.../Come rain or come..	BRUNSWICK	05636	£ 4 – 6
57	Let me sing and I'm happy/It all depends on you		05672	£ 2 – 4
57	With these hands/My Mammy		05693	£ 2 – 4
57	By myself/No one		05710	£ 2 – 4
58	Sad sack/Shine on your shoes		05727	£ 2 – 4
58	Dormi, dormi, dormi/Love is a lonely thing		05756	£ 2 – 4
59	Song from "The Geisha Boy"/The more I see you		05777	£ 2 – 4

JERRY LEE LEWIS
57ø	Whole lotta shakin' goin' on/It'll be me	LONDON	HLS 8457	£ 9 – 12
57ø	Great balls of fire/Mean woman blues		HLS 8529	£ 9 – 12
58	You win again/I'm feeling sorry		HLS 8559	£12 – 18
58ø	Breathless/Down the line		HLS 8592	£ 9 – 12
58	Break–up/I'll make it all up to you		HLS 8700	£ 9 – 12
59ø	High school confidential/Fools like me		HLS 8780	£ 9 – 12
59ø	Lovin' up a storm/Big blon' baby		HLS 8840	£ 9 – 12
59	Let's talk about us/The ballad of Billy Joe		HLS 8941	£ 6 – 9
59	Little Queenie/I could never be ashamed of you		HLS 8993	£ 6 – 9
60	I'll sail my ship alone/It hurt me so		HLS 9083	£ 6 – 9
60ø	Baby, baby, bye bye/Old Black Joe		HLS 9131	£ 6 – 9
60	John Henry/Hang up my rock and roll shoes		HLS 9202	£ 6 – 9

JOE "CANNONBALL" LEWIS
51	Train whistle nightmare/Trust me again	M–G–M	MGM 430 º	£ 6 – 9

MONICA LEWIS
56	I wish you love/Stay after school (Scalintella)	PARLOPHONE	R 4224	£ 2 – 4

PATTI LEWIS
56	Happiness Street (corner Sunshine Square)/Earthbound ..	COLUMBIA	DB 3825	£ 2 – 4
57	Your wild heart/A poor man's roses (or a rich man's....)		DB 3923	£ 2 – 4
57	Speak for yourself John/Pull down de shade		DB 3967	£ 2 – 4

RICHARD LEWIS
60	Hey, little boy/Hey, little girl	DOWNBEAT	CHA 1	£ 9 – 12

SMILEY LEWIS
53	Big Mamou/Play girl	LONDON	L 1189 º	£12 – 18
56	One night/Ain't gonna do it		HLU 8312	£120–160
56	Down yonder we go ballin'/Don't be that way (Please....)		HLU 8337	£120–160
57	Shame, shame, shame/No, no		HLP 8367	£90 –120

TINY LEWIS
59	Too much rockin'/I get weak	PARLOPHONE	R 4617	£40 – 60

VIC LEWIS & HIS ORCH.
54	Happy hornblowers/Bark for Barksdale	DECCA	F 10260	£ 2 – 4
56	Intermission rock/Natal		FJ 10803	£ 2 – 4

JOHN LEYTON
60	Tell Laura I love her/Goodbye to teenage love	TOP RANK	JAR 426	£12 – 18
60	The girl on the floor above/Terry Brown's in love with..	H.M.V.	POP 798	£ 9 – 12

LIBERACE

55ø	Unchained melody/The bridges at Toko-Ri	PHILIPS	PB 430 º	£ 2 - 4
56ø	I don't care (as long as you care for..)/As time goes by	COLUMBIA	DB 3834	£ 4 - 6

JOE LIGGINS & HIS HONEYDRIPPERS

50	I've got a right to cry/Blue moods	PARLOPHONE	R 3309 º	£12 - 18

TERRY LIGHTFOOT'S (NEW ORLEANS) JAZZMEN

57	I saw Mommy kissing Santa Claus/Winter wonderland	COLUMBIA	DB 4032	£ 2 - 4
58	My bucket's got a hole in it/Good time swing	PYE JAZZ	7NJ 2018	£ 2 - 4
60	The preacher/The onions	COLUMBIA	DB 4519	£ 2 - 4

KATHY LINDEN

58	Billy/If I could hold you in my arms	FELSTED	AF 102	£ 2 - 4
58	You'd be surprised/Why oh why		AF 105	£ 2 - 4
58	Oh! Johnny, Oh! Johnny Oh!/Georgie		AF 108	£ 2 - 4
58	Kissin' conversation/Just a sandy haired boy called.....		AF 111	£ 2 - 4
59	Goodbye Jimmy, goodbye/Heartaches at sweet sixteen		AF 122	£ 2 - 4
59	You don't know girls/So close to my heart		AF 124	£ 2 - 4
60	Think love/Mary Lou Wilson and Johnny Brown		AF 130	£ 2 - 4

THE LINDYS

60	The train of love/You know how things get around	DECCA	F 11253	£ 2 - 4
60	Boy with the eyes of blue/Someone else's roses		F 11272	£ 2 - 4

LITTLE ABNER

57	Not here, not there/You mean everything to me	ORIOLE	CB 1380 º	£ 4 - 6

LITTLE ANTHONY & THE IMPERIALS

58	Tears on my pillow/Two people in the world	LONDON	HLH 8704	£12 - 18
59	So much/Oh yeah		HL 8848	£12 - 18
60	Shimmy, shimmy, ko-ko bop/I'm still in love with you ..	TOP RANK	JAR 256	£ 6 - 9
60	My empty room/Bayou, Bayou, baby		JAR 366	£ 6 - 9

LITTLE BILL & THE BLUENOTES

59	I love an angel/Bye, bye baby	TOP RANK	JAR 176	£ 6 - 9

THE LITTLE DIPPERS

60	Forever/Two by four	PYE INT.	7N 25051	£ 2 - 4

LITTLE JOE *& THE THRILLERS

60	Stay*/Cherry	FONTANA	H 281	£ 9 - 12

LITTLE JOHNNY & THE THREE TEENAGERS

58	Baby lover/Rickety rackety rendezvous	DECCA	F 10990	£ 4 - 6

LITTLE LEMMY & BIG JOE

58	Kwela No. 5/Little Lemmy kwela	DECCA	F 11054	£ 2 - 4

LITTLE RICHARD

56ø	Rip it up/Ready Teddy	LONDON	HLO 8336	£18 - 25
57ø	Long tall Sally/Tutti frutti		HLO 8366	£18 - 25
57ø	The girl can't help it/She's got it		HLO 8382	£18 - 25
57ø	Lucille/Send me some lovin'		HLO 8446	£ 9 - 12
57ø	Jenny, Jenny/Miss Ann		HLO 8470	£ 9 - 12
57ø	Keep a knockin'/Can't believe you wanna leave		HLO 8509	£ 9 - 12
58ø	Good golly Miss Molly/Hey-hey-hey-hey		HLU 8560	£ 9 - 12
58ø	Ooh! my soul/True, fine Mama		HLO 8647	£ 9 - 12
58ø	Baby face/I'll never let you go		HLU 8770	£ 9 - 12
59ø	By the light of the silvery Moon/Early one morning		HLU 8831	£ 9 - 12
59ø	Kansas City/She knows how to rock		HLU 8868	£ 9 - 12
60	Baby/I got it		HLU 9065	£ 9 - 12

LITTLE TONY & HIS BROTHERS

59	Who's that knockin'/The beat	DURIUM	DC 16639	£ 9 - 12
59	I can't help it/Arrivederci baby	DECCA	F 11164	£ 4 - 6
59	The hippy hippy shake/Hey little girl		F 11169	£ 6 - 9

59ø	Too good/Foxy little Mama		F 11190	£ 4 – 6
60	I love you/The magic of love		F 21218	£ 4 – 6
60	Princess/I love you		F 21223	£ 4 – 6
60	Teddy girl/Kiss me, kiss me		F 21247	£ 6 – 9

LITTLE WALTER
60	My babe/Blue midnight	LONDON	HLM 9175	£12 – 18

"BIG" TINY LITTLE
57	School day/That's the only way to live	V-CORAL	Q 72263	£ 9 – 12

JERRY LLOYD
60	Be faithful, be true/Sooner or later	TOP RANK	JAR 411	£ 2 – 4

JIMMY LLOYD
58	The Prince of players/Ever since I met Lucy	PHILIPS	PB 795	£ 2 – 4
58	Witch doctor/For your love		PB 827	£ 2 – 4
58	The end/Street in the rain		PB 871	£ 2 – 4
60	Teenage sonata/Falling		PB 1010	£ 2 – 4
60	I double dare you/Just for a thrill		PB 1055	£ 2 – 4

KATHY LLOYD (*& TED HEATH MUSIC)
54	Tomorrow night/It worries me	DECCA	F 10386	£ 2 – 4
54	Teach me tonight/It's a woman's world		F 10418	£ 2 – 4
55	Our future has only begun/Unsuspecting heart		F 10464	£ 2 – 4
55	This must be wrong/Experience unnecessary		*F 10567	£ 2 – 4

HANK LOCKLIN
60ø	Please help me, I'm falling/My old home town	R.C.A.	RCA 1188	£ 2 – 4

MALCOLM LOCKYER & HIS STRICT TEMPO MUSIC FOR DANCING
54	I'm gonna rock, rock, rock/Changing partners	DECCA	F 10304 º	£ 4 – 6

LAURIE LOMAN
54	Whither thou goest/I was the last one to know	LONDON	HL 8101	£12 – 18

ALAN LOMAX & THE RAMBLERS
56	Dirty old town/Hard case	DECCA	F 10787	£ 6 – 9

AL LOMBARDY & HIS ORCH.
54	The blues/The boogie	LONDON	HL 8076	£12 – 18
55	In a little Spanish town/Flying home		HL 8127	£12 – 18

EDDIE LONDON & THE CHIMES
57	Song of the moonlight/I'll thank you	DECCA	F 10859	£ 2 – 4

JOE LONDON
59	It might have been/Lonesome whistle	LONDON	HLW 9008	£ 4 – 6

JULIE LONDON
56ø	Cry me a river/S'wonderful	LONDON	HLU 8240	£18 – 25
56	Baby, baby all the time/Shadow woman		HLU 8279	£12 – 18
57	The meaning of the blues/Now! Baby, now!		HLU 8394	£12 – 18
57	The boy on a dolphin/Tall boy		HLU 8414	£ 4 – 6
58	Saddle the wind/It had to be you		HLU 8602	£ 4 – 6
58	My strange afffair/It's easy		HLU 8657	£ 4 – 6
58	Man of the West/Blue Moon		HLU 8769	£ 4 – 6
59	Must be catchin'/Come on-a my house		HLU 8891	£ 4 – 6

LAURIE LONDON (*& GITTE)
57ø	He's got the whole world in His hands/The cradle rock .	PARLOPHONE	R 4359	£ 4 – 6
58	Handed down/She sells sea shells		R 4388	£ 2 – 4
58	The Gospel train/Boomerang		R 4408	£ 2 – 4
58	Casey Jones/I gotta robe		R 4426	£ 2 – 4
58	Joshua (fit the battle of Jericho)/Basin Street blues .		R 4450	£ 2 – 4
58	My Mother/Darktown Strutters' Ball		R 4474	£ 2 – 4

58	3 o'clock/Up above my head		R 4499	£ 2 –	4
59	Boom–ladda–boom–boom/Pretty–eyed baby*		·R 4557	£ 2 –	4
59	Old time religion/God's little acre		R 4601	£ 2 –	4
60	Roll on Spring/I'm afraid		R 4635	£ 2 –	4
60	Banjo boy/Hear them bells		R 4662	£ 2 –	4

DENISE LOR

54	If I give my heart to you/Hallo darling	PARLOPHONE MSP 6120		£ 2 –	4
55	And one to grow on/Every day of my life	MSP 6148		£ 2 –	4

KENNY LORAN

59	Mama's little baby/Magic star	CAPITOL	CL 15081	£ 4 –	6

JERRY LORDAN (qv LEE & JAY ELVIN)

59ø	I'll stay single/Can we kiss .... '	PARLOPHONE R 4588		£ 4 –	6
60ø	Who could be bluer?/Do I worry?	R 4627		£ 4 –	6
60ø	Sing like an angel/Ev'ry time	R 4653		£ 4 –	6
60	Ring, write or call/I've still got you	R 4695		£ 4 –	6

SOPHIA LOREN (qv PETER SELLERS)

58	Love song from "Houseboat"/Bing! Bang! Bong!	PHILIPS	PB 857	£ 2 –	4

MYRNA LORRIE (*& BUDDY DeVAL)

55	Underway/I'm your man, I'm your gal*	LONDON	HLU 8187	£12 –	18
56	Life's changing scene/Listen to my heartstrings	HLU 8294		£ 9 –	12

DICK LORY

56	Cool it baby/Ball room baby	LONDON	HLD 8348	£60 –	90

JOE LOSS & HIS ORCH.

	Numerous releases on H.M.V.	all valued at under £ 2	

DENNIS LOTIS (& *TED HEATH MUSIC/+THE JOHNSTON BROTHERS)

54	Such a night/Cuddle me	DECCA	+*F 10287	£ 6 –	9
54	Honey love/Manhattan mambo		*F 10392	£ 4 –	6
55	Chain reaction/Go, go, go		*F 10471	£ 4 –	6
55	Face of an angel, heart of a devil/The golden ring		F 10469	£ 2 –	4
57	Tammy/I complain	COLUMBIA	DB 3993	£ 2 –	4
58	Good mornin' life/Valentina		DB 4056	£ 2 –	4
58	Gretna Green/I may never pass this way again		DB 4090	£ 2 –	4
58	The only man on the island/Guess what the neighbours'll.		DB 4158	£ 2 –	4
58	Belonging to someone/Safe in the arms of my darling ...		DB 4182	£ 2 –	4
59	Moonlight serenade/Danger within		DB 4277	£ 2 –	4
59	Who is? You are!/Too much		DB 4339	£ 2 –	4
60	I wish it were you/Love me a little		DB 4432	£ 2 –	4
60	Strangers when we meet/Two wrongs don't make a right ..		DB 4507	£ 2 –	4

PETER LOTIS

60	Doo–dah/You're singing our love song to somebody else .	EMBER	EMB S110	£ 2 –	4

BONNIE LOU (*& RUSTY YORK)

53	Seven lonely days/Dancin' with someone	PARLOPHONE MSP 6021		£ 9 –	12
53	Hand–me–down heart/Scrap of paper	MSP 6036		£ 9 –	12
53ø	Tennessee wig walk/Just out of reach	R 3730 º		£ 4 –	6
53ø	*as above*	MSP 6048		£12 –	18
53	Pa–paya mama/Since you said goodbye	MSP 6051		£ 9 –	12
54	The Texas polka/No heart at all	MSP 6072		£ 9 –	12
54	Don't stop kissing me goodnight/The welcome mat	MSP 6095		£ 9 –	12
54	Huckleberry pie/No one	MSP 6108		£ 9 –	12
54	Blue Tennessee rain/Wait for me, darling	MSP 6117		£ 9 –	12
54	Two step – side step/Please don't laugh when I cry	MSP 6132		£ 9 –	12
55	Tennessee mambo/Train whistle blues	MSP 6151		£ 9 –	12
55	Tweedle dee/The finger of suspicion points at you	MSP 6157		£12 –	18
55	A rusty old halo/Danger! Heartbreak ahead	R 4012 º		£ 4 –	6
55	Drop me a line/Old faithful and true love	MSP 6173		£ 9 –	12
55	The barnyard hop/Tell the world	MSP 6178		£ 9 –	12

55	Dancin' in my socks/Daddy-O		MSP 6188	£12 - 1?
56	Miss the love (that I've been dreaming of)/Darlin' why		MSP 6223	£ 6 - ?
56	Bo weevil (A country song)/Chaperon		MSP 6234	£ 9 - 1?
56	Lonesome lover/Little Miss Bobby Sox		MSP 6253	£ 9 - 1?
56	No rock 'n roll tonight/One track love		R 4215	£ 9 - 1?
57	Runnin' away/Teenage wedding		R 4350	£ 9 - 1?
58	La dee dah/Let the school bell ring ding-a-ling		*R 4409	£25 - 4(

THE LOUVIN BROTHERS
59	Knoxville girl/I wish it had been a dream	CAPITOL	CL 14989	£ 4 - ?
59	You're learning/My curly headed baby		CL 15078	£ 4 - ?

THE LOVERS
58	I wanna' be loved/Let's elope	VOGUE	V 9111	£40 - 6(

JIM LOWE
55	Close the door/Nuevo Laredo	LONDON	HLD 8171	£18 - 2?
56	Blue suede shoes/Maybellene		HLD 8276	£40 - 6C
56	Love is the $64,000 question/Rene la Rue		HLD 8288	£18 - 2?
56ø	The green door/The little man in Chinatown		HLD 8317	£12 - 1?
57	By you, by you, by you/I feel the beat		HLD 8368	£12 - 1?
57	Four walls/Talkin' to the blues		HLD 8431	£ 9 - 12
57	Rock-a-chicka/The bright light		HLD 8538	£40 - 6C
60	He'll have to go/(This life is just a) Dress rehearsal		HLD 9043	£ 4 - 6

PETER LOWE
56	Hear my song of love/Toula	PARLOPHONE	R 4199	£ 2 - 4
57	The banana boat song/The wisdom of a fool		R 4270	£ 2 - 4
57	Tingle/Ca, c'est l'amour		R 4380	£ 2 - 4

JEREMY LUBBOCK
58	Catch a falling star/The man who invented love	PARLOPHONE	R 4399	£ 2 - 4
58	Lemon twist/Tonight		R 4421	£ 2 - 4
58	Odd man out/Too bad you're not around		R 4473	£ 2 - 4

BUDDY LUCAS BAND
60	I want to know/Deacon John	PYE INT.	7N 25045	£ 4 - 6

FRED LUCAS
56	Friendly persuasion (Thee I love)/A thing of beauty	COLUMBIA	DB 3861	£ 2 - 4

JOHNNY LUCK
58	Play rough/Buzz, buzz, buzz	FONTANA	H 110 ℓ	£ 4 - 6

ROBIN LUKE
58ø	Susie darlin'/Living's loving you	LONDON	HLD 8676	£ 6 - 9
58	Chicka chicka honey/My girl		HLD 8771	£ 9 - 12

BOB LUMAN
60	Dreamy doll/Buttercup	WARNER-B	WB 12	£ 4 - 6
60ø	Let's think about living/You've got everything		WB 18	£ 4 - 6
60ø	Why, why, bye, bye/Oh, lonesome me		WB 28	£ 4 - 6

TED LUNE
60	Mr. Custer/Time machine	PHILIPS	PB 1068	£ 2 - 4

DON LUSHER BAND
55	Rock 'n roll/On with the Don	DECCA	F 10560	£ 4 - 6
56	Fast and furious/Let's do it		F 10740	£ 2 - 4

NELLIE LUTCHER
54	Blues in the night/Breezin' along with the breeze	BRUNSWICK	05352	£ 4 - 6
55	It's been said/Please come back		05437	£ 4 - 6
55	Whose honey are you/If I didn't love you like I do		05497	£ 4 - 6
59	My Mother's eyes/The heart of a clown	CAPITOL	CL 15106	£ 2 - 4

LUTHER & LITTLE EVA
57 Love is strange/Ain't got no home	PARLOPHONE	R 4292	£40 - 60

FRANK LUTHER
60 The little red hen (Song story)	DECCA	F 9050	£ 2 - 4
60 The three billy goats Gruff (Song story)		F 9051	£ 4 - 6

ARTHUR LYMAN GROUP
59 Taboo/Dahil sayo	VOGUE	V 9153	£ 2 - 4

FRANKIE LYMON (& THE TEENAGERS)
56ø Why do fools fall in love/Please be mine	COLUMBIA	DB 3772 ọ	£ 4 - 6
56ø as above		SCM 5265	£18 - 25
56 I'm not a know it all/I want you to be my girl		SCM 5285	£18 - 25
56 I promise to remember/Who can explain?		DB 3819	£18 - 25
56 The ABCs of love/Share		DB 3858	£12 - 18
57ø Baby, baby/I'm not a juvenile delinquent		DB 3878	£12 - 18
57 Teenage love/Paper castles		DB 3910	£ 9 - 12
57 Out in the cold again/Miracle in the rain		DB 3942	£ 9 - 12
57ø Goody goody/Creation of love		DB 3983	£ 9 - 12
57 My girl/So goes my love		DB 4028	£12 - 18
58 Footsteps/Thumb thumb		DB 4073	£ 6 - 9
58 Portable on my shoulder/Mama don't allow it		DB 4134	£ 9 - 12
59 Melinda/The only way to love		DB 4245	£ 6 - 9
59 Up jumped a rabbit/No matter what you've done		DB 4295	£ 9 - 12
60 Little bitty pretty one/Creation of love		DB 4499	£ 9 - 12

LEWIS LYMON & THE TEENCHORDS
58 Too young/Your last chance	ORIOLE	CB 1419	£40 - 60

KENNY LYNCH
60ø Mountain of love/Why do you treat me this way?	H.M.V.	POP 751	£ 2 - 4
60 Slowcoach/You make love so well		POP 786	£ 2 - 4

VERA LYNN (& *FRANK WEIR & HIS SAXOPHONE/+THE JOHNSTON BROTHERS)
52ø Auf wiederseh'n, sweetheart/The parting song	DECCA	F 9927 ọ	£ 1 - 2
52ø The homing waltz/Yours		F 9959 ọ	£ 1 - 2
52ø Forget-me-not/When swallows say goodbye		F 9985 ọ	£ 1 - 2
53ø The Windsor waltz/The Lambeth waltz		F 10092 ọ	£ 1 - 2
54 Two Easter Sunday sweethearts/Du bist mein Liebeshoen		F 10253	£ 4 - 6
54 The homecoming waltz/Humble people		F 10290	£ 4 - 6
54ø My son, my son/Our Heaven on Earth		*F 10372	£ 6 - 9
54 "Vera Lynn's Party Sing-Song" medley		F 10411	£ 2 - 4
55 Addio amore+/I do		F 10463	£ 4 - 6
55 Doonaree/Show me the way		F 10535	£ 2 - 4
55 "Vera Lynn Popular Medley, No. 4"		F 10561	£ 2 - 4
55 Ev'ry day of my life/My lonely lover		F 10566	£ 2 - 4
55 Riding my bike/Shopping		F 10613	£ 2 - 4
55 With your love/Unfaithful you		F 10622	£ 2 - 4
56 Last love/Such a day		F 10688	£ 2 - 4
56ø Who are we?/I'll be true to you		F 10715	£ 6 - 9
56 Walk hand in hand/Come back to me		F 10737	£ 2 - 4
56ø A house with love in it/Little lost dog		F 10799	£ 6 - 9
57ø The faithful Hussar (Don't cry my...)/The one beside you		F 10846	£ 6 - 9
57ø Travellin' home/Dear to me		F 10903	£ 6 - 9
57 Across the bridge/If I were you		F 10940	£ 2 - 4
57 I'll remember today/Home for the holidays		F 10963	£ 2 - 4
58 Say/My shining star		F 10995	£ 2 - 4
58 Another time, another place/We're not talking		F 11008	£ 2 - 4
58 Every hour, every day of my life/The wind cannot read		F 11038	£ 2 - 4
58 A window/Be happy		F 11082	£ 2 - 4
59 "Vera Lynn Sings Today's Pop Hits" medley		F 11106	£ 2 - 4
59 Walk with faith in your heart/Glory of love		F 11112	£ 2 - 4
59 Have I told you lately that I.../I'm a fool to forgive..		F 11129	£ 2 - 4
59 Morgen (One more sunrise)/Time marches on		F 11157	£ 2 - 4

```
59ø Auf wiederseh'n, sweetheart/The parting song  ..........      F  9927  £ 6 -  9
60  Travellin' home/The gathering of the clans  ............     F 11249  £ 2 -  4
60  Accordeon/Again  .......................................  M–G–M  MGM 1104  £ 2 -  4

     BARBARA LYON
55ø Stowaway/The pendulum song  ...........................  COLUMBIA  DB 3619 º £ 2 -  4
55  Yes you are/I love to dance with you  .................          SCM 5186  £ 4 -  6
55  Whisper/Where you are  ................................          SCM 5207  £ 4 -  6
56  Band of gold/Such a day  .............................          SCM 5232  £ 4 -  6
56  The birds and the bees/Puppy love  ...................          SCM 5276  £ 4 -  6
56  It's better in the dark/A heart without a sweetheart  ..        DB 3826  £ 4 -  6
56ø Letter to a soldier/Falling in love  .................          DB 3865  £ 6 -  9
57  Fire down below/C'est la vie  ........................          DB 3931  £ 2 -  4
57  Third finger — left hand/Thanks for the loan of a dream         DB 4026  £ 2 -  4
58  Red was the Moon/Ring on a ribbon  ...................          DB 4137  £ 2 -  4
60  My Charlie/Tell me  ..................................  TRIUMPH  RGM 1027  £ 9 - 12

     RICHARD LYON
59  All my own/Private eye  ..............................  FONTANA   H  206  £ 2 -  4

     JIMMY LYTELL
59  Hot cargo/A blues serenade  .........................  LONDON   HL 8873  £ 4 -  6

     HUMPHREY LYTTELTON & HIS BAND (or *"MELODY MAKER" ALL STARS/+THE LYTTELTON PASEO
                             BAND/=& GEORGE BROWNE/qv SHIRLEY ABICAIR)
53  Out of the gallion/The old grey mare  ...............  PARLOPHONE MSP 6001  £ 4 -  6
53  Muskrat ramble/Mamzelle Josephine=  ..................         +MSP 6023  £ 4 -  6
53  Maryland, my Maryland/Blue for Waterloo  .............          MSP 6033  £ 4 -  6
53  Shake it and break it/Jail break  ...................          MSP 6034  £ 4 -  6
53  Kater Street rag/Red for Piccadilly  ................          MSP 6045  £ 4 -  6
53  Martiniquen song (Last year)/Ain't cha got music  ......       MSP 6061  £ 4 -  6
54  East Coast trot/Breeze  .............................          MSP 6076  £ 4 -  6
54  Just once for all time/Joshua, fit the Battle of Jericho       MSP 6093  £ 4 -  6
54  Mainly traditional/Oh! Dad  .........................         *MSP 6097  £ 4 -  6
54  Mezzy's tune/Jelly bean blues  ......................          MSP 6128  £ 4 -  6
56  When the Saints go marching in/Careless love  ........  TEMPO    A  10  £ 4 -  6
56ø Bad penny blues/Close your eyes  ....................  PARLOPHONE R 4184 º £ 4 -  6
56  Love, love, love/Echoing the blues  .................          R 4212  £ 4 -  6
56  The thin red line/Melancholy blues  .................  ESQUIRE  10–491 º £ 4 -  6
56  First of many/Blues for two  ........................          10–494 º £ 4 -  6
57  It's Mardi Gras/Sweet and sour  .....................  PARLOPHONE R 4262  £ 2 -  4
57  Baby doll/Red beans and rice  .......................          R 4277  £ 2 -  4
57  Elizabeth/Blue for Waterloo  ........................  ESQUIRE  10–501 º £ 4 -  6
57  Early call (Bermondsey bounce)/Creole serenade  ........  PARLOPHONE R 4333  £ 2 -  4
57  Dixie theme/Blues at dawn  ..........................          R 4368  £ 2 -  4
57  Cake walkin' babies/If you see me comin'  ...........  ESQUIRE  10–511 º £ 4 -  6
58ø Bad penny blues/Baby doll  ..........................  PARLOPHONE CMSP 41  £18 - 25
58  Buona sera/Blues in the afternoon  ..................          R 4392  £ 2 -  4
58  Hand me down love/Here and gone (Blues in 1890)  .....        R 4428  £ 2 -  4
58  La paloma/Bodega  ...................................  DECCA    F 11058  £ 2 -  4
59  Saturday jump/The bear steps out  ...................  PARLOPHONE R 4519  £ 2 -  4
59  Summertime/Manhunt  .................................          R 4578  £ 2 -  4

     M–G–M STUDIO ORCHESTRA
55  Rock around the clock/"Blackboard Jungle" love theme  ..  M–G–M   SP 1144  £ 4 -  6

     THE M.J.6
60  Tracy's theme/Private eye  ..........................  DECCA    F 11212  £ 2 -  4

     DAVID MACBETH
59ø Mr. Blue/Here's a heart  ............................  PYE      7N 15231  £ 2 -  4
60  Tell her for me/Livin' dangerously  .................          7N 15250  £ 2 -  4
60  Once upon a star/Unhappy  ...........................          7N 15274  £ 2 -  4
60  Pigtails in Paris/Blue blue blue  ...................          7N 15291  £ 2 -  4
```

THE MACK SISTERS
56 Long range love/Stop what you're doing .... LONDON   HLU 8331   £12 – 18

WARNER MACK
58 Rock-a-chicka/Since I lost you .... BRUNSWICK   05728   £60 – 90

GISELE MacKENZIE
53ø Seven lonely days/Till I waltz again with you	CAPITOL	CL 13920 º	£ 1 – 2
55 Hard to get/Boston fancy	H.M.V.	7M 318	£ 2 – 4

KEN MACKINTOSH & HIS ORCH. (*& KENNY BARDELL)
53ø The creep/Tottle-lo-siana	H.M.V.	BD 1295 º	£ 2 – 4
55 Creeping Tom/Lovers in the dark		7M 343	£ 2 – 4
56 Start walking/Curtain call		7M 359	£ 2 – 4
56 Come next Spring*/Blues in the night		7M 379	£ 2 – 4
56 Rock jangle boogie/Touch and go		POP 197 º	£ 4 – 6
56 Sleepwalker/The Berkeley Hunt		7M 403	£ 2 – 4
56 Dizzy fingers/The policeman's holiday		7M 417	£ 2 – 4
56 Highway Patrol/Soft Summer breeze		POP 270	£ 2 – 4
57 Regimental rock/The Buccaneers		POP 287	£ 6 – 9
57 Apple-jack/Slow walk		POP 300	£ 9 – 12
57 Rock man rock/Almost Paradise		POP 327	£ 9 – 12
57 Keep it movin'/Pony tail		POP 358	£ 4 – 6
57 Six-five blues/Marching along to the blues		POP 396	£ 4 – 6
57ø Raunchy/Mojo		POP 426	£ 4 – 6
58 The stroll/The swingin' shepherd blues		POP 441	£ 4 – 6
58 Big guitar/Squatty		POP 464	£ 4 – 6
58 The swivel/Muchacha		POP 506	£ 2 – 4
59 Rock-a-conga/Hampden Park		POP 592	£ 2 – 4
59 Sleep walk/Morgen (One more sunrise)		POP 656	£ 2 – 4
60ø No hiding place/Tally ho!		POP 713	£ 2 – 4

GORDON MacRAE (*& RAY ANTHONY)
54 C'est magnifique/How do you speak to an angel?	CAPITOL	CL 14168	£ 4 – 6
54 Count your blessings instead.../Never in a million years		CL 14193	£ 4 – 6
55 Here's what I'm here for/Love can change the stars		CL 14222	£ 4 – 6
55 Stranger in Paradise/High on a windy hill		CL 14276	£ 4 – 6
55 You forgot (to tell me that you...)/Tik-a-tee, tik-a-tay		CL 14293	£ 4 – 6
55 Jim Bowie/Why break the heart that loves you		CL 14334	£ 4 – 6
55 Bella notte/Blame it on my youth		CL 14361	£ 4 – 6
56 Follow your heart/Fate		CL 14526	£ 2 – 4
56 Never before and never again/Don't blame me		CL 14548	£ 2 – 4
56 Who are we?/There's a lull in my life		CL 14576	£ 2 – 4
56 One misty morning/I asked the Lord		CL 14606	£ 2 – 4
56 The surrey with the fringe.../People will say we're in..		*CL 14613	£ 2 – 4
56 A woman in love/I don't want to walk without you		CL 14622	£ 2 – 4
56 Without love/Obey		CL 14650	£ 2 – 4
57 Endless love/When you kiss me		CL 14743	£ 2 – 4
58 Lonely/Sayonara		CL 14818	£ 2 – 4
58 Now/Till we meet again		CL 14841	£ 2 – 4
58 I've grown accustomed to her face/Never till now		CL 14864	£ 2 – 4
58 The secret/A man once said		CL 14920	£ 2 – 4
59 Fly little bluebird/Little do you know		CL 14983	£ 2 – 4
59 Palace of love/The stranger		CL 15021	£ 2 – 4

JOSH MACRAE
60ø Talking army blues/Talking guitar blues	TOP RANK	JAR 290	£ 4 – 6
60 Original talkin' blues/Talkin' thro' the mill	PYE	7N 15306	£ 2 – 4
60 Let Ramensky go/Sky high Joe		7N 15307	£ 2 – 4
60ø Wild side of life/Dear John		7N 15308	£ 4 – 6

JOHNNY MADARA
57 Be my girl/Love sick	H.M.V.	POP 389	£ 4 – 6

REMEMBER! – THE SYMBOL ø AFTER THE YEAR OF ISSUE INDICATES A BRITISH CHART ENTRY

JOHNNY MADDOX (& HIS ORCH.)

53	Johnny Maddox boogie/Little grass shack	VOGUE	V 9047 º	£ 4 -	6
55	The Crazy Otto (Medley)/Humoresque	LONDON	HL 8134	£12 -	18
55	Do, do, do/When you wore a tulip		HLD 8203	£12 -	18
56	Hands off/Hop scotch boogie		HLD 8277	£12 -	18
56	Dixieland band/Heart and soul		HLD 8347	£ 9 -	12
58	Yellow dog blues/Sugar train		HLD 8540	£ 4 -	6
59	The hurdy gurdy song/Old fashioned love		HLD 8826	£ 2 -	4

ROSE MADDOX

59	Gambler's love/What makes me hang around	CAPITOL	CL 15023	£ 4 -	6

BETTY MADIGAN

54	That was my heart you heard!/Always you	M-G-M	SP 1109	£ 2 -	4
55	And so I walked home/Be a little darlin'		SP 1119	£ 2 -	4
55	The wheels of love/A salute		SP 1131	£ 2 -	4
55	I had a heart/Wonderful words		SP 1137	£ 2 -	4
55	Teddy bear/Strangers		SP 1138	£ 2 -	4
56	Where in the world/The test of time		MGM 924	£ 2 -	4
58	Dance everyone dance/My symphony of love	CORAL	Q 72337	£ 2 -	4
58	A lovely night/True love gone (Come on home)		Q 72348	£ 2 -	4

THE MAGNA JAZZ BAND

57	Buddy's habits/Flat foot	PARLOPHONE	R 4387	£ 2 -	4

MAKADOPOULOS & HIS GREEK SERENADERS

60ø	Never on Sunday/Yasou	PALETTE	PG 9005	£ 2 -	4

PETER MAKANA & HIS RHYTHM BOYS (*& BLACK DUKE)

58	Baboon shepherd*/Black John	ORIOLE	CB 1445	£ 2 -	4
58	Cool mood/Sweet baby		CB 1446	£ 2 -	4

THE MALAGON SISTERS & THE CHA CHA RHYTHM BOYS

59	In a little Spanish town/Lessons in cha-cha-cha	PYE INT.	7N 25008	£ 2 -	4

SIV MALMKVIST

59	Sermonette/The preacher	ORIOLE	CB 1486	£ 2 -	4

HENRY MANCINI & HIS ORCH.

59	Peter Gunn theme/The brothers go to Mother's	R.C.A.	RCA 1134	£ 2 -	4

MANDRAKE

60	The witch's twist/Mandrake	PHILIPS	PB 1093	£ 2 -	4

THE MANHATTAN BROTHERS

55	Lovely lies/Kilimanjaro	DECCA	F 10665	£ 2 -	4

CARL MANN

59	Mona Lisa/Foolish one	LONDON	HLS 8935	£ 9 -	12
59	Pretend/Rockin' love		HLS 9006	£ 9 -	12
60	South of the border/I'm comin' home		HLS 9170	£ 9 -	12

GLORIA MANN

56	Why do fools fall in love/Partners for life	BRUNSWICK	05569	£ 6 -	9
56	It happened again/My secret sin		05610	£ 2 -	4

LORIE MANN

59	Dream lover/A penny a kiss, a penny a hug	TOP RANK	JAR 116	£ 2 -	4
59	Just keep it up/You made me care		JAR 148	£ 2 -	4
59	So many ways/I wonder		JAR 237	£ 2 -	4

BOB MANNING

54	It's all right with me/I'm a fool for you	CAPITOL	CL 14190	£ 4 -	6
55	The very thought of you/Just for laughs		CL 14220	£ 4 -	6
55	Majorca (Isle of love)/It's my life		CL 14256	£ 4 -	6

5	My love song to you/After my laughter came tears		CL 14234	£ 4 – 6
5	The Mission San Michel/You are there		CL 14288	£ 4 – 6
5	What a wonderful way to die/Why didn't you tell me? ...		CL 14318	£ 4 – 6

EDDIE MANNION
0	Just driftin'/Quiet girl	H.M.V.	POP 804	£ 2 – 4

WINGY MANONE
57	Party doll/Real gone	BRUNSWICK	05655	£ 9 – 12

TONY MANSELL (*& JOHNNY DANKWORTH ORCH.)
54	Hold my hand/The high and the mighty	*PARLOPHONE	MSP 6130	£ 2 – 4
56	Zambezi (Sweet African)/11th hour melody		*MSP 6222	£ 4 – 6
58	Impossible/Who are they to say		R 4471	£ 2 – 4

EDDY MANSON
55	Oh! No!/The lovers	H.M.V.	7M 325	£ 2 – 4

MANTOVANI & HIS ORCH. (qv VICO TORRIANI/DAVID WHITFIELD/VARIOUS ARTISTS)
52ø	White Christmas/Adeste fideles	DECCA	F 10017 º	£ 1 – 2
53ø	The song from Moulin Rouge/Vola Colomba		F 10094 º	£ 1 – 2
54ø	Swedish rhapsody/Jamaican rumba		F 10168	£ 4 – 6
54	Luxembourg polka/Music box tango		F 10233	£ 2 – 4
54	Shadow waltz/Moonlight serenade		F 10250	£ 2 – 4
54	Bewitched/Dream, dream, dream		F 10292	£ 2 – 4
54ø	Lonely ballerina/Lazy gondolier		F 10395	£ 4 – 6
55	We'll gather lilacs/Come back to me (Reviens)		F 10439	£ 2 – 4
55	Ma chere amie/Our dream waltz		F 10455	£ 2 – 4
55	Softly, softly/Longing		F 10468	£ 2 – 4
55	Stranger in Paradise/The deserted ballroom		F 10495	£ 2 – 4
57ø	Around the world/The heart of Budapest		F 10888	£ 2 – 4
60	Charmaine/Diane		F 9696	£ 1 – 2

MANUEL & THE MUSIC OF THE MOUNTAINS (actually Geoff Love)
59ø	The honeymoon song/Proud matador	COLUMBIA	DB 4323	£ 1 – 2
60ø	Never on Sunday/The Portuguese washerwomen		DB 4515	£ 1 – 2

LUCILLE MAPP
57	Mangos/On Treasure Island	COLUMBIA	DB 3916	£ 4 – 6
57	Jamie boy/Moonlight in Vermont		DB 3949	£ 2 – 4
57	I'm available/Lovin' ya, lovin' ya, lovin' ya		DB 4040	£ 4 – 6
58	Love is/The early birdie		DB 4071	£ 2 – 4
58	Remember when/I'm a dreamer, aren't we all?		DB 4168	£ 2 – 4
59	Chinchilla/Follow me		DB 4261	£ 2 – 4

TOMMY MARA
55	Pledging my love/Honey bunch	M–G–M	SP 1128	£ 4 – 6
58	Where the blue of the night/What makes you so lovely ..	FELSTED	AF 109	£ 2 – 4
59	You don't know/Marie		AF 116	£ 2 – 4
59	Until I hear from you/Now is the hour		AF 123	£ 2 – 4

(JOSEPH) MARAIS & MIRANDA
53	Old Johnnie Goggabee/The Zulu warrior	COLUMBIA	SCM 5025	£ 2 – 4
59	I-Ha-She/The Queen Bee	FONTANA	H 225	£ 2 – 4

MUZZY MARCELLINO
56	Mary Lou/MR. FORD & MR. GOON-BONES: Ain't she sweet ...	LONDON	HLU 8355	£12 – 18

GLORIA MARCH
58	Baby of mine/Nippon wishing well	LONDON	HLB 8568	£ 4 – 6

HAL MARCH
57	Hear me good/One dozen roses	LONDON	HLD 8534	£ 9 – 12

REMEMBER! – THE SYMBOL º AFTER THE CATALOGUE NUMBER INDICATES A 78 rpm RECORD

JO MARCH
| 58 | Dormi, dormi, dormi/Fare thee well, oh honey | .... | LONDON | HLR 8696 | £ 2 – 4 |
| 58 | The Virgin Mary had one son/I, said the donkey | .... | | HLR 8763 | £ 2 – 4 |

JANIE MARDEN (*& FRANK WEIR & HIS SAXOPHONE)
55	Soldier boy/Hard to get	....	DECCA	F 10600	£ 2 – 4
55	I'll come when you call/Thank you for the waltz	....		*F 10605	£ 2 – 4
56	A teen age prayer/You are my love	....		F 10673	£ 2 – 4
56	Allegheny Moon/Magic melody	....		F 10765	£ 2 – 4

CHARLES MARGULIS
| 59 | Gigi/Malaguena | .... | LONDON | HLL 8774 | £ 2 – 4 |

THE MARILYN SISTERS (qv SUZI MILLER)
55	Bubbles/No chance	....	DECCA	F 10518	£ 2 – 4
55	Genuine love/Everything is big way down in Texas	......		F 10552	£ 2 – 4
55	D-a-r-l-i-n'/The Kinkajou	....		F 10604	£ 2 – 4

THE MARINERS
| 55 | (I love you) Fair dinkum/At the Steamboat River Ball | .. | LONDON | HLA 8201 | £12 – 18 |
| 58 | I heard ya the first time/I live for you | .... | FONTANA | H 127 | £ 2 – 4 |

MARINO MARINI & HIS QUARTET
58	Guitar boogie/Armen's theme	....	DURIUM	DC 16631	£ 4 – 6
58ø	Come prima/Volare (Nel blu dipinto di blu)	....		DC 16632	£ 4 – 6
59ø	Ciao ciao bambina/Avevamo la stessa eta'	....		DC 16636	£ 4 – 6

THE MARK II
| 60 | Night theme/Confusion | .... | COLUMBIA | DB 4549 | £ 4 – 6 |

THE MARK IV
59	I got a wife/Ah-ooo-gah	....	MERCURY	AMT 1025	£ 6 – 9
59	Move over Rover/Dante's inferno	....		AMT 1045	£ 6 – 9
59	Ring, ring, ring those bells/Mairzy doats	....		AMT 1060	£ 2 – 4

MICKI MARLO (*& PAUL ANKA)
54	I'm gonna rock-rock-rock/Love's like that	....	CAPITOL	CL 14086 º	£ 6 – 9
55	Prize of gold/Foolish notion	....		CL 14271	£ 6 – 9
57	What you've done to me*/That's right	....	LONDON	HL 8481	£12 – 18

MARION MARLOWE
| 56 | The hands of time/Ring, phone, ring | .... | LONDON | HLA 8306 | £12 – 18 |

STEVIE MARSH
59ø	If you were the only boy in the world/Leave me alone	..	DECCA	F 11181	£ 4 – 6
60	You don't have to tell me (I know)/Wish	....		F 11209	£ 2 – 4
60	A girl in love/Over and done with	....		F 11244	£ 2 – 4

GARY MARSHAL
| 60 | Oh you beautiful doll/Large as life | .... | PARLOPHONE | R 4636 | £ 2 – 4 |
| 60 | The silent stranger/Lady love | .... | | R 4685 | £ 2 – 4 |

FREDYE MARSHALL
| 57 | Witchcraft/Blue prelude | .... | H.M.V. | POP 407 | £ 2 – 4 |

JACK MARSHALL ORCH. & CHORUS
| 58 | Thunder Road chase/Finger poppin' | .... | CAPITOL | CL 14888 | £ 6 – 9 |

MARY MARSHALL
| 58 | Kiss, kiss, kiss/My island home | .... | COLUMBIA | DB 4163 | £ 2 – 4 |

RALPH MARTERIE & HIS ORCH.
53	Crazy man, crazy/Go away	....	ORIOLE	CB 1199 º	£ 6 – 9
54	Dig that crazy Santa Claus/Rock, rock	....	MERCURY	MB 3176 º	£ 6 – 9
55	Chicken boogie/Silver Moon	....		MB 3220 º	£ 4 – 6
58	Shish-kebab/Tricky	....		7MT 158	£ 4 – 6

58	Tequila/Pop corn		7MT	204	£ 4 - 6
58	Night stroll/Trombone blues		7MT	213	£ 4 - 6
58	Cha-hua-hua/Torero		7MT	232	£ 4 - 6
58	Pretend cha cha/Flighty		AMT	1009	£ 2 - 4
59	Compulsion/Words of love		AMT	1042	£ 2 - 4
59	Wampum/Cleopatra's dream		AMT	1056	£ 2 - 4
59	In the mood/Bwana		AMT	1074	£ 2 - 4

CHRIS MARTIN

59	Lonely street/Swing a little lover	H.M.V.	POP	664	£ 2 - 4
60	I don't regret a thing/Point of no return		POP	692	£ 2 - 4

DEAN MARTIN (& *JERRY LEWIS/+NAT "KING" COLE/=LINE RENAUD)

52	Santa Lucia/Hold me	VOGUE	V	9040	º £ 6 - 9
53ø	Kiss/There's my lover	CAPITOL	CL	13893	º £ 1 - 2
53ø	That's amore/You're the right one		CL	14008	º £ 1 - 2
54	Hey brother pour the wine/I'd cry like a baby		CL	14123	£ 6 - 9
54ø	Sway/Pretty as a picture		CL	14138	£ 9 - 12
54ø	How do you speak to an angel?/Ev'ry street's a boulevard*		CL	14150	£ 9 - 12
54	The peddler man (Ten I loved)/Try again		CL	14170	£ 6 - 9
54	If I could sing like Bing/One more time		CL	14180	£ 6 - 9
55ø	Let me go, lover/The naughty lady of Shady Lane		CL	14226	£ 9 - 12
55ø	Mambo Italiano/That's all I want from you		CL	14227	£ 9 - 12
55	Belle from Barcelona/Confused		CL	14253	£ 6 - 9
55ø	Under the bridges of Paris/What could be more beautiful		CL	14255	£ 9 - 12
55	Open up the doghouse (Two cats are......)/Long, long ago		+CL	14215	£ 9 - 12
55	Chee chee-oo chee (sang the little....)/Ridin' into love		CL	14311	£ 6 - 9
55	Relax-ay-voo/Two sleepy people		=CL	14356	£ 6 - 9
55	Simpatico/Love is all that matters		CL	14367	£ 6 - 9
55	In Napoli/I like them all		CL	14370	£ 6 - 9
56	When you pretend/The lucky song		CL	14505	£ 2 - 4
56ø	Innamorata/You look so familiar		CL	14507	£ 6 - 9
56ø	Young and foolish/Just one more chance		CL	14519	£ 6 - 9
56ø	Memories are made of this/Change of heart		CL	14523	£ 6 - 9
56	Watching the world go by/The lady with the big umbrella		CL	14586	£ 2 - 4
56	The test of time/I'm gonna steal you away		CL	14624	£ 2 - 4
56	The wind, the wind/Me 'n' you 'n' the Moon		CL	14625	£ 2 - 4
56	Give me a sign/Mississippi dreamboat		CL	14656	£ 2 - 4
57ø	The man who plays the mandolino/I know I can't forget		CL	14690	£ 4 - 6
57	Bamboozled/Only trust your heart		CL	14714	£ 2 - 4
57	I can't give you anything but love/I never had a chance		CL	14737	£ 2 - 4
57	Beau James/Write to me from Naples		CL	14758	£ 2 - 4
57	Promise her anything/The triche trache		CL	14782	£ 2 - 4
57	Just kiss me/The look		CL	14801	£ 2 - 4
57	Good mornin' life/Makin' love ukelele style		CL	14813	£ 2 - 4
58ø	Return to me/Forgetting you		CL	14844	£ 4 - 6
58	Angel baby/I'll gladly make the same mistake again		CL	14890	£ 2 - 4
58ø	Volare/Outta my mind		CL	14910	£ 4 - 6
58	Once upon a time (it happened)/The magician		CL	14943	£ 2 - 4
59	It takes so long (to say goodbye)/You were made for love		CL	14990	£ 2 - 4
59	Rio Bravo/My rifle, my pony and me		CL	15015	£ 2 - 4
59	You can't love 'em all/On an evening in Roma		CL	15039	£ 2 - 4
59	Ain't gonna lead this life/Maybe		CL	15064	£ 2 - 4
59	(Love is a) Career/For you		CL	15102	£ 2 - 4
60	Who was that lady?/Love me, my love		CL	15127	£ 2 - 4
60	Buttercup a golden hair/Napoli		CL	15145	£ 2 - 4
60	Just in time/Humdinger		CL	15155	£ 2 - 4
60	Sogni d'oro (Golden dreams)/How sweet it is		CL	15172	£ 2 - 4

GRADY MARTIN & THE SLEWFOOT FIVE

56	Nashville/Don't take your love from me	BRUNSWICK	05535	£ 9 - 12

JANIS MARTIN

60	Here today and gone tomorrow love/Hard times ahead	PALETTE	PG 9000	£18 - 25

KERRY MARTIN
58 Stroll me/Cold hands, warm heart .... PARLOPHONE R 4449 £ 4 – 6

MILLICENT MARTIN
58 Our language of love/Seriously .... COLUMBIA DB 4171 £ 2 – 4
60 Tintarella di Luna/I can dream, can't I? .... DB 4466 £ 2 – 4

RAY MARTIN & HIS CONCERT ORCH. (qv RAY BURNS)
52ø Blue tango/Unforgettable .... COLUMBIA DB 3051 º £ 1 – 2
53ø Blue tango/Belle of the ball .... SCM 5001 £ 6 – 9
53ø Swedish rhapsody/Hi-Lili, hi-lo .... DB 3346 º £ 1 – 2
53ø *as above* .... SCM 5063 £ 6 – 9
56ø The carousel waltz/Port au Prince .... DB 3771 º £ 1 – 2
56ø *as above* .... SCM 5264 £ 4 – 6
59ø *as above* .... SCD 2123 £ 2 – 4

STEVE MARTIN
56 Only you/Lola .... COLUMBIA SCM 5212 £ 4 – 6
58 Stairway of love/Chanson d'amour .... PHILIPS   PB 820 £ 2 – 4
58 The man inside/Blue-eyed Sue .... PB 853 £ 2 – 4

TONY MARTIN
53 Tenement symphony (both sides) .... H.M.V.   7M 105 £ 4 – 6
53 The golden years/April in Portugal .... 7M 136 £ 4 – 6
53 Please, please/You're so dangerous .... 7M 137 £ 4 – 6
53 Sorta on the border/Unfair .... 7M 158 £ 4 – 6
54 I could write a book/Here .... 7M 203 £ 4 – 6
54 That's what a rainy day is for/Look out, I'm romantic . 7M 210 £ 4 – 6
54 Uno/Let's try again .... 7M 254 £ 4 – 6
54 I love Paris/Boulevard of Nightingales .... 7M 258 £ 4 – 6
55 My bambina/Angels in the sky .... 7M 283 £ 4 – 6
55ø Stranger in Paradise/Vera Cruz .... B 10849 º £ 1 – 2
55ø *as above* .... 7M 302 £ 9 – 12
55 What's the time in Nicaragua/Domani .... 7M 320 £ 4 – 6
56 Love, you funny thing/Just a gigolo ....'. 7M 376 £ 4 – 6
56ø Walk hand in hand/Flamenco love .... POP 222 º £ 1 – 2
56ø *as above* .... 7M 414 £ 6 – 9
56 It's better in the dark/Your place in the Sun .... POP 257 £ 4 – 6
57 All of you/Moderation .... POP 282 £ 4 – 6
57 The rainmaker/My Budapest .... POP 319 £ 2 – 4
57 The man from Idaho/One is a lonely number .... R.C.A.   RCA 1002 £ 2 – 4
59 She is not thinking of me/(by GOGI GRANT) .... RCA 1101 £ 2 – 4

VINCE MARTIN (*& THE TARRIERS)
56ø Cindy, oh Cindy/Only if you praise the Lord .... LONDON *HLN 8340 £12 – 18
59 Old grey goose (Aunt Rhodie)/Goodnight, Irene .... H.M.V.   POP 594 £ 2 – 4

MARTINAS & HIS MUSIC (actually MARTIN SLAVIN)
58ø Cha cha Momma Brown/My bonnie lies over the ocean ..... COLUMBIA DB 4223 £ 2 – 4

WINK MARTINDALE
59ø Deck of cards/Now you know how it feels .... LONDON   HLD 8962 £ 4 – 6
60 Life gits tee-jus don't it?/I never see Maggie alone .. HLD 9042 £ 2 – 4

AL MARTINO
52ø Take my heart/I never cared .... CAPITOL CL 13769 º £ 2 – 4
52ø Here in my heart/I cried myself to sleep .... CL 13779 º £ 1 – 2
52ø Now/Say you'll wait for me .... CL 13835 º £ 1 – 2
53ø Rachel/One lonely night .... CL 13879 º £ 1 – 2
54ø Wanted/There'll be no teardrops tonight .... CL 14128 £ 9 – 12
54 Give me something to go with../On and on (in love with.) CL 14148 £ 6 – 9
54ø The story of Tina/Destiny (no one can change) .... CL 14163 £ 9 – 12
54 I still believe/When? .... CL 14192 £ 4 – 6
54 Not as a stranger/No one but you .... CL 14202 £ 4 – 6
55 Don't go to strangers/Say it again .... CL 14224 £ 4 – 6
55 The snowy, snowy mountains/Love is eternal .... CL 14284 £ 4 – 6

55ø	The man from Laramie/To please my lady		CL 14343	£ 9 – 12
55	Come close to me/Small talk		CL 14379	£ 4 – 6
56	Journey's end/Sound advice		CL 14550	£ 2 – 4
56	The girl I left in Rome/Some cloud above		CL 14614	£ 2 – 4
57	I'm sorry/A love to call my own		CL 14680	£ 2 – 4
59	I can't get you out of my../Two hearts are better than..	TOP RANK	JAR 108	£ 2 – 4
59	Darling I love you/The memory of you		JAR 187	£ 2 – 4
60ø	Summertime/I sold my heart		JAR 312	£ 2 – 4
60	Mama/Dearest (Cara)		JAR 337	£ 2 – 4
60	Why do I love you?/Sunday		JAR 418	£ 2 – 4
60	Our concerto/It's all over but the crying	EMBER	EMB S119	£ 2 – 4

MARVIN & JOHNNY

57	Yak yak/Pretty eyes	VOGUE	V 9074	£60 – 90
58	Smack, smack/You're in my heart		V 9099	£40 – 60

SPOKES MASHIYANE (& *BEN NKOSI/+FRANCE PILANE)

58	Jika spokes*/Boys of Jo'burg+	ORIOLE	CB 1441	£ 2 – 4

GLEN MASON

56	Hot diggity (dog ziggity boom)/Baby girl of mine	PARLOPHONE	MSP 6240	£ 4 – 6
56ø	Glendora/Love, love, love		R 4203	£ 6 – 9
56ø	The green door/Why must you go, go, go		R 4244	£ 6 – 9
57	Don't forbid me/Amore		R 4271	£ 4 – 6
57	Round and round/Walking and whistling		R 4291	£ 2 – 4
57	Crying my heart out for you/Why don't they understand .		R 4334	£ 2 – 4
57	By my side/By the fireside		R 4357	£ 2 – 4
58	What a beautiful combination/I'm alone because I love...		R 4390	£ 2 – 4
58	I may never pass this way again/A moment ago		R 4415	£ 2 – 4
58	I know where I'm going/Autumn souvenir		R 4451	£ 2 – 4
58	The end/Fall in love		R 4485	£ 2 – 4
59	The Battle of New Orleans/I don't know		R 4562	£ 4 – 6
60	You got what it takes/If there's someone		R 4626	£ 4 – 6
60	I like it when it rains/That's what I want!		R 4723	£ 2 – 4

MARLIN MASON

56	The mystery of love/Don't throw my love away	V-CORAL	Q 72168	£ 2 – 4

SAMMY MASTERS

60ø	Rockin' Red Wing/Lonely weekend	WARNER-B	WB 10	£12 – 18

VALERIE MASTERS

58	Sharing/The secret of happiness	FONTANA	H 132	£ 2 – 4
58	(Well-a, well-a) Ding-dong/Merci beaucoup		H 145	£ 2 – 4
59	Dreams end at dawn/Wonder		H 175	£ 2 – 4
59	Jack O'Diamonds/Say when		H 195	£ 2 – 4
59	If there are stars in my eyes/Just squeeze me		H 224	£ 2 – 4
60	No one understands/Oh, Gee		H 238	£ 2 – 4
60	Banjo boy/Cow cow boogie		H 253	£ 2 – 4
60	Sweeter as the day goes by/Fools fall in love		H 268	£ 2 – 4

JOHNNY MATHIS

57	Chances are/The twelfth of Never	PHILIPS	JK 1029	£ 6 – 9
58	Wild is the wind/No love (but your love)	FONTANA	H 103	£ 2 – 4
58	Come to me/When I am with you		H 117	£ 2 – 4
58ø	Teacher, teacher/Easy to love		H 130	£ 4 – 6
58ø	A certain smile/Let it rain		H 142	£ 4 – 6
58ø	Winter wonderland/Sleigh ride		H 165	£ 4 – 6
58	Call me/Stairway to the sea		H 163	£ 2 – 4
59	Let's love/You'd be so nice to come home to		H 186	£ 2 – 4
59ø	Someone/They say it's wonderful		H 199	£ 2 – 4
59ø	The best of everything/Cherie		H 218	£ 4 – 6
59ø	Misty/The story of our love		H 219	£ 4 – 6
59	It's not for me to say/Warm and tender		H 220	£ 2 – 4
60ø	You are beautiful/Very much in love		H 234	£ 2 – 4

```
60ø Starbright/All is well  ..................................           H   254    £ 2 -  4
60ø My love for you/Oh that feeling  ......................           H   267    £ 2 -  4
60  The twelfth of Never/Get me to the church on time  .....          H   248    £ 2 -  4
```

BRIAN MATTHEW & PETE MURRAY
```
60  What's it all about eh?/Gee Ma I wanna go home  ........   DECCA     F 11305   £ 2 -  4
```

BILLY MAY & HIS ORCH.
```
54  Rudolph the red-nosed reindeer Mambo/Loop-de-loop mambo   CAPITOL   CL 14210  £ 4 -  6
55  How important can it be?/Let it happen  ................             CL 14266  £ 4 -  6
55  Shaner Maidel/The cha cha cha  .........................             CL 14308  £ 4 -  6
55  Hernando's Hideaway/Just between friends  ..............             CL 14353  £ 4 -  6
56ø Main title & Suzette from "The Man With the Golden Arm"              CL 14551  £ 4 -  6
56  Nightmare/The beat  ....................................             CL 14609  £ 6 -  9
```

BILL MAYNARD
```
57  Who needs you/Hey Liley, Liley lo  .....................   DECCA     F 10868   £ 2 -  4
57  Hey Liley, Liley, lo/Lonely road  ......................             F 10902   £ 2 -  4
```

LES McCANN LTD.
```
60  Vakushna/Fish this week  ...............................   VOGUE     V  2417   £ 2 -  4
```

BUDD McCOY
```
59  Hiawatha/The midnight ride of Paul Revere  .............   R.C.A.    RCA 1106  £ 4 -  6
```

JOE McCOY
```
59  One in a hundred/One more greasing  ....................   COLLECTOR JDL 81    £ 4 -  6
```

JIMMY McCRACKLIN & HIS BAND
```
58  The walk/I'm to blame  .................................   LONDON    HLM 8598  £18 - 25
```

CHAS McDEVITT (SKIFFLE GROUP) (& *NANCY WHISKEY/+SHIRLEY DOUGLAS/qv CRANES SKIFFLE)
```
57ø Freight train*/The cotton song  .........................   ORIOLE    CB 1352   £ 9 - 12
57  It takes a worried man/The House of the Rising Sun  ....             CB 1357   £ 6 -  9
57ø Green back dollar*/I'm satisfied  .......................             CB 1371   £ 9 - 12
57  Face in the rain*/Sporting life  .......................             CB 1386   £ 6 -  9
57  My old man/Sing, sing, sing  ...........................             CB 1395   £ 6 -  9
57  Across the bridge+/Deep down  ..........................             CB 1405   £ 6 -  9
57  Johnny-O*/Bad Man Stack-O-Lee  .........................             CB 1403   £ 6 -  9
58  Real love+/Juke-box jumble  ............................             CB 1457   £ 6 -  9
59  Teenage letter+/SHIRLEY DOUGLAS: Sad little girl  ......             CB 1511   £ 4 -  6
60  Dream talk/Forever  ....................................   TOP RANK +JAR 338   £ 2 -  4
```

SKEETS McDONALD
```
56  Fallen angel/It'll take me a long, long time  ..........   CAPITOL   CL 14566  £18 - 25
```

BOB McFADDEN & DOR
```
59  The Mummy/The beat generation  .........................   CORAL     Q 72378   £ 4 -  6
```

BROWNIE McGHEE (qv SONNY TERRY)
```
51  Me and my dog/Secret mojo blues  .......................   MELODISC    1127 º £ 6 -  9
```

BILL McGUFFIE TRIO
```
53  Concerto for boogie/Begin the beguine  ...............   PARLOPHONE MSP 6040  £ 4 -  6
```

THE McGUIRE SISTERS
```
54  Muskrat ramble/Lonesome polecat  .......................   V-CORAL   Q  2028   £ 4 -  6
55ø Sincerely/No more  .......................................             Q 72050   £ 9 - 12
55  Melody of love/Open up your heart  .....................             Q 72052   £ 4 -  6
55  Something's gotta give/It may sound silly  .............             Q 72082   £ 4 -  6
55  He/Christmas alphabet  .................................             Q 72108   £ 4 -  6
56  Young and foolish/Doesn't anybody love me?  ............             Q 72117   £ 4 -  6
56  Missing/Be good to me (Baby, baby)  ....................             Q 72145   £ 4 -  6
56ø Delilah Jones/Picnic  ....................................             Q 72161   £ 9 - 12
56  In the alps/Weary blues  ...............................             Q 72188   £ 4 -  6
```

6	Endless/My baby's got such lovin' ways		Q 72201	£ 4 - 6
6	Tip toe through the tulips with me/Do you remember when?		Q 72209	£ 4 - 6
7	Goodnight my love, pleasant dreams/Mommy		Q 72216	£ 4 - 6
7	Heart/Sometimes I'm happy		Q 72238	£ 4 - 6
7	Without him/Kid stuff		Q 72249	£ 4 - 6
7	Beginning to miss you/Rock bottom		Q 72265	£ 4 - 6
7	Interlude/He's got time		Q 72272	£ 4 - 6
7	Forgive me/Kiss them for me		Q 72296	£ 4 - 6
8	Sugartime/Banana split	CORAL	Q 72305	£ 6 - 9
8	Ding dong/Since you went away to school		Q 72327	£ 4 - 6
8	Volare/Do you love me like you kiss me?		Q 72334	£ 4 - 6
9	May you always/Achoo-cha-cha		Q 72356	£ 4 - 6
9	Peace/Summer dreams		Q 72370	£ 2 - 4
9	Red River Valley/Compromise		Q 72379	£ 2 - 4
0	Livin' dangerously/Lovers' lullaby		Q 72387	£ 2 - 4
0	"The Unforgiven" theme (The need for love)/I give thanks		Q 72399	£ 2 - 4
0	Nine o'clock/The last dance		Q 72406	£ 2 - 4
0	To be loved/I don't know why		Q 72415	£ 2 - 4

RAY McKINLEY & HIS ORCH. (*or THE NEW GLENN MILLER ORCH.)

56	Flaggin' the train (to Tuscaloosa)/Airizay	BRUNSWICK	05541	£ 2 - 4
58	Falling leaves/So sweet	R.C.A.	*RCA 1034	£ 2 - 4

ROD McKUEN

57	Happy is a boy named me/Jaydee	LONDON	HLU 8390	£ 9 - 12
60	Two brothers/Time after time	BRUNSWICK	05828	£ 2 - 4

HAL McKUSICK QUINTET/SEXTET

57	When I fall in love/Kelly and me	V-CORAL	Q 72258	£ 2 - 4

OSCAR McLOLLIE & HIS HONEYJUMPERS

55	Take your shoes off, Pop/Love me tonight	LONDON	HL 8130	£40 - 60

CHARLIE McNAIR JAZZ GROUP (mis-titled SKIFFLE)

56	Hiawatha/Meadow Lane stomp	BELTONA	BL 2670 º	£ 2 - 4

BIG JAY McNEELY & BAND w. LITTLE SONNY

59	...Back...Shack...Track/There is something on your mind	TOP RANK	JAR 169	£ 9 - 12

CLYDE McPHATTER

56	Seven days/I'm not worthy of you	LONDON		HLE 8250	£40 - 60
56ø	Treasure of love/When you're sincere			HLE 8293	£40 - 60
57	Just to hold my hand/No matter what			HLE 8462	£40 - 60
57	Long lonely nights/Heartaches			HLE 8476	£25 - 40
57	Rock and cry/You'll be there			HLE 8525	£25 - 40
58	Come what may/Let me know			HLE 8707	£18 - 25
58	A lover's question/I can't stand up alone			HLE 8755	£12 - 18
59	(I'm afraid) The masquerade is over/I told myself a lie	M-G-M	MGM 1014	£ 9 - 12
59	Lovey dovey/My island of dreams	LONDON		HLE 8878	£12 - 18
59	Since you've been gone/Try try baby			HLE 8906	£12 - 18
59	Twice as nice/Where did I make my mistake	M-G-M	MGM 1040	£ 9 - 12
59	You went back on your word/There you go	LONDON		HLE 9000	£12 - 18
59	Bless you/Let's try again	M-G-M	MGM 1048	£ 9 - 12
60	Just give me a ring/Don't dog me	LONDON		HLE 9079	£12 - 18
60	Think me a kiss/When the right time comes along	M-G-M	MGM 1061	£ 9 - 12
60	Ta ta/I ain't givin' up nothin' (if I can't get some-..)	MERCURY	AMT 1108	£ 6 - 9
60	You're for me/I just want to love you		AMT 1120	£ 6 - 9

CARMEN McRAE (qv SAMMY DAVIS)

55	Love is here to stay/This will make you laugh	BRUNSWICK	05502	£ 2 - 4
56	You don't know me/Never loved him anyhow		05588	£ 2 - 4
56	Star eyes/I'm a dreamer (aren't we all)		05632	£ 2 - 4
57	Whatever Lola wants (Lola gets)/Ooh (what 'cha doin'...)		05652	£ 2 - 4
57	The party's over/It's like getting a donkey to gallop .		05723	£ 2 - 4
58	As I love you/Passing fancy		05738	£ 2 - 4

58	Namely you/I'll love you (till I die)		05761	£ 2 – 4
59	Play for keeps/Which way is love	LONDON	HLR 8837	£ 2 – 4
59	Come on, come in/I love the ground you walk on	BRUNSWICK	05789	£ 2 – 4
60	The very thought of you/Oh! Look at me now	MERCURY	AMT 1122	£ 2 – 4

CARL McVOY

58	Tootsie/You are my sunshine	LONDON	HLU 8617	£40 – 60

JOE MEDLIN

59	I kneel at your throne/Out of sight, out of mind	MERCURY	AMT 1032	£ 4 – 6

MICHAEL MEDWIN (& *BERNARD BRESSLAW, ALFIE BASS & LESLIE FYSON/+NORMAN ROSSINGTON)

58ø	The Army Game/What do we do in the Army?	H.M.V.	*POP 490	£ 6 – 9
59	Blankety–blankety–blank/Do it yourself		+POP 645	£ 2 – 4

THE MEGATRONS

59	Velvet waters/The merry piper	TOP RANK	JAR 146	£ 4 – 6
59	Tootie flootie/Whispering winds		JAR 236	£ 2 – 4

(George) MELACHRINO ORCHESTRA

56ø	Autumn concerto/A woman in love	H.M.V.	B 10958	£ 6 – 9

GEORGE MELLY

51	Rock Island line/Send me to the 'lectric chair	TEMPO	A 96 ª	£ 6 – 9
52	Kitchen man/Jazzbo Brown from Memphis Town		A 104 ª	£ 4 – 6
55	Frankie and Johnny/I'm down in the dumps	DECCA	F 10457	£ 4 – 6
56	Jenny's ball/Muddy water	TEMPO	A 144	£ 4 – 6
56	I'm a ding dong Daddy/Kingdom coming	DECCA	F 10763	£ 4 – 6
56	Waiting for a train/Railroadin' man		FJ 10779	£ 4 – 6
56	My canary has circles under his eyes/Heebie jeebies ...		FJ 10806	£ 4 – 6
56	Death letter/Cemetery blues	TEMPO	A 147	£ 4 – 6
57	Black bottom/Magnolia	DECCA	FJ 10840	£ 4 – 6
59	Abdul Abulbul Amir/Get away, old man, get away		F 11115	£ 2 – 4
60	Ise a muggin'/Run come see Jerusalem	PYE	7N 15253	£ 2 – 4

LORD MELODY

59	Rock 'n' roll calypso/Bo bo man	KALYPSO	XX 14	£ 4 – 6

THE MEMOS

59	The biddy leg/My type of girl	PARLOPHONE	R 4616	£ 9 – 12

MEMPHIS SLIM (& HIS R&B BAND)

53	Harlem bound/ST.LOUIS JIMMY R&B BAND: Holiday for boogie	ESQUIRE	10–319 ª	£ 6 – 9
60	Pinetop's blues/How long	COLLECTOR	JDN 102	£ 4 – 6

IAN MENZIES & HIS NEW STOMPERS/*CLYDE VALLEY STOMPERS

59	Polly wolly doodle/In a Persian market	PYE JAZZ	7NJ 2027	£ 2 – 4
59	Bill Bailey won't you please../Hot time in the old town.		7NJ 2028	£ 2 – 4
60ø	The fish man/Salty dog		*7NJ 2031	£ 2 – 4

ETHEL MERMAN (& *JIMMY DURANTE/+RAY BOLGER/=DAN DAILEY)

54	A husband – a wife*/The lake song+	BRUNSWICK	05346	£ 4 – 6
55	There's no business like show...../Play a simple melody=		05381	£ 4 – 6
58	A new–fangled tango/Mutual admiration society	R.C.A.	RCA 1039	£ 2 – 4

RAY MERRELL

60	Why did you leave me?/Teenage love	EMBER	EMB S113	£ 2 – 4

BOB MERRILL

58	Nairobi/Jump when I say frog	COLUMBIA	DB 4086	£ 4 – 6

MARILYN MICHAELS

60	Tell Tommy I miss him/Everyone was there but you	R.C.A.	RCA 1208	£ 4 – 6

REMEMBER! – THE SYMBOL ø AFTER THE YEAR OF ISSUE INDICATES A BRITISH CHART ENTRY

MICKEY & KITTY (Mickey Baker & Kitty Noble)

60	Buttercup/My reverie	LONDON	HLE 9054	£ 9 - 12

MICKEY & SYLVIA (Mickey Baker & SYLVIA ROBBINS/Robinson)

57	Love is strange/I'm going home	H.M.V.	POP 331	£40 - 60
58	Rock and stroll room/Bewildered	R.C.A.	RCA 1064	£18 - 25
60	Sweeter as the day goes by/Mommy out de light		RCA 1206	£ 9 - 12

MIKI & GRIFF

59ø	Hold back tomorrow/Deedle-dum-doo-die-day	PYE	7N 15213	£ 2 - 4
60ø	Rockin' alone (in an old....)/I'm here to get my baby...		7N 15296	£ 2 - 4

BOBBY MILANO

55	A king or a slave/If you cared	CAPITOL	CL 14252	£ 4 - 6
55	If tears could bring you back/Make me a present of you		CL 14309	£ 4 - 6

AMOS MILBURN

57	Every day of the week/Girl of my dreams	VOGUE	V 9064	£25 - 40
57	Rum and coca cola/Soft pillow		V 9069	£25 - 40
57	Thinking of you baby/If I could be with you (one hour..)		V 9080	£25 - 40
60	One scotch, one bourbon, one beer/Bad. bad whiskey		V 9163	£40 - 60

BERNARD MILES

56	At the Rose and Crown/Still going strong	DECCA	F 10687	£ 2 - 4
57	The titlark song/As I was driving		F 10872	£ 2 - 4

GARRY MILES

60	Look for a star/Afraid of love	LONDON	HLG 9155	£ 4 - 6

PETER MILES

58	My little girl/Goodnight, God bless, sleep tight	COLUMBIA	DB 4117	£ 2 - 4

BETTY MILLER

59	Pearly gates/Old time religion	TOP RANK	JAR 115	£ 2 - 4
59	(It took) One kiss/Jack O'Diamonds		JAR 127	£ 2 - 4

CHUCK MILLER

56	Rogue River Valley/No baby like you	CAPITOL	CL 14543	£ 4 - 6
57	Bye, bye love/Rang tang ding dong	MERCURY	MT 157 º	£ 4 - 6
57	Plaything/After yesterday		MT 181 º	£ 4 - 6
58	The auctioneer/Me head's in de barrel		7MT 153	£12 - 18
58	Down the road a-piece/Mad about her blues		7MT 215	£18 - 25
59	The auctioneer/Baby doll		AMT 1026	£ 9 - 12

FRANKIE MILLER

59	Black land farmer/True blue	MELODISC	1519	£ 9 - 12
59	Family man/Poppin' Johnnie		1529	£ 6 - 9
60	Baby rocked her dolly/Rain, rain		1552	£ 6 - 9

GARY MILLER (*& MARION RYAN)

55ø	The Yellow Rose of Texas/Man from Laramie	PYE	N 15004 º	£ 2 - 4
56ø	Robin Hood/Ballad of Davy Crockett		N 15020 º	£ 2 - 4
57ø	Garden of Eden/Since I met you baby		N 15070 º	£ 2 - 4
57ø	Wonderful, wonderful!/Love letters in the sand		N 15094 º	£ 2 - 4
58ø	The story of my life/Put a light in the window		7N 15120	£ 4 - 6
58	Lollipop/Dancing with my shadow		7N 15136	£ 4 - 6
58	On the street where you live/That's for me		7N 15140	£ 2 - 4
58	A couple of crazy kids*/Ivanhoe of England		7N 15151	£ 2 - 4
58	The first Christmas day/Nearest and dearest		7N 15164	£ 2 - 4
59	Jezebel/The railroad song		7N 15188	£ 2 - 4
59	Someone to come home to/Sing along		7N 15207	£ 2 - 4
59	Marina/Hold me, thrill me, kiss me		7N 15239	£ 2 - 4
60	Mission bell/Happy together		7N 15277	£ 2 - 4

REMEMBER! - THE SYMBOL º AFTER THE CATALOGUE NUMBER INDICATES A 78 rpm RECORD

GLENN MILLER & HIS ORCH. (qv RAY McKINLEY)
```
46ø Moonlight serenade/American patrol  ...................  H.M.V.    BD 5942 º £ 2 -  4
54  I got rhythm/Sleepy time gal  ..........................  COLUMBIA SCM 5086   £ 6 -  9
54  Little brown jug/Don't sit under the apple tree  .......  H.M.V.     7M  195   £ 9 - 12
58  American patrol/Little brown jug  ......................  R.C.A.    RCA 1096   £ 4 -  6
59  Boom shot/You say the sweetest things, baby  ...........  TOP RANK  JAR 114   £ 4 -  6
59  Chattanooga choo choo/Serenade in blue  ................            TR 5003   £ 4 -  6
```

JIMMY MILLER & THE (NEW) BARBECUES
```
57  Free wheelin' baby/Sizzlin' hot  .......................  COLUMBIA  DB 4006   £12 - 18
58  Jelly baby/Cry, baby, cry  .............................            DB 4081   £12 - 18
```

MANDY MILLER
```
56  Nellie the elephant/It's time to dream  ................  PARLOPHONE R 4219   £ 4 -  6
```

MAX MILLER
```
58  With a little bit of luck/Be sincere  ..................  PYE       7N 15141  £ 2 -  4
```

MITCH MILLER & HIS ORCH.
```
53  Horn belt boogie/(by GUY MITCHELL)  ....................  COLUMBIA SCM 5037   £12 - 18
55ø The yellow rose of Texas/Blackberry winter  ............  PHILIPS   PB  505 º £ 1 -  2
```

RUSS MILLER
```
57  I sit in my window/Wait for me, my love  ...............  H.M.V.    POP  391  £12 - 18
```

SUZI MILLER (& *THE JOHNSTON BROTHERS/+THE KEYNOTES/=MARILYN SISTERS)
```
54  The Tennessee wig walk/Bimbo*  .........................  DECCA    F 10264 º £ 4 -  6
54ø Happy days and lonely nights/Tell me, tell me  .........          *F 10389   £ 9 - 12
54  Two step, side step*/I'll hang my heart on a Christmas.+           F 10423   £ 4 -  6
55  Tweedlee-dee*/That's all I want from you  ..............           F 10475   £ 6 -  9
55  Dance with me Henry (Wallflower)*/Butterfingers=  ......           F 10512   £ 6 -  9
55  The banjo's back in town/Go on by  .....................           F 10593   £ 4 -  6
56  Ay-ay-Senores/Reckless  ................................           F 10677   £ 4 -  6
56  Get up! Get up! (You sleepy head)/The key to my heart  .          F 10722   £ 4 -  6
57  I love my baby/The money tree  .........................           F 10848   £ 4 -  6
```

SPIKE MILLIGAN (qv THE GOONS)
```
58  Wish I knew/Will I find my love today?  ................  PARLOPHONE R 4406   £ 2 -  4
```

LUCKY MILLINDER & HIS ORCH.
```
51  I'm waiting just for you/Bongo boogie  .................  VOGUE     V  9007 º £ 9 - 12
51  The grape vine/No one else could be  ...................            V  9021 º £ 9 - 12
52  Ram-bunk-shush/Let it roll again  ......................            V  2138 º £ 9 - 12
```

THE MILLS BROTHERS (qv PEGGY LEE)
```
52ø The glow worm/After all  ...............................  BRUNSWICK  05007 º £ 2 -  4
54  How blue?/Why do I keep lovin' you?  ...................             05325   £ 4 -  6
55  Paper Valentine/The urge  ..............................             05390   £ 4 -  6
55  Smack dab in the middle/Opus one  ......................             05439   £ 9 - 12
55  Yes you are/You're nobody till somebody loves you  .....             05452   £ 4 -  6
55  Gum drop/Mi muchacha (Little girl)  ....................             05487   £12 - 18
55  Suddenly there's a valley/That's all I ask of you  .....             05488   £ 4 -  6
56  I've changed my mind a thousand.../All the way 'round...            05522   £ 4 -  6
56  Dream of you/In a mellow tone  .........................             05550   £ 4 -  6
56  Ninety-eight cents/King Porter stomp  ..................             05600   £ 4 -  6
56  That's right/Don't get caught (short on love)  .........             05606   £ 6 -  9
57  That's all I need/Tell me more  ........................             05631   £ 2 -  4
57  In de banana tree/The knocked out nightingale  .........             05664   £ 2 -  4
57  My troubled mind/Queen of the Senior prom  .............             05680   £ 2 -  4
58  Get a job/I found a million dollar baby  ...............  LONDON   HLD 8553   £ 9 - 12
60  I got you/Highways are happy ways  .....................           HLD 9169   £ 2 -  4
```

GARRY MILLS
```
59  Hey baby (you're pretty)/You alone  ....................  TOP RANK  JAR 119   £ 6 -  9
59  Seven little girls sitting in.../The night you became 17           JAR 219   £ 4 -  6
59  Living Lord/Big story breaking  ........................  ORIOLE    CB 1529   £ 2 -  4
```

59	I am the Great I Am/Rhythm in religion		CB 1530	£ 2 – 4
60	Running Bear/Teen angel	TOP RANK	JAR 301	£ 4 – 6
60ø	Look for a star/Footsteps		JAR 336	£ 4 – 6
60	Comin' down with love/I'm gonna find out		JAR 393	£ 4 – 6
60ø	Top teen baby/Don't cheat me again		JAR 500	£ 4 – 6

SAL MINEO

57ø	Start movin' (in my direction)/Love affair	PHILIPS	PB 707 º	£ 4 – 6
57ø	as above		JK 1024	£12 – 18
57	Lasting love/You shouldn't do that		PB 733 º	£ 4 – 6
57	Party time/The words that I whisper		PB 764 º	£ 4 – 6
58	Little pigeon/Cuttin' in	FONTANA	H 118	£ 9 – 12
58	Seven steps to love/A couple of crazy kids		H 135	£ 9 – 12

CORINA MINETTE

60	He'll have to stay/TOMMY THOMAS ORCH.: Young at cha cha.	H.M.V.	POP 752	£ 2 – 4

THE MINORBOPS

58	Need you tonight/Want you for my own	VOGUE	V 9110	£40 – 60

THE MINTS

57	Night air/KEN COPELAND: Pledge of love	LONDON	HLP 8423	£40 – 60

GUY MITCHELL (*& MINDY CARSON)

51	My heart cries for you/Me and my imagination	COLUMBIA	DB 2800 º	£ 2 – 4
51	The roving kind/You're not in my arms tonight		DB 2816 º	£ 2 – 4
51	Sparrow in the tree top/Christopher Columbus		DB 2831 º	£ 2 – 4
51	My truly, truly fair/Who knows love		DB 2885 º	£ 2 – 4
51	Belle, Belle, my Liberty Belle/Sweetheart of yesterday		DB 2908 º	£ 2 – 4
52	There's a pawnshop on the corner in../The doll with a...		DB 3056 º	£ 2 – 4
52	Cabaret/I've got a frame without a picture	VOGUE	V 9033 º	£ 4 – 6
52ø	Feet up (pat him on the po-po)/Angels cry	COLUMBIA	DB 3151 º	£ 2 – 4
53ø	Feet up (pat him on the po-po)/Jenny kissed me		SCM 5018	£12 – 18
53ø	She wears red feathers/Why should I go home?		DB 3238 º	£ 2 – 4
53	Train of love/'Cause I love ya, that's a-why		*SCM 5022	£12 – 18
53ø	Pretty little black-eyed Susie/(by MITCH MILLER)		DB 3255 º	£ 2 – 4
53ø	She wears red feathers/Why should I go home?		SCM 5032	£12 – 18
53ø	Pretty little black-eyed Susie/(by MITCH MILLER)		SCM 5037	£12 – 18
53ø	Look at that girl/Wise man or fool	PHILIPS	PB 162 º	£ 2 – 4
53ø	Chicka-boom/Hannah Lee		PB 178 º	£ 2 – 4
53ø	Cloud Lucky Seven/Sippin' soda		PB 210 º	£ 2 – 4
54ø	The cuff of my shirt/Strollin' blues		PB 225 º	£ 2 – 4
54ø	A dime and a dollar/Tear down the mountain		PB 248 º	£ 2 – 4
56ø	Singing the blues/Crazy with love		PB 650 º	£ 1 – 2
56ø	as above		JK 1001	£12 – 18
57ø	Knee deep in the blues/Take me back baby		PB 669 º	£ 1 – 2
57ø	as above		JK 1005	£12 – 18
57ø	Rock-a-Billy/Got a feeling		PB 685 º	£ 1 – 2
57ø	as above		JK 1015	£12 – 18
57ø	Sweet stuff/In the middle of a dark, dark night		PB 712 º	£ 1 – 2
57ø	as above		JK 1023	£ 9 – 12
57ø	Call Rosie on the phone/Cure for the blues		PB 743 º	£ 1 – 2
57ø	as above		JK 1027	£ 9 – 12
58	C'mon let's go/The unbeliever		PB 766	£ 6 – 9
58	Wonderin' and worryin'/If ya don't like it, don't knock.		PB 798	£ 4 – 6
58	Hangin' around/Honey brown eyes		PB 830	£ 4 – 6
58	Let it shine, let it shine/Butterfly doll		PB 858	£ 4 – 6
58	My heart cries for you/Till we're engaged		PB 885	£ 4 – 6
59	Pride o' Dixie/Alias Jesse James		PB 915	£ 4 – 6
59ø	Heartaches by the number/Two		PB 964	£ 4 – 6
60	The same old me/Build my gallows high		PB 998	£ 2 – 4
60	Cry hurtin' heart/Symphony of Spring		PB 1026	£ 2 – 4
60	My shoes keep walking back to.../Silver Moon upon the...		PB 1050	£ 4 – 6
60	Sunshine guitar/One way street		PB 1084	£ 2 – 4

MALCOLM MITCHELL (& HIS ORCH./TRIO)
54	The Jones boy/Granada	PARLOPHONE	MSP 6084	£ 2 – 4
55	Debut/I can't believe that you're in love with me	DECCA	F 10465	£ 2 – 4
55	Little brown jug mambo/Rites of swing		F 10503	£ 2 – 4
60	The wanted man/The blues	ORIOLE	CB 1572	£ 2 – 4

RONNIE MITCHELL
60	How many times/The only love	LONDON	HLU 9220	£ 4 – 6

ROBERT MITCHUM
57	What is this generation coming to?/Mama looka boo boo	CAPITOL	CL 14701	£ 2 – 4

THE MODERNAIRES (& *GEORGIE AULD/+BOB CROSBY BOB CATS/qv THE FOUR GUYS)
54	New juke box Saturday night/Bugle call rag	V–CORAL	Q 2035	£ 4 – 6
54	Mood indigo/Teach me tonight		*Q 2024	£ 4 – 6
55	Birds and puppies and tropical fish/Mine! Mine! Mine!		Q 72069	£ 4 – 6
55	Sluefoot/Wine, women and gold		+Q 72084	£ 4 – 6
55	At my front door/Alright, okay, you win		Q 72112	£ 6 – 9
56	"Let's Dance" medley (both sides)		Q 72135	£ 4 – 6
56	Go on with the wedding/Ain't she sweet		Q 72158	£ 4 – 6
56	April in Paris/Hi–diddlee–i–di		Q 72169	£ 2 – 4

DOMENICO MODUGNO
58ø	Volare (Nel blu dipinto di blu)/Nisciuno po' sape'	ORIOLE	ICB 5000	£ 4 – 6
58ø	as above		CB 1460	£ 4 – 6
58	Come prima (More than ever)/Mariti in citta		CB 1475	£ 2 – 4
59ø	Ciao, ciao bambina (Piove)/Resta cu 'mme		CB 1489	£ 4 – 6

THE MONOGRAMS
59	Juke box cha cha/The greatest mistake of my life	PARLOPHONE	R 4515	£ 4 – 6
59	Crystal/Teach me		R 4545	£ 2 – 4

THE MONOTONES
58	Book of love/You never loved me	LONDON	HLM 8625	£18 – 25

MATT MONRO
56	Ev'rybody falls in love with../Out of sight, out of mind	DECCA	F 10816	£ 4 – 6
57	The Garden of Eden/Love me do		F 10845	£ 4 – 6
57	My house is your house/The bean song (Which way to.....)		F 10870	£ 4 – 6
58	The story of Ireland/Another time another place	FONTANA	H 122	£ 2 – 4
58	Prisoner of love/Have guitar, will travel		H 167	£ 2 – 4
60	Love walked in/I'll know her	PARLOPHONE	R 4638	£ 2 – 4
60ø	Portrait of my love/You're the top of my Hit Parade		R 4714	£ 2 – 4

BILL MONROE & HIS BLUE GRASS BOYS
56	New John Henry blues/Put my little shoes away	BRUNSWICK	05567	£ 4 – 6
57	Four walls/A fallen star		05681	£ 4 – 6
59	Gotta travel on/No one.but my darlin'		05776	£ 4 – 6

MARILYN MONROE (qv JANE RUSSELL)
53	Diamonds are a girl's best friend/Bye bye baby	M–G–M	MGM 663 º	£ 6 – 9
54	I'm gonna file my claim/The river of no return	H.M.V.	7M 232	£ 9 – 12
55	Heat wave/After you get what you want (you don't want..)		B 10847 º	£ 4 – 6
59	I wanna be loved by you/I'm thru' with love	LONDON	HLT 8862	£ 6 – 9

VAUGHN MONROE (& HIS ORCH.)
53	Ruby/Less than tomorrow (but more than yesterday)	H.M.V.	7M 144	£ 2 – 4
53	Small world/Don't you care		7M 148	£ 2 – 4
53	I know for sure/(All roads lead to) The fiesta		7M 165	£ 2 – 4
54	They were doin' the mambo/Mister Sandman		7M 247	£ 4 – 6
55	The butterscotch mop/Goodnight, Mrs. Jones		7M 287	£ 4 – 6
55	Black denim trousers and motorcycle boots/All by myself		7M 332	£12 – 18
57	Wringle wrangle/Westward ho the wagons!		POP 354	£ 2 – 4
59	The battle of New Orleans/Hercules	R.C.A.	RCA 1124	£ 2 – 4
60	Ballerina/Love me forever	LONDON	HLT 9123	£ 2 – 4

LOU MONTE

54	A baby cried/One moment more	H.M.V.	7M 176	£ 2 - 4
54	Darktown Strutters' Ball (Italian..)/I know how you feel		7M 190	£ 2 - 4
54	Somewhere there is someone/Won't you forgive me?		7M 217	£ 2 - 4
54	Vera's veranda/Chain reaction		7M 249	£ 2 - 4
54	In my dreams/When I hold you in my arms		7M 276	£ 2 - 4
58	Lazy Mary (Luna mezzo mare)/Angelique—o	R.C.A.	RCA 1048	£ 2 - 4
59	Santa Nicola/All because it's Christmas		RCA 1161	£ 2 - 4
60	Oh! Oh! Rosie/(The new) Dark Town Strutters' Ball	COLUMBIA	DB 4500	£ 2 - 4

VINNIE MONTE

59	Summer spree/I'll walk you home	LONDON	HLU 8947	£ 6 - 9

ART MOONEY & HIS ORCH. (& THE CLOVERLEAFS/etc./& *CATHY RYAN/+OCIE SMITH)

53	I played the fool/I just couldn't take it, baby	M-G-M	*SP 1037	£ 2 - 4
53	Baby don't do it/Believe in me		*SP 1045	£ 2 - 4
56	"East Of Eden" & "Rebel Without A Cause" themes		MGM 923	£ 2 - 4
57	Giant/There's never been anyone else but you		MGM 943	£ 2 - 4
57	Rock and roll tumbleweed/Is there a teenager in the....+		MGM 951	£12 - 18

THE MOONGLOWS (qv HARVEY & THE MOONGLOWS)

57	I knew from the start/Over and over again	LONDON	HLN 8374	£120-160

MERRILL MOORE

54	The House of Blue Lights/Bell bottom boogie	CAPITOL	CL 14057 º	£ 9 - 12
54	Nola/Fly right boogie		CL 14130 º	£ 9 - 12
55	Hard top race/Five foot two, eyes of blue		CL 14369	£40 - 60

SHELLEY MOORE

55	In the wee small hours of the.../When you lose the one..	COLUMBIA	SCM 5197	£ 2 - 4
58	Gone on the guy/You've tied me up	STARLITE	ST.45 002	£ 2 - 4
58	Where is the bluebird?/Everything is gonna be all right.		ST.45 003	£ 2 - 4

THE MORGAN BROTHERS

59	Nola/Guiding star	M-G-M	MGM 1007	£ 2 - 4
59	Milk from the coconut (Honey..)/Kissin' on the red light		MGM 1026	£ 2 - 4

THE MORGAN TWINS

58	TV hop/Let's get goin'	R.C.A.	RCA 1083	£40 - 60

AL MORGAN

58	Jealous heart/Foolish tears	LONDON	HLU 8741	£ 2 - 4

JANE MORGAN (*& THE TROUBADORS/qv ROGER WILLIAMS)

55	Why - oh why/The heart you break (may be your own)	LONDON	HL 8148	£12 - 18
57	From the first hello to the..../Come home, come home,...		HLR 8395	£ 6 - 9
57	Around the world/It's not for me to say		HLR 8436	£ 4 - 6
57	Fascination*/Why don't they leave us alone		HLR 8468	£ 4 - 6
58	I'm new at the game of romance/It's been a long long....		*HLR 8539	£ 2 - 4
58	I've got bells on my heart/Only one love		HLR 8611	£ 2 - 4
58	Enchanted island/Once more, my love, once more		HLR 8649	£ 2 - 4
58ø	The day the rains came/Le jour ou la pluie viendra		HLR 8751	£ 4 - 6
59ø	If I could only live my life again/To love and be loved		HLR 8810	£ 4 - 6
59	With open arms/I can't begin to tell you		HLR 8925	£ 2 - 4
59	Happy anniversary/C'est la vie, c'est l'amour		HLR 8999	£ 2 - 4
60	My love doesn't love me at all/The bells of St. Mary's		HLR 9087	£ 2 - 4
60ø	Romantica/I am a heart		HLR 9120	£ 2 - 4
60	Lord and master/Where's the boy (I never met)		HLR 9210	£ 2 - 4
60	Somebody/The angry sea		HLR 9249	£ 2 - 4

JAYE P. MORGAN

55	Swanee/The longest walk	H.M.V.	7M 327	£ 2 - 4
55	Pepper hot baby/If you don't want my love		7M 348	£ 6 - 9
56	My bewildered heart/Not one goodbye		7M 365	£ 2 - 4
56	Have you ever been lonely?/Baby don't do it	BRUNSWICK	05519	£ 2 - 4

57	You, you Romeo/Graduation ring	R.C.A.	RCA 1014	£ 2 – 4
59	Are you lonesome tonight?/Miss you	M-G-M	MGM 1005	£ 2 – 4
59	My reputation/(It took) One kiss		MGM 1021	£ 2 – 4
59	Somebody loses, somebody wins/Somebody else is taking...		MGM 1039	£ 2 – 4
60	I walk the line/Wondering where you are		MGM 1093	£ 2 – 4

MARY MORGAN

56	Jimmy Unknown/You are my love	PARLOPHONE	MSP 6204	£ 2 – 4
56	From the candy store on the corner../No-one was there..		R 4227	£ 2 – 4
57	A call to arms/One for sorrow, two for joy		R 4348	£ 2 – 4

MORRIS & MITCH

57	Cumberland Gap/I'm not a juvenile delinquent	DECCA	F 10900	£ 6 – 9
57	What is a skiffler?/The Tommy Rot story		F 10929	£ 6 – 9
58	Bird dog/Highway Patrol		F 11086	£ 6 – 9

THE MORRIS FAMILY & THE GOSPEL JUBILEERS

60	Wake up Jonah/He never complained	TOP RANK	JAR 322	£ 2 – 4

JOE MORRIS (& HIS ORCH.)

54	Just your way baby/I had a notion	LONDON	HL 8088 º	£ 9 – 12
54	Travelin' man/No, it can't be done		HL 8098 º	£ 9 – 12

LIBBY MORRIS

56	When Liberace winked at me/None of that now	PARLOPHONE R 4225	£ 2 – 4

BUDDY MORROW & HIS ORCH. (*& SHAYE COGAN)

51	The boogie woogie march/On the old potato farm	H.M.V.	B 10199 º	£ 6 – 9
52ø	Night train/Vereda Tropical		B 10347 º	£ 4 – 6
53	Heap big beat/I can't get started		7M 151	£ 4 – 6
53	Dragnet/Your mouth's got a hole in it		7M 162	£ 4 – 6
54	Knock on wood*/All night long		7M 216	£ 4 – 6
54	Rock-a-beatin' boogie/Mr. Sandman	MERCURY	MB 3170 º	£ 4 – 6
60	Staccato's theme/Scraunchy	R.C.A.	RCA 1167	£ 2 – 4

ELLA MAE MORSE

52	Tennessee Saturday night/A little further down the road.	CAPITOL	CL 13666 º	£ 9 – 12
52	Oakie boogie/Love ya' like mad		CL 13754 º	£ 9 – 12
53	Jump back honey/Greyhound		CL 13853 º	£ 6 – 9
53	Big Mamou/Is it any wonder		CL 13930 º	£ 6 – 9
53	Forty cups of coffee/Oh! You crazy Moon		CL 13960 º	£ 6 – 9
55	Bring my baby back to me/Lovey dovey		CL 14223	£25 – 40
55	Smack dab in the middle/Yes, yes I do		CL 14303	£18 – 25
55	Heart full of hope/Livin', livin', livin'		CL 14332	£18 – 25
55	Razzle-dazzle/Ain't that a shame		CL 14341	£40 – 60
55	Seventeen/Piddily patter song		CL 14362	£25 – 40
55	Birmin'ham/An occasional man		CL 14376	£18 – 25
56	Sing-ing-ing-ing/When boy kiss girl (it's love)		CL 14508	£ 9 – 12
56	Rock and roll wedding/Down in Mexico		CL 14572	£18 – 25
57	What good'll it do me/Mister Memory Maker		CL 14726	£ 9 – 12
57	I'm gone/Sway me		CL 14760	£ 9 – 12

AZIE MORTIMER

60	Lips/Wrapped up in a dream	LONDON	HLX 9237	£ 2 – 4

JELLY ROLL MORTON (& HIS RED HOT PEPPERS)

53	Tank Town bump/The chant	H.M.V.	7M 132	£ 4 – 6
54	Fat Frances/Pep		7M 178	£ 4 – 6
54	Smoke-house blues/Wild man blues		7M 187	£ 4 – 6
54	Jungle blues/Harmony blues		7M 207	£ 4 – 6
54	Burnin' the iceberg/Fussy Mabel		7M 256	£ 4 – 6

THE MOST BROTHERS (Mickie Most & ALEX MURRAY)

57	Whistle bait/I'm comin' home	DECCA	F 10968	£ 9 – 12
58	Whole lotta woman/Teen angel		F 10998	£ 9 – 12
58	Don't go home/Dottie		F 11040	£ 6 – 9

KEN MOULE SEVEN

55	Hallelujah!/I'm beginning to see the light	DECCA	F 10478	£ 2 - 4
55	Main stem/High lift		F 10508	£ 2 - 4

MICKEY MOZART QUINTET

59	Little dipper/Mexican hop	COLUMBIA	DB 4308	£ 4 - 6

THE MUDLARKS

58	Mutual Admiration Society/A new love	COLUMBIA	DB 4064	£ 2 - 4
58ø	Lollipop/Young dove's calling		DB 4099	£ 6 - 9
58ø	Book of love/Yea, yea		DB 4133	£ 6 - 9
58	There's never been a night/Light'nin' never strikes.....		DB 4190	£ 4 - 6
58	Which witch doctor/My Grandfather's clock		DB 4210	£ 4 - 6
59ø	The love game/Abdul the Bulbul Amer cha cha		DB 4250	£ 4 - 6
59	Tell him no/Time flies		DB 4291	£ 2 - 4
59	Waterloo/Mary		DB 4331	£ 2 - 4
59	True love, true love/Tennessee		DB 4374	£ 2 - 4
60	Never marry a fishmonger/Candy		DB 4417	£ 2 - 4
60	(You've got to) Move two mountains/You're free to go ..		DB 4513	£ 2 - 4

THE MULCAYS

55	Harbour lights/Dipsy doodle	LONDON	HLF 8188	£12 - 18

MOON MULLICAN (*& BOYD BENNETT & HIS ROCKETS)

51	Cherokee boogie/Love is the light that leads me home ..	VOGUE	V 9013 º	£12 - 18
56	Honolulu rock-a roll-a/Seven nights to rock	*PARLOPHONE	R 4195 º	£18 - 25
56	as above	*MSP	6254	£120-160

GERRY MULLIGAN (QUARTET/COMBO/etc.) (& *-PAUL DESMOND QUARTET/+LEE KONITZ)

56	Frenesi/Nights at the turntable	VOGUE	V 2157	£ 2 - 4
56	Freeway/Bernie's tune		V 2158	£ 2 - 4
56	Lullaby of the leaves/Walkin' shoes		V 2225	£ 2 - 4
56	Carioca/My funny Valentine		V 2159	£ 2 - 4
56	Darn that dream/I'm beginning to see the light		V 2257	£ 2 - 4
56	Swing house/I may be wrong		V 2258	£ 2 - 4
56	Jeru/Love or leave me		V 2259	£ 2 - 4
56	Bark for Barksdale/Moonlight in Vermont		V 2260	£ 2 - 4
56	Carson City stage/Cherry		V 2304	£ 2 - 4
56	I can't believe that you're in love with me/Lady be good		+V 2305	£ 2 - 4
56	Makin' whoopee/Motel		V 2306	£ 2 - 4
56	Soft shoe/Aren't you glad you're you?		V 2324	£ 2 - 4
56	Line for Lyons/Limelight		V 2337	£ 2 - 4
59	I want to live - theme/Black nightgown	LONDON	HLT 8901	£ 2 - 4
60	Line for Lyons/Standstill	H.M.V.	*POP 734	£ 2 - 4
60	I'm gonna go fishin' (both sides)		POP 769	£ 2 - 4
60	News from Blueport/Utter chaos	PHILIPS	JAZ 102	£ 2 - 4

MICK MULLIGAN JAZZ BAND

56	In a shanty in old Shanty Town/Snag it	TEMPO	A 139	£ 2 - 4
56	Oriental strut/Big house blues		A 143	£ 2 - 4
56	Raver's edge/Beale Street blues		A 152	£ 2 - 4
57	St. James' Infirmary/After a while		A 155	£ 2 - 4
57	Old Stack-O-Lee blues/Double dee		A 164	£ 2 - 4

GENE MUMFORD

58	More than you know/Please give me one more chance	PHILIPS	PB 862	£ 4 - 6

HAL MUNRO (actually NEVILLE TAYLOR)

58	Breathless/Wear my ring around your neck	EMBASSY	WB 284	£ 4 - 6
59	C'mon everybody/It's late		WB 336	£ 4 - 6

JANET MUNRO & SEAN CONNERY

59	Pretty Irish girl/Ballamaquilty's Band	TOP RANK	JAR 163	£ 2 - 4

ARTHUR MURPHY

59	Sixteen candles/Molly Malone	PARLOPHONE	R 4523	£ 2 - 4

MARK MURPHY

57	Goodbye baby blues/The right kind of woman	BRUNSWICK	05701	£ 2 – 4
58	Belong to me/Don't cry my love	CAPITOL	CL 14962	£ 2 – 4
60	Send for me/Come to me		CL 15117	£ 2 – 4

ROSE MURPHY

53	Little red monkey/Time on my hands	LONDON	L 1176 º	£ 4 – 6

ALEX MURRAY (qv THE MOST BROTHERS)

60	Teen angel/Paper doll	DECCA	F 11203	£ 4 – 6
60	All on my own/String along		F 11225	£ 2 – 4

RUBY MURRAY (& *ANNE WARREN/+BRENDAN O'DOWDA/qv RAY BURNS/NORMAN WISDOM)

54ø	Heartbeart/He's a pal of mine	COLUMBIA	DB 3542 º	£ 2 – 4
55ø	Softly, softly/What could be more beautiful		DB 3558 º	£ 2 – 4
55ø	as above		SCM 5162	£12 – 18
55ø	Let me go lover/Happy days and lonely nights		DB 3577 º	£ 2 – 4
55ø	If anyone finds this, I love you*/Before we know it		DB 3580 º	£ 2 – 4
55ø	as above		SCM 5169	£ 9 – 12
55ø	Evermore/Bambino		DB 3617 º	£ 2 – 4
55ø	as above		SCM 5180	£ 9 – 12
55ø	I'll come when you call/It's the Irish in me		DB 3643 º	£ 2 – 4
56	Oh, please make him jealous/For now, for ever		SCM 5225	£ 6 – 9
56ø	You are my first love/Honestly, I do		DB 3770 º	£ 2 – 4
56	It only hurts for a little while/Teddy O'Neil		DB 3810	£ 4 – 6
56	True love/Knock on any door		DB 3849	£ 4 – 6
56	In love/O'Malley's tango		DB 3852	£ 4 – 6
57	Heart/From the first hello – to the last goodbye		DB 3911	£ 2 – 4
57	Pretty, pretty/Mr. Wonderful		DB 3933	£ 2 – 4
57	Scarlet ribbons/Macushla mine		DB 3955	£ 2 – 4
57	Passing strangers/Little white lies		DB 3994	£ 2 – 4
57	I'll remember today/Ain't that a grand and glorious		DB 4042	£ 2 – 4
58	Forgive me my darling/Keep smiling at trouble		DB 4075	£ 2 – 4
58	In my life/Nora Malone (Call me by 'phone)		DB 4108	£ 2 – 4
58ø	Real love/Little one		DB 4192	£ 4 – 6
59	Who knows/Nevertheless (I'm in love with you)		DB 4266	£ 2 – 4
59ø	Goodbye Jimmy, goodbye/The humour is on me now		DB 4305	£ 4 – 6
59	A pretty Irish girl/Connemara		+DB 4326	£ 2 – 4
59	A message from Jimmy/A voice in the choir		DB 4379	£ 2 – 4
60	Forever/Congratulations		DB 4426	£ 2 – 4
60	Sweetheart of all my dreams/My little corner of the		DB 4497	£ 2 – 4

VIDO MUSSO & HIS ORCH.

54	Vido's boogie/Blue night	LONDON	HL 8077 º	£ 6 – 9

BOOTS MUSSULLI QUARTET

54	Diga diga doo/Lullaby in rhythm	CAPITOL	KC 65002	£ 4 – 6

BILLY MYLES

57	The joker (that's what they call me)/Honey bee	H.M.V.	POP 423	£ 9 – 12

MEG MYLES

56	Sing on, baby/Will you shed a tear for me?	CAPITOL	CL 14555	£ 2 – 4

THE MYSTICS

59	Hushabye/Adam and Eve	H.M.V.	POP 646	£12 – 18
59	Don't take the stars/So tenderly	TOP RANK	JAR 243	£ 9 – 12

GENE NASH

59	I'm an Eskimoo too/Ja, ja, ja (Deutsche rock 'n roll)	CAPITOL	CL 15042	£ 9 – 12

JOHNNY NASH

57	Ladder of love/I'll walk alone	H.M.V.	POP 402	£ 4 – 6
58	Won't you let me share my love....../A very special love		POP 435	£ 2 – 4
58	It's easy to say/My pledge to you		POP 475	£ 2 – 4
58	Almost in your arms/Midnight moonlight		POP 553	£ 2 – 4

59 Walk with faith in your heart/Roots of Heaven		POP 597	£ 2 – 4
59 As time goes by/Voice of love		POP 620	£ 2 – 4
59 And the angels sing/Baby, baby, baby		POP 651	£ 2 – 4
59 Take a giant step/Imagination		POP 673	£ 2 – 4
60 A place in the Sun/Goodbye		POP 746	£ 2 – 4
60 Somebody/Kisses		POP 822	£ 2 – 4

THE NATURALS (qv DEBBIE REYNOLDS)

55 The finger of suspicion points.../You forgot to remember	M-G-M	SP 1123	£ 2 – 4
57 The Buccaneers/The ballad of Sir Lancelot		MGM 939	£ 2 – 4

BERNIE NEE *or* KNEE (QUARTETTE)

55 Scrape off de bark/Chocolate whiskey and vanilla gin ..	H.M.V.	*7M 306	£ 2 – 4
58 Lend me your comb/Medal of honour	PHILIPS	PB 794	£ 4 – 6

THE NELSON TRIO

57 Tear it up/Roll the carpet up	ORIOLE	CB 1360	£ 4 – 6
60 All in good time/The town crier	LONDON	HLL 9019	£ 2 – 4

CLARE NELSON

59 The valley of love/You are my sunshine	M-G-M	MGM 1025	£ 2 – 4

EARL NELSON

59 No time to cry/Come on	LONDON	HLW 8950	£ 4 – 6

RICKY NELSON

57 I'm walkin'/A teenager's romance	H.M.V.	POP 355	£40 – 60
57 You're my one and only love/BARNEY KESSEL: Honey rock .		POP 390	£25 – 40
57 Be-bop baby/Have I told you lately that I love you? ...	LONDON	HLP 8499	£12 – 18
58ø Stood up/Waitin' in school		HLP 8542	£ 9 – 12
58 Believe what you say/My bucket's got a hole in it		HLP 8594	£ 9 – 12
58ø Poor little fool/Don't leave me this way		HLP 8670	£ 6 – 9
58ø Someday/I got a feeling		HLP 8732	£ 4 – 6
58 Lonesome town/My babe		HLP 8738	£ 6 – 9
59ø It's late/Never be anyone else but you		HLP 8817	£ 6 – 9
59ø Just a little too much/Sweeter than you		HLP 8927	£ 4 – 6
60ø I wanna be loved/Mighty good		HLP 9021	£ 4 – 6
60ø Young emotions/Right by my side		HLP 9121	£ 4 – 6
60ø *as above*		HLP 9121 º	£ 9 – 12
60 Yes, sir, that's my baby/I'm not afraid		HLP 9188	£ 4 – 6
60 *as above*		HLP 9188 º	£ 9 – 12

SANDY NELSON

59ø Teen beat/Big jump	TOP RANK	JAR 197	£ 4 – 6
59 Drum party/The big noise from Winnetka	LONDON	HLP 9015	£ 4 – 6
60 Bouncy/I'm walkin'		HLP 9214	£ 4 – 6

NERVOUS NORVUS

56 Ape call/Wild dog of Kentucky	LONDON	HLD 8338	£40 – 60
57 Dig/Bullfrog hop		HLD 8383	£40 – 60

MR. NEW & MR. WU

56 "Rock'n Roll Party" medley	ORIOLE	CB 1343 º	£ 4 – 6

NEW ORLEANS ALL STAR BAND

56 Struttin' with some barbecue/Basin Street blues	VOGUE	V 2380	£ 2 – 4
56 Christopher Columbus/Bugle call rag		V 2368	£ 2 – 4

NEW ORLEANS BOOTBLACKS

54 Flat foot/Mad dog	COLUMBIA	SCM 5090	£ 4 – 6

ANTHONY NEWLEY

59ø I've waited so long/Sat'day night rock-a-boogie	DECCA	F 11127	£ 4 – 6
59 Idle on parade/Idle rock-a-boogie		F 11137	£ 6 – 9
59ø Personality/My blue angel		F 11142	£ 4 – 6

59	Someone to love/It's all over		F 11163	£ 2 – 4
59ø	Why/Anything you wanna do		F 11194	£ 2 – 4
60ø	Do you mind/Girls were made to love and kiss		F 11220	£ 2 – 4
60ø	If she should come to you/Lifetime of happiness		F 11254	£ 2 – 4
60ø	Strawberry Fair/A boy without a girl		F 11295	£ 2 – 4

JIMMY NEWMAN

57	A fallen star/I can't go on this way	LONDON	HLD 8460	£12 – 18
59	What'cha gonna do/So soon	M–G–M	MGM 1009	£ 4 – 6
59	Grin and bear it/The ballad of Baby Doe		MGM 1037	£ 4 – 6
60	A lovely work of art/What about me		MGM 1085	£ 4 – 6

JOE NEWMAN SEXTET

57	Cocktails for two/Later for the happenings	V–CORAL	Q 72244	£ 2 – 4

MARTIN NEWMAN

55	A man without a star/Skid-a-me-oo-ri-ay	BRUNSWICK	05434	£ 2 – 4

RED NICHOLS & HIS (NEW) ORCH./*PENNY SYMPHONY

55	Lights of Vienna (Viennese lantern)/While you're away	CAPITOL	*CL 14365	£ 4 – 6
56	Glory, glory/Bugler's lament		CL 14544	£ 2 – 4
56	Corky/The wail of the winds		CL 14560	£ 2 – 4
56	The beautiful girls of Vienna/Speak easy		CL 14596	£ 2 – 4
56	Cool tango/Indiana		CL 14617	£ 2 – 4

THE NIGHT–HAWKS

58	Cool for cats/Time will tell	FONTANA	H 120 º	£ 4 – 6

THE NIGHTBIRDS

59	The square/Cat on a cool tin roof	ORIOLE	CB 1490	£ 2 – 4

THE NILSSON TWINS

57	Rain on my window/I dance when I walk	CAPITOL	CL 14698	£ 2 – 4

NINA & FREDERIK (qv LOUIS ARMSTRONG)

59ø	Listen to the ocean/I would amor her	COLUMBIA	DB 4332	£ 2 – 4
59ø	Mary's boy child/Oh, sinner man!		DB 4375	£ 2 – 4
60ø	Little donkey/Je ne crois plus au Pere Noel		DB 4536	£ 1 – 2

NITE ROCKERS

58	Nite rock (Lonely train)/Oh! Baby	R.C.A.	RCA 1079	£40 – 60

LISA NOBLE

58	Maggie! – Yes Ma!/Who's sorry now	DECCA	F 11006	£ 2 – 4
58	It's a boy/The Saints		F 11051	£ 2 – 4

NICK NOBLE

60	The tip of my fingers/Sweet love	CORAL	Q 72403	£ 2 – 4
60	Excuse me (I think I've got a heartache)/Island farewell		Q 72413	£ 2 – 4

THE NOBLEMEN

59	Thunder wagon/Dragon walk	TOP RANK	JAR 155	£ 4 – 6

THE NOCTURNES

55	Whodat (Buck dance)/Hey Punchinello	M–G–M	SP 1120	£ 2 – 4
55	Birmin'ham/Toodle-oo igaloo		SP 1148	£ 2 – 4

DICK NOEL

56	The birds and the bees/Birth of the blues	LONDON	HLH 8295	£ 9 – 12

TERRY NOLAND

58	Oh baby! Look at me/Puppy love	CORAL	Q 72311	£40 – 60

GENE NORMAN'S "JUST JAZZ" No. 3

56	Blue Lou (both sides)	VOGUE	V 2047	£ 2 – 4

MONTY NORMAN
5	The shifting, whispering sands/Bonnie blue gal	H.M.V.	7M	349	£ 2 – 4
7	The Garden of Eden/Priscilla		POP	281	£ 4 – 6

THE NU TORNADOS
8	Philadelphia U.S.A./Magic record	LONDON	HLU	8756	£ 4 – 6

THE NUGGETS
5	Quirl up in my arms/So help me, I love you	CAPITOL	CL	14216	£ 6 – 9
5	Shtiggy boom/Anxious heart		CL	14267	£ 6 – 9

THE NUTTY SQUIRRELS
59	Uh! Oh! – Parts 1 & 2	PYE INT.	7N	25044	£ 4 – 6

HUGH O'BRIAN
58	Legend of Wyatt Earp/Down in the meadow	H.M.V.	POP	539	£ 2 – 4
58	I'm looking for a girl/Ain't got a nickel	ORIOLE	CB	1480	£ 2 – 4

ERIN O'BRIEN
58	Padre/Honey boy	CORAL	Q	72321	£ 2 – 4

ANITA O'DAY
56	You're the top/Honeysuckle Rose	H.M.V.	POP	245	£ 2 – 4
60	Tea for two/Sweet Georgia Brown		POP	821	£ 2 – 4

PAT O'DAY
55	Earth angel (will you be mine?)/A rusty old halo	M-G-M	SP	1129	£ 4 – 6
55	Soldier boy/Annie Oakley		SP	1142	£ 4 – 6
60	I'll build a stairway to Paradise/No one understands....	PYE INT.	7N	25048	£ 2 – 4

RONNIE O'DELL & HIS ORCH.
57	Melody of Napoli/Struttin' down Jane Street	LONDON	HLD	8439	£ 4 – 6

JAMES O'GWYNN
59	How can I think of tomorrow/Were you ever a stranger ..	MERCURY	AMT	1052	£ 2 – 4

JOHNNY O'KEEFE
58	Shake baby shake/Real wild child	CORAL	Q	72330	£40 – 60

MATTY O'NEIL
54	Don't sell Daddy any more whiskey/Little Rusty	LONDON	L	1037	£12 – 18

JOHNNY O'NEILL
59	Wagon train/Somebody, just like you	R.C.A.	RCA	1114	£ 2 – 4

GENE O'QUIN
51	Boogie woogie fever/RAMBLIN' JIMMY DOLAN: Wine, women...	CAPITOL	CL	13600 º	£ 9 – 12

THE OBERNKIRCHEN CHILDREN'S CHOIR
54ø	The happy wanderer/Evensong	PARLOPHONE	R	3799	£ 1 – 2

JOHNNY OCTOBER
59	Growin' prettier/Young and in love	CAPITOL	CL	15070	£ 4 – 6
60	There'll always be a feeling/So mean		CL	15121	£ 4 – 6

THE OLD TIMERS SKIFFLE GROUP
58	The woman who loved a swine/The lynching of Jeff Buckner	FONTANA	H	105 º	£ 4 – 6

JOHNNY OLENN & HIS BAND/*THE BLOCKBUSTERS
57	I ain't gonna cry no more/My idea of love	LONDON	HLU	8388	£40 – 60
59	Born reckless/You lovable you	MERCURY	*AMT	1050	£18 – 25

JOHNNY OLIVER
56	Chain gang/These hands	M-G-M	SP	1165	£ 4 – 6
60	What a kiss won't do/That's all I'm living for	MERCURY	AMT	1095	£ 4 – 6

SY OLIVER & HIS ORCH.
59 In a little Spanish town cha-cha/The Mardi Gras march . LONDON HLJ 8776 £ 2 - 4

THE OLYMPICS
58ø Western movies/Well!	H.M.V.	POP 528	£ 9 - 12
58 (I wanna) Dance with the teacher/Everybody needs love .		POP 564	£ 9 - 12
59 Private eye/(Baby) Hully gully	COLUMBIA	DB 4346	£ 9 - 12
60ø I wish I could shimmy like my sister Kate/Workin' hard	VOGUE	V 9174	£ 6 - 9

ROY ORBISON
60ø Only the lonely (know how...)/Here comes that song again	LONDON	HLU 9149	£ 4 - 6
60ø as above		HLU 9149 º	£ 9 - 12
60ø Blue angel/Today's teardrops		HLU 9207	£ 4 - 6

ORIGINAL NEW ORLEANS RHYTHM KINGS
54 Golden leaf strut/She's crying for me .... COLUMBIA SCM 5113 £ 4 - 6

THE ORIOLES
53 Hold me, thrill me, kiss me/Teardrops on my pillow	LONDON	L 1180 º	£ 9 - 12
53 Crying in the chapel/Don't you think I ought to know ..		L 1201 º	£ 9 - 12
54 In the Mission of St. Augustine/Write and tell me why .		HL 8001 º	£ 9 - 12

KID ORY & HIS CREOLE JAZZ/DIXIELAND BAND
53 Mahogany Hall stomp/At a Georgia camp meeting	COLUMBIA	SCM 5047	£ 2 - 4
53 Tiger rag/The world's jazz crazy, Lawdy so am I		SCM 5069	£ 2 - 4
56 Dippermouth blues/Savoy blues	TEMPO	A 106	£ 2 - 4
56 High society/Ballin' the Jack		A 107	£ 2 - 4
56 Tiger rag/Eh, la-bas	VOGUE	V 2011	£ 2 - 4
56 12th Street rag/Savoy blues		V 2012	£ 2 - 4
56 When the Saints go marching in/Muskrat ramble	G.T.J.	GV 2322	£ 2 - 4
56 St. James Infirmary/Bill Bailey, won't you please come..		GV 2339	£ 2 - 4

THE JOHNNY OTIS SHOW/#ORCH. (& *MARIE ADAMS/+MEL WILLIAMS/=MARCI LEE)
50 Harlem nocturne#/(by SLIM GAILLARD)	PARLOPHONE	R 3291 º	£ 6 - 9
57ø Ma (he's makin' eyes at me)/Romance in the dark	CAPITOL	*CL 14794	£ 6 - 9
58ø Bye bye baby*/Good golly		CL 14817	£ 9 - 12
58 All I want is your love/The light still shines in my....		*CL 14837	£ 6 - 9
58 Well, well, well, well!/You just kissed me goodbye		+CL 14854	£ 6 - 9
58 The Johnny Otis hand jive/Ring-a-ling		CL 14875	£ 9 - 12
59 Willie did the cha cha/Crazy country hop		CL 14941	£ 9 - 12
59 My dear/You		+CL 15008	£ 6 - 9
59 Castin' my spell/Telephone baby		=CL 15018	£ 6 - 9
59 Three girls named Molly doin' the hully.../I'll do the..		CL 15057	£ 6 - 9
60 Mumblin' Mosie/Hey, baby, don't you know?		CL 15112	£ 6 - 9

REG OWEN & HIS ORCH.
56 Comin' thru' the rye bread/Harlem swing	PARLOPHONE	R 4217	£ 2 - 4
57 Easy now/Sweeping the floor		R 4303	£ 2 - 4
59ø Manhattan spiritual/Ritual blues	PYE INT.	7N 25009	£ 4 - 6
59 Ginchy/Kazoo		7N 25040	£ 2 - 4
60ø Obsession/Sunday morn	PALETTE	PG 9004	£ 2 - 4

BUCK OWENS
59 Second fiddle/Everlasting love	CAPITOL	CL 15009	£ 2 - 4
60 Above and beyond/Til these dreams come true		CL 15123	£ 2 - 4
60 Excuse me (I think I've got a...)/I've got a right to...		CL 15162	£ 2 - 4

DONNIE OWENS
58 Need you/If I'm wrong .... LONDON HLU 8747 £ 4 - 6

HAL PAGE & THE WAILERS
60ø Going back to my home town/After hours blues .... MELODISC 1553 £ 6 - 9

HOT LIPS PAGE & HIS ORCH.
55 Ain't nothing wrong with that,....../The Cadillac song PARLOPHONE MSP 6172 £ 4 - 6

LARRY PAGE

7	Start movin' (in my direction)/Cool shake	COLUMBIA	DB 3965	£ 6 -	9
7	That'll be the day/Please don't blame me		DB 4012	£ 6 -	9
8	Under control/This is my life		DB 4080	£ 6 -	9
9	Big blon' baby/I vibrate	SAGA	SAG 45-2902	£ 6 -	9
9	How'm I doing, hey, hey/Throw all your lovin' my way ..		SAG 45-2903	£ 6 -	9
9	Little old fashioned love/Marilyn		SAG 45-2904	£ 4 -	6

PATTI PAGE

1	The Tennessee waltz/Long, long ago	ORIOLE	CB 1046 º	£ 4 -	6
2	I went to your wedding/You belong to me		CB 1129 º	£ 4 -	6
3ø	(How much is) That doggie in the window/My jealous eyes		CB 1156 º	£ 2 -	4
8	My, how the time goes by/I'll remember today	MERCURY	7MT 184	£ 4 -	6
8	Bring us together/Belonging to someone		7MT 200	£ 4 -	6
8	These wordly wonders/Another time, another place		7MT 206	£ 4 -	6
8	Left right out of your heart/Longing to hold you again		7MT 223	£ 6 -	9
8	Fibbin'/You will find your love (in Paris)		AMT 1000	£ 2 -	4
9	Trust in me/Under the Sun Valley Moon		AMT 1022	£ 2 -	4
9	The walls have ears/My promise		AMT 1038	£ 2 -	4
9	My Mother's eyes/With my eyes wide open I'm dreaming ..		AMT 1054	£ 2 -	4
0	Promise me Thomas/2,000, 200, 23 miles		AMT 1089	£ 2 -	4
0	One of us (will weep tonight)/What will my future be ..		AMT 1102	£ 2 -	4
0	I wish I'd never been born/I need you		AMT 1112	£ 2 -	4

ROSALIND PAIGE

55	When the Saints go marching in/Nobody's sweetheart now	LONDON	HL 8120	£ 9 -	12
56	Love, oh careless love/That funny melody	M-G-M	MGM 937	£ 2 -	4

MORTY PALITZ & HIS ORCH.

59	The grocer's cha cha cha/Eso es al amor	LONDON	HLJ 8778	£ 2 -	4

EARL PALMER & HIS TEN PIECE ROCKIN' BAND

58	Drum village - Parts 1 & 2	CAPITOL	CL 14859	£ 6 -	9

THE PALMETTO KINGS

50	Ten rum bottles/Home cookin' Mama	STARLITE	ST.45 021	£ 4 -	6

NIKKI PAPAS

59	49 State rock/Try again	PARLOPHONE	R 4590	£ 4 -	6
50	By the river/Don't leave me alone		R 4652	£ 4 -	6

THE PARADONS

60	Diamonds and pearls/I want love	TOP RANK	JAR 514	£ 6 -	9

NORRIE PARAMOR & HIS ORCH. (qv HARRY GOLD)

60ø	Theme from "A Summer Place"/Half pint	COLUMBIA	DB 4419	£ 1 -	2

THE PARAMOUNT ALL STARS

50	Hometown skiffle (both sides)	TEMPO	R 20 º	£ 6 -	9

CHARLIE PARKER QUARTET

60	Cosmic rays/Kim	H.M.V.	POP 747	£ 2 -	4

EDDIE PARKER

55	Far away from everybody/Bella notte	COLUMBIA	SCM 5211	£ 2 -	4
56	Rich in love/Love me as though there were no tomorrow .		DB 3804	£ 2 -	4

EULA PARKER (qv FRANK WEIR)

57	Silhouettes/Hedgehopper	ORIOLE	CB 1411	£ 4 -	6

FESS PARKER

57	Wringle wrangle/Ballad of John Colter	ORIOLE	CB 1378	£ 2 -	4

SONNY PARKER (qv LIONEL HAMPTON)

56	Disgusted blues/My soul's on fire	VOGUE	V 2392	£60 -	90

JIMMY PARKINSON

56ø	The great pretender/Hand in hand	COLUMBIA	DB 3729	º	£ 2 – 4
56ø	*as above*		SCM 5236		£ 9 – 12
56ø	Walk hand in hand/Cry baby		DB 3775	º	£ 2 – 4
56ø	*as above*		SCM 5267		£ 9 – 12
56	A lover's quarrel/Gina		DB 3808		£ 4 – 6
56ø	In the middle of the house/You to me		DB 3833		£ 9 – 12
57	But you/Together (you and I)		DB 3876		£ 4 – 6
57	Whatever Lola wants (Lola gets)/Round and round		DB 3912		£ 4 – 6

BERNICE PARKS

55	Only love me/Lovin' machine	V–CORAL	Q 72056	£ 4 – 6

JACK PARNELL & HIS BAND/ORCH./etc. (& *DENNIS HALE/+ANNIE ROSS)

53	Night train/The Hawk talks	PARLOPHONE	MSP 6031	£ 2 – 4
53	Dragnet/Fuller bounce		MSP 6054	£ 2 – 4
54	The creep/Route 66		MSP 6066	£ 2 – 4
54	Skin deep/Devil's eyes*		MSP 6078	£ 2 – 4
54	Knock out/Blowin' wild*		MSP 6094	£ 2 – 4
54	The bandit*/Annie's blues+		MSP 6102	£ 2 – 4
58	Topsy/Cha cha rock		R 4500	£ 2 – 4
59	Kansas City/The golden striker	H.M.V.	POP 630	£ 2 – 4
60	77 Sunset Strip/Teen ride	PHILIPS	PB 1005	£ 2 – 4

BILL PARSONS (actually BOBBY BARE)

59ø	The all American boy/Rubber dolly	LONDON	HL 8798	£ 9 – 12

THE PASSIONS

58	Jackie Brown/My aching heart	CAPITOL	CL 14874	£ 9 – 12
59	Just to be with you/Oh melancholy me	TOP RANK	JAR 224	£ 4 – 6
60	I only want you/This is my love		JAR 313	£ 4 – 6

TONY PASTOR & HIS ORCH.

60	Begin the beguine/Indian love call	TOP RANK	TR 5014	£ 2 – 4

JOHNNY PATE (QUINTET)

58	Swinging shepherd blues/The elder	PARLOPHONE	R 4404	£ 2 – 4
58	Pretty one/Muskeeta		R 4437	£ 2 – 4

PATIENCE & PRUDENCE

56ø	Tonight you belong to me/A smile and a ribbon	LONDON	HLU 8321	£12 – 18
57ø	Gonna get along without ya now/The money tree		HLU 8369	£12 – 18
57	We can't sing rhythm and blues/Dreamer's Bay		HLU 8425	£ 9 – 12
57	You tattletale/Very nice is Bali Bali		HLU 8493	£ 6 – 9
58	Tom Thumb's tune/Golly oh gee		HLU 8773	£ 4 – 6

OTTILIE PATTERSON (w. CHRIS BARBER'S JAZZ BAND)

55	I hate a man like you/Reckless blues	DECCA	F 10472	£ 4 – 6
55	Nobody knows you when you're down../Weeping willow blues		F 10621	£ 4 – 6
57	Kay–Cee rider/I love my baby	PYE	7N 15109	£ 2 – 4
58	Beale Street blues/Jail–house blues		7NJ 2015	£ 2 – 4
58	Trombone cholly/Lawdy, Lawdy blues		7NJ 2025	£ 2 – 4

BUNNY PAUL

54	New love/You'll never leave my side	COLUMBIA	SCM 5102	£ 2 – 4
54	Such a night/I'm gonna have some fun		SCM 5112	£ 4 – 6
54	Lovey dovey/Answer the call		SCM 5131	£ 4 – 6
54	You came a long way from St../You are always in my heart		SCM 5151	£ 2 – 4
55	Please have mercy (on a fool...)/These are the things...	CAPITOL	CL 14279	£ 4 – 6
55	Two castanets/Leave my heart alone		CL 14304	£ 4 – 6
55	Song of the dreamer/For the very first time		CL 14368	£ 4 – 6

GLEN PAUL

58	Lifetime/Running late	MERCURY	7MT 217	£ 2 – 4

LES PAUL (& MARY FORD/+& HIS TRIO) (qv GENE AUSTIN)

51	Guitar boogie/Steel guitar rag	BRUNSWICK	+04798 º	£ 6 - 9
53ø	Vaya con Dios/Deep in the blues	CAPITOL	CL 13943 º	£ 2 - 4
54	Guitar boogie/Steel guitar rag	BRUNSWICK	+05311 º	£ 4 - 6
54	Mandolino/Whither thou goest	CAPITOL	CL 14185	£ 9 - 12
54	Mister Sandman/That's what I like		CL 14212	£ 9 - 12
55	Song in blue/Someday sweetheart		CL 14233	£ 9 - 12
55	Genuine love/No letter today		CL 14300	£ 9 - 12
55	Hummingbird/Goodbye my love		CL 14342	£ 9 - 12
56	Texas lady/Alabamy bound		CL 14502	£ 4 - 6
56	Amukiriki (The Lord willing)/Magic melody		CL 14521	£ 4 - 6
56	Theme from "The Threepenny Opera" (Moritat)/Nuevo Laredo		CL 14534	£ 4 - 6
56	Say the words I love to hear/Send me some money		CL 14577	£ 4 - 6
56	Cimarron (Roll on)/San Antonio rose		CL 14593	£ 4 - 6
56	Runnin' wild/Blow the smoke away		CL 14665	£ 4 - 6
57	Cinco robles (Five oaks)/Ro-Ro-Robinson		CL 14710	£ 4 - 6
57	Hummin' and waltzin'/Tuxedos and flowers		CL 14738	£ 4 - 6
57	Strollin' blues/I don't want you no more		CL 14776	£ 6 - 9
57	A pair of fools/Fire (I'm keeping my heart away from...)		CL 14809	£ 4 - 6
58	Bewitched/The night of the Fourth		CL 14839	£ 4 - 6
58	Small island/More and more each day		CL 14858	£ 4 - 6
58	Put a ring on my finger/Fantasy	PHILIPS	PB 873	£ 4 - 6
59	Jealous heart/Big eyed gal		PB 882	£ 4 - 6
59	At the Sav-A-Penny Super Store/All I need is you		PB 906	£ 4 - 6

THE PAULETTE SISTERS

55	Dreamboat/Leave my honey be	CAPITOL	CL 14294	£ 6 - 9
55	Ring-a-dang-a-doo/Lonely one		CL 14310	£ 6 - 9
55	You win again/Mama, el baion		CL 14347	£ 6 - 9

RONNIE PEARSON

58	Flippin' over you/Teen-age fancy	H.M.V.	POP 489	£40 - 60

BOBBY PEDRICK

58	White bucks and saddle shoes/Stranded	LONDON	HLX 8740	£12 - 18

DONALD PEERS (& *THE VERNONS GIRLS/+JANET OSBORNE)

58	Oh! Oh! I'm falling in love again/I need somebody	ORIOLE	CB 1431	£ 2 - 4
59	Roses from Venice/If there are stars in my eyes (you...)	COLUMBIA	DB 4369	£ 2 - 4
60	St. Christopher/The miracle of love		*DB 4427	£ 2 - 4
60	Papa, he loves Mama+/The house of love		DB 4488	£ 2 - 4

TRACY PENDARVIS

60	A thousand guitars/Is it too late	LONDON	HLS 9059	£ 9 - 12
60	Is it me/South bound line		HLS 9213	£ 9 - 12

THE PENGUINS

55	Earth angel/Hey senorita	LONDON	HL 8114	£200 ++

THE PENNY SERENADERS

58	Whistle kwela/Fluitjie vastrap	COLUMBIA	DB 4164	£ 2 - 4

HANK PENNY

56	Bloodshot eyes/Wham! Bam! Thank you ma'am	PARLOPHONE	MSP 6202	£12 - 18

CARL PERKINS

56ø	Blue suede shoes/Honey don't	LONDON	HLU 8271	£40 - 60
57	Matchbox/Your true love		HLS 8408	£40 - 60
57	Glad all over/Forever yours		HLS 8527	£25 - 40
58	Lend me your comb/That's right		HLS 8608	£25 - 40
59	I don't see me in your eyes..../One ticket to loneliness	PHILIPS	PB 983	£ 4 - 6

TONY PERKINS

57	Moonlight swim/First romance	R.C.A.	RCA 1018	£ 2 - 4

THE PERRI'S
59 Jerri—Lee/Ballad of a happy heart .... ORIOLE   CB 1481   £ 4 —

THE PERRY SISTERS
59 Willie boy/Fabian .... BRUNSWICK   05802   £12 — 18

MAL PERRY
58 Make me a miracle/That's when your heartaches begin ... FONTANA   H   133   £ 2 —
58 Too young to love/Who are they to say ....   H   149   £ 2 —
58 Things I didn't say/The girl next door ....   H   157   £ 2 —

STEVE PERRY
60ø Step by step/Because they're young .... H.M.V.   POP   745   £ 4 —

JANICE PETERS
58 This little girl's gone rockin'/Kiss cha cha .... COLUMBIA   DB 4222   £12 — 18
59 A girl likes/You're the one ....   DB 4276   £ 9 — 12

BOBBY PETERSON QUINTET
59 The hunch/Love you pretty baby .... TOP RANK   JAR 232   £ 9 — 12

OSCAR PETERSON (QUARTET) (qv ELLA FITZGERALD)
57 Soft sands/Echoes .... H.M.V.   POP   366   £ 2 — 4
60 Jive at five/Blues for Basie ....   POP   706   £ 2 — 4

FAY PETERSON
59ø The wonder of you/I'm gone .... R.C.A.   RCA 1131   £ 6 — 9
59 Come and get it/Shirley Purley ....   RCA 1154   £ 6 — 9
60ø Answer me/Goodnight my love, pleasant dreams ....   RCA 1175   £ 4 — 6
60 Tell Laura I love her/Wedding day ....   RCA 1195   £ 6 — 9
60ø Corrine, Corrina/Be my girl .... LONDON   HLX 9246   £ 4 — 6

THE PETITES
60 Get your Daddy's car tonight/Sun showers .... PHILIPS   PB 1035   £ 4 — 6

THE PETS (qv SEPH ACRE)
58 Cha—hua—hua/Cha—kow—ski .... LONDON   HL 8652   £ 9 — 12
59 (You wandered) Beyond the sea/Wow—ee!!! .... PYE INT.   7N 25004   £ 4 — 6

NORMAN PETTY TRIO
54 Mood indigo/Petty's little polka .... H.M.V.   7M 274   £ 4 — 6

CONFREY PHILLIPS (TRIO)
56 Love and marriage/The others I like .... COLUMBIA SCM 5223   £ 2 — 4
57 Am I going out of your mind?/Afterglow .... DECCA   F 10835   £ 2 — 4
57 Hokey—kokey rock 'n' roll/Shotgun rock 'n' roll ....   F 10866   £ 6 — 9

LESLIE PHILLIPS
59 The Navy Lark/The disc .... PARLOPHONE R 4610   £ 2 — 4

PHIL PHILLIPS (& THE TWILIGHTS)
59 Sea of love/Juella .... MERCURY   AMT 1059   £ 9 — 12
60 Verdie Mae/Take this heart ....   AMT 1072   £ 4 — 6
60 What shall I tell my heart/Your true love once more ....   AMT 1093   £ 6 — 9

SID PHILLIPS & HIS BAND
56 Bugle call rag/Memories of you .... H.M.V.   7M 372   £ 2 — 4
56 Rockin' thru' the rye/Everybody step ....   7M 396   £ 2 — 4
56 Juke box baby/My honey's lovin' arms ....   7M 406   £ 2 — 4
56 Mamma don't allow/Glad rag doll ....   7M 418   £ 2 — 4
56 Farewell blues (Rock 'n' roll style)/It goes like this   POP 269   £ 2 — 4

STU PHILLIPS
58 The Champlain and St. Lawrence.../The priest who slept.. LONDON   HL 8673   £ 4 — 6

TEDDY PHILLIPS & HIS ORCH.
54 Ridin' to Tennessee/Alone tonight .... LONDON   HL 8032   £12 — 18

WOOLF PHILLIPS & HIS ORCH. (& *LEE YOUNG/+DENNIS MORLEY)
Rock, rock, rock/Merci beaucoup .... MELODISC   *1284 º £ 4 – 6
Count your blessings instead of.../Your heart, my heart+ DECCA   F 10416   £ 2 – 4

EDITH PIAF
ø Milord/Je sais comment .... COLUMBIA DC 754   £ 2 – 4

PIANO RED
Hey, good lookin'/Just right bounce .... H.M.V.   B 10246 º £ 9 – 12
Bouncin' with Red/Count the days I'm gone ....   B 10316 º £ 9 – 12
Rockin' with Red/Red's boogie ....   7M 108   £40 – 60

WEBB PIERCE (qv RED SOVINE)
Teenage boogie/Any old time .... BRUNSWICK   05630   £60 – 90
Bye, bye love/Honky tonk song   05682   £18 – 25
I ain't never/Shanghied   05809   £ 6 – 9
No love have I/Whirlpool of love   05820   £ 4 – 6
Drifting Texas sand/All I need is you   05842   £ 4 – 6

RAY PILGRIM
Gambler's guitar/Baby doll .... ORIOLE   CB 1557   £ 2 – 4

THE PILTDOWN MEN
ø McDonald's cave/Brontosaurus stomp .... CAPITOL CL 15149 £ 4 – 6

SIR HUBERT PIMM (qv THE DUKE & DUCHESS)
Honky tonk train blues/Goodnight and cheerio .... LONDON   HL 8155 £18 – 25

THE PINETOPPERS
Yale boola song/Notre Dame victory march .... V-CORAL   Q 72059 £ 2 – 4

"PING PING" & AL VERLANE
ø Sucu sucu/Maria Della Montagna .... ORIOLE   CB 1589   £ 4 – 6

PINKY & PERKY
Tom Dooley/The velvet glove (Pinky & Perky theme) ..... DECCA   F 11095   £ 2 – 4
Does your chewing gum lose its.../The little mountaineer   F 11116   £ 2 – 4
"Pinky & Perky's Party Sing-Song" medley ....   F 11174   £ 2 – 4
Cradle of love/Clinkerated chimes ....   F 11229   £ 2 – 4
Eeny meeny miney mo/The ugly duckling .... COLUMBIA DB 4538   £ 2 – 4

THE PLANETS
Like party/Ippy yippy beatnik .... PALETTE   PG 9008   £ 4 – 6
Chunky/Screwball .... H.M.V.   POP 818 £ 4 – 6

EDDIE PLATT & HIS ORCH.
Tequila/Popcorn .... COLUMBIA DB 4101   £ 2 – 4

THE PLATTERS (*feat. TONY WILLIAMS/qv LINDA HAYES)
(You've got) The magic touch/Winner take all .... MERCURY   MT 107 º £ 2 – 4
ø Only you (and you alone)/The great pretender ....   MT 117 º £ 2 – 4
ø My prayer/Heaven on Earth ....   MT 120 º £ 2 – 4
ø You'll never never know/It isn't right ....   MT 130 º £ 2 – 4
On my word of honor/One in a million ....   MT 143 º £ 4 – 6
ø I'm sorry/He's mine ....   MT 145 º £ 2 – 4
My dream/I wanna ....   MT 156 º £ 4 – 6
Helpless/Indiff'rent ....   7MT 197 £ 9 – 12
Don't let go/Are you sincere ....   7MT 205 £12 – 18
ø Twilight time/Out of my mind ....   7MT 214 £ 6 – 9
You're making a mistake*/My old flame ....   7MT 227 £ 6 – 9
I wish/It's raining outside ....   AMT 1001 £ 4 – 6
ø Smoke gets in your eyes/No matter what you are ....   AMT 1016 £ 4 – 6
Enchanted/The sound and the fury ....   AMT 1039 £ 4 – 6
ø Remember when/Love of a lifetime ....   *AMT 1053 £ 4 – 6
My blue Heaven/Wish it were me ....   AMT 1066 £ 4 – 6
My secret/What does it matter ....   AMT 1076 £ 4 – 6

60ø	Harbour lights/(By the) Sleepy lagoon		AMT 1081	£ 4 -
60	(I'll be with you in) Apple blossom time/Ebb tide		*AMT 1098	£ 4 -
60	Red sails in the sunset/Sad river		*AMT 1106	£ 4 -
60	To each his own/Down the River of Golden Dreams		AMT 1118	£ 4 -

THE PLAYBOYS
58	Over the weekend/Double talk	LONDON	HLU 8681	£12 -

THE PLAYGIRLS
59	Young love swings the world/Hey sport	R.C.A.	RCA 1133	£ 6 -

THE PLAYMATES
57	Barefoot girl/Pretty woman	COLUMBIA	DB 3941	£ 4 -
57	Darling, it's wonderful/Island girl		DB 4033	£ 2 -
58	Jo—Ann/You can't stop me from dreaming		DB 4084	£ 4 -
58	Let's be lovers/Give me another chance	'	DB 4127	£ 2 -
58	Don't go home/Can't you get it through your head		DB 4151	£ 4 -
58	The day I died/While the record goes around		DB 4207	£ 2 -
58	Beep beep/Your love		DB 4224	£ 4 -
59	Star love/The thing-a-ma-jig		DB 4288	£ 2 -
59	What is love?/I am		DB 4338	£ 6 -
59	On the beach/First love		DB 4389	£ 2 -
60	Parade of pretty girls/Jubilation T. Cornpone		DB 4468	£ 2 -
60	Wait for me/Eyes of an angel		DB 4551	£ 2 -

BOBBY PLEASE (*Apart from 78s, possibly only 45 rpm DEMOS exist*)
57	Your driver's license, please/Heartache Street	LONDON	HLB 8507	£18 -

JACK PLEIS & HIS ORCH. (& *BONNIE LAKE & HER BEAUX/+RALPH YOUNG)
56	The trouble with Harry*/Pauline	BRUNSWICK	05534	£ 2 -
56	Giant+/Lonesome without you		05634	£ 2 -

THE POLKA DOTS (*& LAURIE JOHNSON ORCH./qv TEDDY JOHNSON)
58	Don't make small talk baby/There will never be another..	PYE	7N 15144	£ 2 -
59	Hey Liley, Liley lo/Go chase a moonbeam		7N 15194	£ 2 -
59	Girls in arms/You've done something to my heart		*7N 15211	£ 2 -

THE PONI—TAILS
58ø	Born too late/Come on Joey, dance with me	H.M.V.	POP 516	£ 6 -
58	Close friends/Seven minutes in Heaven		POP 558	£ 4 -
59ø	Early to bed/Father Time		POP 596	£ 6 -
59	Moody/Oom pah polka		POP 644	£ 4 -
59	I'll be seeing you/I'll keep tryin'		POP 663	£ 4 -

THE POUND HOUNDS (qv PEGGY LEE)
55	Home sweet home/THE MELLOMEN: Lady	BRUNSWICK	05484	£ 4 -

JANE POWELL
53	Something wonderful/I whistle a happy tune	M—G—M	SP 1061	£ 2 -
53	Hello, young lovers/We kiss in a shadow		SP 1062	£ 2 -
56	True love/Mind if I make love to you	H.M.V.	POP 267	£ 2 -

DUFFY POWER
59	That's my little Suzie/Dream lover	FONTANA	H 194	£ 4 -
59	Kissin' time/Ain't she sweet		H 214	£ 4 -
59	Starry—eyed/Prettier than you		H 230	£ 4 -
60	Whole lotta shakin' goin' on/If I can dream		H 279	£ 4 -

PEREZ "PREZ" PRADO & HIS ORCH.
54	Skokiaan/The high and the mighty	H.M.V.	7M 255	£ 2 -
55ø	Cherry pink and apple blossom white/Maria Elena		B 10833 ⁹	£ 1 -
55ø	*as above*		7M 295	£ 6 -
58ø	Patricia/Why wait	R.C.A.	RCA 1067	£ 4 -
58	Guaglione/Paris		RCA 1082	£ 2 -
59	Tic toc polly woc/My Roberta		RCA 1129	£ 2 -
60	Rockambo baby/Oh, oh, Rosie		RCA 1199	£ 2 -

LOU PREAGER & HIS ORCH.

58	Marchin' drummer blues/Fedora	COLUMBIA	DB	4115	£ 2 – 4

ELVIS PRESLEY

56ø	Heartbreak Hotel/I was the one	H.M.V.	POP	182 º	£ 9 – 12
56ø	*as above*		7M	385	£40 – 60
56ø	Blue suede shoes/Tutti frutti		POP	213 º	£ 9 – 12
56ø	*as above*		7M	405	£60 – 90
56ø	I want you, I need you, I love you/My baby left me		POP	235 º	£ 9 – 12
56ø	*as above*		7M	424	£40 – 60
56ø	Hound dog/Don't be cruel		POP	249	£40 – 60
56ø	Love me tender/Any way you want me (that's how I will..)		POP	253	£40 – 60
56ø	Blue moon/I don't care if the Sun don't shine		POP	272	£40 – 60
57ø	Mystery train/Love me		POP	295	£60 – 90
57ø	Rip it up/Baby, let's play house		POP	305	£60 – 90
57ø	Too much/Playin' for keeps		POP	330	£40 – 60
57ø	All shook up/That's when your heartaches begin		POP	359	£25 – 40
57ø	Paralyzed/When my blue Moon turns to gold again		POP	378	£25 – 40
57ø	(Let me be your) Teddy bear/Loving you	R.C.A.	RCA	1013	£ 9 – 12
57ø	Party/Got a lot o' livin' to do		RCA	1020	£ 9 – 12
57ø	Lawdy, Miss Clawdy/Tryin' to get to you	H.M.V.	POP	408	£25 – 40
57ø	Santa bring my baby back (to..)/Santa Claus is back in..	R.C.A.	RCA	1025	£ 9 – 12
57ø	I'm left, you're right, she's../How do you think I feel?	H.M.V.	POP	428	£18 – 25
58ø	Jailhouse rock/Treat me nice	R.C.A.	RCA	1028	£ 6 – 9
58ø	Don't/I beg of you		RCA	1043	£ 6 – 9
58ø	Wear my ring around your neck/Doncha' think it's time .		RCA	1058	£ 6 – 9
58ø	Hard headed woman/Don't ask me why		RCA	1070	£ 6 – 9
58ø	King Creole/Dixieland rock		RCA	1081	£ 6 – 9
58	All shook up/Heartbreak Hotel		RCA	1088	£12 – 18
58	Hound dog/Blue suede shoes		RCA	1095	£12 – 18
59ø	One night/I got stung		RCA	1100	£ 6 – 9
59ø	A fool such as I/I need your love tonight		RCA	1113	£ 4 – 6
59ø	A big hunk o' love/My wish came true		RCA	1136	£ 4 – 6
60ø	Stuck on you/Fame and fortune		RCA	1187	£ 4 – 6
60ø	*as above*		RCA	1187 º	£12 – 18
60ø	A mess of blues/The girl of my best friend		RCA	1194	£ 4 – 6
60ø	*as above*		RCA	1194 º	£12 – 18
60ø	It's now or never/Make me know it		RCA	1207	£ 2 – 4
60ø	*as above*		RCA	1207 º	£12 – 18

JOHNNY PRESTON

60ø	Running Bear/My heart knows	MERCURY	AMT	1079	£ 4 – 6
60ø	Cradle of love/City of tears		AMT	1092	£ 4 – 6
60ø	Feel so fine/I'm starting to go steady		AMT	1104	£ 6 – 9
60ø	Charming Billy/Up in the air		AMT	1114	£ 4 – 6

MIKE PRESTON

58	My lucky love/A house, a car and a wedding ring	DECCA	F	11053	£ 4 – 6
58	Why, why, why/Whispering grass		F	11087	£ 4 – 6
59	In Surabaya/Dirty old town		F	11120	£ 4 – 6
59ø	Mr. Blue/Just ask your heart		F	11167	£ 4 – 6
60	A girl like you/Too old		F	11222	£ 4 – 6
60ø	I'd do anything/Where is love?		F	11255	£ 4 – 6
60ø	Togetherness/Farewell my love		F	11287	£ 4 – 6

LLOYD PRICE

57	Just because/Why	LONDON	HL	8438	£12 – 18
59ø	Stagger Lee/You need love	H.M.V.	POP	580	£ 6 – 9
59ø	Where were you (on our wedding day)/Is it really love?		POP	598	£ 4 – 6
59ø	Personality/Have you ever had the blues?		POP	626	£ 4 – 6
59ø	I'm gonna get married/Three little pigs		POP	650	£ 4 – 6
59	Wont'cha come home/Come into my heart		POP	672	£ 4 – 6
60ø	Lady Luck/Never let me go		POP	712	£ 4 – 6
60	For love/No if's – no and's		POP	741	£ 4 – 6
60	Question/If I look a little blue		POP	772	£ 4 – 6
60	Just call me (and I'll understand)/Who coulda' told you.		POP	799	£ 4 – 6

(ROCKIN') RED PRICE (*& HIS ROCKIN' RHYTHM)

56	Rocky Mountain gal/Rock o' the North	DECCA	*F 10822	£ 4 – 6
58	Weekend/The sneeze	PYE	7N 15169	£ 4 – 6
60	Wow!/My baby's door		7N 15262	£ 4 – 6

RIKKI PRICE

58	Tom Dooley/(It looks like rain in) Cherry Blossom Lane	FONTANA	H 162	£ 2 – 4
59	Honey, Honey/The very thought of you		H 171	£ 2 – 4
59	Mr. Blue/Man on my trail		H 217	£ 2 – 4

DICKIE PRIDE

59	Slippin' 'n' slidin'/Don't make me love you	COLUMBIA	DB 4283	£ 9 – 12
59	Fabulous cure/Midnight oil		DB 4296	£ 9 – 12
59ø	Primrose Lane/Frantic		DB 4340	£ 9 – 12
60	Betty, Betty (go steady with me)/No John		DB 4403	£ 6 – 9
60	You're singin' our love song to some-./Bye bye blackbird		DB 4451	£ 4 – 6

LOUIS PRIMA (& HIS ORCH.) (*& KEELY SMITH/+SAM BUTERA'S WITNESSES)

50	Oh babe!*/Piccolina Lena	POLYGON	P 1001 º	£ 6 – 9
54	Take a little walk around the block*/Oh! Cumari	COLUMBIA	SCM 5092	£ 9 – 12
54	The happy wanderer/Until sunrise*	BRUNSWICK	05314 º	£ 4 – 6
56	5 months, 2 weeks, 2 days/Banana split for my baby	CAPITOL	CL 14669	£12 – 18
58ø	Buona sera/Beep! Beep!		CL 14821	£ 9 – 12
59	Bei mir bist du schon/I don't know why	LONDON	*HLD 8923	£ 4 – 6
60	I'm confessin' (that I love you)/Night and day		*HLD 9084	£ 4 – 6
60	Ol' Man Moses+/Wonderland by night		HLD 9230	£ 4 – 6

THE PRINCE SISTERS

55	A rusty old halo/Beautiful love	DECCA	F 10500	£ 2 – 4
55	The Bible tells me so/St. Catherine	BELTONA	BL 2633	£ 2 – 4

RED PRYSOCK

57	Teen-age rock/Paquino walk	MERCURY	MT 154 º	£ 6 – 9
59	Chop suey/Margie		AMT 1028	£ 4 – 6

DANNY PURCHES

55	Mama/Just one more time	COLUMBIA	SCM 5183	£ 2 – 4
56	You can't run away from it/You don't know me		DB 3860	£ 2 – 4
58	The shrine on the second floor/He		DB 4129	£ 2 – 4

THE QUAKER CITY BOYS

59	Teasin'/Won't y' come out, Mary Ann	LONDON	HLU 8796	£ 4 – 6

THE QUARTER NOTES

57	Ten minutes to midnight/My fantasy	PARLOPHONE	R 4365	£ 4 – 6

CARMEL QUINN

57	Who are you foolin' now?/You can't run away from your...	M–G–M	MGM 967	£ 2 – 4

OSCAR RABIN & HIS BAND (*& MEL GAYNOR)

53	Crazy man crazy/Forgive me*	POLYGON	P 1086 º	£ 4 – 6

THE RAGPICKERS

59	Fifi/Cat on a cool tin roof	SAGA	SAG 45–2906	£ 2 – 4

THE RAINBEAUS

60	That's all I'm asking of you/Maybe it's wrong	VOGUE	V 9161	£ 4 – 6

THE RAINDROPS

59	Italian style/Along came Jones	PARLOPHONE	R 4559	£ 2 – 4
60	Let's make a foursome/If I had my life to live over.....	ORIOLE	CB 1544	£ 2 – 4
60	Banjo boy/Crazy rhythm		CB 1555	£ 2 – 4

LORRY RAINE

54	You broke my broken heart/I'm in love with a guy	LONDON	HL 8043	£12 – 18
55	Love me tonight/What would I do		HL 8132	£12 – 18

MARVIN RAINWATER (*& Sister PATTY/qv CONNIE FRANCIS)

Year	Title	Label	Cat. No.	Price
56	Albino (Pink-eyed) stallion/Tennessee houn' dog yodel .	M-G-M	MGM 876 º	£ 4 - 6
56	*as above*		SP 1150	£18 - 25
56	What am I supposed to do/Why did you have to go and.....		MGM 929	£ 9 - 12
57	Gonna find me a bluebird/So you think you've got........		MGM 961	£ 6 - 9
58ø	Whole lotta woman/Baby, don't go		MGM 974	£ 6 - 9
58ø	I dig you baby/Two fools in love*		MGM 980	£ 6 - 9
58	Dance me Daddy/Because I'm a dreamer*		MGM 988	£ 6 - 9
59	Half-breed/A song of new love		MGM 1030	£ 4 - 6
60	Nothin' needs nothin' (like I...)/The valley of the Moon		MGM 1052	£ 4 - 6

FREDDY RANDALL & HIS BAND

Year	Title	Label	Cat. No.	Price
53	Clarinet marmalade/Original Dixieland one-step	PARLOPHONE	MSP 6007	£ 2 - 4
53	At the Jazz Band Ball/Way down yonder in New Orleans .		MSP 6030	£ 2 - 4
53	Twelve for six/Copenhagen		MSP 6043	£ 2 - 4
54	Carolina in the morning/Tin roof blues		MSP 6087	£ 2 - 4
54	Muskrat ramble/Shine		MSP 6098	£ 2 - 4
54	Someday sweetheart/Hotter than that		MSP 6137	£ 2 - 4
56	Sugar/That da da strain		R 4223	£ 2 - 4
57	Esox/Jealousy		R 4322	£ 2 - 4

TEDDY RANDAZZO

Year	Title	Label	Cat. No.	Price
59	It's magic/Richer than I	H.M.V.	POP 578	£ 2 - 4
60	Journey to love/Misery		POP 806	£ 2 - 4

SUE RANEY

Year	Title	Label	Cat. No.	Price
57	The careless years/What's the good word, Mr. Bluebird .	CAPITOL	CL 14757	£ 2 - 4
57	Please hurry home/Don't take my happiness		CL 14792	£ 2 - 4
58	My, my, how the time goes by/Periwinkle blue		CL 14923	£ 2 - 4
59	Ever/The restless sea		CL 14980	£ 2 - 4
59	Swingin' in a hammock/I don't look right without you ..		CL 15045	£ 2 - 4
60	Biology/I stayed too long at the fair		CL 15132	£ 2 - 4

KENNY RANKIN

Year	Title	Label	Cat. No.	Price
60	Sure as you're born/Teasin' heart	BRUNSWICK	05845	£ 2 - 4

JOHNNY RAPHAEL

Year	Title	Label	Cat. No.	Price
58	We're only young once/The lonely road to nowhere	VOGUE	V 9104	£ 4 - 6

CARL RAVAZZA

Year	Title	Label	Cat. No.	Price
51	Rock, rock, rock/Like a dream	H.M.V.	B 10202 º	£ 4 - 6

PAUL RAVEN (became Gary Glitter)

Year	Title	Label	Cat. No.	Price
60	Alone in the night/Too proud	DECCA	F 11202	£12 - 18

THE RAVENS

Year	Title	Label	Cat. No.	Price
53	Rock me all night long/Write me one sweet letter	ORIOLE	CB 1148 º	£12 - 18
53	Begin the beguine/Looking for my baby		CB 1149 º	£ 9 - 12
54	Who'll be the fool?/Rough ridin'		CB 1258 º	£ 9 - 12

CLYDE RAY

Year	Title	Label	Cat. No.	Price
57	Follow me/Steady as a rock	COLUMBIA	DB 3875	£ 2 - 4
58	Locked in the arms of love/I'm not afraid anymore		DB 4106	£ 2 - 4

JOHNNIE RAY (*& THE FOUR LADS/qv DORIS DAY/FRANKIE LAINE)

Year	Title	Label	Cat. No.	Price
52	Cry*/The little white cloud that cried	COLUMBIA	DB 2995 º	£ 4 - 6
52	Please, Mr. Sun*/(Here am I) Broken hearted		DB 3006 º	£ 2 - 4
52ø	Walkin' my baby back home/What's the use?*		DB 3060 º	£ 2 - 4
52ø	Faith can move mountains/A sinner am I		DB 3154 º	£ 2 - 4
53ø	Walkin' my baby back home/The lady drinks champagne* ..		SCM 5015	£12 - 18
53ø	Somebody stole my gal/Glad rag doll	PHILIPS	PB 123 º	£ 2 - 4
53	Tell the lady I said goodbye/Whiskey and gin	COLUMBIA	SCM 5041	£ 9 - 12
53	Please don't talk about me when../Coffee and cigarettes*		SCM 5074	£ 9 - 12
54ø	Such a night/An orchid for the lady	PHILIPS	PB 244 º	£ 2 - 4
54	Nobody's sweetheart/I can't escape from you	COLUMBIA	SCM 5111	£ 9 - 12
54	I'm just a shadow of myself/She didn't say nothin' at...		SCM 5122	£ 9 - 12

55ø	If you believe/Alexander's Ragtime Band	PHILIPS	PB	379	º £ 2 - 4
55ø	Paths of Paradise/Parade of broken hearts		PB	441	º £ 2 - 4
55	Flip flop and fly/Thine eyes are as the eyes of a dove		PB	449	º £ 4 - 6
55ø	Hey there/Hernando's Hideaway		PB	495	º £ 2 - 4
55ø	Song of the dreamer/I've got so many million years		PB	516	º £ 2 - 4
56ø	Who's sorry now?/A heart comes in handy		PB	546	º £ 2 - 4
56ø	Ain't misbehavin'/Walk along with Kings		PB	580	º £ 2 - 4
56ø	Just walking in the rain/In the candlelight		PB	624	º £ 1 - 2
57ø	Look homeward, angel/You don't owe me a thing		PB	655	º £ 1 - 2
57ø	as above		JK	1004	£12 - 18
57	So long/I miss you so		JK	1011	£ 9 - 12
57ø	Yes tonight, Josephine/No wedding today		PB	686	º £ 1 - 2
57ø	as above		JK	1016	£12 - 18
57ø	Build your love (on a strong........)/Street of memories		PB	721	º £ 2 - 4
57ø	as above		JK	1025	£12 - 18
57	Pink sweater angel/Texas tambourine		PB	762	º £ 2 - 4
57	as above		JK	1033	£12 - 18
58	Miss me just a little/Soliloquy of a fool		PB	785	£ 4 - 6
58	Strollin' girl/Plant a little seed		PB	808	£ 4 - 6
58	Lonely for a letter/Endlessly		PB	829	£ 4 - 6
58	Up until now/No regrets		PB	849	£ 4 - 6
58	What more can I say/You're the one who knows		PB	884	£ 4 - 6
59	When's your birthday, baby/One man's love song is		PB	901	£ 4 - 6
59	Here and now/Call me yours		PB	918	£ 2 - 4
59ø	I'll never fall in love again/You're all that I live for		PB	952	£ 4 - 6
60	When it's Springtime in the Rockies/Wagon wheels		PB	990	£ 2 - 4
60	Before you/I'll make you mine		PB	1025	£ 2 - 4
60	Tell me/Don't leave me now		PB	1047	£ 2 - 4
60	In the heart of a fool/Let's forget it now	LONDON	HLA	9216	£ 2 - 4

MARGIE RAYBURN

56	The wedding song/That's the chance I've got to take	CAPITOL	CL	14532	£ 2 - 4
57	I'm available/If you were	LONDON	HLU	8515	£ 6 - 9
58	I would/Alright, but it won't be easy		HLU	8648	£ 4 - 6

BILLY RAYMOND

58	Makin' love/I would	H.M.V.	POP	503	£ 2 - 4
58	One in particular/Seven daughters		POP	526	£ 2 - 4
59	Charlie is their darling/Loch Lomond		POP	614	£ 2 - 4

LEE RAYMOND & THE COSTELLO SISTERS

55	Foolishly yours/Baby darling	BRUNSWICK	05438	£ 2 - 4

TONY RAYMOND

59	Broken-hearted melody/This Earth is mine	FONTANA	H	213	£ 2 - 4

JULIE RAYNE

59	Love where can you be?/Waltz me around	H.M.V.	POP	665	£ 2 - 4
60	Bim bam bom/One more time		POP	785	£ 2 - 4

THE RAYS

57	Silhouettes/Daddy Cool	LONDON	HLU	8505	£18 - 25

AL READ

56	What is a home? (A shanty in old..)/We haven't any money	H.M.V.	POP	278	£ 2 - 4
59	That's life/Our Maggie's going to get married		POP	575	£ 2 - 4

PAT READER

60	Dear Daddy/Ricky	TRIUMPH	RGM	1024	£ 9 - 12

BERTICE READING

55	Frankie and Johnnie/My one sin (in life)	PARLOPHONE	R 4045	º £ 4 - 6
55	Bessie Smith blues/Everybody's somebody's fool		R 4064	º £ 4 - 6
57	No flowers by request/September in the rain	DECCA	F 10965	£ 4 - 6
58	Rock baby rock/It's a boy	PARLOPHONE	R 4462	£12 - 18
58	My big best shoes/No more in life		R 4487	£ 4 - 6

THE REBS
58 Bunky/Renegade .... CAPITOL CL 14932 £ 6 - 9

GENE REDD & THE GLOBE TROTTERS
59 Red River Valley rock/Kentucky home rock .... PARLOPHONE R 4584 £ 4 - 6

TEDDY REDELL
60 Judy/Can't you see .... LONDON HLK 9140 £ 9 - 12

DIZZY REECE QUINTET
56 Chorous/Basie line .... TEMPO A 140 £ 2 - 4

CHUCK REED
57 Whispering heart/Another love has ended .... BRUNSWICK 05646 £ 4 - 6
58 No school tomorrow/Let's put our hearts together ...... COLUMBIA DB 4113 £ 9 - 12

DEAN REED
59 The search/Annabelle .... CAPITOL CL 14986 £ 2 - 4
59 I kissed a Queen/A pair of scissors (and a pot of glue)   CL 15030 £ 2 - 4

JERRY REED
58 Bessie baby/Too young to be blue .... CAPITOL CL 14851 £40 - 60

JIMMY REED
60 Baby what you want me to do/Caress me baby .... TOP RANK JAR 333 £ 4 - 6
60 Found love/Where can you be .... JAR 394 £ 4 - 6
60 Hush-hush/Going by the river .... JAR 533 £ 4 - 6

DELLA REESE
58 You gotta love everybody/I wish .... LONDON HLJ 8687 £ 4 - 6
59 Sermonette/Dreams end at dawn .... HLJ 8814 £ 4 - 6
59 Not one minute more/Soldier won't you marry me .... R.C.A. RCA 1160 £ 2 - 4
60 Someday/Let's get away from it all .... RCA 1185 £ 2 - 4
60 Everyday/There's no two ways about it .... RCA 1192 £ 2 - 4
60 And now/There's nothing like a boy .... RCA 1204 £ 2 - 4

TONY REESE
59 Just about this time tomorrow/Lesson in love .... LONDON HLJ 8987 £ 2 - 4

JIM REEVES
54 Bimbo/Gipsy heart .... LONDON HL 8014 £25 - 40
54 Mexican Joe/I could cry .... HL 8030 £25 - 40
54 Butterfly love/It's hard to love just one .... HL 8055 £25 - 40
54 Echo Bonita/Then I'll stop loving you .... HL 8064 £25 - 40
54 Padre of old San Antone/Mother went a-walkin' .... HL 8105 £25 - 40
55 Penny candy/I'll follow you .... HL 8118 £25 - 40
55 Drinking tequila/Red-eyed and rowdy .... HL 8159 £40 - 60
55 Tahiti/Give me one more kiss .... HLU 8185 £25 - 40
56 The wilder your heart beats the../Where does a broken... HLU 8351 £25 - 40
57 Four walls/I know and you know .... R.C.A. RCA 1005 £ 4 - 6
58 Blue boy/Theme of love .... RCA 1074 £ 4 - 6
59 Partners/I'm beginning to forget you .... RCA 1144 £ 2 - 4
60ø He'll have to go/In a mansion stands my love .... RCA 1168 £ 4 - 6
60 I'm getting better/I know one .... RCA 1197 £ 2 - 4
60 Am I losing you/I missed me .... RCA 1214 £ 2 - 4

JOAN REGAN (& *THE SQUADRONAIRES/+JOHNSTON BROTHERS/=TED HEATH MUSIC/#MAX BYGRAVES/
%RUSTY REGAN/qv VARIOUS ARTISTS)
53ø Ricochet/Merry-go-rounds and swings .... DECCA *F 10193 º £ 2 - 4
54ø Someone else's roses/The love I have for you .... F 10257 º £ 2 - 4
54ø Wait for me, darling+/Two kinds of tears .... F 10362 £ 9 - 12
54ø If I give my heart to you/Faded flowers .... F 10373 £ 9 - 12
54 This ole house/Can this be love? .... F 10397 £ 9 - 12
55ø Prize of gold/When you're in love .... F 10432 £ 9 - 12
55ø Open up your heart and let the..%/If you learn to love.. F 10474 £ 9 - 12

55	Danger! Heartbreak ahead/Don't be afraid of love		F 10505	£ 6 – 9
55	Just say you love her/Nobody danced with me		F 10521	£ 6 – 9
55	The shepherd boy/The rose and the flame		F 10598	£ 6 – 9
56ø	Cross of gold (Croce di oro)/Love and marriage		F 10659	£ 9 – 12
56	Don't take me for granted/The boy with the magic guitar		F 10710	£ 4 – 6
56	Honestly/I'd never leave you, baby+		F 10742	£ 4 – 6
56	Sweet heartaches/Second fiddle		=F 10757	£ 4 – 6
56	Gone/Make me a child again		F 10801	£ 4 – 6
57	Nearer to me/Cross my ever–loving heart		F 10871	£ 2 – 4
57	Wonderful! Wonderful!/Speak for yourself John		F 10911	£ 2 – 4
57	7½ cents/Good evening friends		#F 10934	£ 2 – 4
57	Love me to pieces/Soft sands		F 10942	£ 2 – 4
58	I may never pass this way..../Breezing along with the...		F 11009	£ 2 – 4
58	Love like ours/Take me in your arms	H.M.V.	POP 555	£ 2 – 4
59ø	May you always/Have you ever been lonely?		POP 593	£ 2 – 4
59ø	Happy anniversary/So close to my heart	PYE	7N 15238	£ 2 – 4
60	If only you'd be mine/O Dio mio		7N 15259	£ 2 – 4
60ø	Papa loves Mama/When you know someone loves you		7N 15278	£ 2 – 4
60ø	One of the lucky ones/My thanks to you		7N 15310	£ 2 – 4
60ø	Must be Santa/Will Santa come to Shanty Town		7N 15303	£ 2 – 4

RUSS REGAN
59	Adults only/Just the two of us	CAPITOL	CL 15084	£ 2 – 4

THE REGENT BALLROOM ORCHESTRA
54	Midnight tango/Desire	DECCA	F 10402	£ 2 – 4
54	If I give my heart to you/A sky–blue shirt and a rain–..		F 10409	£ 2 – 4
55	No one but you/The "Mama–doll" song		F 10445	£ 2 – 4
55	Mister Sandman/I love Paris		F 10446	£ 2 – 4
55	A blossom fell/Finger of suspicion		F 10482	£ 2 – 4
55	Softly, softly/Let me go, lover!		F 10487	£ 2 – 4

DJANGO REINHARDT
53	Le soir/Deccaphonie	DECCA	F 10219 º	£ 4 – 6

JOE REISMAN & HIS ORCH.
55	Bo Diddley/Bubble boogie	H.M.V.	B 10891 º	£ 6 – 9
56	Robin Hood/His name was Judas		7M 364	£ 2 – 4

LINE RENAUD (qv DEAN MARTIN)
53	April in Portugal/The song from Moulin Rouge	COLUMBIA	SCM 5055	£ 2 – 4
55	If I love/Pam–pou–de (Pam–poo–day)	CAPITOL	CL 14230	£ 4 – 6
56	Flamenco love/To you, my love	COLUMBIA	SCM 5268	£ 2 – 4
56	You can't keep running/Strange		DB 3824	£ 2 – 4
58	Disc–donc, disc–donc/Irma La Douce		DB 4193	£ 2 – 4
60	Jeremy/Mon coeur au Portugal		DB 4485	£ 2 – 4

THE RENAULTS
60	Melancolie/Stella	WARNER–B	WB 11	£ 2 – 4

GOOGIE RENE
60	Forever/Ez–zee	LONDON	HLY 9056	£ 9 – 12

DON RENNIE
56	To love to love is wonderful/One girl – One boy	PARLOPHONE	MSP 6218	£ 2 – 4
56	Who are we?/Can you find it in your heart?		MSP 6237	£ 2 – 4
56	This is only the beginning/Ev'rybody falls in love with.		R 4249	£ 2 – 4

JOHNNY RESTIVO
59	The shape I'm in/Ya ya	R.C.A.	RCA 1143	£ 9 – 12
59	I like girls/Dear Someone		RCA 1159	£ 4 – 6

THE REVELS
59	Midnight stroll/Talking to my heart	TOP RANK	JAR 235	£ 4 – 6

REX (Morris) & THE MINORS
60	Chicken sax/Snake eyes	TRIUMPH	RGM 1023	£ 9 – 12

LITTLE BOBBY REY & HIS BAND
60	Rockin' "J" bells/Dance of the New Year	TOP RANK	JAR 525	£ 4 – 6

DEBBIE REYNOLDS (& *CARLETON CARPENTER/+THE NATURALS)
51	Aba dada honeymoon/Row, row, row	M–G–M	*MGM 350 º	£ 2 – 4
55	Carolina in the morning/Never mind the noise in the....+		SP 1127	£ 2 – 4
56	Love is the tender trap/Canoodlin' rag		SP 1155	£ 2 – 4
57ø	Tammy/French heels	V–CORAL	Q 72274	£ 6 – 9
57	All grown up/Wall flower	M–G–M	MGM 968	£ 2 – 4
58	A very special love/I saw a country boy	CORAL	Q 72297	£ 2 – 4
58	This happy feeling/Hillside in Scotland		Q 72324	£ 2 – 4
58	Faces there are fairer/Hungry eyes		Q 72345	£ 2 – 4
59	The mating game/Right away	M–G–M	MGM 1019	£ 2 – 4
59	It started with a kiss/Love is a gamble		MGM 1043	£ 2 – 4
60	Ask me to go steady/Am I that easy to forget?	LONDON	HLD 9028	£ 2 – 4
60	City lights/Just for a touch of your love		HLD 9128	£ 2 – 4

DONN REYNOLDS
57	Hasta luego/Lorelei	H.M.V.	POP 314	£ 2 – 4
57	Rose of Ol' Pawnee/All alone (with no one by my side)	M–G–M	MGM 971	£ 2 – 4
58	Bella Belinda/Blue eyes crying in the rain		MGM 996	£ 2 – 4

JODY REYNOLDS
58	Endless sleep/Tight capris	LONDON	HL 8651	£12 – 18

TODD RHODES ORCHESTRA
55	Specks/Silver sunset	PARLOPHONE	MSP 6171	£ 9 – 12

THE RHYTHMETTES
59	I'll be with you in apple blossom../Page from the future	CORAL	Q 72358	£ 4 – 6

CHARLIE RICH
60	Lonely weekends/Everything I do is wrong	LONDON	HLU 9107	£ 9 – 12

DAVE RICH
58	City lights/Burn on love fire	R.C.A.	RCA 1092	£ 4 – 6

CLIFF RICHARD (& THE SHADOWS/*DRIFTERS)
58ø	Move it!/Schoolboy crush	COLUMBIA	*DB 4178	£ 9 – 12
58ø	High class baby/My feet hit the ground		*DB 4203	£ 6 – 9
59ø	Livin' lovin' doll/Steady with you		*DB 4249	£18 – 25
59ø	Mean streak/Never mind		*DB 4290	£ 6 – 9
59ø	Living doll/Apron strings		*DB 4306	£ 4 – 6
59ø	Travellin' light/Dynamite		DB 4351	£ 4 – 6
60ø	A voice in the wilderness/Don't be mad at me		DB 4398	£ 4 – 6
60ø	as above		DB 4398 º	£ 9 – 12
60ø	Fall in love with you/Willie and the hand jive		DB 4431	£ 4 – 6
60ø	as above		DB 4431 º	£ 9 – 12
60ø	Please don't tease/Where is my heart		DB 4479	£ 4 – 6
60ø	as above		DB 4479 º	£ 9 – 12
60ø	Nine times out of ten/Thinking of our love		DB 4506	£ 4 – 6
60ø	as above		DB 4506 º	£ 9 – 12
60ø	I love you/"D" in love		DB 4547	£ 2 – 4
60ø	as above		DB 4547 º	£ 9 – 12

ANN RICHARDS (qv STAN KENTON)
58	I'd do it all again/Nobody knows the trouble I've seen	CAPITOL	CL 14897	£ 2 – 4

RUSTY RICHARDS
60	Middle hand road/Golden moon (China night)	TOP RANK	JAR 297	£ 2 – 4

REMEMBER! – THE SYMBOL ø AFTER THE YEAR OF ISSUE INDICATES A BRITISH CHART ENTRY

TRUDY RICHARDS
57	Wishbone/Hangin' around	CAPITOL	CL 14728	£ 4 – 6
57	I want a big butter and egg man/Weaker than wise		CL 14744	£ 2 – 4
58	The night when love was born/Somebody just like you ...		CL 14857	£ 2 – 4

JANET RICHMOND
60	You got what it takes/Not one minute more	TOP RANK	JAR 288	£ 2 – 4
60	June bride/My one and only love		JAR 378	£ 2 – 4

BERESFORD RICKETTS
60	Cherry baby/I want to know	STARLITE	ST.45 025	£ 6 – 9
60	Baby baby/When I woke up		ST.45 029	£ 6 – 9

NELSON RIDDLE & HIS ORCH. (& *BOB GRAHAM/+PAT AULD)
55	Vera Cruz/You won't forget me	CAPITOL	CL 14241	£ 4 – 6
55	The pendulum song/Brother John		CL 14262	£ 4 – 6
55	Run for cover*/Make believe that you're in love with me+		CL 14305	£ 4 – 6

JACKIE RIGGS
56	The great pretender/His gold will melt	LONDON	HLF 8244	£12 – 18

BOB RILEY
58	The midnight line/Wanda Jean	M–G–M	MGM 977	£18 – 25

SHANE RIMMER (*& THE SPINNERS)
59	(Roll along) Wagon train/A touch of pink	COLUMBIA	DB 4293	£ 2 – 4
59	The three bells (Jimmy Brown..)*/I want to walk you home		DB 4343	£ 2 – 4

RINKY DINKS
59	Choo choo cha cha/Catch a little moonbeam	CAPITOL	CL 14999	£ 2 – 4

AUGIE RIOS
58	¿Donde esta Santa Claus?/Ol' Fatso	M–G–M	MGM 999	£ 2 – 4

TEX RITTER
52	High noon/Boogie woogie cowboy	CAPITOL	CL 13778 ♀	£ 6 – 9
54	Is there a Santa Claus?/Old Tex Kringle		CL 14175	£ 4 – 6
55	A whale of a tale/High on a mountain top		CL 14277	£ 4 – 6
55	Marshal of Wichita/September song		CL 14335	£ 4 – 6
56	The last frontier/These hands		CL 14536	£ 2 – 4
56ø	The wayward wind/Gunsmoke		CL 14581	£ 9 – 12
56	The Searchers (Ride away)/Remember the Alamo		CL 14605	£ 2 – 4
56	The last wagon/Paul Bunyan love		CL 14660	£ 2 – 4
57	Green grow the lilacs/The touch of the Master's hand ..		CL 14684	£ 2 – 4
57	I leaned on a man/Children and fools		CL 14715	£ 2 – 4
57	Here was a man/It came upon the midnight clear		CL 14805	£ 2 – 4
58	Burning sand/Jealous heart		CL 14900	£ 2 – 4
58	I look for a love/The history song		CL 14933	£ 2 – 4
59	Rye whisky/Conversation with a gun		CL 15041	£ 2 – 4

BOB RITTERBUSH
59	Darling Corey/I wish that you were mine	TOP RANK	JAR 118	£ 2 – 4

DANNY RIVERS
60	I got/Hawk	TOP RANK	JAR 408	£ 4 – 6
60ø	Can't you hear my heart/I'm waiting for tomorrow	DECCA	F 11294	£ 6 – 9

MAVIS RIVERS
60	Longing, longing, longing/So rare	CAPITOL	CL 15120	£ 2 – 4

THE RIVIERAS
60	Moonlight cocktails/Blessing of love	H.M.V.	POP 773	£ 6 – 9

MARTY ROBBINS
56	Long tall Sally/Mr. Teardrop	PHILIPS	PB 590 ♀	£ 9 – 12
57	A white sport coat (and a pink carnation)/Grown-up tears		PB 696 ♀	£ 2 – 4
57	*as above*		JK 1019	£ 9 – 12

57	Please don't blame me/Teen-age dream		PB 741 [9]	£ 2 - 4
58	The story of my life/Once-a-week date	FONTANA	H 102 [9]	£ 2 - 4
58	Stairway of love/Just married		H 128	£ 4 - 6
58	Sittin' in a tree house/She was only seventeen		H 150	£ 4 - 6
59	The hanging tree/The blues country style		H 184	£ 4 - 6
59	Cap and gown/Last night about this time		H 212	£ 2 - 4
59ø	Big iron/Cool water		H 229	£ 4 - 6
59ø	El Paso/Running gun		H 233	£ 4 - 6
60	I told my heart/Is there any chance		H 263	£ 2 - 4
60	Ballad of the Alamo/Five brothers		H 270	£ 2 - 4

MEL ROBBINS
| 59 | Save it/To know you .... | LONDON | HLM 8966 | £40 - 60 |

SYLVIA ROBBINS (qv MICKEY & SYLVIA)
| 60 | Frankie and Johnny/Come home .... | LONDON | HLJ 9118 | £ 9 - 12 |

KENNY ROBERTS
| 57 | I'm looking for the bully of the.../Broken teenage heart | BRUNSWICK | 05638 | £ 2 - 4 |

DON ROBERTSON (*& LOU DINNING)
| 56ø | The happy whistler/You're free to go* .... | CAPITOL | CL 14575 | £ 6 - 9 |
| 56 | Every day that I live*/You .... | | CL 14629 | £ 2 - 4 |

PAUL ROBESON
| 52 | Ol' Man River/I suits me .... | H.M.V. | 7P 113 | £ 2 - 4 |

IVO ROBIC
| 59ø | Morgen/Ay, ay, ay Paloma .... | POLYDOR | NH 23923 | £ 4 - 6 |

TINA ROBIN
57	Over somebody else's shoulder/Lady fair	V-CORAL	Q 72284	£ 9 - 12
57	Never in a million years/Ca c'est l'amour		Q 72294	£ 4 - 6
58	Believe me/Everyday	CORAL	Q 72309	£ 4 - 6
58	No school tomorrow/Sugar blues		Q 72323	£ 6 - 9

THE ROBINS
| 60 | Cherry lips/Out of the picture .... | VOGUE | V 9168 | £25 - 40 |
| 60 | Just like that/Whole lot imagination .... | | V 9173 | £25 - 40 |

FLOYD ROBINSON
| 59ø | Makin' love/My girl .... | R.C.A. | RCA 1146 | £ 4 - 6 |
| 60 | I believe in love/Tattletale .... | | RCA 1179 | £ 2 - 4 |

HARRY ROBINSON "STRING SOUND"
| 60 | The skirl/Wimoweh .... | TOP RANK | JAR 325 | £ 2 - 4 |

CARSON ROBISON & HIS PLEASANT VALLEY BOYS/etc.
| 53 | Lady round the lady/Pokeberry promenade .... | M-G-M | SP 1004 | £ 4 - 6 |
| 53 | Square dance jitterbug/Keep on circlin' 'round .... | | SP 1024 | £ 9 - 12 |

THE ROCK BROTHERS
| 56 | Dungaree doll/Livin' it up .... | PARLOPHONE | MSP 6201 | £12 - 18 |

THE ROCK-A-TEENS
| 59 | Woo-hoo/Untrue .... | COLUMBIA | DB 4361 | £ 9 - 12 |

ROCK-OLGA
| 60 | Red sails in the sunset/My Dixieland doll .... | EMBER | EMB S105 | £ 2 - 4 |

THE ROCKERS
| 59 | Get cracking/Counter melody .... | ORIOLE | CB 1501 | £ 4 - 6 |

THE ROCKETS
| 59 | Gibraltar rock/Walkin' home .... | PHILIPS | PB 982 | £ 4 - 6 |

THE ROCKIN' R's
59	The beat/Crazy baby	LONDON	HL 8872	£18 – 25

THE ROCKIN' SAINTS
60	Cheat on me, baby/Half and half	BRUNSWICK	05843	£18 – 25

LORD ROCKINGHAM'S XI
58	Fried onions/The squelch	DECCA	F 11024	£ 4 – 6
58ø	Hoots mon/Blue train		F 11059	£ 4 – 6
59ø	Wee Tom/Lady Rockingham, I presume?		F 11104	£ 4 – 6
59	Ra-ra Rockingham/Farewell to Rockingham		F 11139	£ 4 – 6

RODD, KEN & THE CAVALIERS
60	Magic wheel/Happy valley	TRIUMPH	RGM 1001	£18 – 25

EILEEN RODGERS
58	Careful, careful/I'm alone because I love you	FONTANA	H 136	£ 2 – 4
58	Treasure of your love/A little bit bluer		H 156	£ 2 – 4

JIMMIE RODGERS
57ø	Honeycomb/Their hearts were full of Spring	COLUMBIA	DB 3986	£ 9 – 12
57ø	Kisses sweeter than wine/Better loved you'll never be .		DB 4052	£ 6 – 9
58ø	Oh-oh, I'm falling in love again/The long hot Summer ..		DB 4078	£ 6 – 9
58	Secretly/Make me a miracle		DB 4130	£ 2 – 4
58	The wizard/Are you really mine		DB 4175	£ 2 – 4
58ø	Woman from Liberia/Girl in the wood		DB 4206	£ 4 – 6
59	Bimbombey/You understand me		DB 4235	£ 2 – 4
59	Because you're young/I'm never gonna tell		DB 4281	£ 2 – 4
59	Soldier, won't you marry me?/Ring-a-ling-a-lario		DB 4327	£ 2 – 4
59	Tucumcari/The night you became seventeen		DB 4362	£ 2 – 4
60	Waltzing Matilda/T.L.C. – Tender love and care		DB 4401	£ 2 – 4
60	Joshua fit the Battle of Jericho/Just a closer walk.....		DB 4447	£ 2 – 4

ERIC ROGERS
54	"Six Hits Of The Day – Piano Medley No. 5"	DECCA	F 10376	£ 2 – 4

PAULINE ROGERS
54	Spinning the blues/But good	COLUMBIA	SCM 5106	£ 4 – 6

SHORTY ROGERS & HIS ORCH. (qv BUD SHANK)
54	Tale of an African lobster/Sweetheart of Sigmund Freud	H.M.V.	7M 267	£ 2 – 4
60	Tarzan is trapped/Los primitivos	M-G-M	MGM 1084	£ 2 – 4

TIMMIE ROGERS
57	Back to school again/I've got a dog who loves me	LONDON	HLU 8510	£18 – 25
58	Take me to your leader/Fla-ga-la-pa		HLU 8601	£18 – 25

JAN ROHDE
60	Come back baby/So shy	QUALITON	PSP 7128	£ 4 – 6

DICK ROMAN
59	Party girl/My greatest mistake	M-G-M	MGM 1004	£ 2 – 4

CHAN ROMERO
59	The hippy hippy shake/If I had a way	COLUMBIA	DB 4341	£18 – 25
60	My little Ruby/I don't care now		DB 4405	£25 – 40

RONALD & RUBY
58	Lollipop/Fickle baby	R.C.A.	RCA 1053	£ 4 – 6

RONNIE RONALDE (qv VARIOUS ARTISTS)
53	Song of the mountains/If I were a blackbird	COLUMBIA	SCM 5006	£ 4 – 6
53	In a monastery garden/Bells across the meadow		SCM 5007	£ 4 – 6
54	We'll always remember/On the quarter deck		SCM 5101	£ 4 – 6
54	My starlight lullaby/Safe in the harbour		SCM 5116	£ 4 – 6

54	Ave Maria/Angels sing		SCM 5141	£ 4 − 6
55	"Christmastide With Ronnie Ronalde"		SCM 5205	£ 2 − 4
56	Ballad of Davy Crockett/Hair of gold		SCM 5214	£ 4 − 6
56	Robin Hood/Happy trails		SCM 5241	£ 4 − 6
56	The Yarmouth song/Macnamara's Band		SCM 5262	£ 2 − 4
56	The happy whistler/The lady from Luxembourg		SCM 5275	£ 4 − 6
57	The mountain climber/The Buccaneers		DB 3892	£ 2 − 4
57	The Alpine polka/A bird sings		DB 4003	£ 2 − 4
57	"Christmas At Home" medley		DB 4020	£ 2 − 4
57	"Party Rhymes"		DB 4036	£ 2 − 4
58	Innocent sinners/Sweetwater Mountain		DB 4092	£ 2 − 4
59	The pleasant peasant/When it's Springtime in the Rockies		DB 4320	£ 2 − 4
59	Morning star/Christmas lullaby		DB 4367	£ 2 − 4

THE RONDELLS
58	Good good/Dreamy	LONDON	HLU 8716	£18 − 25

DON RONDO
56	Two different worlds/He made you mine	COLUMBIA	DB 3854	£ 2 − 4
57	The love I never had/Don't		DB 3909	£ 2 − 4
57	White silver sands/Stars fell on Alabama	LONDON	HLJ 8466	£ 4 − 6
58	What a shame/Made for each other		HLJ 8567	£ 4 − 6
58	I've got bells on my heart/School dance		HLJ 8610	£ 4 − 6
58	Blonde bombshell/Her hair was yellow		HLJ 8641	£ 4 − 6
58	Dormi, dormi, dormi/In Chi Chi Chihuahua		HLJ 8695	£ 2 − 4
58	City lights/I could be a mountain		HLJ 8749	£ 2 − 4
59	Song from "The Geisha Boy"/Gretna Green		HLJ 8808	£ 2 − 4
60	The King of Holiday Island/Wanderlust		HLL 9217	£ 2 − 4

RONNIE & ROY
59	Big fat Sally/Here I am	CAPITOL	CL 15028	£25 − 40

EDMUNDO ROS & HIS ORCH. (*& JOHNSTON BROTHERS/qv ANNETTE KLOOGER/VARIOUS ARTISTS)
54	Istanbul*/Blowin' wild	DECCA	F 10214	£ 4 − 6
54	Somebody bad stole de wedding bell/Chili sauce		F 10263	£ 4 − 6
55	Cherry pink and apple blossom white/Ole mambo		F 10480	£ 4 − 6
56	Sixteen tons/Robin Hood		F 10669	£ 4 − 6
56	Mister Cuckoo/Don't ringa da bell		F 10716	£ 2 − 4
57	I saw Esau/Jamaica farewell (Kingston Town)		F 10834	£ 2 − 4

ROSITA ROSANO
57	Queer things/Little boy	MELODISC	1436	£ 4 − 6

ANDY ROSE
58	Lov-a lov-a love/Just young	LONDON	HLU 8761	£12 − 18

DAVID ROSE & HIS ORCH. (& *WOODY HERMAN/+BERYL DAVIS/=RUSH ADAMS)
53	Harlem nocturne*/Vanessa	M-G-M	SP 1009	£ 2 − 4
53	Beautiful music to love by+/Satan and the Polar Bear		SP 1019	£ 2 − 4
54	I live for you=/Migraine melody		SP 1083	£ 2 − 4

DUSTY ROSE
55	The birds and the bees/It makes me so mad	LONDON	HLU 8162	£25 − 40

JOHNNY ROSE
60	Linda Lea/The last one to know	CAPITOL	CL 15166	£ 4 − 6

FRANK ROSOLINO SEXTET
54	That old black magic/Yo yo	CAPITOL	KC 65001	£ 4 − 6

ANNIE ROSS (qv TONY CROMBIE/JACK PARNELL)
55	The fish/Mama (he treats your daughter mean)	DECCA	F 10514	£ 4 − 6
56	Only you/Cry me a river		F 10680	£ 4 − 6

DAVE ROSS
58	Everybody's got a girl but Tino/Pit-a-patter boom boom	ORIOLE	CB 1416	£ 4 − 6

GENE ROSS
58 Endless sTeep/The only one .... PARLOPHONE R 4434 £12 – 18

SPENCER ROSS (& HIS ORCH.)
60 Tracy's theme/Thanksgiving Day parade .... PHILIPS   PB 992 £ 2 – 4
60 Theme of a lonely evening/Bobby's blues .... LONDON   HLX 9141 £ 2 – 4

THE ROVERS
55 Ichi-bon Tami Dachi/Why oh-h (Why do you lie to me?) .. CAPITOL CL 14283 £ 4 – 6

DEREK ROY (w. BOB MONKHOUSE, RICHARD MURDOCH, JON PERTWEE, TED RAY & Others)
57 "Derek Roy's All-Star Party" .... ORIOLE   CB 1415 £ 2 – 4

CENTRAL BAND OF THE ROYAL AIR FORCE
55ø The Dam Busters march/Lilliburlero .... H.M.V.   B 10877 º £ 1 – 2
56 "Reach For The Sky" theme/The jolly airman .... ›   B 10957 £ 2 – 4
61ø The Dam Busters march/Lilliburlero .... 7P 287 £ 2 – 4

THE ROYAL HOLIDAYS
58 Margaret/I'm sorry (I did you wrong) .... LONDON   HLU 8722 £12 – 18

THE ROYAL ROCKERS
60 Jet II/Swinging mambo .... TOP RANK JAR 329 £ 6 – 9

THE ROYAL TEENS
58 Short shorts/Planet rock .... H.M.V.   POP 454 £12 – 18
59 Believe me/Little cricket .... CAPITOL CL 15068 £ 6 – 9

THE ROYALTONES
58 Poor boy/Wail! .... LONDON   HLJ 8744 £ 9 – 12

LITA ROZA (& *TED HEATH MUSIC/+JOHNSTON BROS./=THE STARGAZERS/qv VARIOUS ARTISTS)
52 Oakie boogie/Raminay .... DECCA   *F 9955 º £ 6 – 9
53ø (How...) That doggie in the window/Tell me we'll meet... F 10070 º £ 2 – 4
53 Crazy man, crazy/Oo! What you do to me .... *F 10144 º £ 4 – 6
54 Skinnie Minnie (Fishtail)/My kid brother .... F 10363 º £ 4 – 6
54 Changing partners/Just a dream or two ago= .... F 10240 £ 4 – 6
54 Bell bottom blues+/Make love to me .... *F 10269 £ 6 – 9
54 Secret love/Young at heart .... F 10277 £ 6 – 9
54 The "Mama-Doll" song/Call off the wedding .... F 10393 £ 4 – 6
54 Heartbeat/Leave me alone .... F 10427 £ 4 – 6
55 Let me go, lover!/Make yourself comfortable .... F 10431 £ 6 – 9
55 Tomorrow/Foolishly .... F 10479 £ 4 – 6
55 Two hearts, two kisses (make one love)/Keep me in mind F 10536 £ 6 – 9
55 The man in the raincoat/Today and ev'ry day .... F 10541 £ 4 – 6
55ø Hey there/Hernando's Hideaway .... F 10611 £ 9 – 12
56ø Jimmy Unknown/The rose tattoo .... F 10679 £ 9 – 12
56 Too young to go steady/You're not alone .... F 10728 £ 4 – 6
56 But love me (Love but me)/No time for tears .... F 10761 £ 4 – 6
56 Innismore/The last waltz .... F 10792 £ 4 – 6
56 Julie/Hey! Jealous lover .... F 10830 £ 4 – 6
57 Lucky lips/Tears don't care who cries them .... F 10861 £ 6 – 9
57 Tonight my heart she is crying/Five oranges, four apples F 10884 £ 4 – 6
57 I need you/You've changed .... F 10921 £ 2 – 4
58 Ha-ha-ha!/Pretend you don't see him .... PYE   7N 15119 £ 2 – 4
58 You're the greatest/I need somebody .... 7N 15133 £ 2 – 4
58 I could have danced all..../The wonderful season of love 7N 15139 £ 2 – 4
58 Hillside in Scotland/Sorry, sorry, sorry .... 7N 15149 £ 2 – 4
58 Nel blu dipinto di blu (Volare)/It's a boy .... 7N 15155 £ 2 – 4
59 This is my town/Oh dear what can the matter be .... 7N 15190 £ 2 – 4
59 Allentown Jail/Once in a while .... 7N 15204 £ 2 – 4
59 Let it rain, let it rain/Maybe you'll be there .... 7N 15241 £ 2 – 4

BARBARA RUICK
52 Tick tock boogie/Serenade to a lemonade .... M-G-M MGM 550 º £ 4 – 6
53 The price I paid for loving you/Delishious .... SP 1044 £ 2 – 4

ANDY RUSSELL
58	A certain smile/Seven daughters	R.C.A.	RCA 1076	£ 0 - 2

CONNIE RUSSELL
54	No one but you/One Arabian night	CAPITOL	CL 14171	£ 6 - 9
54	Love me/Papa's puttin' the pressure on		CL 14197	£ 4 - 6
55	Foggy night in San Francisco/This is my love		CL 14214	£ 4 - 6
55	Green fire/Snow dreams		CL 14246	£ 4 - 6
55	Ayuh, ayuh/I'm making believe		CL 14236	£ 6 - 9
55	Farewell, farewell/The magnificent matador		CL 14268	£ 4 - 6
57	All of you/This is my love		CL 14676	£ 2 - 4

JANE RUSSELL (& *BOB LOWERY/+MARILYN MONROE)
53	Please do it again/Two sleepy people*	COLUMBIA	SCM 5043	£ 4 - 6
53	A little girl from Little Rock/When love goes wrong (..)	M-G-M	+MGM 662 º	£ 6 - 9
56	If you wanna see Mamie tonight/Keep your eyes on the....	CAPITOL	CL 14590	£ 4 - 6

JOHNNY RUSSELL
60	Lonesome boy/Baby won't you tell me so	M-G-M	MGM 1074	£ 4 - 6

RUSTY & DOUG
59	Hey Mae!/Why don't you love me	ORIOLE	CB 1510	£25 - 40
59	I like you (like this)/Dancing shoes	LONDON	HL 8972	£ 9 - 12

CATHY RYAN (qv ART MOONEY)
53	If I had you/Show me the way to go home	M-G-M	SP 1051	£ 2 - 4

MARION RYAN (qv RAY ELLINGTON/GARY MILLER)
56	Why do fools fall in love/Hot diggity (dog ziggity boom)	PYE	N 15058 º	£ 2 - 4
57	Ding dong rock-a-billy wedding/That's happiness		N 15105 º	£ 2 - 4
58ø	Love me forever/Make the man love me		7N 15121	£ 4 - 6
58	Oh oh, I'm falling in love again/Always and forever ...		7N 15130	£ 4 - 6
58	Stairway of love/I need you		7N 15138	£ 4 - 6
58	The world goes around and..../Please don't say goodnight		7N 15157	£ 2 - 4
58	as above (STEREO version)		7NSR 15157	£ 4 - 6
59	Wait for me/Jeepers creepers		7N 15184	£ 2 - 4
59	Jo-Jo the dog-faced boy/Doin' what comes natur'lly		7N 15200	£ 4 - 6
59	Too much/Promise me		7N 15216	£ 2 - 4
60	Sixteen reasons/Mangos	COLUMBIA	DB 4448	£ 2 - 4
60ø	It's you that I love/Somebody		DB 4550	£ 2 - 4

BOBBY RYDELL
59	Kissin' time/You'll never tame me	TOP RANK	JAR 181	£ 4 - 6
59	We got love/I dig girls		JAR 227	£ 4 - 6
60ø	Wild one/Little bitty girl	COLUMBIA	DB 4429	£ 4 - 6
60ø	Swingin' school/Ding-a-ling		DB 4471	£ 4 - 6
60ø	Volare/I'd do it again		DB 4495	£ 4 - 6
60ø	Sway/Groovy tonight		DB 4545	£ 2 - 4

THE SAFARIS
60	The girl with the story in her eyes/Summer nights	TOP RANK	JAR 528	£ 4 - 6
60	Image of a girl/Four steps to love		JAR 424	£ 4 - 6

THE SAGA SATELLITES (*& ex-R.S.M. BRITTAIN)
59	Regimental rock*/Swingin' sporrans	SAGA	SAG 45-2901	£ 4 - 6

MIKE SAGAR & THE CRESTERS
60ø	Deep feeling/You know	H.M.V.	POP 819	£ 4 - 6

THE SAINTS JAZZ BAND
51	I want a girl just like the../(by CRANE RIVER JAZZ BAND)	PARLOPHONE	R 3427 º	£ 6 - 9
53	Who walks in when I walk out?/Hey lawdy Papa		MSP 6042	£ 2 - 4
56	Mahogany Hall stomp/Stack O' Lee blues		R 4240	£ 2 - 4
57	Blue turning grey over you/'Till we meet again		R 4260	£ 2 - 4
57	How come you do me like you do/Willie the weeper		R 4304	£ 2 - 4
58	I've found a new baby/Swingin' the blues		R 4417	£ 2 - 4

RUSS SAINTY & THE NU-NOTES
60	Happy-go-lucky-me/Standing around	TOP RANK	JAR 381	£ 2 - 4
60	Race with the Devil/Too shy	DECCA	F 11270	£ 4 - 6

SAMMY SALVO
58	Oh Julie/Say yeah	R.C.A.	RCA 1032	£ 9 - 12
59	Afraid/Marble heart	LONDON	HLP 8997	£ 4 - 6

DAVE SAMPSON & THE HUNTERS
60ø	Sweet dreams/It's lonesome	COLUMBIA	DB 4449	£ 9 - 12
60	If you need me/See you around		DB 4502	£ 9 - 12

TOMMY SAMPSON & HIS STRONGMEN
58	Rockin'/Rock 'n' roll those big brown eyes	MELODISC	1411	£ 6 - 9

JERRY SAMUELS (became Napoleon XIV)
56	Puppy love/The chosen few	H.M.V.	7M 411	£ 4 - 6

JODI(E) SANDS
57	With all my heart/More than only friends	LONDON	HL 8456	£ 4 - 6
57	Please don't tell me (.....)/If you're not completely...		HL 8530	£ 4 - 6
58	All I ask of you/The way I love you	STARLITE	ST.45 005	£ 4 - 6
58ø	Someday (you'll want me to want you)/Always in my heart	H.M.V.	POP 533	£ 4 - 6

SHIRLEY SANDS
59	I surrender/I'm yours	DECCA	F 11134	£ 2 - 4

SYLVIA SANDS
59	Love me now! Love me now!..../More, more, more romancing	COLUMBIA	DB 4321	£ 2 - 4

TOMMY SANDS (*& THE RAIDERS)
57	Hep dee hootie (Cutie wootie)/Teen-age crush	CAPITOL	CL 14695	£ 9 - 12
57	Ring-a-ding-a-ding/My love song		CL 14724	£ 6 - 9
57	Goin' steady/Ring my 'phone		CL 14745	£ 6 - 9
57	Let me be loved/Fantastically foolish		CL 14781	£ 4 - 6
57	Man, like wow!/A swingin' romance		CL 14811	£ 6 - 9
58	Sing, boy, sing/Crazy 'cause I love you		CL 14834	£ 6 - 9
58	Hawaiian rock/Teen-age doll		CL 14872	£ 9 - 12
58	After the Senior Prom/Big date		CL 14889	£ 4 - 6
58	Blue ribbon baby/I love you because		*CL 14925	£ 9 - 12
59	Bigger than Texas/The worryin' kind		CL 14971	£12 - 18
59	Is it ever gonna happen/I ain't gittin' rid of you		CL 15013	£ 9 - 12
59	Sinner man/Bring me your love		CL 15047	£ 4 - 6
59	That's the way I am/I'll be seeing you		CL 15071	£ 4 - 6
60	I gotta have you/You hold the future		CL 15109	£ 4 - 6
60ø	The old oaken bucket/These are the things you are		CL 15143	£ 4 - 6

SANTO & JOHNNY
59ø	Sleep walk/All night diner	PYE INT.	7N 25037	£ 4 - 6
60ø	Teardrop/The long walk home	PARLOPHONE	R 4619	£ 4 - 6
60	Caravan/Summertime		R 4644	£ 4 - 6

THE SARATOGA JAZZ BAND
60	Milord/Dinjan	EMBER	EMB S117	£ 2 - 4

DON SARGENT
60	St. James' Infirmary/Gypsy boots	VOGUE	V 9160	£60 - 90

THE SATISFIERS
57	Where'll I be tomorrow night?/Come away, love	V-CORAL	Q 72247	£ 4 - 6

LONNIE SATTIN
56	Trapped (in the web of love)/Your home can be a castle	CAPITOL	CL 14552	£ 4 - 6
56	High steel/What time does the Sun go down?		CL 14638	£ 2 - 4
57	I'll never stop loving you/Whoo-pie shoo-pie		CL 14771	£ 2 - 4
58	Ring around the Moon/My heart's your home		CL 14831	£ 2 - 4
60	I'll fly away/Any more than I	WARNER-B	WB 15	£ 2 - 4

THE SAUTER-FINEGAN ORCHESTRA (*& SALLY SWEETLAND)
```
54  The Moon is blue*/"O" (Oh!) .......................... H.M.V.      7M  177   £ 2 -  4
54  Where's Ace?*/Hit the road to Dreamland ..............             7M  192   £ 2 -  4
```

EDNA SAVAGE
```
55  Stars shine in your eyes/A star is born ............. PARLOPHONE MSP 6175   £ 4 -  6
55  Candlelight/In the wee small hours of the morning ....            MSP 6181   £ 4 -  6
55ø Arrivederci darling/Bella notte .......................           R 4097 º  £ 2 -  4
55ø  as above ...........................................             MSP 6189   £ 9 - 12
56  Please hurry home/Tell me, tell me, tell me that you....          MSP 6217   £ 4 -  6
56  My prayer/Me 'n' you 'n' the Moon ....................            R 4226   £ 6 -  9
57  Never leave me/Don't ever go (I need you) ............            R 4253   £ 4 -  6
57  Me head's in de barrel/Five oranges, four apples ......           R 4301   £ 4 -  6
57  Let me be loved/Diano Marina .........................            R 4360   £ 4 -  6
58  My shining star/Once .................................            R 4420   £ 2 -  4
58  Why, why, why/Near you ...............................            R 4489   £ 2 -  4
59  Maybe this year/Beautiful love .......................            R 4572   £ 2 -  4
60  All I need/Every day .................................            R 4648   £ 2 -  4
```

JOAN SAVAGE
```
57  Five oranges, four apples/Bamboozled .................. COLUMBIA  DB 3929   £ 4 -  6
57  With all my heart/Love letters in the sand ...........            DB 3968   £ 4 -  6
57  Shake me, I rattle/Lula rock-a-hula ..................            DB 4039   £ 9 - 12
58  Hello happiness, goodbye blues/Left right out of my.....          DB 4159   £ 4 -  6
```

"ACE" DINNING SAX
```
59  Mulholland Drive/My love ............................. TOP RANK  JAR 184   £ 2 -  4
```

AL SAXON (qv THE LANA SISTERS)
```
58  Where the black-eyed Susans grow/She screamed ......... FONTANA    H  138   £ 2 -  4
58ø You're the top-cha/The day the rains came .............           H  164   £ 4 -  6
59  Chattanooga Choo-Choo/Chip off the old block ..........            H  188   £ 2 -  4
59ø Only sixteen/I'm all right, Jack .....................            H  205   £ 4 -  6
59  Linda Lu/Heart of stone ..............................            H  222   £ 2 -  4
59  Marina/Me without you ................................            H  231   £ 2 -  4
60  The piper of love/Believe me .........................            H  244   £ 2 -  4
60  I've heard that song before/Someone like you ..........           H  261   £ 2 -  4
60ø Blue-eyed boy/Don't push your luck ...................            H  278   £ 2 -  4
```

THE SCAMPS
```
59  Petite fleur/Naomi ................................... LONDON    HLW 8827   £ 4 -  6
```

CHARLES FRANCIS SCARRATT III
```
59  Two innocent lovers/Lovemobile ....................... FELSTED    AF  113   £ 2 -  4
```

HAL SCHAEFFER ORCH. & CHORUS
```
58  March of the Vikings/March of the Parisian bakers ..... LONDON    HLT 8692   £ 2 -  4
```

MURRAY SCHAFF'S ARISTOCRATS
```
54  Believe me/I'm waiting for the ships that never come in  COLUMBIA SCM 5148   £ 2 -  4
```

IVY SCHULMAN & THE BOWTIES
```
57  Rock, pretty baby/THE BOWTIES: Ever since I can remember LONDON   HLN 8372   £25 - 40
```

The Voices Of WALTER SCHUMANN
```
54  Haunted house/I only have eyes for you ............... H.M.V.     7M  229   £ 2 -  4
55  The man from Laramie/Let me hear you whisper .........            7M  323   £ 2 -  4
```

BILLY SCOTT
```
58  You're the greatest/That's why I was born ............ LONDON    HLU 8565   £ 4 -  6
60  Carole/Stairway to the stars ......................... TOP RANK  JAR 270   £ 4 -  6
```

BOBBY SCOTT
```
56  Chain gang/Shadrack .................................. LONDON    HL  8254   £12 - 18
```

JACK SCOTT

58ø	My true love/Leroy	LONDON	HLU 8626	£ 9 – 12
58	With your love/Geraldine		HLU 8765	£ 9 – 12
59	Goodbye baby/Save my soul		HLL 8804	£ 9 – 12
59	I never felt like this/Bella		HLL 8851	£ 9 – 12
59ø	The way I walk/Midgie		HLL 8912	£ 9 – 12
59	There comes a time/Baby Marie		HLL 8970	£ 9 – 12
60ø	What in the world's come over you/Baby, baby	TOP RANK	JAR 280	£ 4 – 6
60ø	Burning bridges/Oh, little one		JAR 375	£ 4 – 6
60	Cool water/It only happened yesterday		JAR 419	£ 4 – 6
60	Patsy/Old time religion		JAR 524	£ 4 – 6

JOHN SCOTT

60	Hi-flutin' boogie/Peace pipe	PARLOPHONE	R 4697	£ 2 – 4

JOHN *or JOHNNY SCOTT

60	Darlin'/Why don't you write?	ORIOLE	*CB 1542	£ 2 – 4
60	They say/How about that	PHILIPS	PB 1056	£ 2 – 4

JUDY SCOTT

57	Game of love (A-one and a-two)/With all my heart	BRUNSWICK	05687	£ 2 – 4
57	Parlour piano theme/A tender word		05704	£ 2 – 4

RONNIE SCOTT ORCHESTRA/*NEW QUINTET

56	Basie talks/Flying home	DECCA	FJ 10712	£ 2 – 4
57	I'll take romance/Speak low	TEMPO	*A 153	£ 2 – 4

JOHN SEBASTIAN

54	Inca dance/Foolish waltz	LONDON	HL 8029	£ 9 – 12
55	Stranger in Paradise/Autumn leaves		HL 8131	£ 9 – 12

HARRY SECOMBE (qv THE GOONS)

55ø	On with the motley/Strange harmony of contrasts	PHILIPS	PB 523 º	£ 1 – 2

MIKE SECREST

57	The gift/Do you promise	M-G-M	MGM 960	£ 2 – 4

NEIL SEDAKA

59	The diary/No vacancy	R.C.A.	RCA 1099	£ 4 – 6
59ø	I go ape/Moon of gold		RCA 1115	£ 6 – 9
59	You gotta learn your rhythm and.../Crying my heart out..		RCA 1130	£ 6 – 9
59	Ring a rockin'/Fly don't fly on me	LONDON	HLW 8961	£18 – 25
59ø	Oh! Carol/One way ticket	R.C.A.	RCA 1152	£ 4 – 6
60ø	Stairway to Heaven/Forty winks away		RCA 1178	£ 2 – 4
60ø	You mean everything to me/Run Samson run		RCA 1198	£ 2 – 4

PEGGY SEEGER

57	Freight train/Cumberland Gap	TOPIC	TRC 107 º	£ 4 – 6

PETE SEEGER

60	Careless love/LEON BIBB: Times are getting hard	TOP RANK	TR 5020	£ 2 – 4

VIVIENNE SEGAL & HAROLD LANG

54	Den of iniquity/BARBARA ASHLEY: That terrific rainbow	COLUMBIA	SCM 5114	£ 2 – 4

RONNIE SELF

58	Bop-a-Lena/Ain't I'm a dog	PHILIPS	PB 810 º	£25 – 40

PETER SELLERS (*& SOPHIA LOREN/qv THE GOONS)

57ø	Any old iron/Boiled bananas and carrots	PARLOPHONE	R 4337	£ 4 – 6
58	I'm so ashamed/A drop of the hard stuff		R 4491	£ 4 – 6
59	Puttin' on the smile/My old Dutch		R 4605	£ 4 – 6
60ø	Goodness gracious me!*/Grandpa's grave		R 4702	£ 4 – 6

SEMPRINI

53	Variations on boogie/Kitten on the keys	H.M.V.	7M 104	£ 2 – 4

RAY SENDIT & HIS ROCKEY TEAM
57 Rocket 0869/Spike's rock .... FELSTED   SD 80052   £ 4 - 6

SERINO
60 I had the craziest dream/I'm walkin' through the ruins.. PYE INT. 7N 25055   £ 2 - 4

DAVID SEVILLE & HIS ORCH./*THE CHIPMUNKS (qv ALFI & HARRY)
56 Armen's theme/Carousel in Rome .... LONDON   HLU 8359   £ 9 - 12
57 The gift/The donkey and the schoolboy ....   HLU 8411   £ 4 - 6
57 Gotta get to your house/Camel rock ....   HLU 8485   £ 6 - 9
58 Bonjour tristesse/Dance from "Bonjour Tristesse" ......   HLU 8582   £ 2 - 4
58ø Witch doctor/Don't whistle at me baby ....   HLU 8619   £ 4 - 6
58 The bird on my head/Hey there Moon ....   HLU 8659   £ 4 - 6
58 Take five/Little brass band ....   HLU 8736   £ 2 - 4
58 Almost good/(by THE CHIPMUNKS) ....   HLU 8762   £ 2 - 4
59 Alvin's harmonica*/Mediocre ....   HLU 8823   £ 2 - 4
59 Judy/Maria from Madrid ....   HLU 8893   £ 2 - 4
59ø Ragtime Cowboy Joe*/Flip side ....   HLU 8916   £ 2 - 4
60 Alvin's orchestra*/Copyright 1960 ....   HLG 9061   £ 2 - 4
60 Coming 'round the mountain/Sing a goofy tune ....   *HLG 9125   £ 2 - 4
60 Alvin for President*/Sack time ....   HLG 9193   £ 2 - 4

THE SHADES & THE KNOTT SISTERS
58 Sun glasses/KNOTT SISTERS: Undivided attention .... LONDON   HLX 8713   £ 9 - 12

THE SHADOWS (U.K.) (qv THE DRIFTERS/CLIFF RICHARD)
59 Lonesome fella/Saturday dance .... COLUMBIA DB 4387   £12 - 18
60ø Apache/Quatermasster's stores ....   DB 4484   £ 4 - 6
60ø *as above* ....   DB 4484 º £12 - 18
60ø (Theme from) Man of mystery/The stranger ....   DB 4530   £ 4 - 6

THE SHADOWS (U.S.)
58 Jungle fever/Under stars of love .... H.M.V.   POP 563   £ 9 - 12

THE ALEXANDRA SHAMBER BOYS
58 Dintho - Kwela/Holom toe - Kwela .... H.M.V.   POP 496   £ 2 - 4

DAVE SHAND & HIS ROCKIN' RHYTHM
56 You can't chop your.... (Lizzie Borden)/Rockin' the boat ORIOLE   CB 1321 º £ 4 - 6

JIMMY SHAND (& HIS BAND)
52ø Bluebell polka/The veleta .... PARLOPHONE F 3436 º £ 1 - 2
56ø "Sing With Jimmy Shand" medley ....   R 4242   £ 2 - 4

THE SHANE SISTERS
60 Presents on the Christmas tree/My Mommy told me .... EMBER   EMB S115   £ 2 - 4

DICK SHANE
59 Don't come back again/When your heart is only 17 years.. DECCA   F 11122   £ 2 - 4

VALERIE SHANE
58 When the boys talk about the girls/Careful, careful ... PHILIPS   PB 833   £ 2 - 4
58 One billion seven million thirty-three/Meet me tonight..   PB 879   £ 2 - 4
59 Make love to me/Baisez moi (Kiss me) ....   PB 929   £ 2 - 4

BUD SHANK (& *BILL PERKINS QUINTET/+BOB BROOKMEYER/=SHORTY ROGERS QUINTET)
56 Royal Garden blues/It had to be you .... VOGUE   *V 2376   £ 2 - 4
56 When your lover has gone/There's a small hotel ....   +V 2383   £ 2 - 4
56 Shank's pranks/Left bank ....   =V 2385   £ 2 - 4

JOHNNY SHANLY
60 This day I promise/Makin' love to you .... COLUMBIA DB 4425   £ 2 - 4
60 I wonder/It happens that way ....   DB 4526   £ 2 - 4

DEAN SHANNON
60 Blinded with love/Jezebel .... H.M.V.   POP 820   £ 4 - 6

LINDA SHANNON
59	Goodbye Charlie, goodbye/If you only knew	PARLOPHONE R 4603	£ 2 – 4

SHARI
58	Going home for Christmas/Count every star	DECCA F 11069	£ 2 – 4

SHARKEY'S KINGS OF DIXIELAND
57	Look sharp, be sharp/Sharkey strut	CAPITOL CL 14767	£ 2 – 4

RAY SHARPE
59	Linda Lu/Red sails in the sunset	LONDON HLW 8932	£18 – 25

BOB SHARPLES & HIS (DANCE) MUSIC
55	Capitano/Time remembered	DECCA F 10450	£ 2 – 4
56	Hurricane boogie/Concetta	F 10707	£ 4 – 6
56	The Portuguese washerwomen/Sadie's shawl	F 10748	£ 2 – 4

THE SHARPS (qv THURSTON HARRIS)
57	Love is here to stay/Lock my heart	VOGUE V 9086	£40 – 60
58	Shufflin'/What will I gain	V 9096	£40 – 60

GEORGIE SHAW (qv KITTY KALLEN)
55	Give me the right/Yearning (just for you)	BRUNSWICK 05356	£ 2 – 4
55	Unsuspecting heart/Let me go, devil	05362	£ 2 – 4
55	I'll step aside/The water tumbler tune	05426	£ 2 – 4
55	Banjo woogie/I can tell	05476	£ 4 – 6
55	No arms can ever hold you/Do it now	05489	£ 2 – 4
56	Look to your heart/There's an old saying	05517	£ 2 – 4
56	Fallen angel (are you sorry)/The proverb	05547	£ 2 – 4
57	Suddenly (The meeting)/City of tears	05686	£ 2 – 4

ROLAND SHAW ORCH. (*& KIM BENNETT)
54	No one but you*/The high and the mighty	DECCA F 10407	£ 2 – 4
55	Softly, softly*/A trumpeter's lullaby	F 10449	£ 2 – 4

SANDY SHAW
58	Hello, goodbye/TERRY TAYLOR: The only way	STARLITE ST.45 007	£ 2 – 4

GEORGE SHEARING (QUINTET) (*& TEDDI KING/qv PEGGY LEE/DAKOTA STATON)
53	I'll remember April/Jumping with Symphony Sid	M-G-M SP 1006	£ 2 – 4
53	There's a lull in my life/Bassic English	SP 1017	£ 2 – 4
53	Night flight/Love (your magic spell is everywhere)* ...	SP 1031	£ 2 – 4
53	How high the Moon/So this is Cuba	SP 1035	£ 2 – 4
53	Body and soul/The lady is a tramp	SP 1046	£ 2 – 4
53	Love is just around the corner/Point and counterpoint .	SP 1047	£ 2 – 4
54	Tiempo de Cencerro (both sides)	SP 1066	£ 2 – 4
54	Rap your troubles in drums/Love is here to stay	SP 1080	£ 2 – 4
54	Spring is here/Easy to love	SP 1090	£ 2 – 4
54	Mambo Inn/I've never been in love before	SP 1103	£ 2 – 4
54	Lullaby of Birdland/Get off my Bach	SP 1113	£ 2 – 4
56	I'll never smile again/If you were the only girl in the.	SP 1161	£ 2 – 4
56	I wished on the Moon/It's easy to remember	*SP 1171	£ 2 – 4
56	Cherokee/Four bars short	VOGUE V 2043	£ 2 – 4
56	Over the rainbow/Appreciation	M-G-M MGM 919	£ 2 – 4
57	I don't stand a ghost of a chance with you/Mood for Milt	MGM 947	£ 2 – 4
60	Honeysuckle rose/East of the Sun	CAPITOL CL 15157	£ 2 – 4

THE SHEIKS
59	Tres chic/Little French doll	LONDON HLW 9012	£ 4 – 6

ANNE SHELTON
53	Answer me (Mutterlein)/The Bridge of Sighs	H.M.V. 7M 164	£ 6 – 9
54	The Book/Why does it have to be me	7M 186	£ 6 – 9
54	Cross over the bridge/(O baby mine) I get so lonely ...	7M 197	£ 6 – 9
54	Goodnight, well it's time to go/If I give my heart to...	7M 240	£ 6 – 9
54	My gypsy heart/Teach me tonight	7M 279	£ 6 – 9

55ø	Arrivederci darling (Goodbye to Rome)/Song of the trees		POP 146 º	£ 2 – 4
56ø	Seven days/The great pretender	PHILIPS	PB 567 º	£ 2 – 4
56ø	Lay down your arms/Daydreams		PB 616 º	£ 1 – 2
57	Absent friends/Seven stages of man		JK 1012	£ 6 – 9
58	Until they sail/Ha! Ha!		PB 779	£ 2 – 4
58	The girl he left behind/Sail along, silv'ry moon		PB 815	£ 2 – 4
58	Volare/Do you love me like you kiss me?		PB 852	£ 2 – 4
58	Hurry home/I.T.A.L.Y. (I trust and love you)		PB 878	£ 2 – 4
59	Just love me/Could I love you more		PB 920	£ 2 – 4
59	Now hear this!/To love and be loved		PB 956	£ 2 – 4
59ø	The village of St. Bernadette/You're not living in vain		PB 969	£ 2 – 4
60	The angels' lullaby/Where can I go		PB 994	£ 2 – 4
60	Come back again/Papa loves Mama		PB 1042	£ 2 – 4

JO SHELTON

59	Tread softly (you're step–..)/More, more, more romancing	TOP RANK	JAR 124	£ 2 – 4
59	If there are stars in my eyes/I need your arms around me		JAR 245	£ 2 – 4

BILLY SHEPARD *or SHEPHARD

54	The bandit/Oh, Donna Clara	COLUMBIA	SCM 5108	£ 2 – 4
59	You call everybody darling/Somebody stole my gal	FELSTED	*AF 117	£ 2 – 4

JEAN SHEPARD

59	Jeopardy/Better love next time	CAPITOL	CL 15031	£ 2 – 4

THE SHEPHERD BOYS (*& GIRLS)

56	Teenage love/Little girls and little boys	*COLUMBIA	SCM 5282	£ 4 – 6
56	Summer sweetheart/Song for a Summer night		DB 3816	£ 2 – 4

THE SHEPHERD *or SHEPPARD SISTERS

57ø	Alone (why must I be alone)/Congratulations to someone	H.M.V.	POP 411	£ 6 – 9
58	Gettin' ready for Freddy/The best thing there is (is...)	MERCURY	*7MT 196	£ 6 – 9
58	Eating pizza/A boy and a girl		*7MT 218	£ 4 – 6
58	Dancing baby/Is it a crime?		AMT 1005	£ 4 – 6

BILL SHEPHERD ORCHESTRA

58	Big guitar/Tequila	PYE	7N 15137	£ 4 – 6
58	Inn Of The 6th..../DR. BARNARDO'S CHILDREN: This old man		7N 15180	£ 2 – 4

PAULINE SHEPHERD

57	Love me to pieces/Just between you and me	COLUMBIA	DB 4019	£ 2 – 4

BOBBIE SHERWOOD

55	The Kentuckian song/Far away places	V-CORAL	Q 72097	£ 2 – 4

ROBERTA SHERWOOD

56	Lazy river/This train	BRUNSWICK	05572	£ 2 – 4
57	Tears don't care.who cries.../You're nobody till some–..		05654	£ 2 – 4
57	What does it matter/Mary Lou		05670	£ 2 – 4

THE SHIELDS

58	You cheated/That's the way it's gonna be	LONDON	HLD 8706	£12 – 18

THE SHIRELLES

58	I met him on a Sunday/I want you to be my boyfriend ...	BRUNSWICK	05746	£12 – 18
60	Tonight's the night/The dance is over	LONDON	HL 9233	£ 9 – 12

SHIRLEY & LEE

56	Let the good times roll/Do you mean to hurt me so	VOGUE	V 9059	£18 – 25
57	I feel good/Now that it's over		V 9063	£18 – 25
57	That's what I wanna do/When I saw you		V 9067	£18 – 25
57	Rock all nite/Don't you know I love you		V 9072	£25 – 40
57	Rockin' with the clock/The flirt		V 9084	£25 – 40
58	Feel so good/You'd be thinking of me		V 9094	£18 – 25
58	I want to dance/Marry me		V 9088	£18 – 25

58	I'll thrill you/Love no one but you		V	9103	£18 – 25
58	Everybody's rockin'/Don't leave me here to cry		V	9118	£18 – 25
59	Come on and have your fun/All I want to do is cry		V	9129	£18 – 25
59	A little word/That's what I'll do		V	9135	£18 – 25
59	I'll do it/Lee's dream		V	9137	£18 – 25
59	True love/When day is done		V	9156	£18 – 25
60	I've been loved before/Like you used to do	LONDON	HLI	9186	£ 9 – 12
60	Let the good times roll/Keep loving me		HLI	9209	£ 9 – 12

JOYCE SHOCK
58	Take your foot from the door!/I've got bells on my heart	PHILIPS	PB	824	£ 2 – 4
58	Hoopa hoola/You're not losing a daughter, Mama		PB	872	£ 2 – 4
59	Personality/I can't love you any more		PB	934	£ 2 – 4
59	Cry, baby, cry/Dear diary		PB	957	£ 2 – 4

DINAH SHORE
53	Keep it a secret/Bella musica	H.M.V.	7M	119	£ 6 – 9
53	Sweet thing/Three-cornered tune		7M	139	£ 4 – 6
54	Changing partners/Think		7M	183	£ 4 – 6
54	Come back to my arms/This must be the place		7M	221	£ 4 – 6
54	Three coins in the fountain/Pakistan		7M	236	£ 4 – 6
54	If I give my heart to you/Let me know		7M	250	£ 4 – 6
56	Love and marriage/Compare		7M	352	£ 4 – 6
57	The cattle call/Promises, promises (Skip redwine)	R.C.A.	RCA	1003	£ 2 – 4
58	Thirteen men/I'll never say "Never again" again		RCA	1054	£ 2 – 4
58	The secret of happiness/I've never left your arms		RCA	1060	£ 2 – 4

PETER SHRAYDER
60	Where's the girl for me/Take me back baby	CAPITOL	CL	15174	£ 2 – 4

MORT SHUMAN
59	I'm a man/Turn me loose	DECCA	F	11184	£12 – 18

THE SILHOUETTES
58	Get a job/I am lonely	PARLOPHONE	R	4407	£18 – 25
58	Headin' for the poorhouse/Miss Thing		R	4425	£25 – 40

THE SILVER SISTERS
60	Waiting for the stars to shine/When a boy meets a girl	PARLOPHONE	R	4669	£ 2 – 4

EDDIE SILVER
58	Seven steps to love/Put a ring on her finger	PARLOPHONE	R	4439	£ 4 – 6
58	Rockin' robin/The ways of a woman in love		R	4483	£ 6 – 9

VICTOR SILVESTER & HIS BALLROOM ORCH./*ROCK 'N' ROLL RHYTHM
	Numerous releases on COLUMBIA .... except as below, all worth under £ 2				
58	Society rock/Rockin' rhythm roll	COLUMBIA	*DB	3888	£ 2 – 4
58	Off beat rock/Alligator roll		*DB	3907	£ 2 – 4

HARRY SIMEONE CHORALE
59ø	The little drummer boy/THE JUNIOR CHOIR: Die Lorelei ..	TOP RANK	JAR	101	£ 2 – 4
60ø	Onward Christian soldiers/The little drummer boy	EMBER	EMB	S118	£ 2 – 4

NINA SIMONE
59	I loves you Porgy/Love me or leave me	PARLOPHONE	R	4583	£ 4 – 6
59	Chilly winds don't blow/Solitaire	PYE INT.	7N	25029	£ 4 – 6

HOKE SIMPSON
58	I finally found you/Gi-Gi	H.M.V.	POP	442	£ 4 – 6

THE SIMS-WHEELER VINTAGE JAZZ BAND
60	Never on Sunday/Ma curly headed baby	POLYDOR	NH	66638	£ 2 – 4

CHUCK SIMS
58	Little pigeon/Life isn't long enough	LONDON	HLR	8577	£60 – 90

KELLY SIMS
```
60  Betrayed by love/A girl in love  ......................  TOP RANK  JAR 321    £ 2 -  4
```

FRANK SINATRA (& *CELESTE HOLM/+KEELY SMITH/qv BING CROSBY)
```
53  The birth of the blues/Why try to change me now?  ......  COLUMBIA SCM 5052   £ 9 - 12
53  You do something to me/Lover  ........................           SCM 5060   £ 9 - 12
53  Santa Claus is comin' to town/My girl  ...............           SCM 5076   £ 9 - 12
54ø Young-at-heart/Take a chance  ........................  CAPITOL  CL 14064   £ 9 - 12
54ø Three coins in the fountain/I could have told you  .....           CL 14120   £ 9 - 12
54  The Christmas waltz/White Christmas  ..................           CL 14174   £ 6 -  9
54  When I stop loving you/It worries me  ................           CL 14188   £ 6 -  9
55  The gal that got away/Someone to watch over me  .......           CL 14221   £ 6 -  9
55  Melody of love/I'm gonna live till I die  .............           CL 14238   £ 6 -  9
55  S'posin'/How deep is the ocean  ......................  COLUMBIA SCM 5167   £ 9 - 12
55ø You, my love/Just one of those things  ...............  CAPITOL  CL 14240   £ 9 - 12
55  Don't change your mind about me/Why should I cry over...           CL 14270   £ 6 -  9
55  Two hearts, two kisses (make one love)/From the bottom..           CL 14292   £ 9 - 12
55ø Learnin' the blues/If I had three wishes  ..............           CL 14296   £ 9 - 12
55ø Not as a stranger/How could you do a thing like that to.           CL 14326   £ 9 - 12
55  My funny Valentine/I get a kick out of you  ...........           CL 14352   £ 6 -  9
55  In the wee small hours of the../It never entered my mind           CL 14360   £ 6 -  9
55  Fairy tale/Same old Saturday night  ...................           CL 14373   £ 6 -  9
56ø Love and marriage/Look to your heart  ................           CL 14503   £ 6 -  9
56ø (Love is) The tender trap/Weep they will  .............           CL 14511   £ 6 -  9
56  Flowers mean forgiveness/You'll get yours  ............           CL 14564   £ 4 -  6
56  Five hundred guys/(How little it....) How little we know           CL 14584   £ 2 -  4
56  "Johnny Concho" theme (Wait for me)/Hey! Jealous lover            CL 14607   £ 2 -  4
56  The impatient years/Our town  ........................           CL 15620   £ 2 -  4
56  Who wants to be a millionaire?*/Mind if I make love to..           CL 14644   £ 4 -  6
56  You're sensational/You forgot all the words  ..........           CL 14646   £ 2 -  4
57  Can I steal a little love?/Your love for me  ..........           CL 14696   £ 2 -  4
57  So long, my love/Crazy love  .........................           CL 14719   £ 2 -  4
57  Something wonderful happens in Summer/You're cheatin'...           CL 14750   £ 2 -  4
57ø All the way/Chicago  .................................           CL 14800   £ 2 -  4
57  Mistletoe and holy/Jingle bells  .....................           CL 14804   £ 2 -  4
58  I could write a book/Nevertheless (I'm in love with you) FONTANA  H  109 º £ 4 -  6
58ø Witchcraft/Tell her you love her  ....................  CAPITOL  CL 14819   £ 2 -  4
58  How are ya' fixed for love?/Nothing in common  ........          +CL 14863   £ 2 -  4
58  The same old song and dance/Monique (Song from "Kings..)           CL 14904   £ 2 -  4
58  If I forget you/I'm a fool to want you  ...............  FONTANA  H  140   £ 4 -  6
58ø Mr. Success/Sleep warm  ..............................  CAPITOL  CL 14956   £ 2 -  4
59ø French Foreign Legion/Time after time  ...............           CL 14997   £ 2 -  4
59  To love and be loved/No one ever tells you  ...........           CL 15006   £ 2 -  4
59ø High hopes/All my tomorrows  .........................           CL 15052   £ 2 -  4
59  They came to Cordura/Talk to me  .....................           CL 15086   £ 2 -  4
60ø It's nice to go trav'ling/Brazil  ....................           CL 15116   £ 2 -  4
60ø River, stay 'way from my door/It's over, it's over,.....           CL 15135   £ 2 -  4
60ø Nice 'n' easy/This was my love  ......................           CL 15150   £ 2 -  4
60ø Ol' MacDonald/You'll always be the one I love  ........           CL 15168   £ 2 -  4
```

THE SINGING BELLES
```
60  Someone loves you, Joe/The empty mailbox  .............  TOP RANK  JAR 350   £ 4 -  6
```

THE SINGING DOGS
```
55ø Pat-a-cake/Three blind mice/Jingle bells//Oh! Susanna  .  PYE      N 15009 º £ 2 -  4
56  Barking dog boogie/Rock around the dogs  ..............           N 15065 º £ 6 -  9
```

THE SINGING REINDEER (qv DANCER, PRANCER & NERVOUS)
```
60  I wanna be an Easter bunny/The happy birthday song  ....  CAPITOL  CL 15124   £ 2 -  4
```

MARGIE SINGLETON
```
60  The eyes of love/Angel hands  ........................  MELODISC     1544   £ 4 -  6
```

THE SIX TEENS
```
56  A casual look/Teen age promise  ......................  LONDON   HLU 8345   £60 - 90
```

JIMMIE SKINNER

59	Walkin' my blues away/Dark hollow	MERCURY	AMT 1030	£ 4 – 6
59	John Wesley Hardin/Misery loves company		AMT 1062	£ 4 – 6
60	Riverboat gambler/Married to a friend		AMT 1088	£ 2 – 4
60	Reasons to live/I'm a lot more lonesome now		AMT 1117	£ 2 – 4

SKIP & FLIP (actually Gary Paxton & Clyde Batton)

59	It was I/Lunch hour	TOP RANK	JAR 156	£ 6 – 9
59	Fancy Nancy/It could be		JAR 248	£ 6 – 9
60	Cherry pie/(I'll quit) Cryin' over you		JAR 358	£ 6 – 9

THE SKYLINERS

59	Since I don't have you/One night, one night	LONDON	HLB 8829	£12 – 18
59	This I swear/Tomorrow		HLU 8924	£ 9 – 12
59	It happened today/Lonely way		HLU 8971	£ 9 – 12
60	I'll be seeing you/Pennies from Heaven	POLYDOR	NH 66951	£ 6 – 9

MARTIN SLAVIN & HIS GANG (qv MARTINAS)

60	Rock-a-Charleston/The Charleston's gonna rock the hop...	ORIOLE	*CB 1587	£ 2 – 4

THE SLEEPWALKERS

59	Sleep walk/Golden mile	PARLOPHONE	R 4580	£ 4 – 6

JOAN SMALL

56	Come next Spring/Change of heart	PARLOPHONE	MSP 6219	£ 2 – 4
56	Autumn concerto/Love is a stranger		R 4211	£ 2 – 4
57	You can't say I love you to a R&R tune/Gonna get along..		R 4269	£ 4 – 6
58	Afraid/How many times (can I fall in love)		R 4431	£ 2 – 4
59	The big hurt/Ask me to go steady		R 4622	£ 2 – 4

MARY SMALL

56	None of that now/Dino	V-CORAL	Q 72196	£ 2 – 4

CHARLES SMART

55	Solemn melody/Evensong	DECCA	F 10466	£ 2 – 4

HAROLD SMART QUARTET

54	Happy tango/Messenger boy	DECCA	F 10391	£ 2 – 4

SMILIN' JOE

54	A.B.C.'s – Parts 1 & 2	LONDON	HL 8106 º	£ 9 – 12

THE (*FIVE) SMITH BROTHERS

54	A.B.C. boogie/Veni-vidi-vici	DECCA	*F 10403	£ 6 – 9
55	You're as sweet today (as yesterday)/Paper Valentine ..		*F 10507	£ 4 – 6
55ø	I'm in favour of friendship/Don't worry		*F 10527	£ 9 – 12
56	You took my heart (My only heart)/The grass is green ..		*F 10698	£ 2 – 4
56	Bacon barbecue/Smith (what a name to be stuck with) ...		F 10759	£ 2 – 4

ARTHUR (Guitar Boogie) SMITH & HIS CRACKERJACKS

50	Guitar boogie/Be bop rag	M-G-M	MGM 329 º	£ 4 – 6
51	Mandolin boogie/The Memphis blues		MGM 363 º	£ 4 – 6
52	Guitar and piano boogie/Banjo buster		MGM 518 º	£ 4 – 6
53	Guitar boogie/Be bop rag		SP 1008	£18 – 25
53	Five string banjo boogie/South		SP 1021	£12 – 18
53	Express train boogie/River rag		SP 1039	£12 – 18
53	In memory of Hank Williams/(by HANK WILLIAMS)		MGM 630 º	£ 6 – 9
53	Big mountain shuffle/KEN CURTIS: The call of the far–...		MGM 660 º	£ 4 – 6
53	Three D boogie/He went that-a-way		MGM 695 º	£ 4 – 6
54	Oh, baby mine, I get so lonely/Outboard		SP 1096	£12 – 18
54	Redheaded stranger/Texas hop		SP 1110	£12 – 18
55	Hi lo boogie/Truck stop grill		SP 1122	£12 – 18

BEASLEY SMITH & HIS ORCH.

56	Goodnight, sweet dreams/Parisian rag	LONDON	HLD 8235	£ 9 – 12
56	My foolish heart/Old spinning wheel		HLD 8273	£ 9 – 12

BETTY SMITH QUINTET/GROUP/*SKIFFLE

57	There's a blue ridge round my heart,...../Double shuffle	TEMPO	*A 162	£ 4 – 6
57	Sweet Georgia Brown/Little white lies		A 163	£ 2 – 4
58	Hand jive/Bewitched	DECCA	F 10986	£ 4 – 6
58	Will the angels play their harps for me/Betty's blues .		F 11031	£ 2 – 4
58	Begin the beguine/Song of the boulevards		F 11071	£ 2 – 4
59	Song of India/Stormy weather		F 11124	£ 2 – 4

CARL SMITH

59	Ten thousand drums/The tall, tall gentleman	PHILIPS	PB 943	£ 2 – 4

EDDIE SMITH (& THE *CHIEFS/+HORNETS)

55	Silver Star stomp/Stumbling	*PARLOPHONE	MSP 6186	£ 9 – 12
60	Upturn/Border beat	TOP RANK	+JAR 285	£ 6 – 9

ETHEL SMITH

55	Hernando's Hideaway/Lemon merengue	BRUNSWICK	05470	£ 2 – 4
59	The Spanish marching song/Rico vacilon		05793	£ 2 – 4

GLORIA SMITH

59	Playmates/Don't take your love from me	LONDON	HLU 8903	£ 2 – 4

HUEY "PIANO" SMITH & THE CLOWNS (qv FRANKIE FORD)

58	Don't you just know it/High blood pressure	COLUMBIA	DB 4138	£12 – 18
60	Don't you know Yockomo/(by FRANKIE FORD)	TOP RANK	JAR 282	£ 9 – 12

JENNIE SMITH

59	Huggin' my pillow (Sweet side & sweet beat side)	PHILIPS	PB 924	£ 2 – 4

KEELY SMITH (*& LOUIS PRIMA/qv FRANK SINATRA)

57	Hurt me/High school affair	CAPITOL	CL 14717	£ 2 – 4
57	Young and in love/You better go now		CL 14739	£ 2 – 4
57	Good behaviour/You'll never know		CL 14754	£ 2 – 4
57	Autumn leaves/I keep forgetting		CL 14803	£ 2 – 4
58	Foggy day/The lip*		CL 14862	£ 2 – 4
58	The whippoorwill/Sometimes		CL 14885	£ 2 – 4
58	That old black magic*/You are my love		CL 14948	£ 2 – 4
59	I've got you under my skin*/Don't take your love from me		CL 14994	£ 2 – 4
59	If I knew I'd find you/Don't let the stars get in your..	LONDON	HLD 8984	£ 4 – 6
60	Here in my heart/Close		HLD 9240	£ 2 – 4

LOU SMITH

60	Cruel love/Close to my heart	TOP RANK	JAR 520	£ 2 – 4

MURIEL SMITH

53ø	Hold me, thrill me, kiss me/I'd love to fall asleep ...	PHILIPS	PB 122 º	£ 2 – 4
55	Dat's love/JUNE HAWKINS: Beat out dat rhythm on a drum	BRUNSWICK	05370	£ 2 – 4

OCIE SMITH (qv ART MOONEY)

57	Lighthouse/Too many :.................................	LONDON	HLA 8480	£12 – 18

RAY SMITH

60	Rockin' little angel/That's all right	LONDON	HL 9051	£12 – 18

ROY SMITH (*& THE STARGAZERS)

55	Red roses (for my lady fair)/The Devil's in your eyes .	DECCA	*F 10529	£ 2 – 4
55	He/Glengarry		F 10644	£ 2 – 4

SOMETHIN' SMITH & THE REDHEADS

58	I don't want to set the world on.../You made me love you	FONTANA	H 154	£ 4 – 6

TAB SMITH & HIS ORCH.

53	Ace high/Deejay special	VOGUE	V 2172 º	£ 4 – 6
54	Down beat/Boogie joogie		V 2203 º	£ 4 – 6
54	Cuban boogie/Red hot and blue		V 2282 º	£ 4 – 6
55	All my life/Seven up		V 2299 º	£ 2 – 4

56	Jump time/Rock City		V 2410	£ 9 - 12
59	My happiness cha–cha/Smoke gets in your eyes	LONDON	HLM 8801	£ 4 - 6
60	My Mother's eyes/These foolish things	VOGUE	V 2416	£ 2 - 4
62	All my life/Seven up		V 2299	£ 2 - 4

TRIXIE SMITH

51	He likes it slow/Black bottom stomp	TEMPO	R 42 º	£ 6 - 9
52	Freight train blues/Trixie blues	VOCALION	V 1006 º	£ 6 - 9
52	My Daddy rocks me (both sides)		V 1017 º	£ 6 - 9

GLORIA SMYTHE

60	I'll be over after while/Gee baby ain't I good to you .	VOGUE	V 9159	£ 2 - 4

THE SNAPPERS

59	Big Bill/If there were	TOP RANK	JAR 167	£ 6 - 9

THE SNEAKY PETES

60	Savage – Parts 1 & 2	DECCA	F 11199	£ 4 - 6

HANK SNOW

52	My two timin' woman/The rhumba boogie	H.M.V.	B 10284 º	£ 6 - 9
59	Old Shep/The last ride	R.C.A.	RCA 1151	£ 2 - 4

BILL SNYDER & HIS ORCH. (*& RALPH STERLING)

53	Bewitched/Drifting sands*	PARLOPHONE	MSP 6005	£ 2 - 4

THE SOHO SKIFFLE GROUP

57	Give me a big fat woman/The Midnight Special	MELODISC	1403 º	£ 4 - 6
57	Frankie and Johnny/Streamline train		1421 º	£ 4 - 6

THE SOLITAIRES

58	Walking along/Please kiss this letter	LONDON	HLM 8745	£12 - 18

VIRGINIA SOMERS

54	Cross over the bridge/Lovin' spree	DECCA	F 10301	£ 2 - 4

JOANIE SOMMERS

60	Be my love/Why don't you do right?	WARNER-B	WB 23	£ 2 - 4

ROY SONE

59	Jenny/Why do they doubt our love	DECCA	F 11159	£ 2 - 4

THE SONGSTERS

54	Bahama buggy ride/It isn't right	LONDON	HL 8100	£12 - 18

JERI SOUTHERN

54	Remind me/Little boy grown tall	BRUNSWICK	05343	£ 2 - 4
55	The man that got away/Speak softly to me		05367	£ 2 - 4
55	An occasional man/It's d'lovely		05490	£ 2 - 4
56	Where walks my true love?/Don't explain		05529	£ 2 - 4
57ø	Fire down below/Smoke gets in your eyes		05665	£ 4 - 6
57	Scarlet ribbons (for her hair)/Would I		05709	£ 2 - 4
57	Bells are ringing/Just in time		05722	£ 2 - 4
58	I waited so long/The mystery of love		05737	£ 2 - 4
59	Senor Blues/Take me back again	CAPITOL	CL 14993	£ 2 - 4
59	Run/Don't look at me that way		CL 15054	£ 2 - 4

JOHNNY SOUTHERN & HIS WESTERN RHYTHM KINGS

57	She's long, she's tall/Lonesome whistle	MELODISC	1434	£ 4 - 6
58	We will make love/Crazy heart		1413	£ 4 - 6

THE SOUTHLANDERS

55	Ain't that a shame/Have you ever been lonely	PARLOPHONE	MSP 6182	£12 - 18
56	Hush–a–bye rock/The wedding of the lucky black cat ...		MSP 6236	£ 9 - 12
57ø	Alone/Swedish polka	DECCA	F 10946	£ 4 - 6
57	Peanuts/I never dreamed		F 10958	£ 6 - 9

58ø	Put a light in the window/Penny loafers and bobby socks		F 10982	£ 9 – 12
58	Down deep/Wishing for your love		F 11014	£ 4 – 6
58	I wanna jive tonight/Torero		F 11032	£ 9 – 12
58	The mole in a hole/Choo–choo–choo–choo cha–cha–cha		F 11067	£ 4 – 6
60	Charlie/Imitation of love	TOP RANK	JAR 403	£ 2 – 4

RED SOVINE (*& WEBB PIERCE)

56	Why baby why?*/Sixteen tons	BRUNSWICK	05513	£18 – 25

THE SPACEMEN

59	The lonely jet pilot/The clouds	TOP RANK	JAR 228	£ 4 – 6

MUGSY SPANIER'S DIXIELAND BAND (qv SIDNEY BECHET)

56	Tin roof blues/Muskrat ramble	TEMPO	A 36	£ 2 – 4

RANDY SPARKS

59	Birmingham train/A girl like you	H.M.V.	POP 683	£ 4 – 6

SONNY SPENCER

59	Oh boy/Gilee	PARLOPHONE	R 4611	£ 9 – 12

THE SPIDERS

54	I'm slippin' in/I'm searching	LONDON	HL 8086 º	£12 – 18

THE SPINNERS (qv SHANE RIMMER)

59	The "I had a dream, dear" rock/Pedro the fisherman	COLUMBIA	DB 4267	£ 2 – 4

THE SPIRALS

58	The rockin' cow/Everybody knows	CAPITOL	CL 14958	£ 9 – 12

THE SPOTLIGHTERS

59	Please be my girl friend/Whisper	VOGUE	V 9130	£40 – 60

BILLY SPROUD & THE ROCK 'N' ROLL SIX

57	Rock Mr. Piper/If you're so smart (how come you ain't..)	COLUMBIA	DB 3893	£12 – 18

THE SPROUTS

58	Teen Billy baby/Goodbye, she's gone	R.C.A.	RCA 1031	£18 – 25

DOROTHY SQUIRES

53ø	I'm walking behind you/Is there any room in your heart?	POLYGON	P 1068 º	£ 2 – 4
57	Song of the valley/Our song	COLUMBIA	DB 3985	£ 2 – 4
58	Bewitched/A secret that's never been told		DB 4070	£ 2 – 4
58	Torremolinos/This is my Mother's day	PYE	7N 15154	£ 2 – 4
59	Sticks and stones/Don't search for love		7N 15199	£ 2 – 4
60	This place called home/Trust in me	DECCA	F 11262	£ 2 – 4

ROSEMARY SQUIRES

56	Band of gold/Where you are	DECCA	F 10685	£ 2 – 4
56	You can't run away from it/Love is here to stay		F 10812	£ 2 – 4
58	Happy is the bride/Give me the simple life	H.M.V.	POP 462	£ 2 – 4
58	There goes my lover/Please be kind		POP 541	£ 2 – 4
59	Must be catching/Love is a simple thing		POP 628	£ 2 – 4

CLARENCE STACY

59	Just your love/Lonely guy	PYE INT.	7N 25025	£ 4 – 6

JO STAFFORD (*& FRANKIE LAINE)

51	Shrimp boats/Love, mystery and adventure	COLUMBIA	DB 2983 º	£ 2 – 4
52ø	You belong to me/Pretty boy (Pretty girl)		DB 3152 º	£ 1 – 2
52ø	Jambalaya (on the Bayou)/Early Autumn		DB 3169 º	£ 2 – 4
53	Star of hope/Somebody		SCM 5011	£ 6 – 9
53	It is no secret/He bought my soul at Calvary		SCM 5012	£ 9 – 12
53ø	You belong to me/Jambalaya (on the Bayou)		SCM 5013	£12 – 18
53	Settin' the woods on fire/Piece a–puddin'		*SCM 5014	£ 9 – 12

– 183 –

53	Keep it a secret/Once to every heart		SCM 5026	£ 6 - 9
53	Something to remember you by/Blue Moon		SCM 5046	£ 6 - 9
53	Chow, Willy*/September in the rain		SCM 5064	£ 6 - 9
54ø	Make love to me!/Adi-adios amigo	PHILIPS	PB 233 º	£ 2 - 4
55ø	Suddenly there's a valley/Night watch		PB 509 º	£ 2 - 4
57	On London Bridge/Perfect love		JK 1003	£ 6 - 9
58	With a little bit of luck/Wouldn't it be loverly		PB 818	£ 2 - 4
58	Hibiscus/How can we say goodbye		PB 876	£ 2 - 4
59	My heart is from Missouri/It won't be easy		PB 898	£ 2 - 4
59	Pine Top's boogie/All yours		PB 935	£ 4 - 6
60	It is no secret/He bought my soul at Calvary		PB 991	£ 2 - 4
60	Candy/Indoor sport		PB 1034	£ 2 - 4

STAIFFI ET SES MUSTAFA'S

60ø	Mustafa/Zoubida	PYE INT. 7N 25057		£ 2 - 4

ARNOLD STANG

59ø	Ivy will cling/Where ya' calling from, Charlie	FONTANA	H 226	£ 4 - 6

CYRIL STAPLETON & HIS ORCH. (& *JEAN CAMPBELL/+JULIE DAWN/=GORDON LANGHORN/
#DESMOND LANE)

52	Boogie woogie march/What might have been*	DECCA	F 9901 º	£ 4 - 6
54	Long distance love/There'll be no teardrops tonight ...		F 10293	£ 2 - 4
55	Tango mambo/Mexican madness		F 10456	£ 2 - 4
55	Fanfare boogie/Time after time		F 10470	£ 4 - 6
55ø	Elephant tango/Gabrielle		F 10488	£ 6 - 9
55ø	Blue Star (The "Medic" theme)+/Honey babe=		F 10559	£ 6 - 9
56ø	The Italian theme/Come next Spring		F 10703	£ 6 - 9
56ø	The happy whistler#/Tiger tango		F 10735	£ 6 - 9
56	Highway Patrol/Maids of Madrid		F 10793	£ 2 - 4
57	Rock, fiddle, rock/Chantez, chantez		F 10883	£ 2 - 4
57ø	Forgotten dreams/It's not for me to say		F 10912	£ 4 - 6
58	Monday blues - Parts 1 & 2		F 10979	£ 2 - 4

THE STARGAZERS (*& SONNY FARRAR BANJO BAND/qv LITA ROZA/ROY SMITH/DICKIE VALENTINE)

53ø	Broken wings/Make it soon	DECCA	F 10047 º	£ 2 - 4
54ø	I see the Moon/Eh cumpari		F 10213	£ 9 - 12
54ø	The happy wanderer/Till we two are one		F 10259	£ 9 - 12
54	Rose of the Wildwood/Came the morning		F 10412	£ 4 - 6
55ø	Somebody/(My baby don't love me) No more		*F 10437	£ 9 - 12
55ø	The Crazy Otto rag/Hey, Mr. Banjo		F 10523	£ 9 - 12
55	At the Steamboat River Ball/I love you a mountain		*F 10569	£ 2 - 4
55ø	Close the door/I've got four big brothers		F 10594	£ 9 - 12
55ø	Twenty tiny fingers/An old beer bottle		F 10626	£ 9 - 12
56	(Love is) The tender trap/When the swallows say goodbye		F 10668	£ 4 - 6
56	Zambesi/When the swallows say goodbye		F 10696	£ 4 - 6
56ø	Hot diggity (dog ziggity boom)/Rockin' and rollin'		F 10731	£ 9 - 12
56	She loves to rock/John Jacon Jingleheimer Smith		F 10775	£ 9 - 12
57	You won't be around/Mangos		F 10867	£ 4 - 6
57	Honky tonk song/Golly!		F 10898	£ 4 - 6
57	Who is it? (It's the milkman)/Sorry, you'll have to wait		F 10916	£ 4 - 6
57	The skiffling dogs/Out of this world		F 10969	£ 4 - 6
58	Big man/Lonely for a letter		F 11034	£ 2 - 4
59	My blue Heaven/How ja lika		F 11105	£ 2 - 4
60	Manhattan spiritual/Three beautiful words	PALETTE	PG 9003	£ 2 - 4

JIMMY STARR

58	It's only make believe/Ooh crazy	LONDON	HL 8731	£12 - 18

KAY STARR

51	Ain't misbehavin'/Good for nothin' Joe	VOGUE	V 9009 º	£ 4 - 6
51	Them there eyes/What is this thing called love?		V 9010 º	£ 4 - 6
52	Wheel of fortune/Wabash Cannon Ball	CAPITOL	CL 13717 º	£ 2 - 4
52ø	Comes a-long a-love/Three letters		CL 13808 º	£ 2 - 4
53ø	Side by side/Too busy!		CL 13871 º	£ 2 - 4

4ø	Changing partners/I'll always be in love with you		CL 14050 º £ 2 - 4
4ø	Am I a toy or a treasure?/Fortune in dreams		CL 14151 º £ 2 - 4
4	Fool, fool, fool/Allez-vous-en		CL 14167 £ 9 - 12
5ø	Am I a toy or a treasure?/Fortune in dreams		CL 14151 £ 9 - 12
5	If anyone finds this, I love you/Turn right	H.M.V.	7M 300 £ 6 - 9
5	Foolishly yours/For better or worse		7M 307 £ 6 - 9
5	Where, what or when?/Good and lonesome		7M 315 £ 6 - 9
6ø	Rock and roll waltz/I've changed my mind a 1,000 times		POP 168 º £ 2 - 4
6ø	as above		7M 371 º £ 9 - 12
6	Second fiddle/Love ain't right		7M 420 £ 6 - 9
7	A little loneliness/Touch and go		POP 345 £ 4 - 6
7	Jamie boy/The things I never had		POP 357 £ 4 - 6
8	Stroll me/Rockin' chair	R.C.A.	RCA 1065 £ 4 - 6
9	Riders in the sky/Night train	CAPITOL	CL 15105 £ 4 - 6
ø	Wheel of fortune/If you love me (really love me)		CL 15137 £ 4 - 6
ø	Just for a thrill/Out in the cold again		CL 15154 £ 2 - 4

RANDY STARR
57	After school/Heaven high (man so low)	LONDON	HL 8443 £ 9 - 12
58	Count on me/Pink lemonade	FELSTED	AF 106 £ 6 - 9
50	Workin' on the Santa Fe/You're growing up	TOP RANK	JAR 264 £ 4 - 6

THE STARTIME KIDS
59	The railroad song/I don't want to walk without you, baby	FONTANA	H 182 £ 2 - 4

THE STATION SKIFFLE GROUP
57	Don't you rock me Daddy-o/Hugged my honey	ESQUIRE	10-503 º £ 4 - 6
57	Steamboat Bill/Titanic		10-516 º £ 4 - 6

DAKOTA STATON (*& GEORGE SHEARING QUINTET)
55	Don't leave me now/A little you	CAPITOL	CL 14314 £ 4 - 6
55	I never dreamt/Abracadabra		CL 14339 £ 4 - 6
58	Trust in me/The late, late show		CL 14828 £ 2 - 4
58	The party's over/Invitation		CL 14870 £ 2 - 4
58	Confessin' the blues/(I'm left with..) Blues in my heart		*CL 14917 £ 2 - 4
58	My funny Valentine/A foggy day		CL 14931 £ 2 - 4

THE STATUES
60	Blue velvet/Keep the hall burning	LONDON	HLG 9192 £ 4 - 6

ANTHONY STEEL & THE RADIO REVELLERS
54ø	West of Zanzibar/THE RADIO REVELLERS: Who cares	POLYGON	P 1114 º £ 2 - 4
56	as above	PYE	N 15023 º £ 1 - 2

BETTE ANNE STEELE
55	Barricade/Gimme a little kiss will "ya", huh?	CAPITOL	CL 14315 £ 6 - 9

DORIS STEELE
59	Why must I?/Never again	ORIOLE	CB 1468 £ 2 - 4

SONDRA & JON STEELE
55	I'm crazy with love/Fill my heart with happiness	PARLOPHONE	MSP 6166 £ 4 - 6

TOMMY STEELE (& THE STEELMEN) (qv VARIOUS ARTISTS)
56ø	Rock with the caveman/Rock around the town	DECCA	F 10795 £12 - 18
56	Doomsday rock/Elevator rock		F 10808 £12 - 18
56ø	Singing the blues/Rebel rock		F 10819 £ 6 - 9
57ø	Knee deep in the blues/Teenage party		F 10849 £ 9 - 12
57ø	Butterfingers/Cannibal pot		F 10877 £ 6 - 9
57ø	Shiralee/Grandad's rock		F 10896 £ 6 - 9
57ø	Water water/A handful of songs		F 10923 £ 4 - 6
57ø	Hey you!/Plant a kiss		F 10941 £ 4 - 6
58ø	Nairobi/Neon sign		F 10991 £ 4 - 6
58ø	Happy guitar/Princess		F 10976 £ 4 - 6
58	It's all happening/What do you do		F 11026 £ 2 - 4

```
58ø The only man on the island/I puts the lightie on  ......        F 11041    £ 4 –  6
58ø Come on let's go/Put a ring on her finger  ............         F 11072    £ 4 –  6
58  A lovely night/Marriage type love  ...................         F 11089    £ 2 –  4
59  Hiawatha/The trial  ....................................        F 11117    £ 4 –  6
59ø Tallahassee lassie/Give! Give! Give!  ................          F 11152    £ 6 –  9
59  You were mine/Young ideas  ............................         F 11162    £ 2 –  4
59ø Little white bull/Singing time  .......................         F 11177    £ 4 –  6
60ø What a mouth (What a north and south)/Kookaburra  ......        F 11245    £ 2 –  4
60  Happy-go-lucky blues/(The girl with the) Long black hair        F 11275    £ 2 –  4
60ø Must be Santa/Boys and girls  .........................         F 11299    £ 2 –  4


    BILL STEGMEYER & HIS ORCH.
54  On the waterfront/We just couldn't say goodbye  ........  LONDON   HL  8078   £12 – 18


    LOU STEIN
57  Almost Paradise/Soft sands  ..........................  LONDON   HLZ 8419   £ 4 –  6
58  Got a match/Who slammed the door  ....................  MERCURY  7MT  226   £ 4 –  6


    APRIL STEVENS
53  C'est si bon/Soft warm lips  .......................  PARLOPHONE MSP 6060   £ 6 –  9
54  How could Red Riding Hood (have..)/You said you'd do it   MSP 6088   £ 6 –  9


    CHUCK STEVENS
57  Take a walk/The way I do  ...........................  COLUMBIA  DB 3883   £ 2 –  4
57  My London/Couldn't care more  .......................            DB 3938   £ 2 –  4


    CONNIE STEVENS (qv EDWARD BYRNES)
60ø Sixteen reasons/Little sister  .......................  WARNER-B  WB   3   £ 4 –  6
60  Too young to go steady/A little kiss is a kiss is a kiss  WB  17   £ 2 –  4
60  Apollo/Why do I cry for Joey  .......................            WB  25   £ 2 –  4


    DODIE STEVENS
59  Pink shoe laces/Coming of age  ......................  LONDON   HLD 8834   £ 9 – 12
60  No/A-tisket a-tasket  ...............................            HLD 9174   £ 2 –  4


    JOHNNY STEVENS
54  Please opportunity/Not as a stranger  .................  DECCA    F 10413   £ 2 –  4
55  My loving hands/This night is mine  ...................            F 10499   £ 2 –  4


    KIRK STEVENS
57  Once/This silver Madonna  ...........................  DECCA    F 10863   £ 2 –  4


    RAY STEVENS
58  Chickie-chickie wah wah/Crying goodbye  ...............  CAPITOL  CL 14881  £ 4 –  6


    TERRI STEVENS
59  My wish tonight/All alone  ...........................  FELSTED  AF  112   £ 2 –  4
59  Adonis/Vieni, vieni  .................................            AF  126   £ 2 –  4


    ANDY STEWART
60ø Donald, where's your troosers?/Dancing in Kyle  ........  TOP RANK  JAR 427  £ 4 –  6
60ø A Scottish soldier/The muckin' o' Geordie's byre  ......            JAR 512  £ 2 –  4


    BOB STEWART
55  It's a woman's world/I went out of my way  ............  M-G-M    SP 1114   £ 2 –  4


    GRAHAM STEWART SEVEN
58  Roll along prairie Moon/Just gone  ...................  DECCA    FJ 11029   £ 2 –  4


    JOHNNY STEWART
58  Wishing for your love/Promise me  ....................  H.M.V.   POP  480   £ 2 –  4


    SANDY STEWART
58  A certain smile/Kiss me Richard  ....................  LONDON   HLE 8683   £ 4 –  6
```

SONNY STEWART & HIS SKIFFLE KINGS
57	The Northern Line/Black Jack	PHILIPS	PB 719 ♀	£ 6 – 9
57	Let me lie/Mama don't allow it		PB 773 ♀	£ 4 – 6

GARY STITES
59	Lonely for you/Shine that ring	LONDON	HLL 8881	£ 4 – 6
59	Starry eyed/Without your love		HLL 9003	£ 4 – 6
60	Lawdy, Miss Clawdy/Don't wanna say goodbye		HLL 9082	£ 6 – 9

RHET STOLLER
60	Walk don't run/All Rhet	DECCA	F 11271	£ 4 – 6
60ø	Chariot/Night theme		F 11302	£ 4 – 6

MORRIS STOLOFF & COLUMBIA PICTURES ORCH.
56ø	Moonglow & Theme from "Picnic"	BRUNSWICK	05553	£ 4 – 6

CLIFFIE STONE (& HIS ORCH.) (*& BILLY STRANGE & SPEEDY WEST)
55	Barracuda/The popcorn song	CAPITOL	*CL 14330	£25 – 40
59	Blood on the saddle/Cool water		CL 14996	£ 2 – 4

KIRBY STONE QUARTET/FOUR
56	Honey hush/Lassus trombone	V-CORAL	Q 72129	£ 4 – 6
59	That "I Had A Dream, Dear" rock/Sweet nothings	PHILIPS	PB 903	£ 2 – 4

MARK STONE
58	The stroll/Ever since I met Lucy	LONDON	HLR 8543	£18 – 25

THE STOREY SISTERS
58	Bad motorcycle/Sweet Daddy	LONDON	HLU 8571	£18 – 25

BILLY STORM
59	I've come of age/This is always	PHILIPS	PB 916	£ 2 – 4
60	Sure as you're born/In the chapel in the moonlight	LONDON	HLK 9236	£ 4 – 6

GALE STORM
56ø	I hear you knocking/Never leave me	LONDON	HLD 8222	£18 – 25
56	Memories are made of this/A teen-age prayer		HLD 8232	£18 – 25
56	Ivory tower/I ain't gonna worry		HLD 8283	£18 – 25
56	Why do fools fall in love/I walk alone		HLD 8286	£18 – 25
56	Don't be that way (Please listen to me)/Tell me why ...		HLD 8311	£18 – 25
56	A heart without a sweetheart/Now is the hour		HLD 8329	£12 – 18
57	Lucky lips/On Treasure Island		HLD 8393	£18 – 25
57	Orange blossoms/My heart belongs to you		HLD 8413	£ 9 – 12
57	Dark Moon/A little too late		HLD 8424	£ 9 – 12
58	"Farewell To Arms" love theme/I get that feeling		HLD 8570	£ 4 – 6
58	You/Angry		HLD 8632	£ 4 – 6

JERRY STORM
59	Sonny boy/Where do flies go in the Wintertime	ORIOLE	CB 1504	£ 2 – 4

ROBB STORME
60	1000, 900 and when/I don't need your love anymore	DECCA	F 11282	£ 4 – 6

HILLARD STREET
58	River love/It will never happen again	CAPITOL	CL 14960	£ 4 – 6

"TEXAS" BILL STRENGTH
55	Cry, cry, cry/The yellow rose of Texas	CAPITOL	CL 14357	£12 – 18

THE STROLLERS
58	Jumping with Symphony Sid/Swinging yellow rose of Texas	VOGUE	V 9113	£ 4 – 6
58	Little bitty pretty one/Flute cha-lypso		V 9124	£ 4 – 6

BARRETT STRONG
60	Money (that's what I want)/Oh I apologise	LONDON	HLU 9088	£25 – 40

SUGAR & PEE WEE
58	One, two, let's rock/Just a few little words	VOGUE	V 9112	£40 – 60

MAXINE SULLIVAN
54	Boogie woogie Maxixe/Piper in the glen	PARLOPHONE	MSP 6086	£ 4 – 6

PHIL SULLIVAN w. LONZO & OSCAR'S PEAPICKERS
59	Luckiest man in town/Love never dies	MELODISC	1512	£ 2 – 4

BOB or BOBBY SUMMERS
59	Rattle rhythm/Excitement	CAPITOL	CL 15063	£ 4 – 6
60	Little brown jug/Twelfth Street rag		CL 15130	£ 6 – 9

THE SUNNYSIDERS
55	Hey, Mr. Banjo/Zoom, zoom, zoom	LONDON	HL 8135	£12 – 18
55	Oh me oh my oh/(Let's gather round) The parlour piano .		HL 8160	£12 – 18
55	Banjo woogie/She didn't even say goodbye		HLU 8180	£12 – 18
55	I love you fair dinkum/Stay on the sunny side		HLU 8202	£ 9 – 12
56	Doesn't he love me/Humdinger		HLU 8246	£ 9 – 12

MR. *or MRS. SUNSHINE (Carl & Jane Swanson)
56	Along the China coast/Two car garage*	M-G-M	SP 1160	£ 2 – 4

THE SUPERSONICS (*& ARLENE JAMES)
53	New guitar boogie shuffle/The Sheik of Araby	LONDON	L 1197 º	£ 6 – 9
54	Cherokee/Linger awhile*		HL 8022 º	£ 4 – 6

THE SURFERS
59	Mambo jambo/ALAN KALANI: A touch of pink	VOGUE	V 9147	£ 4 – 6

RALPH SUTTON QUARTET
56	Up jumped you with love/Sweet and lovely	BRUNSWICK	05564	£ 2 – 4

PAT SUZUKI
58	Daddy/Just one of those things	R.C.A.	RCA 1069	£ 2 – 4
60ø	I enjoy being a girl/Sunday		RCA 1171	£ 2 – 4

THE SWALLOWS w. SONNY THOMPSON
52	Roll, roll pretty baby/It ain't the meat	VOGUE	V 2136 º	£12 – 18

THE SWE-DANES
60	Scandinavian shuffle/Hot toddy	WARNER-B	WB 7	£ 2 – 4
60	Swe-Dane shuffle/At a Georgia camp meeting		WB 22	£ 2 – 4

JIM SWEENEY
58	The midnight hour/Till the right one comes along	PHILIPS	PB 811	£ 4 – 6

THE SWEET CORPORALS
59	The same old army/Warm and willing	TOP RANK	JAR 217	£ 2 – 4

THE SWINGERS
60	Love makes the world go round/Jackie	VOGUE	V 9158	£ 2 – 4

THE (FABULOUS) SWINGTONES
58	Geraldine/You know baby	H.M.V.	POP 471	£25 – 40

ROOSEVELT SYKES & HIS HONEYDRIPPERS
56	Fine and brown/Too hot to hold	VOGUE	V 2389	£18 – 25
56	Walkin' this boogie/Security blues		V 2393	£25 – 40

SYLVIA SYMS
56	English muffins and Irish stew/The world in my corner .	BRUNSWICK	05592	£ 2 – 4
57	Dancing chandelier/Each day		05643	£ 2 – 4
58	I could have danced all night/Be good (to me)		05744	£ 2 – 4
59	The night they invented champagne/The nature of things		05771	£ 2 – 4

THE (FABULOUS) TALBOT BROTHERS
59 Bloodshot eyes/She's got freckles .... MELODISC   1507   £ 4 - 6

ZIGGY TALENT
55 Cheek to cheek (Cha cha)/Bozooki blues .... BRUNSWICK   05506   £ 2 - 4

TOM TALL (*& RUCKUS TAYLOR/qv GINNY WRIGHT)
55 Give me a chance/Remembering you .... LONDON   HLU 8216   £12 - 18
56 Underway/Goldie Jo Malone ....   HLU 8231   £12 - 18
57 Don't you know/If you know what I know ....   *HLU 8429   £ 9 - 12

THE TANTONES
57 So afraid/Tell me .... VOGUE   V   9085   £60 - 90

THE TARRIERS (qv VINCE MARTIN)
57ø The banana boat song/No hidin' place .... COLUMBIA   DB 3891   £ 4 - 6
57 Tom Dooley/Everybody loves Saturday night ....   DB 3961   £ 2 - 4
57 Dunya/Quinto (My little pony) ....   DB 4025   £ 2 - 4
58 Lonesome traveller/East Virginia .... LONDON   HLU 8600   £ 4 - 6
58 I know where I'm going/Acres of clams .... COLUMBIA   DB 4148   £ 2 - 4

THE TASSELS
59 To a soldier boy/The boy for me .... LONDON   HL 8885   £12 - 18
59 My guy and I/To a young lover .... TOP RANK   JAR 229   £ 9 - 12

PHIL TATE & HIS ORCH.
59 Countdown (Jive)/Green turtle .... ORIOLE   CB 1514   £ 2 - 4

THE TAYLOR MAIDS
55 Theme from "I Am A Camera" (Why do I)/Po-go stick ..... CAPITOL   CL 14322   £ 4 - 6

AUSTIN TAYLOR
60 Push push/A heart that's true .... TOP RANK   JAR 511   £ 2 - 4

EILEEN TAYLOR
56 Love me, love me now/Sing a song of Sunday .... DECCA   F 10700   £ 2 - 4

GLEN TAYLOR
54 Until the day I die/Play, fiddle, play .... COLUMBIA SCM 5137   £ 2 - 4

NEVILLE TAYLOR (qv HAL BURTON/HAL MUNRO)
58 Mercy, mercy, Percy/House of bamboo .... PARLOPHONE R 4447   £ 9 - 12
58 Tears on my pillow/I don't want to set the world on fire   R 4476   £ 4 - 6
58 The miracle of Christmas/A baby lay sleeping ....   R 4493   £ 2 - 4
59 Crazy little Daisy/The first words of love ....   R 4524   £ 9 - 12
60 Dance with a dolly/Free passes .... ORIOLE   CB 1546   £ 4 - 6

SAM "The Man" TAYLOR & HIS CAT MEN
54 This can't be love/Please be kind .... M-G-M   SP 1106   £ 2 - 4

TED TAYLOR FOUR
58 Son of Honky Tonk/Farrago .... ORIOLE   CB 1464   £ 4 - 6
60 M.1./You are my sunshine ....   CB 1573   £ 4 - 6

VERNON TAYLOR
60 Mystery train/Sweet and easy to love .... LONDON   HLS 9025   £18 - 25

VINCE TAYLOR (& HIS PLAYBOYS)
58 Right behind you baby/I like love .... PARLOPHONE R 4505   £12 - 18
59 Brand new Cadillac/Pledging my love ....   R 4539   £12 - 18
60ø Jet black machine/I'll be your hero .... PALETTE   PG 9001   £ 9 - 12

TEACHO & HIS STUDENTS
58 Stop/Rock-et .... FELSTED   AF   104   £ 6 - 9

THE TECHNIQUES
58 Hey! Little girl/In a round about way   ...   .UMBIA   DB 4072   £ 4 – 6

THE TEDDY BEARS
58ø To know him is to love him/Don't you worry my little pet LONDON   HLN 8733   £ 6 – 9
59 I don't need you anymore/Oh why ....   HLP 8836   £ 9 – 12
59 You said goodbye/If you only knew ....   HLP 8889   £ 9 – 12

THE TEEN BEATS feat. DON RIVERS & THE CALIFFS
60 The slop beat/Califf boogie .... TOP RANK   JAR 342   £ 6 – 9

BOBBY TEMPEST
59 Love or leave/Don't leave me .... DECCA   F 11125   £ 4 – 6

BOB TEMPLE
57 Vim vam vamoose/Come back, come back .... PARLOPHONE R 4264   £ 4 – 6

SHIRLEY TEMPLE
59 On the good ship Lollipop/Animal crackers in my soup .. TOP RANK   JAR 139   £ 4 – 6

NINO TEMPO & HIS BAND
57 Tempo's tempo/June's blues .... LONDON   HLU 8387   £40 – 60

THE TEMPOS
59 See you in September/Bless you my love .... PYE INT. 7N 25026   £ 9 – 12

THE TEMPTATIONS
60 Barbara/Someday .... TOP RANK   JAR 384   £ 9 – 12

THE TERRY SISTERS
57 It's the same old jazz/Broken promise .... PARLOPHONE R 4364   £ 9 – 12
58 Sweet thing (tell me that you...)/You forgot to remember   R 4509   £ 4 – 6

TERRY-THOMAS *& THE ROCK 'N' ROLL ROTTERS
56 A sweet old-fashioned boy*/Lay down your arms .... DECCA   F 10804   £ 6 – 9

SONNY TERRY (TRIO) (*& BROWNIE McGHEE)
53 Hootin' blues/TOMMY REILLY: Bop! goes the weasel .... PARLOPHONE MSP 6017   £ 9 – 12
55 Fox chase/John Henry .... VOGUE   V 2326 º £ 4 – 6
60 Talking harmonica blues/Rockin' and whoopin' .... COLUMBIA *DB 4433   £ 4 – 6

THE TEXTOR SINGERS
54 Sobbin' women/Remember me .... CAPITOL   CL 14211   £ 4 – 6

Sister ROSETTA THARPE (qv Rev. KELSEY)
57 When the Saints go marching in/Cain't no grave hold my.. MERCURY   MT 126 º £ 4 – 6
57 Up above my head there's music in the air/Jericho ......   MT 185 º £ 4 – 6
60 If I can help somebody/Take my hand, precious Lord .... M–G–M   MGM 1072   £ 2 – 4

DANNY THOMAS
56 Nobody knows but the Lord/It's wonderful when .... BRUNSWICK 05557   £ 2 – 4

RAMBLIN' THOMAS
52 Jig head blues/Hard Dallas blues .... TEMPO   R 51 º £ 6 – 9

HANK THOMPSON (& HIS BRAZOS VALLEY BOYS)
56 Don't take it out on me/Honey, Honey Bee Ball .... CAPITOL   CL 14517   £ 4 – 6
56 The blackboard of my heart/I'm not mad, just hurt .....   CL 14668   £ 4 – 6
58 Li'l Liza Jane/How do you hold a memory ....   CL 14869   £ 4 – 6
58 Squaws along the Yukon/Gathering flowers ....   CL 14945   £ 2 – 4
58 I've run out of tomorrows/You're going back to your old.   CL 14961   £ 2 – 4
59 Total strangers/Anybody's girl ....   CL 15014   £ 2 – 4
59 I didn't mean to fall in love/I guess I'm getting over..   CL 15074   £ 2 – 4
60 A six pack to go/What made her change ....   CL 15114   £ 9 – 12
60 She's just a whole lot like you/There my future goes ..   CL 15156   £ 2 – 4

KAY THOMPSON
56 Eloise/Just one of those things .... LONDON   HLA 8268   £ 9 - 12

LUCKY THOMPSON
56 But not for me/East of the Sun .... VOGUE   V 2388   £ 2 - 4

SONNY THOMPSON & HIS ORCH./R&B BAND (qv THE SWALLOWS)
52 Real, real fine (both sides) .... VOGUE   V 2143 º £12 - 18
53 Houseful of blues/Creepin' .... ESQUIRE 10-320 º £ 9 - 12
53 Screamin' boogie/The fish .... 10-339 º £12 - 18
60 *as above* .... STARLITE ST.45 008   £60 - 90

CLAUDE THORNHILL & HIS ORCH.
54 Pussy-footin'/Adios .... LONDON   HL 8042   £12 - 18

WILLIE MAE "Big Mama" THORNTON
54 Hound dog/Mischievous boogie .... VOGUE   V 2284 º £12 - 18

THE THREE BELLS
60 Steady date/In between (wishing I was sweet sixteen) .. PYE   7N 15252   £ 2 - 4

THE THREE CHUCKLES
55 Runaround/At last you understand .... H.M.V.   7M 292   £ 4 - 6
55 Times two, I love you/Still thinking of you .... 7M 333   £ 4 - 6
57 We're gonna rock tonight/Won't you give me a chance ... POP 292   £25 - 40

THE THREE DOLLS
57 The living end/The octopus song .... M-G-M   MGM 958   £ 4 - 6

THE THREE PROFESSORS
56 Yew stept owt offa dreme/Vulgar boatman rock .... COLUMBIA DB 3845   £ 2 - 4

THE THREE RAYS
55 Mister Clarinet Man/There he goes .... V-CORAL Q 72086   £ 2 - 4

THE THREE SUNS
55 Perdido/For you .... H.M.V.   7M 297   £ 2 - 4
55 Arrivederci darling (Arrivederci Roma)/Cha Cha Joe .... 7M 346   £ 2 - 4
57 Moonlight and roses/Vintage lies .... R.C.A.   RCA 1006   £ 2 - 4

THE THUNDERBIRDS (qv BERT CONVY)
55 Ayuh, ayuh/Blueberries .... LONDON   HL 8146   £12 - 18

JOHNNY TILLOTSON
59 True true happiness/Love is blind .... LONDON   HLA 8930   £ 4 - 6
60 Why do I love you so/Never let me go .... HLA 9048   £ 4 - 6
60 Earth angel/Pledging my love .... HLA 9101   £ 4 - 6
60ø Poetry in motion/Princess, princess .... HLA 9231   £ 2 - 4

AL TIMOTHY & HIS BAND
55 Gruntin' blues/You mad man! .... DECCA   F 10558   £ 4 - 6

TINY TOPSY (*& THE CHARMS)
58 Come on, come on, come on/Ring around my finger .... *PARLOPHONE R 4397   £18 - 25
58 Waterproof eyes/You shocked me .... R 4427   £18 - 25

THE TITANS
58 Don't you just know it/Can it be .... LONDON   HLU 8609   £18 - 25

ART & DOTTIE TODD
52ø Broken wings/Heavenly - Heavenly .... H.M.V.   B 10399 º £ 2 - 4
58 Chanson d'amour/Along the trail with you .... LONDON   HLB 8620   £ 4 - 6
59 Straight as an arrow/Stand there, mountain .... HLN 8838   £ 4 - 6

DICK TODD
55 Tiny hands/Baby girl of mine .... BRUNSWICK 05374   £ 2 - 4

NICK TODD

Year	Title	Label	Cat.	Price
57	Plaything/The honey song	LONDON	HLD 8500	£12 – 18
58ø	At the hop/I do		HLD 8537	£ 6 – 9
59	Tiger/Twice as nice		HLD 8902	£ 6 – 9

SHARKEY TODD & THE MONSTERS (actually WALLY WHYTON)

59	The horror show/Cool gool	PARLOPHONE R 4536		£ 6 – 9

TONY & JOE

58	The freeze/Gonna get a little kissin' tonight	LONDON	HLN 8694	£12 – 18

THE TOPPERS

57	Stashu Pandowski (She's not very much....)/Pots and pans	BRUNSWICK	05678	£ 2 – 4

MEL TORME (*& TED HEATH MUSIC)

56ø	Mountain greenery/Jeepers creepers	V–CORAL	Q 72150	£ 6 – 9
56	Blue Moon/That old black magic		Q 72159	£ 2 – 4
56	Love is here to stay/Goody goody		Q 72185	£ 2 – 4
56	Lulu's back in town/The lady is a tramp	LONDON	HLN 8305	£ 9 – 12
56	I can't give you anything but.../There's no business....	M–G–M	MGM 922	£ 2 – 4
56	All of you/It don't mean a thing	V–CORAL	Q 72202	£ 2 – 4
56	Lullaby of Birdland/I love to watch the moonlight	LONDON	HLN 8322	£ 9 – 12
56	Walkin' shoes/The cuckoo in the clock	DECCA	*F 10800	£ 2 – 4
56	Waltz for young lovers/I don't want to walk without you		F 10809	£ 2 – 4
56	My Rosemarie/How	V–CORAL	Q 72217	£ 2 – 4
60	The white cliffs of Dover/I've got a lovely bunch of....	PHILIPS	PB 1045	£ 2 – 4

MITCHELL TOROK (*& THE TULANE SISTERS)

54	Caribbean/Weep away	LONDON	HL 8004	£12 – 18
54	Hootchy kootchy Henry (from Hawaii)/Gigolo		HL 8048	£12 – 18
54	The haunting waterfall/Dancerette		HL 8083	£12 – 18
55	The world keeps turning around/A peasant's guitar	BRUNSWICK	05423	£ 4 – 6
56ø	When Mexico gave up the rhumba/I wish I was a little....		05586	£ 9 – 12
56ø	Red light, green light*/Havana huddle		05626	£ 9 – 12
57	Drink up and go home/Take this heart		05642	£ 4 – 6
57	Pledge of love/What's behind that strange door		05657	£ 6 – 9
57	Two words (True love)/You're tempting me		05718	£ 2 – 4
60	Pink chiffon/What you don't know (won't hurt you)	LONDON	HLW 9130	£ 4 – 6

VICO TORRIANI w. MANTOVANI ORCH.

55	Remembering/Mandolines are playing	DECCA	F 10498	£ 2 – 4

THE TOWERS feat. *EVELYN KINGSLEY/+FRANK PERRY

58	To know him is to love him*/Let me be the one+	CAPITOL	CL 14944	£ 4 – 6

THE TOWNSEL SISTERS

60	Will I ever/I know	POLYDOR	NH 66954	£ 2 – 4

ED TOWNSEND

58	Over and over again/For your love	CAPITOL	CL 14867	£ 2 – 4
58	When I grow too old to dream/You are my everything		CL 14927	£ 2 – 4
59	Richer than I/Getting by without you		CL 14976	£ 2 – 4
59	Don't ever leave me/Lover come back to me		CL 15020	£ 2 – 4
59	This little love of mine/Hold on		CL 15072	£ 2 – 4
60	Don't get around much anymore/Do nothin' till you hear..		CL 15141	£ 2 – 4
60	Stay with me (a little.....)/I love everything about you	WARNER–B	WB 21	£ 2 – 4

AL TRACE & HIS LITTLE TRACERS w. BETSY GAY

53	Mocking bird boogie/You're only a part-time sweetheart	M–G–M	MGM 693 º	£ 4 – 6

WENDALL TRACY

58	Corrigidor rock/Who's to know	LONDON	HLM 8664	£ 6 – 9

THE TRADEWINDS

59	Furry Murray/Crossroads	R.C.A.	RCA 1141	£ 6 – 9

```
     TRAVIS & BOB
59  Tell him no/We're too young  ........................  PYE INT. 7N 25018   £ 2 -  4

     THE TRENIERS
58  Oo-la-la/Pennies from Heaven  .......................  CORAL     Q 72319   £ 6 -  9
58  Go! Go! Go!/Get out of the car  .....................  FONTANA     H 137   £18 - 25
59  When your hair has turned to silver/Never, never  ....  LONDON   HLD 8858   £ 6 -  9

     TOMMY TRINDER & THE GANG
59  La plume de ma Tante/On the sunny side of the street  ..  FONTANA   H 204   £ 2 -  4

     TRIO LOS PARAGUAYOS
59  Bell bird/Misionera  .................................  PHILIPS  PB 947    £ 2 -  4

     THE TROJANS
58  Man I'm gonna be/Make it up  .........................  DECCA    F 11065    £ 6 -  9

     THE TROOPERS
58  Get out/My resolution  ...............................  VOGUE     V 9087   £40 - 60

     THE TROUBADORS (qv JANE MORGAN)
57  Fascination/Midnight in Athens  ......................  LONDON   HLR 8469   £ 4 -  6
58  The lights of Paris/The flaming rose  ................           HLR 8541   £ 2 -  4

     BOBBY TROUP
54  Julie is her name/Instead of you  ....................  CAPITOL  CL 14219   £ 4 -  6

     BOB TROW QUARTET
54  Soft squeeze baby/I went along for the ride  .........  LONDON    HL 8082   £12 - 18

     THE TU-TONES
59  Still in love with you/Saccharin Sally  ..............  LONDON   HLW 8904   £18 - 25

     ERNEST TUBB (qv RED FOLEY)
56  Thirty days/Answer the phone  ........................  BRUNSWICK   05527   £ 9 - 12
56  So doggone lonesome/If I never have anything else  ....             05587   £ 6 -  9

     LEE TULLY
57  Around the world with Elwood Pretzel - Parts 1 & 2  ....  LONDON   HL 8363   £18 - 25

     THE TUNE ROCKERS
58  The green mosquito/Warm up  ..........................  LONDON   HLT 8717   £12 - 18

     IKE & TINA TURNER
60  A fool in love/The way you love me  ..................  LONDON   HLU 9226   £ 6 -  9

     JESSE LEE TURNER
59  Shake, baby, shake/The little space girl  ............  LONDON   HLL 8785   £25 - 40
60  That's my girl/Teenage misery  .......................  TOP RANK JAR 303   £ 4 -  6
60  I'm the little space girl's...../Valley of lost soldiers  LONDON HLP 9108  £ 6 -  9
60  All right, be that way/Do I worry (Yes I do)  .........  TOP RANK JAR 516   £ 4 -  6

     JOE TURNER
49  Mardi Gras boogie/My heart belongs to you  ...........  M-G-M   MGM 253 º  £12 - 18
56  Corrine Corrina/Morning, noon and night  .............  LONDON  HLE 8301   £60 - 90
56  Boogie woogie country girl/The chicken and the hawk  ...         HLE 8332   £90 -120
57  Lipstick, powder and paint/Rock a while  .............           HLE 8357   £90 -120
60  Honey hush/Tomorrow night  ...........................           HLE 9055   £18 - 25
60  My little honey dripper/Chains of love  ..............           HLK 9119   £12 - 18

     SAMMY TURNER
59  Lavender blue (Dilly, Dilly)/Sweet Annie Laurie  .......  LONDON  HLX 8918   £ 6 -  9
59ø Always/Symphony  .....................................           HLX 8963   £ 4 -  6
60  Paradise/I'd be a fool again  ........................           HLX 9062   £ 2 -  4
```

TITUS TURNER

60	We told you not to marry/Taking care of business	LONDON	HLU 9024	£ 9 – 12

ZEB TURNER

51	Chew tobacco rag/No more nothin'	VOGUE	V 9002 º	£ 9 – 12

WESLEY & MARILYN TUTTLE

55	Jim, Johnny and Jonas/Say you do	CAPITOL	CL 14291	£ 4 – 6

THE TWIN-TONES

58	Jo-Ann/Before you go	R.C.A.	RCA 1040	£18 – 25

THE TWIN TUNES QUINTET

58	Baby lover/The love nest	R.C.A.	RCA 1046	£ 4 – 6

THE TWISTERS

60	Turn the page/Dancing little clown	CAPITOL	CL 15167	£ 2 – 4

CONWAY TWITTY

57	Shake it up/Maybe baby	MERCURY	MT 173 º	£12 – 18
58ø	It's only make believe/I'll try	M-G-M	MGM 992	£ 4 – 6
59ø	The story of my love/Make me know you're mine		MGM 1003	£ 4 – 6
59ø	Hey little Lucy! (don't cha put..)/When I'm not with you		MGM 1016	£ 4 – 6
59ø	Mona Lisa/Heavenly		MGM 1029	£ 4 – 6
59	Rosaleena/Halfway to Heaven		MGM 1047	£ 4 – 6
60	Lonely blue boy/My one and only you		MGM 1056	£ 4 – 6
60	What am I living for/The hurt in my heart		MGM 1066	£ 4 – 6
60ø	Is a blue bird blue/She's mine		MGM 1082	£ 4 – 6
60	What a dream/Tell me one more time		MGM 1095	£ 4 – 6
60	Whole lotta shakin' goin' on/The flame		MGM 1108	£ 4 – 6

THE 2.19 SKIFFLE GROUP

57	Freight train blues/Railroad Bill	ESQUIRE	10-497 º	£ 4 – 6
57	I'm a-lookin' for a home/When the Saints go marching in		10-502 º	£ 4 – 6
57	In the valley/Tom Dooley		10-509 º	£ 4 – 6
57	Where can I go?/Roll the Union on		10-512 º	£ 4 – 6
57	This little light of mine/Union maid		10-515 º	£ 4 – 6

ARLYNE TYE

59	The Universe/Who is the one	LONDON	HLL 8825	£ 4 – 6

BIG "T" TYLER

57	King Kong/Sadie Green	VOGUE	V 9079	£90 –120

JIMMY TYLER & HIS ORCH.

56	Fool 'em Devil/Stardust	PARLOPHONE	MSP 6215	£ 9 – 12

RED TYLER & THE GYROS

60	Junk village/Happy sax	TOP RANK	JAR 306	£ 2 – 4

LESLIE UGGAMS

58	Ice cream man/I'm old enough	COLUMBIA	DB 4160	£ 2 – 4
59	One more sunrise (Morgen)/The eyes of God	PHILIPS	PB 954	£ 2 – 4
60	The carefree years/Lullaby of the leaves		PB 999	£ 2 – 4
60	Love is like a violin/Inherit the wind		PB 1063	£ 2 – 4

MIYOSHI UMEKI

58	Sayonara/On and on	MERCURY	7MT 203	£ 2 – 4

THE UPBEATS

58	Just like in the movies/My foolish heart	LONDON	HLU 8688	£ 4 – 6
59	You're the one I care for/Keep cool crazy heart	PYE INT.	7N 25016	£ 4 – 6
59	Teenie weenie bikini/Satin shoes		7N 25028	£ 4 – 6

REMEMBER! – THE SYMBOL º AFTER THE CATALOGUE NUMBER INDICATES A 78 rpm RECORD

PETER USTINOV
53 Mock Mozart/Phoney folk-lore .... PARLOPHONE MSP 6012 £ 2 - 4

RICKY VALANCE
60ø Tell Laura I love her/Once upon a time .... COLUMBIA DB 4493 £ 4 - 6
60 Movin' away/Lipstick on your lips .... DB 4543 £ 4 - 6

JERRY VALE (*& MARY MAYO)
58 Goodbye now/This is the place .... PHILIPS *PB 826 £ 2 - 4
59 The moon is my pillow/The flame .... PB 963 £ 2 - 4

RITCHIE VALENS
58 Come on, let's go/Dooby dooby wah .... PYE INT. 7N 25000 £18 - 25
59ø Donna/La bamba .... LONDON HL 8803 £ 9 - 12
59 That's my little Suzie/Bluebirds over the mountains ... HL 8886 £ 9 - 12

CATERINA VALENTE
55ø The breeze and I/Jealousy .... POLYDOR BM 6002 º £ 2 - 4
60 Malaguena/Secret love .... NH 66816 £ 2 - 4
60 The breeze and I/Side by side .... NH 66953 £ 2 - 4
60 Till/Amour .... DECCA F 11306 £ 2 - 4

BILLY VALENTINE
55 It's a sin/Your love has got me (reelin' and rockin') . CAPITOL CL 14320 £ 9 - 12

DICKIE VALENTINE (*& THE STARGAZERS/qv VARIOUS ARTISTS)
52ø Broken wings/The homing waltz .... DECCA F 9954 º £ 2 - 4
53ø All the time and everywhere/Why should I go home? ..... F 10038 º £ 2 - 4
53ø In a golden coach/The Windsor waltz .... F 10098 º £ 2 - 4
54ø Endless/I could have told you .... F 10346 £ 9 - 12
54ø The finger of suspicion points at you*/Who's afraid (..) F 10394 £ 9 - 12
54ø Mister Sandman/Runaround .... F 10415 £ 9 - 12
55ø A blossom fell/I want you all to myself (Just you) .... F 10430 £ 9 - 12
55 Ma cherie amie/Lucky waltz .... F 10484 £ 6 - 9
55ø I wonder/You too can be a dreamer .... F 10493 £ 9 - 12
55 Hello Mrs. Jones (is Mary there?)/Lazy gondolier ...... F 10517 £ 4 - 6
55 No such luck/The engagement waltz .... F 10549 £ 4 - 6
55ø Christmas alphabet/Where are you tonight? .... F 10628 £ 9 - 12
55ø The old pi-anna rag/First love .... F 10645 £ 9 - 12
56 Dreams can tell a lie/Song of the trees .... F 10667 £ 4 - 6
56 The voice/The best way to hold a girl .... F 10714 £ 4 - 6
56 My impossible castle/When you came along .... F 10753 £ 4 - 6
56 Day dreams/Give me a carriage with eight white horses . F 10766 £ 4 - 6
56ø Christmas Island/The hand of friendship .... F 10798 £ 9 - 12
56 "Dickie Valentine's Rock 'N' Roll Party" medley .... F 10820 £ 6 - 9
57 Chapel of the Roses/My empty arms .... F 10874 £ 4 - 6
57 Puttin' on the style/Three sides to every story .... F 10906 £ 4 - 6
57 Long before I knew you/Just in time .... F 10949 £ 4 - 6
57ø Snowbound for Christmas/Convicted .... F 10950 £ 6 - 9
58 Love me again/King of Dixieland .... F 11005 £ 2 - 4
58 In my life/Come to my arms .... F 11020 £ 2 - 4
58 Take me in your arms/An old-fashioned song .... F 11066 £ 2 - 4
59ø Venus/Where? (in the old home town) .... PYE 7N 15192 £ 4 - 6
59 A teenager in love/My favourite song .... 7N 15202 £ 2 - 4
59ø One more sunrise (Morgen)/You touch my hand .... 7N 15221 £ 2 - 4
60 Standing on the corner/Roundabout .... 7N 15255 £ 2 - 4
60 Once, only once/A fool that I am .... 7N 15294 £ 2 - 4

ANNA VALENTINO
57 Calypso Joe/You're mine .... LONDON HLD 8421 £ 6 - 9

DANNY VALENTINO
59 Stampede/(You gotta be a) Music man .... M-G-M MGM 1049 £ 9 - 12
60 Biology/A million tears .... MGM 1067 £ 6 - 9
60 Pictures from the past/'Till the end of forever .... MGM 1109 £ 2 - 4

VALERIE (The Rock 'N' Roll Youngster)
56 Tonight you belong to me/The man who owns the sunshine   COLUMBIA DB 3832 £ 6 - 9

JOE VALINO
57ø	The Garden of Eden/Caravan	H.M.V.	POP 283	£ 6 - 9
58	God's little acre/I'm happy with what I've got	LONDON	HLT 8705	£ 4 - 6
60	Hidden persuasion/Back to your eyes	COLUMBIA	DB 4406	£ 2 - 4

JUNE VALLI
54	I understand (just how you.)/Old shoes and a bag of rice	H.M.V.	7M 245	£ 4 - 6
54	Tell me, tell me/Boy wanted		7M 259	£ 2 - 4
55	Wrong, wrong, wrong/Ole Pappy time		7M 284	£ 2 - 4
55	Por favor (Please)/The things they say		7M 347	£ 2 - 4
59	The answer to a maiden's prayer/In his arms	MERCURY	AMT 1033	£ 2 - 4
59	An anonymous letter/Bygones		AMT 1048	£ 2 - 4
60	Apple green/Oh! Why		AMT 1091	£ 2 - 4

THE VAMPIRES
59 Swinging ghosts/Clap trap .... PARLOPHONE R 4599 £ 4 - 6

HARVIE JUNE VAN
54 Can-can skirt/My sins of yesterday .... PARLOPHONE MSP 6141 £ 2 - 4

MAMIE VAN DOREN
58 Something to dream about/I fell in love .... CAPITOL CL 14850 £ 4 - 6

TEDDY VANN
60 Cindy/I'm waiting .... LONDON HLU 9097 £ 4 - 6

PETER VARDAS
59 He threw a stone/Checkerboard love .... TOP RANK JAR 173 £ 2 - 4

VARIOUS ARTISTS
53 "Columbia Cavalcade": MARIE BENSON: Among my souvenirs/STEVE CONWAY: We'll gather lilacs/BEVERLEY SISTERS: Limehouse blues/TEDDY JOHNSON: I'll see you again/STEVE RACE: Dream of Olwen/JOHNNY BRANDON: Lily of Laguna/RONNIE RONALDE: Bells of St. Mary/ ENSEMBLE: If you were the only girl in the world ...... COLUMBIA SCD 2008 £ 4 - 6

56ø "All Star Hit Parade": DICKIE VALENTINE: Out of town/JOAN REGAN: My September love/ WINIFRED ATWELL: Theme from "The Threepenny Opera"/DAVE KING: No other love/LITA ROZA: A tear fell/DAVID WHITFIELD: It's almost tomorrow ..... DECCA F 10752 £ 9 - 12

57ø "All Star Hit Parade No. 2": JOHNSTON BROS.: Around the world/BILLY COTTON: Puttin' on the style/JIMMY YOUNG: When I fall in love/MAX BYGRAVES: A white sport coat/BEVERLEY SISTERS: Freight train/TOMMY STEELE: Butterfly .... DECCA F 10915 £ 6 - 9

57 "Top Ten Special": JIM DALE: Wanderin' eyes/All shook up/THE KING BROTHERS: A handful of songs/Build your love (on a strong foundation)/VIPERS SKIFFLE GROUP: Last train to San Fernando/Putting on the style .... PARLOPHONE R 4356 £ 6 - 9

58 "Star Band Hit Parade": TED HEATH MUSIC: Lollipop/Who's sorry now/MANTOVANI ORCH.: I may never pass this way again/Tulips from Amsterdam/EDMUNDO ROS ORCH.: Swingin' shepherd blues/Tom Hark .... DECCA F 11043 £ 2 - 4

59 CRAIG DOUGLAS: The Battle of New Orleans/Dream lover/BERT WEEDON: Roulette/I need your love tonight/SHEILA BUXTON: Where were you on our wedding day/Personality .... TOP RANK TR 5004 £ 4 - 6

FRANKIE VAUGHAN (*& THE KAYE SISTERS/qv ALMA COGAN)
53ø	Istanbul (not Constantinople)/Cloud lucky seven	H.M.V.	B 10599 º	£ 1 - 2
53ø	as above		7M 167	£ 6 - 9
54	The cuff of my shirt/Heartless		7M 182	£ 2 - 4
54	My son, my son/Cinnamon sinner (selling lollipop lies)		7M 252	£ 2 - 4
54ø	Happy days and lonely nights/Danger signs		B 10783 º	£ 1 - 2
54ø	as above		7M 270	£ 6 - 9
55	Too many heartaches/Unsuspecting heart		7M 298	£ 2 - 4

55ø	Tweedle-dee/Give me the moonlight, give me the girl ...	PHILIPS	PB	423 º	£ 1 -	2
55ø	Seventeen/Meet me on the corner		PB	511 º	£ 1 -	2
56ø	My boy Flat Top/Stealin'		PB	544 º	£ 1 -	2
56ø	The green door/Pity the poor, poor man		PB	640 º	£ 1 -	2
57ø	The Garden of Eden/Priscilla		PB	660 º	£ 1 -	2
57ø	as above		JK	1002	£ 6 -	9
57	What's behind that strange door/Cold, cold shower		JK	1014	£ 4 -	6
57	These dangerous years/Isn't this a lovely evening		JK	1022	£ 4 -	6
57ø	Wanderin' eyes/Man on fire		PB	729 º	£ 1 -	2
57ø	Got-ta have something in the bank, Frank/Single		*PB	751 º	£ 1 -	2
57ø	as above		*JK	1030	£ 6 -	9
57ø	Kisses sweeter than wine/Rock-a-chicka		JK	1035	£ 6 -	9
58ø	as above		PB	775	£ 2 -	4
58ø	We're not alone/Can't get along without you		PB	793	£ 2 -	4
58ø	Kewpie doll/So many women		PB	825	£ 2 -	4
58ø	Wonderful things/Judy		PB	834	£ 2 -	4
58ø	Am I wasting my time on you/So happy in love		PB	865	£ 2 -	4
59ø	That's my doll/Love is the sweetest thing		PB	895	£ 2 -	4
59	Honey bunny baby/The lady is a square		PB	896	£ 2 -	4
59ø	Come softly to me/Say something sweet to your sweetheart		*PB	913	£ 2 -	4
59ø	The heart of a man/Sometime somewhere		PB	930	£ 2 -	4
59ø	Walkin' tall/I ain't gonna lead this life		PB	931	£ 2 -	4
59	Give me the moonlight, give me the girl/Happy go lucky		PB	423	£ 1 -	2
59ø	What more do you want/The very very young		PB	985	£ 2 -	4
60ø	Kookie little Paradise/Mary Lou		PB	1054	£ 2 -	4
60ø	Milord/Do you still love me?		PB	1066	£ 2 -	4

MALCOLM VAUGHAN

55ø	Ev'ry day of my life/Mama	H.M.V.	B	10874	£ 1 -	2
55	More than a millionaire/Take me back again		7M	317	£ 2 -	4
55ø	With your love/Small talk		POP	130 º	£ 1 -	2
55ø	as above		7M	338	£ 6 -	9
56	Only you (and you alone)/I'll be near you		7M	389	£ 4 -	6
56ø	St. Therese of the Roses/Love me as though there were...		POP	250	£ 4 -	6
57ø	The world is mine/Now		POP	303	£ 4 -	6
57ø	Chapel of the Roses/Guardian angel		POP	325	£ 4 -	6
57	What is my destiny/Oh! My Papa		POP	381	£ 2 -	4
57ø	My special angel/The heart of a child		POP	419	£ 4 -	6
58ø	To be loved/My loving arms		POP	459	£ 2 -	4
58	Ev'ry hour, ev'ry day of my life/Miss you		POP	502	£ 2 -	4
58ø	More than ever (Come prima)/A night to remember		POP	538	£ 2 -	4
59ø	Wait for me/Willingly		POP	590	£ 2 -	4
59	You'll never walk alone/The Holy City		POP	687	£ 2 -	4
60	Oh, so wunderbar/For everyone in love		POP	700	£ 2 -	4
60	My love for you/Lady of Spain		POP	739	£ 2 -	4

ROY VAUGHAN BOOGIE TRIO

51	Oval boogie/Rumble. boogie	JAZZ PARADE	B	3 º	£ 6 -	9

SARAH VAUGHAN (& *BILLY ECKSTINE/+COUNT BASIE & JOE WILLIAMS)

57ø	Passing strangers/The door is open	MERCURY	*MT	164 º	£ 2 -	4
58	My darling, my darling/Bewitched		7MT	198	£ 4 -	6
58	Padre/Spin little bottle		7MT	212	£ 4 -	6
58	Too much, too soon/What's so bad about it		7MT	222	£ 4 -	6
58	Everything I do/I ain't hurtin'		AMT	1010	£ 2 -	4
59	Alexander's Ragtime Band/No limit		*AMT	1020	£ 2 -	4
59	Cool baby/Are you certain?		AMT	1029	£ 4 -	6
59	Careless/Separate ways		AMT	1044	£ 4 -	6
59ø	Broken-hearted melody/Misty		AMT	1057	£ 4 -	6
59	Passing stranger*/Smooth operator		AMT	1071	£ 2 -	4
60	You're my baby/Eternally		AMT	1080	£ 2 -	4
60	Sweet affection/Don't look at me that way		AMT	1087	£ 2 -	4
60	Ooh! What a day/My dear little sweetheart	COLUMBIA	DB	4491	£ 2 -	4
60	If I were a bell/Teach me tonight		+DB	4511	£ 2 -	4
60ø	Serenata/Let's		DB	4542	£ 2 -	4

BILLY VAUGHN & HIS ORCH. (*& KEN NORDINE)

55	Melody of love/Joy ride	LONDON	HL 8112	£ 9 - 12
55ø	The shifting whispering sands - Parts 1 & 2		*HLD 8205	£12 - 18
56ø	Theme from "The Threepenny Opera"/I'd give a million....		HLD 8238	£ 9 - 12
56	When the lilac blooms again/Autumn concerto		HLD 8319	£ 9 - 12
56	Petticoats of Portugal/La la Colette		HLD 8342	£ 9 - 12
57	The ship that never sailed/Little Boy Blue		*HLD 8417	£ 4 - 6
57	Johnny Tremain/Naughty Annetta		HLD 8511	£ 4 - 6
57	Raunchy/Sail along silvery Moon		HLD 8522	£ 4 - 6
58	Tumbling tumbleweeds/Trying		HLD 8612	£ 2 - 4
58	Sail along silvery Moon/The singing hills		HLD 8680	£ 2 - 4
58	La paloma/Here is my love		HLD 8703	£ 2 - 4
58	Cimarron (Roll on)/You're my baby doll		HLD 8772	£ 2 - 4
59	Blue Hawaii/Tico tico		HLD 8797	£ 2 - 4
59	Your cheatin' heart/Lights out		HLD 8859	£ 2 - 4
59	All nite long/Blues stay away from me		HLD 8920	£ 2 - 4
59	Morgen (One more sunrise)/Sweet Leilani		HLD 8952	£ 2 - 4
59	(It's no) Sin/After hours		HLD 8996	£ 2 - 4
60	Look for a star/He'll have to go		HLD 9152	£ 2 - 4

CHUCK VEDDER

59	Spanky boy/Arriba	LONDON	HLU 8951	£12 - 18

BOBBY VEE

60	Devil or angel/Since I met you, baby	LONDON	HLG 9179	£ 4 - 6

CHARLIE VENTURA

55	I love you/Intermezzo	V-CORAL	Q 72048	£ 2 - 4

DOLORES VENTURA (*& HER SOUTHERNAIRES)

54	Chopsticks boogie/The robin's return	DECCA	F 10229	£ 2 - 4
54	Ringin' the rag/Two parrots		F 10390	£ 2 - 4
56	The seven hills of Lisbon/When the dog sits on the......	*PARLOPHONE R 4243		£ 2 - 4

THE VENTURES

60ø	Walk don't run/Home	TOP RANK	JAR 417	£ 4 - 6
60ø	Perfidia/No trespassing	LONDON	HLG 9232	£ 4 - 6

FRANK VERNA

56	Innamorata/With you beside me	BRUNSWICK	05520	£ 2 - 4
56	The conqueror/I'd give a million tomorrows (for just...)		05548	£ 2 - 4
58	Oho aha/Everybody loves my baby	H.M.V.	POP 552	£ 2 - 4

LARRY VERNE

60	Mr. Custer/Okeefenokee two step	LONDON	HLN 9194	£ 4 - 6

LYN VERNON

60	Woodchoppers Ball/Caravan	TOP RANK	JAR 323	£ 2 - 4

THE VERNONS GIRLS (*& JIMMY SAVILLE/qv DONALD PEERS)

58	Lost and found/White bucks and saddle shoes	PARLOPHONE R 4497		£ 9 - 12
59	Jealous heart/Now is the month of Maying		R 4532	£ 4 - 6
59	Don't look now but/Who are they to say?		R 4596	£ 4 - 6
60	We like boys/Boy meets girl		R 4624	£ 4 - 6
60	Madison time*/The oo-we		R 4654	£ 2 - 4

MACK VICKERY

60	Fantasy/Hawaiian stroll	TOP RANK	JAR 420	£ 2 - 4

THE VIDELS

60	Mister Lonely/I'll forget you	LONDON	HLI 9153	£ 4 - 6

JOE VINA

59	Marina/That's alright	TOP RANK	JAR 251	£ 2 - 4

GENE VINCENT (& HIS BLUE CAPS) (*& THE BEAT BOYS)

56ø	Be-bop-a-Lula/Woman love	CAPITOL	CL 14599	£12 – 18
56ø	Race with the Devil/Gonna back up baby		CL 14628	£18 – 25
56ø	Bluejean bop/Who slapped John?		CL 14637	£18 – 25
57	Jumps, giggles and shouts/Wedding bells (are breaking..)		CL 14681	£25 – 40
57	Crazy legs/Important words		CL 14693	£25 – 40
57	Five days, five days/B-i-bickey-bi, bo-bo-go		CL 14722	£25 – 40
57	Wear my ring/Lotta lovin'		CL 14763	£12 – 18
57	Dance to the bop/I got it		CL 14808	£12 – 18
58	Walkin' home from school/I got a baby		CL 14830	£12 – 18
58	Baby blue/True to you		CL 14868	£12 – 18
58	Rocky road blues/Yes I love you, baby		CL 14908	£12 – 18
58	Git it/Little lover		CL 14935	£12 – 18
59	Say Mama/Be bop boogie boy		CL 14974	£ 9 – 12
59	Who's pushin' your swing/Over the rainbow		CL 15000	£ 9 – 12
59	Summertime/Frankie and Johnnie		CL 15035	£ 9 – 12
59	Right now/The night is so lonely		CL 15053	£ 9 – 12
59ø	Wild cat/Right here on Earth		CL 15099	£ 9 – 12
60ø	My heart/I've got to get you yet		CL 15115	£ 9 – 12
60ø	Pistol packin' Mama*/Weeping willow		CL 15136	£ 6 – 9
60	Anna-Annabelle/Ac-cent-tchu-ate the positive		CL 15169	£ 9 – 12

EDDIE "Mr. Cleanhead" VINSON & HIS ORCH.

51	Jump and grunt/Queen Bee blues	VOGUE	V 2023 º	£ 9 – 12

THE VIPERS (*SKIFFLE GROUP) (qv WALLY WHYTON/VARIOUS ARTISTS)

56	Ain't you glad/Pick a bale of cotton	*PARLOPHONE	R 4238	£ 9 – 12
57ø	Don't you rock me Daddy-O/10,000 years ago		*R 4261	£ 9 – 12
57	Jim Dandy/Hey liley, liley lo		*R 4286	£ 9 – 12
57ø	The Cumberland Gap/Maggie May		*R 4289	£ 6 – 9
57ø	Streamline train/Railroad steam boat		*R 4308	£ 6 – 9
57	Homing bird/Pay me my money down		*R 4351	£ 6 – 9
57	"Skiffle Party" medley		*R 4371	£ 4 – 6
58	Baby why?/No other baby		R 4393	£ 6 – 9
58	Make ready for love/Nothing will ever change (my love..)		R 4435	£ 4 – 6
58	Summertime blues/Liverpool blues		R 4484	£ 9 – 12

THE VIRTUES

59ø	Guitar boogie shuffle/Guitar in orbit	H.M.V.	POP 621	£ 6 – 9
59	Shufflin' along/Flippin' in		POP 637	£ 6 – 9

FRANK VIRTUOSO ROCKETS

56	Rollin' and rockin'/Rock – Goodbye mambo	MELODISC	1386 º	£ 4 – 6
56	Toodle-oo-kangaroo/Hop-skip-jump mambo		1393 º	£ 4 – 6
58	Rollin' and rockin'/Rock – Goodbye mambo		1386	£ 9 – 12

THE VISCOUNTS (U.K.)

60	Rockin' little angel/That's all right	PYE	7N 15249	£ 4 – 6
60ø	Shortnin' bread/Fee-fi-fo-fum		7N 15287	£ 4 – 6

THE VISCOUNTS (U.S.)

59	Harlem nocturne/Dig	TOP RANK	JAR 254	£ 4 – 6
60	The touch (Le grisbi)/Chug-a-lug		JAR 388	£ 4 – 6
60	Night train/Summertime		JAR 502	£ 4 – 6

THE VOICES

56	"Rock 'N' Roll Hit Parade" medley	BELTONA	BL 2667	£ 6 – 9

WES VOIGHT

59	I'm movin' in/I'm ready to go steady	PARLOPHONE	R 4586	£ 9 – 12

VOXPOPPERS

58	The last drag/Wishing for your love	MERCURY	7MT 202	£18 – 25

REMEMBER! – THE SYMBOL ø AFTER THE YEAR OF ISSUE INDICATES A BRITISH CHART ENTRY

ADAM WADE

60	Tell her for me/Don't cry, my love	TOP RANK	JAR	296	£ 2 – 4
60	Ruby/Too far		JAR	370	£ 2 – 4
60	I had the craziest dream/I can't help it	H.M.V.	POP	764	£ 2 – 4
60	Speaking of her/Blackout the Moon		POP	787	£ 2 – 4
60	In pursuit of happiness/For the want of your love		POP	807	£ 2 – 4

ROBERT WAGNER

57	Almost eighteen/So young	LONDON	HLU 8491		£ 6 – 9

THE WAILERS

59	Tall cool one/Road-runner	LONDON	HL	8958	£ 9 – 12
59	Mau-Mau/Dirty robber		HL	8994	£25 – 40

CHERRY WAINER

58	Itchy twitchy feeling/Cerveza	PYE	7N 15161		£ 4 – 6
59	The happy organ/Spanish marching song		7N 15197		£ 2 – 4
59	Saturday night in Tia Juana/I'll walk the line	TOP RANK	JAR 253		£ 2 – 4
60	Money (that's what I want)/Happy like a bell (Ding dong)	COLUMBIA	DB 4528		£ 4 – 6

JIMMY WAKELY (& *RUTH ROSS/+GLORIA WOOD/qv KAREN CHANDLER)

56	Are you mine*/Yellow roses	V-CORAL	Q 72125		£ 4 – 6
56	Are you satisfied?+/Mississippi dreamboat	BRUNSWICK	05542		£ 9 – 12
56	Folsom Prison blues/That's what the Lord can do		05563		£ 9 – 12

ANTON WALBROOK

53	La ronde de l'amour/BERLIN SYMPHONY ORCH.: The blue...	PARLOPHONE	MSP 6002		£ 2 – 4
54	Always young/S.SWINFORD & J.WARREN: It only took a.....		MSP 6099		£ 2 – 4
54	Strike another match/EVELYN LAYE: A man is a man		MSP 6100		£ 2 – 4

BILLY WALKER

60	Forever/Changed my mind	PHILIPS	PB 1001		£ 4 – 6

JACKIE WALKER

58	Only teenagers allowed/Oh lonesome me	LONDON	HLP 8588		£40 – 60

T-BONE WALKER

54	Baby broke my heart/The hustle is on	LONDON	HL	8087 º	£ 9 – 12

REM WALL & HIS GREEN VALLEY BOYS

60	Heartsick and blue/One more time	TOP RANK	JAR 324		£ 2 – 4

GIG WALLACE & HIS ORCH.

59	Rockin' on the railroad/Show me the way to go home	PHILIPS	PB 981		£ 2 – 4

IAN WALLACE

57	The hippopotamus song/Welcome home	PARLOPHONE	R 4296		£ 2 – 4

JERRY WALLACE

58	With this ring/How the time flies	LONDON	HL	8719	£ 6 – 9
59	Primrose Lane/By your side		HLH 8943		£ 2 – 4
60	Little coco palm/Mission bell blues		HLH 9040		£ 2 – 4
60ø	You're singing our love song to..../King of the mountain		HLH 9110		£ 2 – 4
60	Swingin' down the lane/Teardrop in the rain		HLH 9177		£ 2 – 4

"FATS" WALLER & HIS RHYTHM (*& THE DEEP RIVER BOYS)

50	I'm gonna sit right down and write../Everybody loves my.	H.M.V.	B	9935 º	£ 2 – 4
53	My very good friend the milkman/Shortnin' bread		7M	128	£ 4 – 6
53	Honey hush/You've been reading my mail		7M	142	£ 4 – 6
53	A good man is hard to find/The girl I left behind me ..		7M	157	£ 4 – 6
54	You've been taking lessons in love/I've got a new lease.		7M	208	£ 4 – 6
54	By the light of the silvery Moon/Romance a la mode		*7M	244	£ 4 – 6
60	Dinah/When somebody thinks you're wonderful	R.C.A.	RCA 1189		£ 2 – 4

REMEMBER! – THE SYMBOL º AFTER THE CATALOGUE NUMBER INDICATES A 78 rpm RECORD

BOB WALLIS & HIS STORYVILLE JAZZMEN

60	Bluebird/Captain Morgan	TOP RANK	JAR 331	£ 2 - 4
60	Madison time/Bonne nuit, ma cherie		JAR 365	£ 2 - 4
60	Jingle bells/Chinatown, my Chinatown	PYE JAZZ 7NJ 2039		£ 2 - 4

RUTH WALLIS

57	Donkey is jackass/A sad calypso	BRUNSWICK	05691	£ 2 - 4

SHANI WALLIS (qv THE KIRCHIN BAND)

60	Sixteen reasons (why I love you)/Forever, forever	PHILIPS	PB 1019	£ 2 - 4
60	Where's the boy/And now		PB 1076	£ 2 - 4

THE WANDERER

59	True true happiness/The happy hobo	TOP RANK	JAR 183	£ 2 - 4

THE WANDERERS

60	I could make you mine/I need you more	M-G-M	MGM 1102	£ 4 - 6

BILLY WARD (& THE DOMINO(E)S)

53	Rags to riches/Don't thank me	PARLOPHONE	R 3789 º	£ 9 - 12
54	Three coins in the fountain/Lonesome road		MSP 6112	£60 - 90
56	St. Therese of the Roses/Home is where you hang your....	BRUNSWICK	05599	£18 - 25
57	Evermore/Half a love (is better than none)		05656	£18 - 25
57ø	Stardust/Lucinda	LONDON	HLU 8465	£ 9 - 12
57ø	Deep purple/Do it again		HLU 8502	£ 9 - 12
58	Jennie Lee/Music, Maestro, please		HLU 8634	£12 - 18
59	Please don't say 'No'/Behave, hula girl		HLU 8883	£ 6 - 9

THE HEDLEY WARD TRIO

56	Steamboat rock/My baby's got such lovin' ways	MELODISC	1387 º	£ 2 - 4

FRED WARING & THE PENNSYLVANIANS

59	Dry bones/Way back home	CAPITOL	CL 14981	£ 2 - 4

OZZIE WARLOCK & THE WIZARDS

59	Juke box fury/Wow!	H.M.V.	POP 635	£ 4 - 6

HERB & BETTY WARNER

59	Slowly/"BUGS" BOWER GROUP: Slowly	FELSTED	AF 114	£ 2 - 4

JACK WARNER w. TOMMY REILLY

58	An ordinary copper/On the way up	ORIOLE	CB 1426	£ 2 - 4

GALE WARNING

56	Heartbreak Hotel/Met rock	PYE	N 15061 º	£ 6 - 9
56	Rock those crazy skins/I need your love	ORIOLE	CB 1349 º	£ 4 - 6

ALMA WARREN

56	Stealin'/Now and forever	PARLOPHONE MSP 6200	£ 4 - 6

FRAN WARREN

59	Shame/As long as you believe	M-G-M	MGM 1008	£ 2 - 4

GUY WARREN & ROD SAUNDERS

59	Monkies and butterflies/An African's prayer	BRUNSWICK	05791	£ 2 - 4

DINAH WASHINGTON (qv BROOK BENTON)

59	What a diff'rence a day made/Come on home	MERCURY	AMT 1051	£ 4 - 6
59	Unforgettable/Nothing in the world		AMT 1069	£ 2 - 4
60	This bitter earth/I understand		AMT 1105	£ 2 - 4
60	Love walked in/I'm in Heaven tonight		AMT 1119	£ 2 - 4

SHERI WASHINGTON

57	I got plenty/Ain't I talkin' to you baby	VOGUE	V 9070	£40 - 60

MUDDY WATERS
52	Walkin' blues/Rollin' stone blues	VOGUE	V	2101 º	£12 – 18
54	Long distance call/Hello little girl		V	2273 º	£12 – 18
56	Honey bee/Too young to know		V	2372 º	£ 9 – 12

JOHNNY WATSON & THE KAMPAI KINGS
60	Moshi, moshi, anone! (Hello....)/ABDULLA: Fatima's theme	ORIOLE	CB 1532		£ 2 – 4

LU WATTERS' (YERBA BUENA) JAZZ BAND
56	Muskrat ramble/Frankie and Johnny	VOGUE	V	2125	£ 2 – 4
56	High society/Aunt Hagar's blues		V	2315	£ 2 – 4

NOBLE "THIN MAN" WATTS
58	Hard times (The slop)/Midnight flight	LONDON	HLU 8627	£18 – 25

THE WATUSI WARRIORS
59	Wa-chi-bam-ba/Kalahari	LONDON	HL 8866	£ 4 – 6

CHRIS WAYNE & THE ECHOS
60	Lonely/Counting girls	DECCA	F 11231	£ 2 – 4

JERRY WAYNE
60	Half-hearted love/Ten thousand miles	VOGUE	V 9169	£ 6 – 9

RICKY WAYNE (& *THE FLEE-RAKKERS/+THE OFF-BEATS)
60	Hot chick a'roo/Don't pick on me	TRIUMPH	*RGM 1009	£18 – 25
60	*as above*	TOP RANK	*JAR 432	£ 9 – 12
60	Make way baby/Goodness knows	PYE	+7N 15289	£ 9 – 12

TERRY WAYNE
57	Matchbox/Your true love	COLUMBIA	DB 4002	£ 9 – 12
57	Plaything/Slim Jim tie		DB 4035	£ 9 – 12
58	All Mama's children/Forgive me		DB 4067	£ 9 – 12
58	Oh! Lonesome me/There's only one of you		DB 4112	£ 4 – 6
58	Little brother/Where my baby goes		DB 4205	£ 4 – 6
59	Brooklyn Bridge/She's mine		DB 4312	£ 4 – 6

THOMAS WAYNE
59	Tragedy/Saturday date	LONDON	HLU 8846	£12 – 18

THE WEAVERS
59	Wild goose grasses/Meet the Jonson boys	TOP RANK	JAR 120	£ 2 – 4

DEAN WEBB
59	Hey Miss Fannie/Warm your heart	PARLOPHONE	R 4549	£ 9 – 12
59	Streamline baby/The rough and the smooth		R 4587	£ 6 – 9

DON WEBB
60	Little ditty baby/I'll be back home	CORAL	Q 72385	£40 – 60

JILLA WEBB
56	You gotta love me now/What do you think it does to me?	M-G-M	SP 1180	£ 2 – 4

JOHNNY WEBB
56	Dig/Glendora	COLUMBIA	DB 3805	£ 4 – 6
57	The song of the moonlight/Give me more		DB 3904	£ 2 – 4

LIZBETH WEBB
53	I've never been in love before/If I were a bell	H.M.V.	7M 140	£ 2 – 4

JOAN WEBER
55ø	Let me go lover/Marionette	PHILIPS	PB	389 º	£ 2 – 4

BUDDY WEED & HIS ORCH.
57	The Kent song/For love	VOGUE	V 9075	£ 4 – 6

BERT WEEDON (qv GEORGE CHISHOLM/VARIOUS ARTISTS)

55	China boogie/Stranger than fiction (The big guitar) ...	PARLOPHONE R 4113 º	£ 4 – 6
56	The boy with the magic guitar/Flannel-foot	MSP 6242	£ 4 – 6
57	Theme from ITV's "64,000 Question"/Twilight theme	R 4256	£ 4 – 6
57	The jolly gigolo/Soho Fair	R 4315	£ 4 – 6
57	Play that big guitar/Quiet quiet ssh!	R 4381	£ 4 – 6
58	Big note blues/Rippling tango	R 4446	£ 4 – 6
59ø	Guitar boogie shuffle/Bert's boogie	TOP RANK JAR 117	£ 4 – 6
59	Sing little birdie/The lady is a tramp	JAR 121	£ 2 – 4
59	Petite fleur/My happiness	JAR 122	£ 2 – 4
59	Charmaine/It's time to say goodnight	JAR 123	£ 2 – 4
59	Teenage guitar/Blue guitar	JAR 136	£ 4 – 6
59	Jealousy/Tango tango	JAR 210	£ 2 – 4
59	Stardust/Summertime	JAR 211	£ 2 – 4
59ø	Nashville boogie/King size guitar	JAR 221	£ 4 – 6
60ø	Big beat boogie/Theme from "A Summer Place"	JAR 300	£ 4 – 6
60ø	Twelfth Street rag/Querida	JAR 360	£ 2 – 4
60ø	Apache/Lonely guitar	JAR 415	£ 4 – 6
60ø	Sorry Robbie/Easy beat	JAR 517	£ 4 – 6

FRANK WEIR & HIS ORCH./SAXOPHONE (*& EULA PARKER/qv VERA LYNN/JANIE MARDEN)

54	The happy wanderer/From your lips	DECCA F 10271	£ 2 – 4
54	The bandit/By candlelight	F 10291	£ 2 – 4
55	Theme from Journey Into Space/Serenade to an empty room	F 10435	£ 4 – 6
55	The cuckoo cries/Misty islands of the Highlands	F 10384	£ 2 – 4
55	Hold me in your arms/Too many dreams	F 10473	£ 2 – 4
55	The water tumbler tune/Whispering leaves	F 10530	£ 2 – 4
55	I'm a little echo*/Castles in the air	F 10646	£ 2 – 4
59	Swinging ghosts/The cool spectre	ORIOLE CB 1523	£ 2 – 4
60	Big Ben/Drivin' South	CB 1554	£ 2 – 4
60ø	Caribbean honeymoon/Farewell my love	CB 1559	£ 2 – 4

MOLLY WEIR

57	Glasgow/I'm Aggie from Glasgow toon	PARLOPHONE R 4340	£ 2 – 4

LENNY WELCH

60	You don't know me/I need someone	LONDON HLA 9094	£ 2 – 4

TIM WELCH

60	Weak in my knees/A boy and a girl in love	COLUMBIA DB 4529	£ 4 – 6

ORSON WELLES

59	The courtroom scene from "Compulsion"	TOP RANK TR 5001	£ 2 – 4

JOHNNY WELLS

59	Lonely Moon/The one and only one	COLUMBIA DB 4377	£ 6 – 9

ALEX WELSH & HIS DIXIELANDERS/DIXIELAND BAND

55	Eccentric/I'll build a stairway to Paradise	DECCA F 10538	£ 2 – 4
55	Shoe shiner's drag/Blues my naughty sweetie gives to me	F 10557	£ 2 – 4
55	As long as I live/New Orleans stomp	F 10607	£ 2 – 4
55	Sugar/Smiles	F 10651	£ 2 – 4
55	Hard hearted Hannah/What can I say after I say I'm sorry	F 10652	£ 2 – 4

DANNY WELTON

60	Boogie woogie/To each his own	CORAL Q 72409	£ 2 – 4

TABBY WEST

58	If you promise not to tell/All that I want	CAPITOL CL 14861	£ 2 – 4

JOHNNY WESTERN (*w. RICHARD BOONE)

60	The ballad of Paladin/The guns of Rio Muerto*	PHILIPS PB 1030	£ 2 – 4

THE WESTERNAIRES ORCHESTRA

57	Walking alone in a crowd/Sweet talk (won her loving....)	BRUNSWICK 05692	£ 2 – 4

JILL WESTLAKE
58	Sharin'/Over and over again	COLUMBIA	DB 4132	£ 2 – 4
59	Li per li/Love me, love me		DB 4299	£ 2 – 4

NANCY WHISKEY (*& HER SKIFFLERS) (qv CHAS McDEVITT)
58	He's solid gone/Ella Speed	ORIOLE	*CB 1394	£ 6 – 9
58	I know where I'm goin'/Hillside in Scotland		CB 1452	£ 4 – 6
59	Johnny Blue/Old grey goose		CB 1485	£ 4 – 6

GEORGIA WHITE
54	Was I drunk?/Moonshine blues	VOCALION	V 1038 º	£ 6 – 9

KITTY WHITE *& DAVE HOWARD
54	Jesse James/Scratch my back*	LONDON	HL 8102	£12 – 18

TERRY WHITE & THE TERRIERS
59	Blackout/Rock around the mailbag	DECCA	F 11133	£18 – 25

PAUL WHITEMAN & HIS ORCH. (*& THE "NEW" RHYTHM BOYS)
54	Whispering/You're driving me crazy	V–CORAL	Q 2015	£ 2 – 4
55	Mississsppi mud/Then and now		*Q 72064	£ 2 – 4

DAVID WHITFIELD (*& MANTOVANI ORCH./qv VARIOUS ARTISTS)
53ø	The Bridge of Sighs/I'm the King of broken hearts	DECCA	F 10129 º	£ 1 – 2
53ø	Answer me/Dance, gypsy, dance		F 10192 º	£ 1 – 2
53ø	Rags to riches/Mardi Gras		F 10207 º	£ 1 – 2
54ø	The Book/Heartless		F 10242	£ 9 – 12
54ø	Cara mia/Love, tears and kisses		*F 10327	£ 9 – 12
54	Smile/How, when or where*		F 10355	£ 4 – 6
54ø	Santo Natale/Adeste fideles		F 10399	£ 6 – 9
55ø	Beyond the stars/Open your heart		*F 10458	£ 9 – 12
55ø	Ev'rywhere/Mama		F 10515	£ 9 – 12
55	The lady/Santa Rosa Lea Rose		F 10562	£ 4 – 6
55	I'll never stop loving you/Lady of Madrid		F 10596	£ 4 – 6
55ø	When you lose the one you love/Angelus		*F 10627	£ 6 – 9
56ø	My September love/The rudder and the rock		F 10690	£ 6 – 9
56ø	My son John/My unfinished symphony		F 10769	£ 6 – 9
57ø	The adoration waltz/If I lost you		F 10833	£ 6 – 9
57ø	I'll find you/I'd give you the world		F 10864	£ 6 – 9
57	Without him/Dream of Paradise		F 10890	£ 2 – 4
57	Ev'rything/Martinella		F 10931	£ 2 – 4
58ø	Cry my heart/My one true love		*F 10978	£ 2 – 4
58ø	On the street where you live/Afraid		F 11018	£ 2 – 4
58ø	The right to love/That's when your heartaches begin		F 11039	£ 2 – 4
58	This is Lucia/Love is a stranger		F 11079	£ 2 – 4
59	Willingly/William Tell		F 11101	£ 2 – 4
59	A million stars/Farewell my love		F 11144	£ 2 – 4
59	Oh, tree/Our love waltz		F 11161	£ 2 – 4
60	Song of the dreamer/My only love		F 11196	£ 2 – 4
60	A tear, a kiss, a smile/Angela mia		F 11221	£ 2 – 4
60ø	I believe/Hear my song, Violetta		F 11289	£ 2 – 4

WILBUR WHITFIELD (& THE PLEASERS) (*as LITTLE WILBUR)
57	P.B. Baby/The one I love	VOGUE	V 9078	£40 – 60
57	Plaything/I don't care		*V 9091	£40 – 60
58	Heart to heart/Alone in the night		*V 9097	£40 – 60

MARGARET WHITING
54	My own true love/Can this be love	CAPITOL	CL 14213	£ 4 – 6
55	Heat wave/Come rain or come shine		CL 14242	£ 4 – 6
55	Stowaway/All I want is all there is and then some		CL 14307	£ 4 – 6
55	A man/Mama's pearls		CL 14348	£ 4 – 6
55	Lover, lover/I kiss you a million times		CL 14375	£ 4 – 6
56	I love a mystery/Bidin' my time		CL 14527	£ 2 – 4
56	Old enough/Day in – day out		CL 14591	£ 2 – 4
56	True love/Haunting love		CL 14647	£ 2 – 4

57	The money tree/Maybe I love him	CL 14685	£ 2 – 4
57	Kill me with kisses/Speak for yourself John	LONDON HLD 8451	£ 4 – 6
58	I can't help it/That's why I was born	HLD 8562	£ 4 – 6
58	Hot spell/I'm so lonesome I could cry	HLD 8662	£ 4 – 6

SLIM WHITMAN

52ø	Indian love call/China doll	LONDON L 1149 º	£ 2 – 4
54ø	as above	L 1149	£12 – 18
54	There's a rainbow in every teardrop/Danny boy	L 1214	£12 – 18
54	North wind/Darlin' don't cry	L 1226	£12 – 18
54	Stairway to Heaven/Lord, help me be as Thou	HL 8018	£12 – 18
54	Secret love/Why	HL 8039	£12 – 18
54ø	Rose Marie/We stood at the altar	HL 8061	£12 – 18
54	Beautiful dreamer/Ride away	HL 8080	£12 – 18
54	The singing hills/I hate to see you cry	HL 8091	£12 – 18
55	When I grow too old to dream/Cattle call	HL 8125	£12 – 18
55	Roll on silvery Moon/Haunted hungry heart	HL 8141	£ 9 – 12
55	I'll never stop loving.../I'll never take you back again	HLU 8167	£ 9 – 12
55	Song of the wild/You have my heart	HLU 8196	£ 9 – 12
56ø	Tumbling tumbleweeds/Tell me	HLU 8230	£12 – 18
56ø	I'm a fool/My heart is broken in three	HLU 8252	£ 9 – 12
56ø	Serenade/I talk to the waves	HLU 8287	£ 9 – 12
56	Dear Mary/Whiffenpoof song	HLU 8327	£ 9 – 12
56	I'm casting my lasso towards.../There's a love knot in..	HLU 8350	£ 9 – 12
57ø	I'll take you home again Kathleen/Careless love	HLP 8403	£ 9 – 12
57	Curtain of tears/Smoke signals	HLP 8416	£ 6 – 9
57	Gone/An amateur in love	HLP 8420	£12 – 18
57	Many times/Warm, warm lips	HLP 8434	£ 4 – 6
57	Lovesick blues/Forever	HLP 8459	£ 4 – 6
57	Unchain my heart/Hush-a-bye	HLP 8518	£ 4 – 6
58	A very precious love/Careless hands	HLP 8590	£ 4 – 6
58	Candy kisses/Tormented	HLP 8642	£ 4 – 6
58	Wherever you are/At the end of nowhere	HLP 8708	£ 2 – 4
59	I never see Maggie alone/The letter edged in black	HLP 8835	£ 2 – 4
60	Roll, river, roll/Twilla Lee	HLP 9103	£ 2 – 4

TOMMY WHITTLE & HIS QUARTET

57	The finisher/Cabin in the sky	H.M.V. POP 379	£ 2 – 4

WALLY WHYTON (& *THE VIPERS/+SALLY MILES/qv SHARKEY TODD)

59	Don't tell me your troubles/It's all over now	PARLOPHONE R 4585	£ 4 – 6
60	All over this world/Got me a girl	R 4630	£ 4 – 6
60	It's a rat race/etc./95% of me loves you+/You're going..	PYE *7N 15304	£ 4 – 6

THE WILBURN BROTHERS

59	That silver haired Daddy of mine/A boy's faithful friend	BRUNSWICK 05799	£ 2 – 4

THE WILDCATS

59	Gazachstahagen/Billy's cha cha	LONDON HLT 8787	£ 6 – 9

MARTY WILDE (& HIS WILDCATS)

57	Honeycomb/Wild cat	PHILIPS PB 750 º	£ 4 – 6
57	as above	JK 1028	£12 – 18
58	Love bug crawl/Afraid of love	PB 781 º	£ 4 – 6
58	Oh-oh, I'm falling in love again/Sing, boy, sing	PB 804	£ 6 – 9
58ø	Endless sleep/Her hair was yellow	PB 835	£ 4 – 6
58	My lucky love/Misery's child	PB 850	£ 4 – 6
58	No one knows/The fire of love	PB 875	£ 4 – 6
59ø	Donna/Love-a love-a love-a	PB 902	£ 4 – 6
59ø	A teenager in love/Danny	PB 926	£ 4 – 6
59ø	Sea of love/Teenage tears	PB 959	£ 4 – 6
59ø	Bad boy/It's been nice	PB 972	£ 4 – 6
60ø	Johnny Rocco/My heart and I	PB 1002	£ 2 – 4
60ø	The fight/Johnny at the crossroads	PB 1022	£ 2 – 4
60	Angry/I wanna be loved by you	PB 1037	£ 2 – 4
60ø	Little girl/Your seventeenth Spring	PB 1078	£ 2 – 4

THE WILDER BROTHERS
57	I want you/Teenage angel	H.M.V.	POP	365	£40 - 60

ANDY WILLIAMS
56	Walk hand in hand/Not any more	LONDON	HLA	8284	£12 - 18
56	Canadian sunset/High upon a mountain		HLA	8315	£ 9 - 12
56	Baby doll/Since I've found my baby		HLA	8360	£ 9 - 12
57ø	Butterfly/It doesn't take very long		HLA	8399	£ 9 - 12
57ø	I like your kind of love/Stop teasin' me		HLA	8437	£ 9 - 12
57	Lips of wine/Straight from my heart		HLA	8487	£ 4 - 6
58	Are you sincere/Be mine tonight		HLA	8587	£ 4 - 6
58	Promise me, love/Your hand, your heart, your love		HLA	8710	£ 2 - 4
59	House of bamboo/Hawaiian wedding song		HLA	8784	£ 6 - 9
59	Lonely street/Summer love		HLA	8957	£ 2 - 4
59	The village of St. Bernadette/I'm so lonesome I could...		HLA	9018	£ 2 - 4
60	Wake me when it's over/We have a date		HLA	9099	£ 2 - 4
60	You don't want my love/Don't go to strangers		HLA	9241	£ 2 - 4

AUDREY WILLIAMS
56	Ain't nothing gonna be all../Livin' it up and havin' a..	M-G-M	SP	1179	£ 4 - 6

BILLY WILLIAMS (QUARTET) (*& BARBARA McNAIR)
54	Sh'boom/Whenever wherever	V-CORAL	Q	2012 º	£ 4 - 6
54	Honeydripper/Love me		Q	2039	£ 9 - 12
56	A crazy little palace/Cry baby		Q	72149	£ 9 - 12
56	Pray/You'll reach your star		Q	72180	£ 4 - 6
57	Follow me/Shame, shame, shame		Q	72222	£ 6 - 9
57	Butterfly/The pied piper		Q	72241	£ 6 - 9
57ø	I'm gonna sit right down and write../Date with the blues		Q	72266	£ 6 - 9
57	Got a date with an angel/The Lord will understand		Q	72295	£ 4 - 6
58	Don't let go/Baby. baby	CORAL	Q	72303	£ 6 - 9
58	Steppin' out tonight/There I've said it again		Q	72316	£ 4 - 6
58	I'll get by/It's prayin' time		Q	72331	£ 2 - 4
59	Nola/Tied to the strings of your heart		Q	72359	£ 2 - 4
59	Goodnight Irene/Red hot love		Q	72369	£ 4 - 6
59	Telephone conversation/Go to sleep, go to sleep, go to..		*Q	72377	£ 4 - 6
60	I cried for you/The lover of all lovers		Q	72402	£ 2 - 4
60	Begin the beguine/For you		Q	72414	£ 2 - 4

CHRIS WILLIAMS & HIS MONSTERS
59	The monster/The Eton boating song	COLUMBIA	DB	4383	£ 9 - 12

CLARENCE WILLIAMS & HIS WASHBOARD BAND/ORCH.
54	High society/Left all alone with the blues	COLUMBIA	SCM	5134	£ 4 - 6

DAN WILLIAMS & HIS ORCH.
55	Donkey City/SHAW PARK CALYPSO BAND: Take her to Jamaica	LONDON	CAY	110	£ 6 - 9

GEORGE WILLIAMS & HIS ORCH.
55	The rompin' stomper/Knock-out choo-choo	V-CORAL	Q	72053	£ 2 - 4

HANK WILLIAMS (& HIS DRIFTING COWBOYS)
50	Lovesick blues/Wedding bells	M-G-M	MGM	269 º	£ 4 - 6
51	Moanin' the blues/The blues come around		MGM	381 º	£ 4 - 6
51	Dear John/Fly trouble		MGM	405 º	£ 4 - 6
51	Hey, good lookin'/Howlin' at the Moon		MGM	454 º	£ 4 - 6
51	Cold, cold heart/I'm a long gone Daddy ....:.....		MGM	459 º	£ 4 - 6
52	I can't help it/Baby, we're really in love		MGM	471 º	£ 4 - 6
52	Why don't you love me/I'd still want you		MGM	483 º	£ 4 - 6
52	Honky-tonk blues/I'm sorry for you, my friend		MGM	505 º	£ 4 - 6
52	Half as much/Long gone lonesome blues		MGM	527 º	£ 4 - 6
52	Mind your own business/Nobody's lonesome for me		MGM	553 º	£ 4 - 6
52	Jambalaya (on the Bayou)/Settin' the woods on fire		MGM	566 º	£ 4 - 6
53	I'll never get out of this world.../I could never be....		SP	1016	£12 - 18
53	Kaw-Liga/Take these chains from my heart		SP	1034	£12 - 18

53	I saw the light/(by ARTHUR [G.B.] SMITH)	MGM	630 º	£ 6 – 9
53	Window shopping/You win again	MGM	678 º	£ 4 – 6
53	My bucket's got a hole in it/Let's turn back the years	SP	1048	£12 – 18
53	Ramblin' man/I won't be home no more	SP	1049	£12 – 18
54	Weary blues (from waitin')/I can't escape from you	SP	1067	£12 – 18
54	There'll be no tear drops tonight/Crazy heart	SP	1085	£12 – 18
54	I'm satisfied with you/I ain't got nothin' but time ...	SP	1102	£12 – 18
55	I'm gonna sing/California zephyr	MGM	799 º	£ 4 – 6
56	Your cheatin' heart/A teardrop on a rose	MGM	896 º	£ 4 – 6
56	I wish I had a nickel/There's no room in my heart (for.)	MGM	921	£ 9 – 12
56	Blue love (in my heart)/Singing waterfall	MGM	931	£ 9 – 12
57	Low down blues/My sweet love ain't around	MGM	942	£12 – 18
57	Rootie tootie/Lonesome whistle	MGM	957	£12 – 18
57	Leave me alone with the blues/With tears in my eyes ...	MGM	966	£ 9 – 12

JOE WILLIAMS (qv COUNT BASIE/SARAH VAUGHAN)

60	Somebody/One is a lonesome number	COLUMBIA	DB 4560	£ 2 – 4

LARRY WILLIAMS

57ø	Short fat Fannie/High school dance	LONDON	HLN 8472	£12 – 18
58ø	Bony Moronie/You bug me baby		HLU 8532	£12 – 18
58	Dizzy Miss Lizzy/Slow down		HLU 8604	£12 – 18
59	She said "Yeah"/Bad boy		HLU 8844	£ 9 – 12
60	I can't stop loving you/Steal a little kiss		HLU 8911	£ 6 – 9
60	Baby, baby/Get ready		HLM 9053	£ 9 – 12

MAURICE WILLIAMS & THE ZODIACS

60ø	Stay/Do you believe	TOP RANK	JAR 526	£ 6 – 9

OTIS WILLIAMS & HIS CHARMS

56	Ivory tower/In Paradise	PARLOPHONE	MSP 6239	£40 – 60
56	One night only/It's all over		R 4210	£40 – 60
57	Walkin' after midnight/I'm waiting just for you		R 4293	£40 – 60
58	Don't wake up the kids/The secret		R 4495	£18 – 25

RITA WILLIAMS

58	Love me forever/Looking for someone to love	ORIOLE	CB 1417	£ 2 – 4

ROGER WILLIAMS (*& JANE MORGAN)

55	Autumn leaves/Take care	LONDON	HLU 8214	£ 9 – 12
56	Two different worlds*/I'll always walk with you		HLU 8341	£ 9 – 12
57	Anastasia/A serenade for joy		HLU 8379	£ 6 – 9
57	Almost Paradise/For the first time I've fallen in love		HLR 8422	£ 2 – 4
57	Till/Big town		HLR 8516	£ 2 – 4
58	Arrivederci Roma/The sentimental touch		HLR 8572	£ 2 – 4

SONNY WILLIAMS

59	Bye bye baby goodbye/Lucky Linda	LONDON	HLD 8931	£ 4 – 6

SPARKIE WILLIAMS (1958 Champion Talking Budgerigar)

58	Sparkie Williams/Sparkie the Fiddle	PARLOPHONE	R 4475	£ 2 – 4

TEX WILLIAMS (*& HIS WESTERN CARAVAN) (+& REX ALLEN)

50	Talking boogie/Tamburitza boogie	CAPITOL	*CL 13424 º	£ 6 – 9
54	River of no return/Down in the meadow	BRUNSWICK	05327	£ 6 – 9
54	This ole house+/They were doin' the mambo		05341	£ 9 – 12
55	Money/If you'd believe in me		05393	£ 4 – 6
56	Be sure you're right (and then go ahead)/Old Betsy		05516	£ 4 – 6
57	Talkin' to the blues/Every night		05684	£ 9 – 12
60	The keeper of Boothill/Bummin' around	TOP RANK	JAR 330	£ 4 – 6

CLAUDE WILLIAMSON TRIO

54	All God's chillun got rhythm/Woody'n you	CAPITOL	KC 65003	£ 4 – 6

REMEMBER! – THE SYMBOL ø AFTER THE YEAR OF ISSUE INDICATES A BRITISH CHART ENTRY

CHUCK WILLIS
57	C.C. rider/Ease the pain	LONDON	HLE 8444	£18 – 25
57	That train has gone/Love me Cherry		HLE 8489	£18 – 25
58	Betty and Dupree/My crying eyes		HLE 8595	£18 – 25
58	What am I living for/Hang up my rock and roll shoes ...		HLE 8635	£12 – 18
59	My life/Thunder and lightning		HLE 8818	£12 – 18

RALPH WILLIS
54	Goodbye blues/Lazy woman blues	ESQUIRE	10–370 º	£ 6 – 9
54	Old home blues/Salty dog		10–380 º	£ 6 – 9

THE WILLOWS
56	Church bells may ring/Baby tell me	LONDON	HLL 8290	£90 –120

BOB WILLS & HIS TEXAS PLAYBOYS
51	'Tater pie/Ida Red likes the boogie	M–G–M	MGM 455 º	£ 6 – 9
53	Snatchin' and grabbin'/I want to be wanted		MGM 613 º	£ 6 – 9

DOYLE WILSON
58	Hey–hey/You're the one for me	VOGUE	V 9117	£60 – 90

GADDY WILSON & THE CINDERELLAS
59	Nothin' at night/I'll never be myself again	PHILIPS	PB 980	£ 2 – 4

GARLAND WILSON
53	Just you, just me/Sweet Georgia Brown	H.M.V.	7M 122	£ 2 – 4

JACKIE WILSON
57ø	Reet petite/By the light of the silvery Moon	V–CORAL	Q 72290	£12 – 18
58ø	To be loved/Come back to me	CORAL	Q 72306	£ 6 – 9
58	I'm wanderin'/As long as I live		Q 72332	£ 4 – 6
58	We have love/Singing a song		Q 72338	£ 4 – 6
58	Lonely teardrops/In the blue of the evening		Q 72347	£ 6 – 9
59	That's why/Love is all		Q 72366	£ 4 – 6
59	I'll be satisfied/Ask		Q 72372	£ 4 – 6
59	You better know it/Never go away		Q 72380	£ 4 – 6
59	Talk that talk/Only you, only me		Q 72384	£ 4 – 6
60	Doggin' around/The magic of love		Q 72393	£ 4 – 6
60ø	(You were made..) All my love/A woman, a lover, a friend		Q 72407	£ 4 – 6
60ø	Alone at last/Am I the man		Q 72412	£ 4 – 6

MARTY WILSON & THE STRAT–O–LITES
58	Hey! Eula/Hedge–hopper	BRUNSWICK	05750	£ 9 – 12

PEANUTS WILSON
58	Cast iron arm/You've got love	CORAL	Q 72302	£90 –120

SHIRLEY WILSON
57	Funny what a kiss can do/Tell me	COLUMBIA	DB 3936	£ 2 – 4

SMILEY WILSON
60	Running Bear/Long as little birds fly	LONDON	HLG 9066	£ 4 – 6

JOHNNY WILTSHIRE & HIS TREBLETONES
59	If the shoe fits/Cha cha choo choo	ORIOLE	CB 1494	£12 – 18

ERIC WINSTONE & HIS ORCH.
55	Rhythm and blues/Opus one mambo	POLYGON	P 1173 º	£ 4 – 6
56	*as above*	PYE	N 15032 º	£ 2 – 4

DON WINTERS
60	Someday baby/That's all I need	BRUNSWICK	05827	£ 6 – 9

MIKE & BERNIE WINTERS
57	How do you do?/Does my baby?	PARLOPHONE	R 4384	£ 9 – 12

RONNIE WINTERS
59	Forgotten/I'll close my eyes	COLUMBIA	DB 4297	£ 2 –	4

WYOMA WINTERS
54	Where can I go without you?/Won't you give a repeat.....	H.M.V.	7M 222	£ 2 –	4
54	Shish kebab/Toy balloon		7M 260	£ 2 –	4

NORMAN WISDOM (& *JOYCE GRENFELL/+RUBY MURRAY)
52ø	Don't laugh at me/Once in love with Amy	COLUMBIA	DB 3133 º	£ 2 –	4
52	Narcissus/I don't 'arf love you		*DB 3161 º	£ 2 –	4
56	Two rivers/Boy meets girl		+SCM 5222	£ 6 –	9
57	Up in the world/Me and my imagination		DB 3864	£ 2 –	4
57ø	The wisdom of a fool/Happy ending		DB 3903	£ 4 –	6
59	Follow a star/Give me a night in June	TOP RANK	JAR 246	£ 2 –	4

THE WISE BOYS
60	Why, why, why/My fortune	PARLOPHONE	R 4693	£ 6 –	9

THE WISE GUYS
60	(Little girl) Big noise/As long as I have you	TOP RANK	JAR 271	£ 4 –	6

MAC WISEMAN
55	The Kentuckian song/Wabash cannonball	LONDON	HLD 8174	£18 –	25
56	My little home in Tennessee/I haven't got the right to..		HLD 8226	£18 –	25
56	Fire Ball mail/When the roses bloom again		HLD 8259	£18 –	25
57	Step it up and go/Sundown		HLD 8412	£40 –	60

JIMMY WITHERSPOON
54	Who's been jivin' with you/Rain, rain, rain	VOGUE	V 2295 º	£ 4 –	6
54	It/Highway to happiness	PARLOPHONE	MSP 6125	£ 9 –	12
54	Oh boy/I done told you		MSP 6142	£ 9 –	12
55	Falling by degrees/New Orleans woman	VOGUE	V 2261 º	£ 4 –	6
56	Jump, children/Take me back		V 2356 º	£ 4 –	6
56	Big fine girl/No rollin' blues		V 2060	£ 9 –	12

DEL WOOD
54	Ragtime Annie/Backroom polka	LONDON	HL 8036	£12 –	18

DONALD WOODS
58	Memories of an angel/That much of your love	VOGUE	V 9107	£60 –	90

MAGGI WOODWARD
59	Ali Bama/Zulu warrior	VOGUE	V 9148	£ 4 –	6

SHEB WOOLEY
51	Hoot owl boogie/Country kisses	M–G–M	MGM 439 º	£ 6 –	9
54	Panama Pete/Blue guitar		MGM 757 º	£ 4 –	6
55	38–24–35/I flipped		SP 1130	£ 6 –	9
58ø	The Purple People Eater/Recipe for love		MGM 981	£ 6 –	9
58	Santa and the Purple People Eater/Star of love		MGM 997	£ 4 –	6
59	Sweet chile/More		MGM 1017	£ 4 –	6
60	Luke the Spook/My only treasure		MGM 1081	£ 4 –	6

JIMMY WORK
56	When she said "You all"/There's only one you	LONDON	HLD 8270	£40 –	60
56	You've gotta heart like a merry–go–round/Blind heart ..		HLD 8308	£18 –	25

JOHNNY WORTH
57	Let's go/Just because	COLUMBIA	DB 3962	£ 4 –	6
59	Mean streak/Fort Worth Jail	EMBASSY	WB 338	£ 2 –	4
60	Nightmare/Hold me, thrill me, kiss me	ORIOLE	CB 1545	£ 4 –	6

LINK WRAY & HIS RAY MEN
58	Rumble/The swag	LONDON	HLA 8623	£12 –	18

DALE WRIGHT (& THE ROCK-ITS)
| 58 | She's neat/Say that you care | .... | LONDON | HLH 8573 | £60 – 90 |
| 59 | That's show biz/That's my gal | .... | PYE INT. | 7N 25022 | £18 – 25 |

GINNY WRIGHT (*& TOM TALL/qv T.TOMMY CUTRER)
| 55 | Indian Moon/Your eyes feasted upon her | .... | LONDON | HL 8119 | £18 – 25 |
| 55 | Boom boom boomerang/Are you mine? | .... | | *HL 8150 | £18 – 25 |

RUBY WRIGHT (*& CHARLIE GORE)
53	Till I waltz again with you/When I gave you my love	..	*PARLOPHONE	MSP 6025	£ 9 – 12
54ø	Bimbo/Boy, you got yourself a girl	....		R 3816 º	£ 2 – 4
54ø	as above	....		MSP 6073	£ 9 – 12
54	Santa's little sleigh bells/Toodle loo to you	....		MSP 6133	£ 4 – 6
55	What have they told you?/I had the funniest feeling	...		MSP 6150	£ 4 – 6
56	I fall in love with you ev'ry day/Do you believe?	.....		MSP 6209	£ 4 – 6
59ø	Three stars/I only have one lifetime	....		R 4556	£ 9 – 12
59	You're just a flower from an old..../Sweet night of love			R 4589	£ 2 – 4

STEVE WRIGHT
| 59 | Wild, wild women/Love you | .... | LONDON | HLW 8991 | £25 – 40 |

JANE WYMAN (*& BING CROSBY)
| 52ø | Zing a little zong*/The maiden of Guadalupe | .... | BRUNSWICK | 04981 º | £ 2 – 4 |

MARK WYNTER
| 60ø | Image of a girl/Glory of love | .... | DECCA | F 11263 | £ 2 – 4 |
| 60ø | Kickin' up the leaves/That's what I thought | .... | | F 11279 | £ 2 – 4 |

THE X-RAYS
| 59 | Chinchilla/Out of control | .... | LONDON | HLR 8805 | £ 6 – 9 |

YANA
56	If you don't love me/Climb up the wall	....	H.M.V.	POP 252	£ 4 – 6
57	Mr. Wonderful/Too close for comfort	....		POP 340	£ 4 – 6
58	I need you/I miss you Mama	....		POP 481	£ 2 – 4

YOLANDA
| 60 | With this kiss/Don't tell me not to love you | .... | TRIUMPH | RGM 1007 | £12 – 18 |

RUSTY YORK (qv BONNIE LOU)
| 57 | Peggy Sue/Shake 'em up baby | ..... (DEMOS ONLY EXIST) .. | PARLOPHONE | R 4398 | £120–160 |

YOUNG JESSIE
| 58 | Shuffle in the gravel/Make believe | .... | LONDON | HLE 8544 | £40 – 60 |

FARON YOUNG
55	Live fast, love hard, die young/Forgive me, dear	......	CAPITOL	CL 14336	£ 9 – 12
56	If you ain't lovin' (you ain't livin')/All right	......		CL 14574	£ 6 – 9
56	I've got five dollars and it's Saturday../You're still..			CL 14655	£ 6 – 9
57	He was there/The Shrine of St. Cecilia	....		CL 14735	£ 2 – 4
57	Love has finally come my way/Moonlight Mountain	....		CL 14762	£ 2 – 4
57	Honey stop! (and think of me)/Vacation's over	....		CL 14793	£ 9 – 12
58	Snowball/The locket	....		CL 14822	£ 4 – 6
58	I can't dance/Rosalie (is gonna get married)	....		CL 14860	£ 9 – 12
58	Alone with you/Every time I'm kissing you	....		CL 14891	£ 2 – 4
58	That's the way I feel/I hate myself	....		CL 14930	£ 2 – 4
59	Last night at a party/A long time ago	....		CL 14975	£ 2 – 4
59	That's the way it's gotta be/We're talking it over	....		CL 15004	£ 2 – 4
59	I hear you talkin'/Country girl	....		CL 15050	£ 4 – 6
59	Riverboat/Face to the wall	....		CL 15093	£ 2 – 4
60	Your old used to be/I'll be alright (in the morning)	..		CL 15133	£ 2 – 4
60	Is she all you thought she'd be/There's not any like....			CL 15151	£ 2 – 4
60	A world so full of love/Forget the past	....		CL 15173	£ 2 – 4

REMEMBER! – THE SYMBOL º AFTER THE CATALOGUE NUMBER INDICATES A 78 rpm RECORD

GEORGE YOUNG & THE ROCKIN' BOCS

59	Nine more miles/The sneak	LONDON	HLU 8748	£ 6 - 9

JIMMY YOUNG (qv VARIOUS ARTISTS)

51	Too young/How can I leave you	POLYGON	P 1013 º	£ 2 - 4
52ø	Faith can move mountains/Moon above Malaya	DECCA	F 9986 º	£ 2 - 4
53ø	Eternally/Is it any wonder?		F 10130 º	£ 2 - 4
54	A baby cried/Remember me		F 10232	£ 4 - 6
54	Give me your word/Lonely nightingale		F 10406	£ 4 - 6
55	These are the things we'll share/Don't go to strangers		F 10444	£ 4 - 6
55	If anyone finds this, I love you/The sand and the sea		F 10483	£ 4 - 6
55ø	Unchained melody/Help me forget		F 10502	£ 9 - 12
55ø	The man from Laramie/No arms can ever hold you		F 10597	£ 9 - 12
55ø	Someone on your mind/I look at you		F 10640	£ 9 - 12
56ø	Chain gang/Capri in May		F 10694	£ 9 - 12
56ø	Rich man, poor man/The wayward wind		F 10736	£ 9 - 12
56ø	More/I'm gonna steal you away		F 10774	£ 9 - 12
57	My faith, my hope, my love/Lovin' baby		F 10842	£ 2 - 4
57ø	Round and round/Walkin' after midnight		F 10875	£ 4 - 6
57	Love in the afternoon/Man on fire		F 10925	£ 2 - 4
57	Deep blue sea/Harbour of desire		F 10948	£ 2 - 4
58	Love me again/A very precious love	COLUMBIA	DB 4100	£ 2 - 4
58	Her hair was yellow/The state of happiness		DB 4147	£ 2 - 4
58	Volare (Nel blu dipinto...)/Beats there a heart so true?		DB 4176	£ 2 - 4
58	There! I've said it again/I could be a mountain		DB 4211	£ 2 - 4
59	Golden girl/Watch your heart		DB 4268	£ 2 - 4
59	Soon I'll wed my love/You're wonderful and you're mine		DB 4366	£ 2 - 4
60	Just a little more/If only you'd be mine		DB 4438	£ 2 - 4

LESTER YOUNG QUINTET

56	New Lester leaps in/She's funny that way	VOGUE	V 2362	£ 2 - 4
56	You're driving me crazy/East of the Sun		V 2384	£ 2 - 4

RALPH YOUNG (qv JACK PLEIS)

55	The man from Laramie/The Bible tells me so	BRUNSWICK	05466	£ 2 - 4
55	Bring me a bluebird/A room in Paris		05500	£ 2 - 4
56	The legend of Wyatt Earp/Do you know?		05605	£ 2 - 4

ROY YOUNG

59	Just keep it up/Big fat Mama	FONTANA	H 200	£ 9 - 12
59	Hey little girl/Just ask your heart		H 215	£ 6 - 9
60	I hardly know me/Gilee		H 237	£ 6 - 9
60	Taboo/I'm in love		H 247	£ 4 - 6

VICKI YOUNG (*& JOE "FINGERS" CARR)

54	Riot in cell block number nine/Honey love	CAPITOL	CL 14144 º	£ 4 - 6
55	Hearts of stone/Tweedlee dee		CL 14228	£ 9 - 12
55	Live fast, love hard, die young/Zoom, zoom, zoom		CL 14281	£ 9 - 12
56	Steel guitar/Bye, bye for just a while		CL 14528	£ 4 - 6
56	Spanish Main/Tell me in your own sweet way		*CL 14653	£ 2 - 4

JOHNNY YUKON

60	Made to be loved/Magnolia	TOP RANK	JAR 347	£ 2 - 4

HELMUT ZACHARIAS & HIS ORCH./*HOT CLUB

56	China boogie/Slap happy	POLYDOR	BM 6011 º	£ 4 - 6
57	Rock 'n' roll "Roll-Mops" rock/Barock 'n' roll rock		*BM 6058 º	£ 4 - 6

JOHN ZACHERLE

58	Dinner with Drac - Parts 1 & 2	LONDON	HLU 8599	£12 - 18

TOMMY ZANG

59	Break the chain/I'll put a string on your finger	H.M.V.	POP 611	£ 2 - 4

REMEMBER! - THE SYMBOL ø AFTER THE YEAR OF ISSUE INDICATES A BRITISH CHART ENTRY

THE END!